D0410691

Wartime DISASTERS AT SEA

By the same author:

Damned by Destiny (co-author)
Docks & Ports – Southampton
Sea Traffic Management
Cunard White Star Liners of the 1930s (co-author)
Liners in Battle Dress
Salvage!
Maritime Research & Picture Sources
White's of Cowes
Siege!

As part of our ongoing market research, we are always pleased to receive comments about our books, suggestions for new titles, or requests for catalogues. Please write to: The Editorial Director, Patrick Stephens Ltd, Sparkford, Nr Yeovil, Somerset, BA22 7JJ.

Wartime DISASTERS AT SEA

Every passenger ship loss in World Wars I and II

David Williams

Patrick Stephens Limited

First published 1997

British Library Cataloguing-in-Publication Data:
A catalogue record for this book
is available from the British Library.

ISBN 1 85260 565 0

Library of Congress catalog card number: 97-70199

Patrick Stephens Limited is an imprint of Haynes Publishing, Sparkford, Nr Yeovil, Somerset, BA22 7JJ.

Designed & typeset by G&M,
Raunds, Northamptonshire NN9 6SR.
Printed and bound in Great Britain by
Butler & Tanner Ltd, London and Frome.

CONTENTS

	Introduction	7
	Explanatory Notes	10
Chapter 1	1914: Raiders at Large	13
Chapter 2	1915: All-Out U-Boat War	18
Chapter 3	1916: Some Mines but Mostly Torpedoes	29
Chapter 4	1917: Unrestricted Submarine Warfare	41
Chapter 5	1918: The U-Boat Offensive Continues	67
Chapter 6	1939: Magnetic Mine Menace	86
Chapter 7	1940: Wolf Packs and Surface Raiders	94
Chapter 8	1941: Convoy Casualties as the War Widens	122
Chapter 9	1942: Amphibious Landings Everywhere	140
Chapter 10	1943: Enigma Breaks the U-Boat Ciphers	174
Chapter 11	1944: Aircraft Dominate as 'Overlord' is Launched	197
Chapter 12	1945: 'Hannibal' and the Road to Japan	225
Appendix 1	Summary of Wartime Disasters	241
Appendix 2A	Worst 25 Disasters by Casualties	242
Appendix 2B	Worst 25 Disasters by Size of Vessel	243
Appendix 3	Comparison of Total Losses	244
	Bibliography and Acknowledgements	245
	Index to Ships' Names	246

This book is dedicated to the memory of

Tom Rayner

(1921–1996)

Shiplover, Photographer, Friend

INTRODUCTION

Ten years ago, the book *Disasters at Sea* by Milton Watson was first published, providing a comprehensive account of all ocean-going passenger ship losses in peacetime service since 1900. *Wartime Disasters at Sea* complements this earlier publication and completes the record of all twentieth century passenger ship losses by detailing sinkings that occurred during the two World Wars. Like its companion volume, *Wartime Disasters at Sea* is comprehensive in its coverage. For this reason it does not focus only on ships engaged in war duties, but includes those vessels which continued to make commercial sailings.

Although both books are essentially sources of factual information, it is important to remember that the events they describe involved real people and, all too often, real death and suffering. A quick analysis of the casualties resulting from the incidents covered here, both in human life and shipping, emphasizes that the events recorded were far from inconsequential. Expressed in purely statistical terms, no less than 500 cases of total loss are described, representing some six million tons of shipping and in excess of 60,000 known human casualties. The recent disaster to the ferry *Estonia* stunned the world as news bulletins progressively revealed how almost 1,000 people had drowned in the icy seas of the Baltic in the most horrific circumstances. But imagine the equivalent of such an incident happening every year for each of the past 50 years, for that is how these wartime casualty figures average out, and even then we would only have accounted for a quarter of the tonnage sunk.

But no matter how dramatically they are presented, facts and figures only tell half the story, for they lack the human dimension of these terrible experiences. Regrettably, with the limitations of space imposed on such a project, it has not proved possible to include the first-hand testimonies of those who were directly involved in the disasters described.

Of course, whichever approach one adopts when writing a book about disasters, there are certain incidents for which even the most expressive language or the most detailed personal account prove wholly inadequate in conveying the full tragedy of the event. For example, the torpedoing of the German refugee ships *Wilhelm Gustloff* and *Steuben* in the same area, within ten days of each other, during the closing stages of the Second World War, resulting in a combined death toll of 10,800; or the peacetime loss of the *Titanic*, swallowed up into the ocean's depths on her maiden voyage while two-thirds of her complement drowned for want of sufficient life-saving facilities. For all the words that have been written, nothing can adequately communicate the horror of catastrophes on such a scale as these.

Given the gravity of the book's subject, I felt it was appropriate in this Introduction to review briefly the causes of passenger ship losses, natural, accidental and, in particular, as a result of hostile wartime action, and the steps that have been taken to minimize their likelihood or to prevent them from occurring altogether.

Ever since the beginning of the age of steam at sea, there have been many disasters involving passenger ships on the ocean highways, and these have been accompanied by a mounting death toll. The causes have been manifold, ranging from the vagaries of the weather to mechanical failure, collisions with other vessels, and, very often, fires on board. Indeed, in the early part of this period losses at sea occurred with alarming frequency, and for the traveller brave enough to venture on an ocean voyage the odds on arriving safely at the port of destination were woefully slim. The hazards were numerous, and the remedies, at the time, were very few.

In response to growing public pressure, as well as to the demands of insurance underwriters and organizations such as the Select Committee on Shipwrecks, the process of improving maritime standards began to gather pace. As the years went by the range and scope of measures designed to promote the safety of life at sea constantly increased. A short résumé of just the more important of the devices introduced and the practices adopted, often pioneered on passenger vessels, serves to emphasize the point: hull sub-division, smoke detectors, sprinkler systems, load line rules, 'rules of the road', wireless telegraphy, watertight doors, double bottoms, radio direction finders, radio telephony, life-boat rules, echo sounders, radar, and so on. The list continues right up to the present day, with such modern facilities as satellite navigation and communication systems. With all the advantages of more than 150 years of progress, maritime safety standards today are such that the risks of a disaster occurring at sea have been reduced considerably.

It is totally inappropriate, of course, to talk in the same terms as peacetime disasters when dealing with the much greater casualty rate and loss of human life that occurs during wartime. Whereas in peacetime the hazards to which ships are routinely exposed are largely governed by the unpredictable forces of nature, wartime dangers arise from the deliberate actions of a purposeful and destructive adversary. Under such circumstances the development of effective protection for undefended merchantmen has proved difficult, if not impossible, to achieve. That is not to say that during times of conflict ships have been left entirely to the mercy of the enemy. On the contrary, considerable efforts have been made to devise defences against the rigours of maritime warfare, resulting in some ingenious techniques and contrivances.

A measure of protection is, of course, embodied in the International Conventions governing the conduct of war. The Declaration of Paris of April 1856 laid down the earliest maritime law relating to the operation of merchant vessels in hostile circumstances. Later, in October 1868, the principles set out in the Geneva Convention of August 1864 were adapted to cover maritime conflict. They were subsequently expanded and more widely ratified at the Hague Convention in 1907. These agreements identified protected vessels, and established codes of behaviour concerning offensive action that could be taken against non-combatant ships. However, the escalation of war in the twentieth century, and the tendency of certain régimes to disregard international law, or to interpret it as they see fit, has made these agreements appear rather naïve when judged by today's standards. Certainly they have proved to be a very fragile shield when implemented on the ocean highways.

Nor do the provisions of the Conventions appear to have been entirely without their own anomalies. For instance, ships conveying war materials – whether fighting men, munitions, or armaments – are designated as legitimate targets. Consequently troopships, unlike hospital ships, are not afforded any specific safeguard under the regulations. Yet with their vast and vulnerable cargoes, and being invariably unarmed, some sort of immunity from attack would seem appropriate, especially when their passengers were frequently not troops at all, but evacuees, refugees, or prisoners.

The most successful method of defence employed for merchant ships was the convoy system. Based upon the maxim of strength in numbers, it was originally developed at the time of the Revolutionary and Napoleonic Wars. Re-introduced in 1917, the practice was subsequently used throughout the Second World War. As a result, on the two occasions when Great Britain's back was to the wall and submarine warfare threatened to starve the nation into submission, it helped reduce losses and turn the tide of war in her favour.

In spring 1917, the artist Norman Wilkinson, then employed by the Admiralty, devised one of the most bizarre schemes yet for the protection of merchant ships from submarine attack. Known as 'Dazzle Painting', it was a form of camouflage which relied not on concealment for its effectiveness but on confusion. Wilkinson's idea proved to be quite successful and its application spread to naval vessels. Between the Wars it formed the basis for investigations into a wide range of similar schemes which were eventually employed by the combatant powers during the Second World War.

Another important addition to the anti-submarine war armoury was the Anglo-French invention ASDIC, also introduced in 1917. Named after the initials of the Allied Submarine Detection and Investigation Committee responsible for its development, ASDIC could detect a submerged submarine and pinpoint its range and direction. Limited benefit was derived from the system in the First World War but it was widely and effectively employed from 1939.

If Dazzle Painting and ASDIC were the novelties of the First World War, then de-gaussing was the revolutionary innovation of the Second World War. When examination of a German magnetic mine, picked up intact in the Thames estuary, revealed the principle of its triggering mechanism it permitted the development of a most unusual counter-measure. Huge electric coils, made of copper set in a rubber channel, called 'de-gaussing strips', were fixed around the hulls of ships so that the polarity of their magnetic field could be adjusted and thereby render them invulnerable. The first coils were fitted in the early summer of 1940, virtually neutralizing overnight a menace which, until then, had been one of the most potent weapons in the enemy's arsenal. A similar, but less well-known, device was the noise and vibration generator which could detonate acoustic mines in a ship's path while they were still a safe distance ahead.

Numerous new anti-submarine weapons were also introduced during the Second World War, supplementing the already available offensive capability of the depth-charge. These more sophisticated devices, among them the 'Hedgehog' and 'Squid', were designed to allow blanket attacks against either single submarines or entire U-boat formations.

The single most important technological advance to affect the balance of the war at sea, providing for the first time – as it did during the Second World War – a measure of really effective protection to troop and cargo convoys, was the aircraft. Although, between 1914 and 1918, there had been small coastal airships and early types of naval flying boats, these did not have sufficient range to be of much use. Even in the early period of the Battle of the Atlantic during the Second World War, air cover of the mid-Atlantic gap – the zone beyond the range of land-based aircraft – required special CAM-ships and MAC-ships attached to each convoy. Later, the escort carrier and long-range flying boats such as the Sunderland (the appropriately nicknamed 'flying porcupine'), meant that there was virtually no part of the ocean from which Allied aerial protection was absent.

I have mentioned only a few of the many devices and tactics whose implementation afforded a degree of protection in the otherwise somewhat one-sided war at sea. For the crews whose lives they saved they were a Godsend, but in the final reckoning they amounted to little more than a token contribution.

From a seafarer's point of view, wars are fought in a

hostile environment already fraught with natural hazards. Recognition of this stark reality, and acknowledgement of the vulnerability of merchant ships in wartime, highlights the courageous sacrifice and outstanding bravery of those seamen whose unglamorous but vital contest was fought out on the grey expanse of the oceans. For instance, it is a little-known fact that one in four British merchant seamen lost their lives during the Second World War, a far higher casualty rate than for any of the armed services. Yet there are few memorials to these unsung heroes of the maritime war and, with the passage of time, their brave deeds have tended to diminish in stature. For this reason, I hope that the publication of *Wartime Disasters at Sea* will help to commemorate those many thousands of Merchant Navy officers and seamen of all nationalities, the crews not only of passenger ships but of all types of merchant vessel, who gave their lives in the two World Wars and 'who have no grave but the sea'.

In conclusion, I hope that this book will not only assist the reader in his or her search for information, but that it will also – returning to the point with which I opened this Introduction – give him cause to reflect on the circumstances of these disasters and the experiences of those unfortunate souls who were their victims, passengers and crews alike.

I have endeavoured to include all the ships that warranted inclusion in this book and to exclude those that did not, according to the rules that I set myself (see Explanatory Notes). However, it is likely that I have made mistakes on both counts. I most certainly do not intend to belittle the tragedy of any disaster which has been excluded, either through error of omission or because it has fallen outside of these arbitrarily determined limits, and I request the reader's forbearance for any such errors that may have arisen.

David L. Williams
June 1996

EXPLANATORY NOTES

For reasons of space and apart from a few important exceptions, the contents of this book have been restricted to cover only those disaster incidents which involved engine-propelled, ocean-going passenger ships which were either lost while performing wartime duties in an auxiliary capacity, ie. as troopships, armed merchant cruisers, hospital ships, etc., or by war causes while still engaged in commercial operations.

In general terms, short-sea and coastal passenger ships are not covered by this book. The larger, deep-sea vessels have been concentrated on because, with their normal operational areas so much further removed from the means of rescue and refuge and carrying, on occasions, vast wartime passenger complements, the potential magnitude of a disaster was significantly greater where they were concerned.

For the purposes of this book, a passenger ship has been defined as a vessel which, during peacetime, carried or would have carried a substantial number of passengers in permanent accommodation and on a regular basis. Again, there are certain exceptions to this but, wherever there was uncertainty as to an individual ship's qualification for inclusion, this has been determined by whether she was utilized to a significant extent for passenger transportation. From 1934 onwards, Lloyd's Register of Shipping indicated wherever a vessel held a British Board of Trade Passenger Certificate or the equivalent issued by another country. This has been used to confirm the status of certain ships for inclusion in this book where precise figures for passenger accommodation could not be found.

Apart from losses due to war actions, disasters attributable to natural or accidental causes which occurred during wartime, while vessels were engaged in military duties, are also described.

The subject entries are presented in chronological sequence. Each chapter presents the incidents of a complete year in the range 1914–1918 (World War I) and 1939–1945 (World War II). For each account, the format is as follows:

- the vessel's peacetime name; any former names; if applicable, the name under which she was temporarily operating at the time of the disaster; years of total service.
- name of owners prior to war service and country of registration; name of builders and place where constructed.
- gross registered tonnage (GRT); length, overall (LOA) if stated; overall beam.
- where known, the number of passengers and classes.
- where known, the type of propulsion, number of screws; service speed in knots.
- factual account of the disaster detailing, where known, the date, location and/or position and cause, plus the numbers of casualties and survivors.

The passenger accommodation figures that have been provided are only intended to be indicative and, where available, have been restricted to only the total number of passengers and total number of grades or classes. In most cases this relates to the layout as originally built or following the last major refit. More detailed information has not been given because passenger accommodation changed frequently and no single set of figures would, necessarily, be a fair reflection of most ships' entire working careers.

The identification of Japanese passenger ships lost during World War II presents particular problems because from the mid-1930s the Japanese introduced a change to the system of transliteration of their phonetic language. This is the method by which the sounds of the spoken Japanese can be expressed in written form in Roman characters. The effect of this change, while not altering the Japanese pronunciation, did result in some alterations to the Roman spelling of ships' names. In keeping with the approach adopted by other books, I have used the pre-1937 spellings of Japanese ship names in all cases with, where applicable, the modified version alongside in parentheses, e.g. *Fuji* (*Huzi*) *Maru*.

In some cases, there are conflicting views as to the whereabouts and circumstances of certain disasters, all of which have been clarified where possible. The Lloyds War Loss Records have been used as the basis of the data provided for Allied or neutral vessel losses. Other official or reputable unofficial records have been used for purposes of substantiation, or to complete the details of those non-Allied and non-neutral ships whose losses are described.

Glossary of Terms

Other than those terms and abbreviations already explained in this section, the following additional terms have been used in this book:

CAM	Catapult Aircraft Merchantman, as in CAM-ship
ft	feet
GCHQ	Government Communications Headquarters, Cheltenham
kts	knots
LP	Low Pressure, as in Low Pressure steam turbine
m	metres
MAC	Merchant Aircraft Carrier, as in MAC-ship
RNR	Royal Naval Reserve
SR	Steam Reciprocating, as in SR engines

Chapter One

1914

RAIDERS AT LARGE

There were only six passenger ship losses in the five months between the outbreak of war on 1 August 1914 and 31 December of that year, two of them as a result of causes that had no direct connection with the hostilities. The four remaining sinkings are split equally, two Allied and two German, two of them in the role of auxiliary cruisers and two of them as the victims of surface raiders.

Both Great Britain and Germany saw value in converting passenger ships into naval auxiliaries. The British application took the form of squadrons of patrol vessels, notably the 10th Cruiser Squadron, while the German ships were operated as lone assailants, supported on the high seas by a fleet of replenishment vessels and with dockyard and bunkering facilities established in friendly ports around the world.

The British experience was that passenger ships over a certain size were unwieldy and, therefore, unsuited to this role, so the planned conversions of a number of well-known transatlantic liners were cancelled. The German auxiliaries had a rather more serious 'Achilles' Heel', given their intended function: their enormous coal consumption. The Admiralty knew that by either tracking these raiders or setting up blockade lines and laying in wait for them, sooner or later they would be forced to enter port, where they could be intercepted. It was then simply a matter of overwhelming them with the greater fire-power of conventional warships. In essence, this was the fate which befell the *Kaiser Wilhelm der Grosse* and the *Cap Trafalgar*, although in the latter case it resulted from the only liner versus liner engagement that ever occurred.

Other German raiders breached the blockade of the United States' Atlantic coastline, when their fuel was close to exhaustion, and were interned by what was then a 'neutral' power.

Along with the destruction of the *Tabora* in March 1916, the two liner losses recorded in this chapter amount to the total sinkings of Central Power passenger ships in the whole of the First World War. All the other losses in this period involved requisitioned Allied passenger vessels. Germany's passenger fleet did not suffer major depletion until after the Armistice, when the majority of the surviving German ships were allocated to Great Britain, France, the United States of America, the Netherlands, and so on, as reparations for the huge mercantile losses sustained by the Allies.

The situation was to be very different between 1939 and 1945. Sinkings of former passenger ships while on war service were then almost equally distributed between the Allies and their opponents. Axis shipping casualties were particularly high in the latter half of the Second World War, when Allied air power was dominant.

KAISER WILHELM DER GROSSE (1897–1914)

Norddeutscher Lloyd, Germany; Vulkan, Stettin.
14,349 GRT, 648ft (197.5m) LOA, 66ft (20.1m) beam.
1,749 passengers in three classes.
Triple expansion SR engines, twin screw, 22.5kts.
Date of disaster: 26 August 1914.

The *Kaiser Wilhelm der Grosse* was the first German passenger liner to capture the Atlantic Blue Riband, a feat she achieved in November 1897, shortly after her maiden voyage from Bremerhaven to New York. Her average speed for the record crossing was 22.35kts.

After 17 years on the North Atlantic she was converted into an auxiliary cruiser for the German Navy and from 4 August 1914 she joined the *guerre de course*. In the weeks that followed, the *Kaiser Wilhelm der Grosse*, under the command of Captain Reymann, sank three vessels but allowed the *Galician* and *Arlanza* to continue on their way after first destroying their radio equipment, as they were both carrying passengers.

On 17 August the *Arlanza* came across the cruiser HMS *Cornwall* off Las Palmas and advised her of the raider's whereabouts. The cruiser HMS *Highflyer* finally located the *Kaiser Wilhelm der Grosse* on 26 August, bunkering off Rio del Oro in Spanish West Africa. The *Highflyer* initially refrained from opening fire as the raider and colliers were in Spanish territorial waters. Instead, the German ships were ordered to surrender. Two hours after this was refused, the *Highflyer* opened fire, and the German vessel swiftly responded. After about 90 minutes the *Kaiser Wilhelm der Grosse* sank in shallow water, but there was dispute as to the cause. The British claimed that she sank as a result of the damage they inflicted on her, which had also caused considerable loss of life. For their part, the Germans insisted that the *Kaiser Wilhelm der Grosse* had scarcely been touched in the battle, and that her crew had scuttled her

Top *The* Kaiser Wilhelm der Grosse *as built. She was the first passenger ship to be lost in the First World War.* (A. Duncan)

Above *The partially submerged wreck of the* Kaiser Wilhelm der Grosse *at Rio del Oro.* (L.L. von Münching)

when she ran out of ammunition. Whichever account is true, the survivors of her skeleton crew rowed ashore in the ship's boats and later made good their escape aboard the stores ship *Bethania*, a former Hamburg Amerika Line vessel.

OCEANIC (1899–1914)

White Star Line, Great Britain; Harland & Wolff, Belfast.
17,274 GRT, 704ft (214.6m) LOA, 68ft (20.7m) beam.
1,710 passengers in three classes.
Triple expansion SR engines, twin screw; 21kts.
Date of disaster: 8 September 1914.

The liner *Oceanic* was the first vessel to exceed the length of the *Great Eastern*, a record that had stood for 40 years. She introduced new standards of comfort and spaciousness when she joined the Atlantic service from Liverpool to New York in September 1899. From 1907 she sailed out of Southampton.

White Star's Oceanic, *at one time the largest ship in the world.* (World Ship Society)

At the outbreak of war in 1914, the *Oceanic* was requisitioned for service as an armed merchant cruiser. After conversion she was attached to the 10th Cruiser Squadron, but on 8 September 1914, only weeks after she had been commissioned, the *Oceanic* ran onto the rocks off Foula Island in the Shetlands. Her complement of 400 officers and men was rescued by the trawler *Glenogil.* The accident occurred in dense fog, leaving the *Oceanic* firmly wedged. Three days later she was declared to be a constructive total loss. Breaking up was carried out on the spot, lasting until 1924.

CAP TRAFALGAR (1914)

Hamburg Sud-Amerika Line, Germany; Vulkan, Hamburg.
18,710 GRT, 613ft (186.8m) LOA, 72ft (21.9m) beam.
1,586 passengers in three classes.
Triple expansion SR engines, triple screw, 17.5kts.
Date of disaster: 13 September 1914.

Only five months after entering the Hamburg to South America service, the *Cap Trafalgar* was fitted out at sea as an auxiliary cruiser in August 1914. Having received her

The short-lived Cap Trafalgar. *At the time of her engagement with the* Carmania *she had only two funnels.* (Hamburg Sud-Amerika Line)

Artist's impression of the duel between the Carmania *and the* Cap Trafalgar. *The* Carmania *is the nearer of the two ships.* (University Archives, University of Liverpool)

orders at Buenos Aires, she coaled at Montevideo and then rendezvoused off Bahia Blanca with the gunboat *Eber*, which transferred weapons and other equipment to her. To help conceal her identity, *Cap Trafalgar*'s commander, Captain Wirth, had her third funnel removed.

On 13 September, the *Cap Trafalgar* was interrupted in the act of coaling, off the Brazilian island of Trinidad, by the British armed merchant cruiser *Carmania*. After a brief chase, the two ships engaged one another and initially, at a distance of four miles, the British ship's gunnery was more effective, causing much damage to the *Cap Trafalgar*'s hull. As the range closed, however, the battle became more even and the *Carmania* also began to sustain damage. After nearly two hours of intense action the *Cap Trafalgar* was listing and ablaze from end to end, while the *Carmania*, hit no less than 79 times, was also on fire at her fore-end, and had lost the use of her navigation and communication equipment. Her water main had been ruptured so that fire-fighting was impossible and she had to be escorted to port by the cruiser HMS *Cornwall*. The *Cap Trafalgar* capsized onto her port side and sank bow first. Her survivors were picked up by the *Eleonore Woermann*. In all, 25 men lost their lives in the battle, 16 on the German side, Captain Wirth among them, and nine on the British. There were 279 survivors from the *Cap Trafalgar*.

HIGHLAND HOPE (1903–1914)

Nelson Line, Great Britain; Russell, Port Glasgow.
5,150 GRT, 384ft (117.0m) length, 51ft (15.5m) beam.
Triple expansion SR engine, single screw, 12kts.
Date of disaster: 14 September 1914.

While bound from Liverpool to Buenos Aires in ballast on 14 September 1914, the *Highland Hope* was captured by the German commerce raider *Karlsruhe* near Cape Sao Roque. After removing her crew, stores, and other useful materials, the *Highland Hope* was scuttled, going down in the position 01°03′S–31°45′W.

VANDYCK (1911–1914)

Lamport & Holt Co., Great Britain; Workman Clark, Belfast.
10,328 GRT, 511ft (155.7m) LOA, 60ft (18.3m) beam.
610 passengers in three classes.
Quadruple expansion SR engines, twin screw, 15kts.
Date of disaster: 27 October 1914.

The *Vauban*, *Vandyck*, and *Vestris* were employed on the New York to La Plata service. The *Vandyck* was another

Lamport & Holt's Vandyck*, sunk by the raider* Karlsruhe. (A. Duncan)

The Rohilla *stranded soon after conversion for hospital-ship duties.* (World Ship Society)

victim of the German commerce raider *Karlsruhe.* While bound for New York from Buenos Aires on 26 October 1914, she was intercepted off the coast of Brazil in the position 01°14'S–40°40'W, and arrested after a short chase. Her occupants, including over 200 passengers, were transferred to the *Asuncion,* which had been captured earlier, and were taken to Pará (Belem), arriving there on 1 November. Meanwhile, the *Vandyck*'s cargo was looted, an especially valuable prize being a 1,000-ton consignment of frozen meat. This completed, the *Vandyck* was sunk by explosive charges off Maranhão on 27 October 1914.

ROHILLA (1906–1914)

British India Line, Great Britain; Harland & Wolff, Belfast.
7,409 GRT, 460ft (140.2m) length, 56ft (17.1m) beam.
165 passengers in two classes.
Quadruple expansion SR engines, twin screw, 17kts.
Date of disaster: 30 October 1914.

The steamship *Rohilla,* sister of the *Rewa* (which was to be torpedoed and sunk in January 1918), was taken over as a hospital ship in the First World War. On 30 October 1914, while she was proceeding to Dunkerque from Leith in a gale, the *Rohilla* ran onto the rocks south of Whitby. The lifeboats from Whitby, Redcar, and Upgang went to her aid but, because of the conditions, were unable at first to take off any of the 229 persons aboard her. Ultimately, 143 were rescued, including the *Rohilla*'s master, Captain Neilson, and the entire complement of nurses, but the remainder perished in the rough seas.

Chapter Two

1915

ALL-OUT U-BOAT WAR

By far the majority of the passenger ships lost during 1915 were victims of torpedoes fired by submarines, and the period from February to September 1915 has, in retrospect, been identified as the first of several periods of intensive German submarine warfare. During this nine-month period losses were high amongst all types of vessel, but the most notorious sinking was that of the Cunard express liner *Lusitania*, torpedoed south of Ireland on 7 May while bound for Liverpool on a scheduled Atlantic crossing. The death-toll was massive – 1,198 in total, and all civilians.

At the time, the rules by which war was conducted on the high seas required that ships which were intercepted had to have all their passengers safely evacuated before any sort of attack could be launched. However, the *Lusitania* incident, in demonstrating the willingness of some naval commanders to ignore this code of conduct, indicated the shape of things to come. To be fair, it has to be recognized that in many cases the Allied vessels which were the victims of such attacks were hardly a passive or submissive prey. Equally, the U-boats were themselves being hunted by growing numbers of destroyers and other anti-submarine vessels, and the time required to fulfil the convention protocols was rarely available to German submarines without compromising their own safety.

The Highland Brae *was sunk by the raider* Kronprinz Wilhelm, *herself a former liner.* (Furness Withy Group)

The close proximity of many of these sinkings, and the frequently repeated U-boat identities noted in these disaster accounts, reveal that Germany was already concentrating attacks in particular sea areas, a trend which was to evolve into the 'wolf-pack' tactics employed during the Second World War.

The opening of a front in the Balkans by the Allies in mid-1915, in an ill-conceived attempt to expedite the removal of Turkey from the war, created the circumstances in which many passenger ship losses occurred over a period extending well into the following year. Centred on a bid to seize and control the entrance to the Dardanelles Straits, the campaign commenced with the infamous landings at Gallipoli. However, it proved to be a very costly mistake, politically, militarily and, in particular, in terms of human casualties, both on the battlefield and at sea. Through a combination of submarine attacks and strategically laid minefields, there were heavy losses to troopships ferrying men to the front, as well as to the hospital ships transferring casualties back to Salonica and Malta for treatment. In fact, the worst shipping casualties of the war were sustained in the Mediterranean theatre during the Gallipoli offensive, where just three losses, all French – the *Gallia*, *La Provence*, and *Amiral Magon* – accounted for 24 per cent of all passenger ship casualties in the First World War.

HIGHLAND BRAE (1910–1915)

Nelson Line, Great Britain; Cammell Laird, Birkenhead.
7,634 GRT, 413ft (125.9m) length, 56ft (17.1m) beam.
516 passengers in three classes.
Triple expansion SR engine, single screw, 13kts.
Date of disaster: 31 January 1915.

The *Highland Brae* was one of a group of 10 steamships employed in the South American trade. She was captured by the German auxiliary cruiser *Kronprinz Wilhelm* on 14 January 1915 while bound to Buenos Aires from London with passengers. The *Highland Brae* was kept for two weeks as a source of stores and as accommodation for the prisoners from this and earlier victim ships. She was finally scuttled and sunk on 31 January in the position 02°46'N–24°11'W. Just over a month later the French passenger liner *Guadeloupe* was another of the *Kronprinz Wilhelm*'s victims.

FLORIDE (1907–1915)

French Line (CGT), France; Chantiers et Ateliers de Provence, Port de Bouc.
7,029 GRT, 437ft (133.2m) LOA, 52ft (15.9m) beam.
910 passengers in two classes.
Triple expansion SR engine, single screw, 12.5kts.
Date of disaster: 19 February 1915.

The transatlantic liner *Floride* was intercepted by the German commerce raider *Prinz Eitel Friedrich* on 19 February 1915, north-east of Fernando de Noronha, near Dakar, Senegal, during a voyage from Le Havre to the River Plate. After her 86 passengers and 78 crew were taken off, the ship was shelled and sunk. The *Floride*'s occupants were held prisoner aboard the *Prinz Eitel Friedrich*, herself a converted Norddeutscher Lloyd liner, until she was interned at Newport News, Virginia, on 11 March 1915, after her supplies had run out. By that time she had sunk 11 ships, over half of them sailing vessels.

GUADELOUPE (1906–1915)

French Line (CGT), France; Chantiers de L'Atlantique, St. Nazaire.
6,600 GRT, 433ft (132.0m) length, 52ft (15.9m) beam.
Triple expansion SR engines, twin screw, 16kts.
Date of disaster: 9 March 1915.

The *Guadeloupe* operated on the service from France to the West Indies and Venezuela with a sister ship, the *Perou*. While homeward bound to Bordeaux from Buenos Aires and Rio de Janeiro on 22 February 1915, the *Guadeloupe* was captured by the German auxiliary cruiser *Kronprinz Wilhelm*, the former Norddeutscher Lloyd holder of the Atlantic Blue Riband. The interception took place some 300 miles south-east of Fernando de Noronha, in the position 05°58'S–27°27'W. The raider retained the *Guadeloupe* for two weeks, consuming her stores, eventually sinking her on 9 March. Her occupants, including 143 passengers, were put aboard the British collier *Chasehill*, another captured vessel, and sent to Pernambuco, Brazil, where they arrived on 12 March. By the time she abandoned her raiding activities on 11 April 1915, and was interned at Newport News, Virginia, the *Kronprinz Wilhelm* had sunk 14 Allied merchant vessels.

BAYANO (1913–1915)

Elders & Fyffes, Great Britain; Alexander Stephen, Glasgow.
5,948 GRT, 417ft (127.1m) length, 53ft (16.2m) beam.
Triple expansion SR engines, twin screw, 14kts.
Date of disaster: 11 March 1915.

Although the *Bayano* normally had only limited accommodation for passengers she has been included in this book because she was sunk while carrying a considerably larger number of people. Her peacetime employment was between Jamaica and the United Kingdom. In August 1914, she was taken over for conversion into an auxiliary cruiser and while serving in this capacity she was torpedoed and sunk by the German submarine *U27*, under Lt-Cdr Wegener, on 11 March 1915. The attack took place three miles off Corsewall Point while the *Bayano* was heading for Liverpool to take on coal. The sinking claimed

The Bayano, *owned by Elders & Fyffes*. (World Ship Society)

195 lives, comprising 14 officers and 181 ratings. The steamship *Castlereagh* arrived on the scene to give assistance but, due to the continuing presence of the U-boat, was compelled to abandon a search for other survivors for fear of being torpedoed herself.

FALABA (1906–1915)

Elder Dempster Line, Great Britain; Alexander Stephen, Glasgow.
4,806 GRT, 381ft (116.1m) length, 47ft (14.3m) beam.
210 passengers in two classes.
Triple expansion SR engine, single screw, 14kts.
Date of disaster: 28 March 1915.

One of Elder Dempster's fleet of West African services vessels, the *Falaba* was the victim of a torpedo attack. She sailed from Liverpool bound for Sierra Leone on 27 March 1915. The following day, when some 36 miles south-west by west of the Smalls Lighthouse, she sighted a submarine flying the White Ensign. However, as the submarine approached the *Falaba* it exchanged its flag for the German naval ensign, turning out to be the *U28* under the command of Baron von Forstner. Capt Davis of the *Falaba* considered attempting to outrun the U-boat but decided against it, the *U28* being capable of bettering his best speed on the surface. He therefore hove to and commenced lowering his boats in anticipation of an attack. When only five boats had yet been swung out the *U28* fired a torpedo, which struck the *Falaba* amidships. She sank rapidly, disappearing beneath the water within 10 minutes. In consequence of the inadequate time given to evacuate the ship there were many deaths, a total of 104 perishing out of the 151 passengers and 96 crew aboard. The survivors were picked up by the drifters *Eileen Emma* and *Wenlock*. Among them was Capt Davis, though he died shortly after being picked up.

LUSITANIA (1907–1915)

Cunard Line, Great Britain; John Brown, Clydebank.
31,550 GRT, 787ft (239.9m) LOA, 87ft (26.5m) beam.
2,165 passengers in three classes.
Steam turbine engines, quadruple screw, 26kts.
Date of disaster: 7 May 1915.

The sinking by torpedo of the Cunard express transatlantic liner *Lusitania* was a marine disaster that ranks only with the loss of the *Titanic*, and probably no two other ships have had so much written about the circumstances surrounding their demise. Her loss was one of the two most serious marine casualties that Great Britain sustained during the First World War, the tragedy being made all the more poignant by the fact that she was not engaged in military activities at the time. Unlike her sister ship the *Mauretania*, the *Lusitania* continued with her regular sailing schedule after the outbreak of war, in spite of the known risk of U-boat attacks. Strange as it may seem today, a chivalrous view of warfare was still held at the time, the belief being

The Elder Dempster ship Falaba. (World Ship Society)

Top *The* Lusitania *– a trials view in the Firth of Clyde, August 1907.* (Author's collection)

Above *Norman Wilkinson's dramatic painting of the* Lusitania*'s last moments. The original caption described the torpedo attack as an act of 'wilful and wholesale murder'.* (Illustrated London News)

that conflict could be conducted within agreed rules and that a defenceless ship going about her peaceful business was safe from attack.

The *Lusitania*'s last departure from New York, accompanied by threats of possible attack, was on 1 May 1915. She was bound for Liverpool with 1,959 people on board, including 440 women and 129 children. Six days later, as she was approaching the St George's Channel, she was torpedoed without warning off the Old Head of Kinsale by the submarine *U20*. Those aboard the *Lusitania* said they heard two explosions, while Capt-Lt Schweiger of the *U20* insisted that he had only fired one torpedo. Either way, the liner sank with alarming suddenness, barely 15 minutes after the attack. Although her engines were stopped, she was still going ahead in the water, and this, coupled with the increasing list to starboard, hampered efforts to launch her lifeboats. The trawlers *Bluebell* and *Peel*, accompanied by a flotilla of smaller craft, headed to the scene from the nearby Irish coast, but were able to rescue only a fraction of those who had been aboard. The dead totalled 1,198, among whom were 291 women and 94 children. Capt W.J. Turner, the *Lusitania*'s commander, was among the 761 survivors. Apart from the ignominy of setting a precedent for attacking a civilian passenger vessel without warning, even greater disdain was attached to the manner in which the affair was celebrated in Germany, though it is only fair to point out that the German public were led to believe the *Lusitania* had been engaged in belligerent activities.

Though relatively innocuous compared to some of the horrors subsequently unleashed by twentieth century warfare, the sinking of the *Lusitania*, as one of the first examples of modern 'total war', is symbolic of humankind's ever-deteriorating standards of behaviour.

MERION (1902–1915)

American Line, USA; John Brown, Clydebank.
11,612 GRT, 547ft (166.7m) LOA, 59ft (18.0m) beam.
1,850 passengers in two classes.
Triple expansion SR engines, twin screw, 14kts.
Date of disaster: 30 May 1915.

The steamship *Merion* was lost in rather unusual circumstances in the early summer of 1915. This former transatlantic liner, which had sailed between Liverpool and Philadelphia, was taken over by the British Admiralty on the outbreak of war. She was earmarked for deployment in a special naval decoy fleet and, following conversion, she emerged as the dummy battle cruiser HMS *Tiger*. In this guise she was sent to the Mediterranean, but on 30 May 1915 the German submarine *UB8* torpedoed her in the Aegean Sea, off Mudros, on the island of Lemnos. Presumably she achieved her objective even as a casualty, by misleading the Germans regarding British naval strength.

INDIA (1896–1915)

P&O Line, Great Britain; Caird, Greenock.
7,940 GRT, 500ft (152.4m) length, 54ft (16.5m) beam.
526 passengers in two classes, and/or 2,500 troops.
Triple expansion SR engine, single screw, 18kts.
Date of disaster: 8 August 1915.

The sister ships *Arabia*, *China*, *Egypt*, *India*, and *Persia* were introduced to the England to Australia via India service between 1896 and 1900. The *India* was taken over by the Admiralty in August 1914 and was employed as an auxiliary cruiser under the command of Capt W.G.A. Kennedy. A German submarine attacked the *India* off the island of

The Merion *as built.* (World Ship Society)

The Merion *disguised as HMS* Tiger. (Imperial War Museum, Neg. SP2350)

The steamship India. *The paddle-steamer* Lorna Doone *is in the foreground.* (P&O Group)

Hellevoer, near Bodo, Norway, on 8 August 1915. She sank with the loss of 160 lives (10 officers and 150 ratings). The 141 survivors included her master.

ROYAL EDWARD ex-*CAIRO* (1908–1915)

Royal Line, Great Britain; Fairfield, Glasgow.
11,117 GRT, 545ft (166.1m) LOA, 60ft (18.3m) beam.
1,000 passengers in two classes.
Steam turbine engines, triple screw, 20kts.
Date of disaster: 13 August 1915.

The *Cairo* and the *Heliopolis* were built for the Marseilles to Alexandria service, but as this was unprofitable they were soon laid up. In 1910, they were purchased by the Royal Line (Canadian Northern Steamships) for the Avonmouth to

The Royal Edward *was built as the* Cairo, *as depicted here.* (Tom Rayner)

Montreal service, and renamed *Royal Edward* and *Royal George* respectively. In autumn 1914 both became troopships.

Bound for Mudros from Alexandria, her voyage having started at Avonmouth, the *Royal Edward* was sunk on 13 August 1915 when the German submarine *UB14*, under Lt von Heimburg, torpedoed her six miles west of the island of Kandeliusa, in the Aegean Sea, at position 36°31′N–26°51′E. She sank rapidly by the stern, many of the 1,366 troops and 220 crew aboard losing their lives, including her commander, Capt P.M. Wotton. The hospital ship *Soudan*, accompanied by two French destroyers and some trawlers, arrived on the scene to render assistance, but they were only able to rescue 651 survivors, the casualties numbering 935. Some accounts put the death toll higher, at over 1,000.

ARABIC ex-*MINNEWASKA* (1903–1915)

White Star Line, Great Britain; Harland & Wolff, Belfast.
15,801 GRT, 616ft (187.8m) LOA, 69ft (21.0m) beam.
Quadruple expansion SR engines, twin screw, 17kts.
Date of disaster: 19 August 1915.

Originally ordered for the Atlantic Transport Line, this vessel finally entered service under the White Star houseflag, sailing between Liverpool and Boston or New York. On 19 August 1915 the *Arabic* was torpedoed off the Old Head of Kinsale – the most dangerous area in the Western Approaches for submarine attacks – by *U24*, under the

The Arabic. (World Ship Society)

command of Lt-Cdr Schneider. She was bound for New York, her passengers including a number of American citizens. The torpedo, which hit her starboard side, left the *Arabic* mortally wounded and she sank inside 15 minutes in the position 50°50'N–08°32'W. Prompt action and good discipline prevented a massive loss of life and enabled 390 people to be taken off safely. Even so, a further 44, including some Americans, were killed. The US Government exchanged diplomatic notes with Germany over the affair, demanding an explanation for the apparently un-forewarned attack. In response the Germans claimed that the submarine commander had attacked in self-defence, believing that the *Arabic* was about to ram him. Assurances that such an attack would not be repeated proved sufficient to appease growing public concern in the United States, if only temporarily.

HESPERIAN (1908–1915)

Allan Line, Great Britain; Alexander Stephen, Glasgow.
10,920 GRT, 502ft (153.0m) LOA, 60ft (18.3m) beam.
1,460 passengers in three classes.
Triple expansion SR engines, twin screw, 15kts.
Date of disaster: 4 September 1915.

The *Hesperian* was a sister ship of the *Grampian* (destroyed by fire at Antwerp in March 1921). For her brief life she sailed between Glasgow and Montreal, being torpedoed by the German submarine *U20*, under Cdr W. von Schwieger, on 4 September 1915 when 85 miles south-west of Fastnet, bound for Montreal with 653 passengers and crew and a general cargo. Thirty two people lost their lives in the attack, the remainder safely taking to the boats and being picked up later. The *Hesperian* did not immediately sink, and warships which had gone to her aid took her in tow for Queenstown. However, after proceeding about 40 miles she began to settle, her master, Capt Maine, and his volunteer skeleton crew being forced to abandon her. The position of the attack was 50°03'N–10°10'W. The liner eventually sank about 130 miles west of Malin Head, Donegal.

KONINGIN EMMA (1913–1915)

Nederland Royal Mail Line, Netherlands; Fijenoord, Rotterdam.
9,181 GRT, 470ft (143.3m) length, 57ft (17.4m) beam.
Quadruple expansion SR engines, twin screw, 15kts.
Date of disaster: 22 September 1915.

The *Koningin Emma* and her sister ship, the *Prins der Nederlanden*, plied between Amsterdam and Sumatra and Java in the Dutch East Indies. Returning to Amsterdam from Batavia on 22 September 1915, she struck a mine in the Thames Estuary one mile west of the Sunk Light Vessel, in the position 51°54'N–01°32'E. The wreck was dispersed later.

CARIBBEAN ex-*DUNOTTAR CASTLE* (1890–1915)

Royal Mail Line, Great Britain; Fairfield, Glasgow.
5,825 GRT, 433ft (132.0m) LOA, 49ft (14.9m) beam.

Top *The* Koningin Emma *at Genoa in 1913.* (L.L. von Münching)

Above *The* Koningin Emma, *seen sinking in the Thames estuary after striking a mine laid by the German submarine* UC7. (L.L. von Münching)

350 passengers in three classes.
Triple expansion SR engine, single screw, 16kts.
Date of disaster: 27 September 1915.

Her speed and reliability made the *Dunottar Castle* one of the outstanding units of the Castle Line fleet (after 1900 the Union Castle Line) serving South Africa from Southampton. In 1913 she was sold to the Royal Mail Line for the South America service and was renamed *Caribbean*. The following August she was requisitioned for duties as a transport and armed merchant cruiser. On 27 September 1915, while bound for Scapa Flow, she encountered extremely heavy weather off the aptly named Cape Wrath, Sutherland, and foundered with the loss of 15 lives. An attempt by the cruiser HMS *Birkenhead*, aided by tugs, to tow the disabled *Caribbean* to port was unsuccessful.

This old, somewhat damaged picture shows Red Star's Marquette. (World Ship Society)

MARQUETTE ex-*BOADICEA* (1898–1915)

Red Star Line, Belgium; Alexander Stephen, Glasgow.
7,057 GRT, 486ft (148.1m) length, 52ft (15.9m) beam.
132 passengers in single class.
Triple expansion SR engine, single screw, 14.5kts.
Date of disaster: 23 October 1915.

Typical of the vessels built under the umbrella of the International Mercantile Marine, the *Marquette* was moved freely between the combine's companies. She was built for the Leyland Line, but very soon after completion passed to the Atlantic Transport Line for use on the London to New York route. In 1901 she was transferred again, to the Red Star Line, remaining on the Antwerp to Philadelphia service until the First World War. She was then engaged as a troop transport, in which capacity she was sunk on 23 October 1915 during a voyage from Alexandria to Salonica (Thessaloniki). The *Marquette* was heavily loaded with 610 troops from the Royal Field Artillery and 36 nurses of the New Zealand Stationary Hospital, in addition to her crew. Besides this, she was carrying ammunition and 541 animals, including many horses. The *U35*, under Lt-Cdr Waldemar Kophamel, torpedoed her 36 miles south of Salonica. Though the badly damaged ship did not sink immediately there was heavy loss of life, 88 troops, 11 nurses, and 29 crewmen being killed.

The Ancona *was the first Italian passenger ship to be sunk in the First World War.* (World Ship Society)

ANCONA (1908–1915)

Italia Line (Italia Societa Anonima di Navigazione), Italy; Workman Clark, Belfast.
8,885 GRT, 482ft (146.9m) length, 58ft (17.7m) beam.
Triple expansion SR engines, twin screw, 16kts.
Date of disaster: 7 November 1915.

The *Ancona*, with her sisters *Taormina* and *Verona*, worked the passenger service to New York from Genoa, Naples, Messina, and Palermo. She left Messina for New York on 7 November 1915 carrying 283 passengers and 163 crewmen under Capt Massardo. Off Cape Carbonara she was fired on by a surfaced submarine, flying the Austrian flag, which subsequently torpedoed and sank her. The lifeboats were lowered, but as the ship was still moving ahead most of them capsized as they reached the water. As a result there was a heavy loss of life, 194 people being killed. The survivors were picked up by the French cruiser *Pluton*.

Because the dead included 11 American citizens, the

sinking of the *Ancona* led to a diplomatic exchange between the USA and Austria. The Austrian Government acknowledged that the submarine commander's actions, particularly the shelling of the liner, had exceeded his orders. However, it was later revealed that though she had been displaying the Austrian ensign, the submarine concerned was in fact the German *U38*, commanded by Lt-Cdr Max Valentiner. At the time there existed no state of war between Italy and Germany.

FRANCE (1896–1915)

Soc. Générale des Transports Maritime (SGTM), France;
Forges et Chantiers de la Mediterranée, La Seyne.
4,269 GRT, 397ft (121.0m) length, 42ft (12.8m) beam.
Triple expansion SR engine, single screw, 14kts.
Date of disaster: 7 November 1915.

Returning to Marseilles from Mudros while engaged in carrying French troops to Gallipoli, the steamship *France* was torpedoed and sunk by the German submarine *U38* on 7 November 1915. She foundered in the position 38°30′N–10°00′E. In peacetime she had maintained the passenger service from Marseilles to South America.

CALIFORNIAN (1902–1915)

Leyland Line, GB; Caledon SB Co, Dundee.
6,223 GRT, 448ft (136.4m) length, 54ft (16.4m) beam.
35 passengers in single class.
Triple expansion SR engine, single screw, 14kts.
Date of disaster: 9 November 1915.

Famed as the ship which, allegedly, ignored the distress flares and failed to go to the aid of the sinking *Titanic* on 15 April 1912, the *Californian* was one of many mixed role vessels operated by the Leyland Line across the Atlantic. Although not primarily a passenger ship, she did retain accommodation for a small number of First Class passengers throughout her life. She was torpedoed and sunk off Cape Matapan, in the Mediterranean, on 9 November 1915.

YASAKA MARU (1914–1915)

Nippon Yusen Kaisha, Japan; Kawasaki, Kobe.
10,932 GRT, 523ft (159.4m) LOA, 63ft (19.2m) beam.
512 passengers in three classes.
Triple expansion SR engines, twin screw, 14.5kts.
Date of disaster: 21 December 1915.

The *Yasaka Maru* was the last unit of a five-ship class built for the Japan to Europe service. On 21 December 1915, while bound from the River Tees and London for Yokohama, she was torpedoed by the German submarine *U38*, and sank 60 miles from Port Said in the position 31°53′N–31°10′E. There were no casualties, as her entire complement was able to escape in the boats. The *Yasaka Maru*'s classmates were all sunk during the naval actions of the Second World War.

The Yasaka Maru. (Kawasaki Heavy Industries)

The Persia *was engaged as an armed cruiser in the First World War.* (P&O Group)

VILLE DE LA CIOTAT (1892–1915)

Messageries Maritimes, France; Messageries Maritimes, La Ciotat.
6,378 GRT, 485ft (147.8m) length, 49ft (14.9m) beam.
352 passengers in three classes.
Triple expansion SR engine, single screw, 17.5kts.
Date of disaster: 24 December 1915.

Built for the France to Australia via Suez service, the *Ville de la Ciotat* was switched to the Far East run after the outbreak of war in 1914. While returning to Marseilles from Yokohama on 24 December 1915, she was torpedoed east of Crete by an Austrian submarine, claimed to be the *U34*. She sank with the loss of 35 of her 135 passengers and 45 of her 181 crew. The survivors were taken to Malta, many aboard the British ship *Meroe*.

PERSIA (1900–1915)

P&O Line, Great Britain; Caird, Greenock.
7,974 GRT, 500ft (152.4m) length, 54ft (16.5m) beam.
526 passengers in two classes, and/or 2,500 troops.
Triple expansion SR engine, single screw, 18kts.
Date of disaster: 30 December 1915.

The *Persia* was the last unit of the *India* class, a five-ship group of which only the *China* survived to be broken up for scrap. The *India*, *Arabia*, and *Persia* were victims of submarines, while the *Egypt* sank after a collision in May 1922. Bound from London and Marseilles to Bombay, with a total complement of 501, the *Persia* was torpedoed without warning on 30 December 1915 by the German submarine *U38* under the command of Lt-Cdr Max Valentiner. The attack took place 71 miles south-east of Cape Martello, Crete, in the position 34°01′N–26°00′E. The torpedo struck her on the port side forward, the boiler on that side exploding, and she foundered after only a very short time. In all 334 people lost their lives in the attack, some of the *Persia*'s boats being sucked under as she sank and their occupants drowned. The survivors, in four boats that managed to get away safely, were picked up by a trawler the following day and taken to Alexandria.

Chapter Three

1916

SOME MINES BUT MOSTLY TORPEDOES

The continuing submarine war dominated the year, torpedo attacks accounting for by far the greatest number of passenger ship losses during 1916. The second period of intensification of the German U-boat campaign occurred between March and April, although this is not reflected particularly in the events described below because cargo vessels were the main target.

The Battle of Jutland – in effect the last occasion in history when two entire battle fleets faced one another and decided the issue by an exchange of gunfire – took place in late-May and early-June. Its outcome, which indirectly set the course of the war at sea for the remainder of the conflict, has long been debated by historians. On paper, the German High Seas Fleet would appear to have fared best, sustaining fewer ship losses than the British Grand Fleet. However, it is significant that the German fleet never again ventured to sea with any serious intent. Instead, German naval command resolved that henceforward its strategy for waging war at sea should be predominantly by means of its submarine forces. U-boat construction was stepped up accordingly, offering no respite for Allied merchant seamen struggling to get their vessels and valuable cargoes safely home to port.

NORSEMAN ex-*BRASILIA* (1897–1916)

Dominion Line, Great Britain; Harland & Wolff, Belfast.
9,546 GRT, 516ft (157.3m) LOA, 62ft (18.9m) beam.
2,400 passengers in single class.
Quadruple expansion SR engines, twin screw, 12.5kts.
Date of disaster: 22 January 1916.

This former Hamburg Amerika Line passenger ship was taken over by the Dominion Line in 1900, when she was

The Norseman*'s wreck, lying in shallow water.* (Maritime Photo Library)

The French Line's La Provence *was sunk under the name* Provence II. *Her loss was one of France's worst shipping disasters in the First World War.* (Author's collection)

adapted for a North Atlantic cargo service with passenger accommodation reduced to steerage class only. Later she transferred to a London to Sydney route.

The *Norseman* was torpedoed by the submarine *U39* on 22 January 1916 off Gran Capo, in the Gulf of Salonica, while bound from Plymouth to Salonica with a cargo of mules and munitions. The casualties of the attack are not known. The stricken ship was taken in tow for Mudros, where she was beached. From 1920 onwards she was broken up on the spot by a firm of Italian shipbreakers.

LA PROVENCE as *PROVENCE II* (1906–1916)

French Line (CGT), France; Chantiers et Ateliers de St Nazaire (Penhoët).
13,753 GRT, 627ft (191.1m) LOA, 64ft (19.5m) beam.
1,354 passengers in three classes.
Triple expansion SR engines, twin screw, 21.5kts.
Date of disaster: 26 February 1916.

The *La Provence* was a larger version of the earlier near sister ships *La Lorraine* and *La Savoie*, entering the transatlantic service from Le Havre to New York in April 1906. After the outbreak of the First World War, the *La Provence* entered service with the French Navy as the auxiliary cruiser *Provence II.* She was also employed carrying troops and, during a voyage from Toulon to Greece with 1,700 troops in addition to her crew, she was torpedoed and sunk by the German submarine *U35* on 26 February 1916. She sank rapidly, and 930 of those on board were drowned. Approximately 870 survivors were rescued. The *U35* was commanded by Capt Lothar von Arnauld de la Perière, whose torpedoes were to sink another French liner, the *Gallia*, the following October, with the loss of another 1,350 lives. Between them, the sinking of the *Gallia* and the *Provence II* constituted France's two most serious mercantile losses of the war.

MALOJA (1911–1916)

P&O Line, Great Britain; Harland & Wolff, Belfast.
12,431 GRT, 569ft (173.4m) LOA, 62ft (18.9m) beam.
770 passengers in two classes.
Quadruple expansion SR engines, twin screw, 18.5kts.
Date of disaster: 27 February 1916.

The Maloja, *a mine casualty.* (World Ship Society)

P&O Line's 'M' class consisted of seven passenger vessels built for the London to Sydney service. The *Maloja* was the sixth unit, entering service in February 1912. After the outbreak of war in 1914 she was employed on other routes, and in February 1916 she set out from London on a voyage to Bombay with 121 passengers and 335 crew. On 27 February she struck a mine 2.5 miles south-west of Dover and foundered after only a very brief interval. In order to make the lowering of lifeboats easier, the *Maloja*'s engines were reversed to slow her forward movement and stop her dead. However, the ship's engine compartment was soon flooded and the engines could not be arrested. With the ship now moving astern at some eight knots the launching of her boats remained hazardous and soon became almost impossible, a 75° list adding to the difficulties. The Canadian ship *Empress of Fort William* attempted to get alongside the *Maloja* to assist in the rescue of those aboard, but she too struck a mine and foundered. There were no deaths on the *Empress of Fort William*, but 155 people were killed on the *Maloja*.

ALCANTARA (1913–1916)

Royal Mail Line, Great Britain; Harland & Wolff, Govan.
15,831 GRT, 589ft (179.5m) LOA, 67ft (20.4m) beam.
1,330 passengers in three classes.
Triple expansion SR engines with LP turbine, triple screw, 16kts.
Date of disaster: 29 February 1916.

Sister ship to the *Andes* and *Almanzora*, the *Alcantara* operated with them on the service from Southampton to the Atlantic coast ports of South America. In April 1915, the *Alcantara* joined the 10th Cruiser Squadron as an auxiliary cruiser, in which capacity she was responsible for patrolling between Scapa Flow and the coast of Norway. On 29 February 1916 she intercepted the German raider *Greif*, disguised as a Norwegian vessel named *Reno*, in the entrance to the Skagerrak. Capt T.E. Wardle, master of the *Alcantara*, had been warned of the vessel's possible identity, and his guns were manned in readiness. The *Greif* was requested to stop, and blanks were fired across her bow. As the two ships closed a boat with a boarding party was lowered from the *Alcantara*, at which point the *Greif* suddenly revealed her identity, running up the German battle ensign and opening fire on the British ship, which, at a distance of only 1,000 yards, was a sitting duck. The first German salvo destroyed the *Alcantara*'s steering gear and engine-room telegraph as well as her telephone system, beside causing numerous deaths. Her guns replied, and after a brief but intense exchange both ships were left sinking. The *Alcantara* listed to port, then completely capsized, remaining afloat keel uppermost for a short time before sinking beneath the surface. The *Greif*, which was ablaze from stem to stern, was finished off soon after by the *Alcantara*'s sister liner *Andes*, aided by the cruiser HMS *Comus* and the destroyer HMS *Munster*, which had arrived on the scene to give assistance. Between them they picked up the survivors from both ships. Of the *Alcantara*'s company 69 lost their lives, while 80 out of the 300 men aboard the *Greif* also perished.

TUBANTIA (1914–1916)

Royal Holland Lloyd, Netherlands; Alexander Stephen, Glasgow.
13,911 GRT, 560ft (170.7m) LOA, 65ft (19.8m) beam.
1,520 passengers in four classes.
Quadruple expansion SR engines, twin screw, 16kts.
Date of disaster: 16 March 1916.

The Alcantara *was a victim of the raider* Greif. (World Ship Society)

Royal Holland Lloyd's Tubantia. (L.L. von Münching)

The *Tubantia* sailed between Amsterdam and the River Plate ports with her sister ship *Gelria*. Unlike the *Gelria*, however, the *Tubantia* did not survive the First World War. On 16 March 1916 she was bound from Amsterdam to Buenos Aires with 82 passengers, besides her crew of 296, when the German submarine *UB13* torpedoed her four miles from the Noordhinder lightship in thick fog. The *Tubantia* had been about to anchor owing to the poor visibility. The torpedo penetrated amidships, wrecking the engine-room, and the liner sank some four or so hours later. Before she went down, Dutch torpedo boats took off all on board. An International Committee of Inquiry held at the Hague after the war ordered Germany to pay £800,000 to Royal Holland Lloyd in compensation, an amount which was finally settled in 1922. Throughout the 1920s the wreck of the *Tubantia*, which lay in the position 51°46′N–02°45′E, was the subject of salvage operations, because it was believed that £2 million worth of smuggled gold was concealed in cheeses which had formed the bulk of the ship's cargo.

MINNEAPOLIS (1900–1916)

Atlantic Transport Line, Great Britain; Harland & Wolff, Belfast.
13,543 GRT, 616ft (187.8m) LOA, 65ft (19.8m) beam.
228 passengers in one class.
Quadruple expansion SR engines, twin screw, 16kts.
Date of disaster: 23 March 1916.

Atlantic Transport Line added four new ships – the *Minneapolis*, *Minnehaha*, *Minnetonka*, and *Minnewaska* – to their London to New York service between the years 1900 and 1909, all four being lost in the First World War. The *Minneapolis* was sunk on 23 March 1916 while she was serving as a troopship. The German submarine *U35* torpedoed her 195 miles north-east of Malta while she was bound from Marseilles to Alexandria in a light condition. She remained afloat for almost two days, but after an attempt to tow her to Malta had been abandoned she sank in the position 36°20′N–17°57′E. There were 189 people aboard the *Minneapolis* when she was torpedoed, of whom 12 were killed. The survivors were landed at Valetta.

TABORA (1912–1916)

Deutsche Ost-Africa Line, Germany; Blohm & Voss, Hamburg.
8,022 GRT, 449ft (136.9m) LOA, 54ft (16.5m) beam.
Quadruple expansion SR engines, twin screw, 15kts.
Date of disaster: 23 March 1916.

The German liner *Tabora*, which normally operated between Hamburg and East African ports, was shelled and sunk at Dar-es-Salaam on 23 March 1916 by the British warships HMS *Hyacinth*, *Vengeance*, and *Challenger*.

SIMLA (1894–1916)

P&O Line, Great Britain; Caird, Greenock.
5,884 GRT, 430ft (131.1m) length, 49ft (14.9m) beam.
152 passengers in two classes.
Triple expansion SR engine, single screw, 14.5kts.
Date of disaster: 2 April 1916.

The *Simla*, *Nubia*, and *Malta*, three sister ships introduced to the London to Calcutta service, were often used as troopships, and on the outbreak of war in 1914 the *Simla* was taken over for full time trooping duties. She was torpedoed and sunk by a German submarine on 2 April 1916 while bound from Marseilles to Alexandria via Malta. She was attacked 45 miles west-north-west of Gozo lighthouse in the Maltese Islands. Ten members of her crew were killed.

CHANTALA (1913–1916)

British India Line, Great Britain; Richardson Duck, Stockton.
4,949 GRT, 405ft (123.4m) length, 52ft (15.9m) beam.
Triple expansion SR engine, single screw.
Date of disaster: 5 April 1916.

The British India passenger ship *Chantala* was sunk by a submarine 15 miles north of Cape Bengut, Algeria, in the position 37°12′N–03°48′E, on 5 April 1916. She was bound for Calcutta, having sailed from the River Tees some days earlier, with a call at London. The submarine torpedoed her in the engine-room, the attack having been launched without warning. Capt E. Hamlyn of the *Chantala* ordered his boats away, but as his ship remained afloat he decided to return to her hoping he might save her. At this the submarine surfaced and opened fire on the *Chantala* with its gun, eventually finishing her off with time bombs that were taken aboard. The *Chantala* was not carrying passengers on this voyage but nine members of her crew were killed in the attack, all of them engine-room staff.

The German liner Tabora *was sunk by HMS* Hyacinth. (W.Z. Bilddienst)

CYMRIC (1898–1916)

White Star Line, Great Britain, Harland & Wolff, Belfast.
13,096 GRT, 599ft (182.6m) LOA, 64ft (19.5m) beam.
1,418 passengers in two classes.
Quadruple expansion SR engines, twin screw, 15kts.
Date of disaster: 8 May 1916.

Apart from scheduled voyages between Liverpool and New York or Boston, the *Cymric* also served as a troopship in the

The Cymric. (World Ship Society)

Boer War. After the outbreak of hostilities between Britain and Germany in August 1914, the *Cymric* continued in commercial service regardless of the submarine menace. She was torpedoed on 7 May 1916 by *U20*, under the command of Cdr W. von Schwieger, the same submarine that had been responsible for the sinking of the *Lusitania*. The *Cymric* was returning from New York without passengers but carrying a general cargo, when she was attacked about 140 miles north-west of Fastnet. She sank the following day with the loss of five men from her crew of 110.

GOLCONDA (1877–1916)

British India Line, Great Britain; William Doxford, Sunderland.
5,874 GRT, 438ft (133.5m) LOA, 48ft (14.6m) beam.
102 passengers in two classes.
Triple expansion SR engine, single screw, 13kts.
Date of disaster: 3 June 1916.

The *Golconda* served mainly on the route from England to India via the Suez Canal. She was torpedoed and sunk on 3 June 1916 while bound from the River Tees and London to Calcutta. The attack took place about 6.5 miles east of Orfordness, in the North Sea. Nineteen of the *Golconda*'s crew were lost with her.

PRINCIPE UMBERTO (1909–1916)

Navigazione Generale Italiana, Italy; Cantieri Navali Riuniti, Palermo.
7,838 GRT, 476ft (145.1m) length, 53ft (16.2m) beam.
1,424 passengers in three classes.
Quadruple expansion SR engines, twin screw, 16kts.
Date of disaster: 8 June 1916.

The Italian passenger liner *Principe Umberto* operated on the service from Italy to South America with a sister ship, the *Duca Degli Abruzzi*, although she also made occasional crossings to New York. On 8 June 1916, while proceeding across the lower Adriatic in company with two other troopships and an escorting destroyer, the *Principe Umberto* was sunk when the convoy came under attack from two Austrian submarines. The badly damaged vessel, which was transporting a large number of soldiers to Mudros, remained afloat for only a very brief time and many of her complement were drowned when she went under.

STAMPALIA ex-*OCEANIA* (1909–1916)

La Veloce Line, Italy; Cantieri Navali Riuniti, Spezia.
9,000 GRT, 476ft (145.1m) length, 55ft (16.8m) beam.
2,500 passengers in two classes.
Triple expansion SR engines, twin screw, 16kts.
Date of disaster: 18 August 1916.

The Italian emigrant carrier *Oceania* was renamed *Stampalia* in 1913, even though her entire career was spent under the La Veloce Line houseflag, operating on the route from Genoa to New York. She was lost on 18 August 1916 when an enemy submarine torpedoed and sunk her in the Mediterranean while she was bound from Genoa to Liverpool.

FRANCONIA (1911–1916)

Cunard Line, Great Britain; Swan, Hunter & Wigham Richardson, Newcastle.
18,150 GRT, 625ft (190.5m) LOA, 71ft (21.6m) beam.
2,850 passengers in three classes.
Quadruple expansion SR engines, twin screw, 17kts.
Date of disaster: 4 October 1916.

Cunard introduced the sister ships *Franconia* and *Laconia* to the Liverpool to New York or Boston services in 1911. Four years later, the *Franconia* was requisitioned for war service as a troopship for operations in the Mediterranean. On 4 October 1916, the German submarine *UB47* torpedoed and sank her some 195 miles south-east of Malta when she was bound from Alexandria to Marseilles without troops. Twelve of her crew of 314 were killed. The *Franconia* went down in the position 35°56′N–18°30′E.

GALLIA (1913–1916)

Cie. Sud-Atlantique, France; Forges et Chantiers de la Mediterranée, La Seyne.
14,996 GRT, 600ft (182.9m) LOA, 62ft (18.9m) beam.
1,086 passengers in four classes.
Triple expansion SR engines with LP turbine, quadruple screw, 20kts.
Date of disaster: 4 October 1916.

France's most serious loss of the First World War was the sinking of the *Gallia* 35 miles west of Sardinia. She had been built for the express service between Bordeaux and the River Plate. On 3 October 1916 she sailed from Marseilles bound for Salonica (Thessaloniki), carrying in excess of 2,700 people, mainly French and Serbian troops destined for the battlefields of Gallipoli. She was spotted the following day by the German submarine *U35* under the command of Lt-Cdr Lothar von Arnauld de la Perière, a notorious U-boat commander of French ancestry. Zigzagging at 18kts, the *Gallia* was unescorted and unprotected. The *U35* fired two torpedoes, which caused a massive internal explosion, destroying, among other things, the liner's radio. Discipline on board the *Gallia* was rather poor, and there was much confusion as many of the soldiers jumped into the sea immediately following the attack. The harassed crew were unable to launch all the rafts and lifeboats and many who might otherwise have been saved went down with the ship, which sank very quickly. The following day, 5 October, the French cruiser *Chateaurenault* arrived on the scene, but was only able to rescue 1,362 of those who had been aboard.

ALAUNIA (1913–1916)

Cunard Line, Great Britain; Scott's, Greenock.
13,405 GRT, 540ft (164.6m) LOA, 64ft (19.5m) beam.
2,060 passengers in two classes.
Quadruple expansion engines, twin screw, 16kts.
Date of disaster: 19 October 1916.

Top *Cunard Line's* Franconia. (World Ship Society)

Above *The* Gallia. *Her loss was the worst French shipping disaster of the First World War.* (World Ship Society)

One of three vessels built for either the Liverpool or London service to Boston or Montreal, the *Alaunia*'s sisters were the *Andania* and *Aurania*. None of them survived the First World War. The *Alaunia* struck a mine two miles south of the Royal Sovereign lightship on 19 October 1916 while bound from New York for London. She was carrying 180 passengers and 166 crew. Fortunately only two people were killed.

GALEKA (1899–1916)

Union Castle Line, Great Britain; Harland & Wolff, Belfast.
6,722 GRT, 440ft (134.1m) length, 53ft (16.2m) beam.
210 passengers in two classes.
Triple expansion SR engines, twin screw, 12kts.
Date of disaster: 28 October 1916.

The last vessel to enter service with the Union Line prior to the amalgamation with the Castle Line in 1900 was the *Galeka*. She was the second-to-last ship of a group of six, the last unit, the *Galician*, being completed after the merger. All six operated on the intermediate service to South Africa. On the outbreak of war in 1914 the *Galeka* was taken over as a troopship, but a year later she was commissioned as a hospital ship serving in the Mediterranean. On 28 October 1916 she struck a mine off Cap de le Hogue, three miles north-west of Le Havre, and was beached in a bid to save her. In spite of concerted salvage attempts the *Galeka* became a total wreck.

ARABIA (1898–1916)

P&O Line, Great Britain; Caird, Greenock.
7,933 GRT, 500ft (152.4m) length, 54ft (16.5m) beam.
524 passengers in two classes, and/or 2,500 troops.
Triple expansion engine, single screw, 18kts.
Date of disaster: 6 November 1916.

The *Arabia* was a sister ship of the *Egypt*, which was to become the victim of a tragic collision disaster in May 1922. Other ships of the class, which operated between England, India and Australia, were the *China*, *India*, and *Persia*. The *Arabia* was sunk by a German torpedo on 6 November 1916 as she was returning to London from Sydney under the command of Capt Palmer. She was struck about 112 miles south-west of Cape Matapan in the Mediterranean, in the approximate position 36°00′N–21°00′E. On board were a total of 723 people, of whom two were killed by the initial explosion. The *Arabia* went down rapidly but due to good discipline and an orderly evacuation no other lives were lost.

BURDIGALA ex-*KAISER FRIEDRICH* (1898–1916)

Cie. Sud-Atlantique, France; F. Schichau, Danzig.
12,481 GRT, 600ft (182.9m) LOA, 63ft (19.2m) beam.
1,350 passengers in three classes.
Quadruple expansion SR engines, twin screw, 18kts.
Date of disaster: 14 November 1916.

Late in the nineteenth century Germany mounted its challenge for the Atlantic Blue Riband. Norddeutscher Lloyd ordered two express vessels under an arrangement whereby, if they failed to achieve their designed speed, they could be rejected and returned to the builders. The *Kaiser Wilhelm der Grosse* succeeded and took the speed record. The *Kaiser Friedrich*, however, failed and for 14 years her prospects were uncertain and her career indefinite. Hamburg Amerika Line occasionally chartered her but she was otherwise laid up until bought by the newly established Compagnie Sud-Atlantique in May 1912. She was then operated between Bordeaux and Buenos Aires.

In March 1915 the *Burdigala* entered service with the French Navy as an armed transport. On 14 November 1916 she ran into a minefield, laid by the German submarine *U73* between Mykonos and Tenos in the Aegean Sea, and was sunk. She was the first of three victims of the *U73*'s mines.

BRITANNIC (1915–1916)

White Star Line, Great Britain; Harland & Wolff, Belfast.
48,158 GRT, 903ft (275.2m) LOA, 94ft (28.7m) beam.
2,573 passengers in three classes (designed).
Quadruple expansion SR engines with LP turbine, triple screw, 22kts.
Date of disaster: 21 November 1916.

A model of the White Star Britannic, *showing her intended appearance, with an earlier namesake in the foreground.* (Steamship Historical Society of America)

The hospital ship Britannic. (Titanic Historical Society)

The *Britannic* was the third of White Star Line's great trio of Atlantic express liners conceived before the First World War, the earlier ships being the famed *Olympic* and *Titanic*. When the *Titanic* sank after colliding with an iceberg in April 1912, structural improvements were incorporated into the *Britannic*, which was then still only at the early stages of construction. As a result she was slightly larger and longer than the earlier pair. The modifications to her design also had the effect of delaying her construction, so that at the outbreak of war in August 1914 she was still incomplete.

The following year the Admiralty ordered her completion as a hospital ship and she ran trials in this capacity that December. The *Britannic* was drafted into the Dardanelles campaign and for the next year she sailed between the Greek island of Lemnos and Naples and Southampton, conveying home wounded men brought down from the battlefront in Gallipoli by smaller hospital vessels. On 21 November 1916, the outward bound *Britannic*, on only her sixth round voyage, stuck a mine laid by the German submarine *U73*, four miles west of Port St Nikolo in the Kea Channel. The explosion ripped open her starboard side, breaking two watertight compartments. This, combined with a failure of the watertight door system in the forepart of the ship, spelt disaster for the *Britannic*. In spite of all the additional work to improve her seaworthiness, and the efforts on the part of her master, Capt Bartlett, to beach her, the *Britannic* had disappeared beneath the water only an hour after the explosion.

The loss of the huge ship was tragic, ranking as Britain's biggest mercantile loss of the war, but it was perhaps fortunate that the *Britannic* was heading for Lemnos and not in the other direction, when she would have had a full complement of wounded soldiers aboard. In the event she was carrying 1,125 people, made up of 625 crew and 500 medical officers, nurses, and RAMC personnel. Of these, 21 lost their lives.

CITY OF BIRMINGHAM (1911–1916)

Ellerman Lines, Great Britain; Palmers, Newcastle.
7,498 GRT, 452ft (137.8m) length, 55ft (16.8m) beam.
170 passengers in two classes.
Quadruple expansion SR engine, single screw, 12kts.
Date of disaster: 27 November 1916.

The *City of Birmingham* was sunk in a torpedo attack on 27 November 1916 in mid-Atlantic when bound from Liverpool to Karachi. On board were 315 people, of whom 170 were passengers, many of them women and children. A heavy swell made it difficult to launch the boats but an orderly

The City of Birmingham. (World Ship Society)

evacuation nevertheless ensued and all but four people, all crew members were saved. The *City of Birmingham* sank in the position 36°01'N–16°00'E. Her master, Capt W.J. Haughton, survived the attack even though he went down with his ship.

KARNAK ex-*TOURANE* ex-*ANNAM* (1899–1916)

Messageries Maritimes, France; Messageries Maritimes, La Ciotat.
6,054 GRT, 446ft (135.9m) length, 50ft (15.2m) beam.
Triple expansion SR engines, twin screw, 19kts.
Date of disaster: 27 November 1916.

The steamship *Karnak*, employed on the route from Marseilles to Alexandria, was renamed twice by her owners during her 17-year life. She opened her career under the name *Annam*, operating to the Far East with three sister ships. In 1904 she was renamed *Tourane*, and in 1912, following a major refit, she became the *Karnak*, when she entered the Mediterranean service. The *Karnak* was lost on 27 November 1916 when she was torpedoed and sunk near Malta by the German submarine *U32*. She had been bound from Marseilles to Piraeus at the time of the attack.

MINNEWASKA (1909–1916)

Atlantic Transport Line, Great Britain; Harland & Wolff, Belfast.
14,317 GRT, 616ft (187.8m) LOA, 65ft (19.8m) beam.
330 passengers in single class.
Quadruple expansion SR engines, twin screw, 16kts.
Date of disaster: 29 November 1916.

The fourth vessel of the *Minneapolis* class, the *Minnewaska*, joined her sisters after an interval of seven years. This was because the original *Minnewaska*, which would have entered service for Atlantic Transport Line in 1903, was sold to White Star while still under construction and renamed *Arabic*. In 1915 the second *Minnewaska* was converted into a troopship and took part in the conveyance of soldiers to the Dardanelles battlefront. On 29 November 1916, the *Minnewaska* was nearing Mudros with 1,800 troops from Alexandria when she struck a floating mine about 1.5 miles south-west of Dentero Point in Suda Bay. The severely damaged ship was run ashore in the hope that she might be saved, but the extent of the devastation was such that she was written off as a total loss. Fortunately, no lives were lost in the disaster. The wreck was broken up by an Italian firm from late-1918.

PALERMO ex-*LAZIO* ex-*BRITISH PRINCESS* (1899–1916)

Navigazione Generale Italiana, Italy; Palmers, Newcastle.
9,203 GRT, 470ft (143.3m) length, 56ft (17.1m) beam.
Triple expansion SR engines, twin screw, 12.5kts.
Date of disaster: 2 December 1916.

The Italian transatlantic liner *Palermo* started life as the *British Princess* of British Shipowners Company Ltd, one of

The Minnewaska *was sunk by a mine.* (World Ship Society)

three similar vessels. They passed to NGI ownership in 1906 as the *Campania*, *Sannio*, and *Lazio*. They were further renamed in 1913 when the *Lazio* became the *Palermo*. Their service was from Italy to Halifax and Boston. While returning to Genoa from New York on 2 December 1916, the *Palermo* was torpedoed and sunk in the Mediterranean, about 25 miles from Cape San Sebastian off the east coast of Spain. She was transporting horses and munitions for the Italian war effort, and had a number of passengers aboard besides. However, there seems to have been no loss of life. It was believed that, in addition to her other cargoes, the *Palermo* was carrying a large consignment of gold at the time of her sinking. Salvage operations to recover this valuable treasure were undertaken in May 1956 but whether they were fruitful or not is unknown.

VOLTAIRE (1907–1916)

Lamport & Holt Co, Great Britain; D. & W. Henderson, Glasgow.
8,618 GRT, 501ft (152.7m) LOA, 58ft (17.7m) beam.
60 passengers in single class.
Triple expansion SR engine, single screw, 12kts.
Date of disaster: 2 December 1916.

Built for a cargo-passenger service to Latin American ports, the *Voltaire* had accommodation for only a small number of passengers, all cabins being to first class standard. In late 1916, while bound from Liverpool to New York, she came upon the German armed raider *Möwe*, which captured her. After removal of her cargo and stores, the *Voltaire* was sunk by her adversary on 2 December 1916, some 650 miles west of Fastnet.

PERUGIA (1901–1916)

Anchor Line, Great Britain, D. & W. Henderson, Glasgow.
4,348 GRT, 375ft (114.3m) length, 47ft (14.3m) beam.
1,400 passengers in single class.
Triple expansion SR engine, single screw; 13kts.
Date of disaster: 3 December 1916.

The small Anchor Line steamship *Perugia* was a steerage class vessel with accommodation for an extensive number of emigrant passengers, serving on the transatlantic route from the Mediterranean to New York. On 3 December 1916 she was torpedoed in the Mediterranean, north-west of Sardinia, while sailing in ballast, and sank in the position 42°56′N–07°56′E.

ALGERIE (1901–1916)

Soc. Générale des Transports Maritimes, France; Forges et Chantiers de la Mediterranée, Le Havre.
4,035 GRT, 397ft (121.0m) length, 42ft (12.8m) beam.
Triple expansion SR engine, single screw, 13.5kts.
Date of disaster: 4 December 1916.

The *Algerie* served South America from Marseilles until the outbreak of the First World War. She was sunk on 4 December 1916 by a submarine while returning to France after a troop carrying voyage to Salonica (Thessaloniki), going down off the island of Malta.

CALEDONIA (1905–1916)

Anchor Line, Great Britain; D. & W. Henderson, Glasgow.
9,223 GRT, 500ft (152.4m) length, 58ft (17.7m) beam.
1,616 passengers in three classes.
Triple expansion SR engines, twin screw, 16kts.
Date of disaster: 4 December 1916.

After serving for nine years on the run from Glasgow to New York, the *Caledonia* was requisitioned in 1914 for troop carrying purposes, with a capacity for 3,074 troops –

The Caledonia *of Anchor Line.* (World Ship Society)

Messageries Maritimes' Magellan. (World Ship Society)

considerably in excess of her peacetime passenger numbers. On 4 December 1916 she was torpedoed and sunk in the Mediterranean by *U65*, which attacked her without warning. The *Caledonia* was on a passage from Salonica to Marseilles, carrying bags of mail. She sank in the position 35°40'N–17°05'E, approximately 125 miles east of Malta. The *Caledonia*'s master, Capt James Blaikie, attempted unsuccessfully to ram and sink his assailant and later, after he was taken prisoner, he was threatened with execution, a fate which had befallen other captured mercantile officers. The British Government, however, advised the German authorities through the offices of the United States ambassador in Berlin, that should this happen, a captive German officer would receive like treatment. In response to this unequivocal stand, Capt Blaikie was reprieved and he spent the remainder of the war incarcerated in a prison camp.

MOUNT TEMPLE (1901–1916)

Canadian Pacific Line, Great Britain; Armstrong Whitworth, Newcastle.
9,792 GRT, 485ft (147.8m) length, 59ft (18.0m) beam.
500 passengers.
Triple expansion SR engine, single screw, 12.5kts.
Date of disaster: 6 December 1916.

The Elder Dempster steamship *Mount Temple* was taken over by Canadian Pacific in April 1903, and sailed in the North Atlantic service with her sister *Montezuma* for 12 years. The only interruption to this came on 1 December 1907, when she ran aground at Lahave, Nova Scotia. Her complement of 600 was got ashore by breeches buoy the same day but the *Mount Temple* remained fast until 16 April 1908, when she was successfully refloated.

On 6 December 1916, during a voyage from Montreal to Brest and London, the *Mount Temple* was captured by the German commerce raider *Möwe*. Her cargo of horses and other merchandise was looted, after which the *Mount Temple* was sunk, some 620 miles south-west of Fastnet. Four days earlier, the *Möwe* had sunk the liner *Voltaire* and, on 10 December, the White Star cargo ship *Georgic* became another of her victims.

MAGELLAN ex-*INDUS* (1897–1916)

Messageries Maritimes, France; Messageries Maritimes, La Ciotat.
6,357 GRT, 446ft (135.9m) length, 50ft (15.2m) beam.
Triple expansion SR engines, twin screw, 19.5kts.
Date of disaster: 11 December 1916.

Built as the *Indus* for the service to the Far East, this ship was renamed *Magellan* in 1904 when she was transferred to the South American trade. In 1912 she reverted once more to the service from Marseilles to the Orient. The *Magellan* continued to make commercial sailings after the outbreak of war and on one such voyage, returning from Yokohama on 11 December 1916, she was torpedoed and sunk by an enemy submarine. She foundered south-east of Pantellaria. The survivors were picked up by the *Magellan*'s fleetmate *Sinai*, which was likewise torpedoed and sunk later the same day, probably by the same U-boat.

Chapter Four

1917

UNRESTRICTED SUBMARINE WARFARE

The war at sea seemed to be settling down into one of attrition, albeit one-sided, just as it already had on land, when, early in 1917, three significant developments occurred.

As early as 1915, Germany had responded to the Royal Navy's stringent blockade conditions by declaring the seas around Britain a war zone in which any ships considered to be belligerent were liable to be sunk on sight. However, faced with a blockade that went well beyond the pre-war interpretations of international law, and which threatened her with economic ruin, Germany felt obliged to tighten the screws even further. As the climax of her attempts to starve Britain into submission before she was herself starved out, Germany declared unrestricted submarine warfare from 1 February 1917. In effect this meant that any vessel, Allied or neutral, was thenceforward regarded as a legitimate target to be sunk without warning. Consequently merchant ship losses began to increase once more.

To counter the growing submarine menace, the Allies were compelled to introduce a range of new defensive measures. These included depth-charges, air patrols, hydrophone detection gear and, most important of all, the introduction of escorted merchant convoys from the beginning of April 1917.

Most welcome of all at this time, however, for Russia, France and Great Britain alike, was the entry into the war on the Allied side of the United States of America, on 6 April.

Nevertheless, 1917 was the worst year of the war for passenger ship losses, as well as for merchant ship losses in general.

IVERNIA (1900–1917)

Cunard Line, Great Britain; Swan Hunter, Newcastle.
14,278 GRT, 600ft (182.9m) LOA, 64ft (19.5m) beam.
1,964 passengers in three classes.
Quadruple expansion SR engines, twin screw, 16kts.
Date of disaster: 1 January 1917.

Cunard placed the *Ivernia* and her sister ship *Saxonia* in the Liverpool to Boston service until around 1911–1912, when

The Cunard passenger liner Ivernia. (World Ship Society)

they were switched to the service from Trieste to New York. The *Ivernia* was commissioned as an auxiliary transport in the First World War. On 1 January 1917 she was taking 2,400 troops to Alexandria when the German submarine *UB47*, commanded by Lt-Cdr Steinbauer, torpedoed and sunk her 48 miles south-east of Cape Matapan. One hundred and twenty people lost their lives when the *Ivernia* went down, 85 military personnel and 35 members of the crew.

QUEBEC ex-*EBRO* (1896–1917)

French Line (CGT), France; Robert Napier, Glasgow.
3,342 GRT, 345ft (105.2m) length, 44ft (13.4m) beam.
Triple expansion SR engine, single screw, 12kts.
Date of disaster: 24 January 1917.

Originally built for the Royal Mail Line, the *Quebec* was purchased in 1903 for the service from France to the West Indies, on which she was joined by one of her former Royal Mail sisters, the *Minho*, which became the *Montreal*. Both ships were lost during the First World War. The *Quebec* struck a mine in the mouth of the River Gironde on 24 January 1917 while returning to Bordeaux from San Juan, Puerto Rico.

AMIRAL MAGON (1904–1917)

Chargeurs Reunis, France; Ateliers et Chantiers de la Loire.
5,566 GRT, 390ft (118.9m) length, 50ft (15.2m) beam.
Triple expansion engine, single screw, 12kts.
Date of disaster: 25 January 1917.

The *Amiral Magon* was one of a large number of similar ships, almost all of which were sunk during the First World War. Their normal service routes placed these vessels beyond the scope of this book, but the disaster which befell the *Amiral Magon* was so severe that it was felt appropriate to include her.

On 25 January 1917 she was en route to Salonica carrying some 900 French troops when she was torpedoed without warning by a German submarine. The damage was so cataclysmic that the *Amiral Magon* remained afloat for only 10 minutes. In these circumstances, evacuation was near impossible and most of those on board went down with her.

Of the *Amiral Magon*'s fleetmates, the *Amiral de Kersaint* was sunk with the loss of eight lives by *U60* under the command of Cdr Robert Wilhelm Moraht on 14 September 1917, after putting up a stout and courageous resistance. The *Amiral Ganteaume* was torpedoed off Cap Gris Nez by *U24*, captained by Lt-Cdr Schneider, on 26 October 1914. Thirty of the 2,000 or so Belgian refugees she was transporting, mostly women and children, were killed, but the *Amiral Ganteaume* made port, under tow, and was later restored. Two other similar ships, the *Amiral Olry* and the *Amiral Zede* were sunk by torpedo on 1 September 1917 and 19 November 1917 respectively.

The Amiral Magon, *another tragic French loss from the Gallipoli campaign.* (Musée de la Marine)

LAURENTIC ex-*ALBERTA* (1909–1917)

White Star Line, Great Britain; Harland & Wolff, Belfast.
14,892 GRT, 565ft (172.2m) LOA, 67ft (20.4m) beam.
1,660 passengers in three classes.
Triple expansion SR engines, triple screw, 17kts.
Date of disaster: 25 January 1917.

The *Laurentic* was laid down as the *Alberta* for the Dominion Line but passed to White Star ownership before she was launched. She entered the Liverpool to Montreal service, on which she remained until 1914, when she became a troopship. Later, as an auxiliary cruiser, she was engaged to carry a large consignment of gold bullion from Liverpool to Halifax, Nova Scotia. Shortly after sailing, on 25 January 1917, the *Laurentic* struck two mines off Malin Head, County Donegal, and sank in under an hour, taking with her 354 men of her complement of 475. Many of these died of exposure in the bitterly cold sea. Her master, Capt R.A. Norton, was among those saved. The minefield into which the *Laurentic* had steamed had been laid by the German submarine *U80*.

After the war, the *Laurentic*'s valuable cargo became the subject of a daring Royal Navy salvage operation and by 1924 the majority of the gold, some 3,186 bars, valued at £5 million, had been recovered. The distorted shape of the gold bars was a graphic reminder of the immense pressures that the divers had to work under to effect the salvage. During August 1952, further salvage operations were undertaken to locate the last 22 gold bars.

White Star's Laurentic. *Of all the wartime losses attributable to mine explosions, the sinking of the* Laurentic *in January 1917 was the worst, claiming 354 lives.* (Tom Rayner)

CALIFORNIA (1907–1917)

Anchor Line, Great Britain; D. & W. Henderson, Glasgow.
8,662 GRT, 485ft (147.8m) LOA, 58ft (17.7m) beam.
1,214 passengers in three classes.
Triple expansion SR engines, twin screw, 17kts.
Date of disaster: 7 February 1917.

The *California* sailed in consort with three similar vessels – the *Caledonia*, *Cameronia*, and *Columbia* – on the route to New York from Glasgow. Nine days after leaving Glasgow, outward bound with 205 people on board, the *California* was torpedoed on 7 February 1917 by a German submarine and sunk some 40 miles south-west of the Irish coast, in the position 51°10′N–09°24′W. She went down with alarming rapidity and some people were killed in lifeboats that capsized in the hasty evacuation. Others had died when the torpedo struck her aft end, 43 people losing their lives in all. The *California*'s master went down with his ship but was later rescued.

MANTOLA (1916–1917)

British India Line, Great Britain; Barclay Curle, Glasgow.
8,260 GRT, 450ft (137.2m) length, 58ft (17.7m) beam.
129 passengers in two classes.
Triple expansion SR engines, twin screw, 13kts.
Date of disaster: 8 February 1917.

A similar ship to the *Malda*, the *Mantola* had a very brief existence and no real opportunity to prove herself on the India run for which she was built. On 8 February 1917, while bound from London to Calcutta under Capt D.J. Chivas, she was torpedoed by a German submarine about 140 miles west-south-west of Fastnet, in the position 49°55′N–12°25′W. The torpedo struck the *Mantola* on her port side and she was soon sinking by the head. Her crew were compelled to abandon ship. The only lives lost were during the launching of the lifeboats, when seven seamen were drowned as a boat capsized. The submarine surfaced at this point and turned her guns on the sinking liner, but when the British destroyer HMS *Laburnam* arrived on the scene the U-boat beat a hasty retreat. The *Laburnam* picked up the survivors (who were later landed at Bantry) and took the *Mantola* in tow, but the tow rope parted in rough seas soon after and the *Mantola* was left to sink.

AFRIC (1899–1917)

White Star Line, Great Britain; Harland & Wolff, Belfast.
11,948 GRT, 570ft (173.7m) LOA, 63ft (19.2m) beam.
350 passengers in single class.
Quadruple expansion SR engines, twin screw, 13.5kts.
Date of disaster: 12 February 1917.

Originally built for the New York to Liverpool run, the *Afric* spent most of her life in the Liverpool to Sydney, Australia, service. She was torpedoed on 12 February 1917 by the submarine *UC66*, 12 miles south-south-west of the Eddystone lighthouse while bound from Liverpool to Devonport and Sydney. There were 22 fatal casualties but 145 of her complement, including the captain, survived the attack.

ATHOS (1914–1917)

Messageries Maritimes, France; Ateliers et Chantiers de France, Dunkerque.
12,692 GRT, 528ft (160.9m) LOA, 61ft (18.6m) beam.
384 passengers in three classes.
Triple expansion SR engines, twin screw, 17.5kts.
Date of disaster: 17 February 1917.

Messageries Maritimes had three ships building for the Marseilles to Far East service immediately prior to the First World War. Only the *Porthos* and *Athos* commenced commercial operations, the third ship, *Sphinx*, being taken over by the French Navy on completion. By 1917 the *Athos* was also employed in an auxiliary capacity. On 17 February

The Afric. (World Ship Society)

1917, as she was returning to Marseilles from Yokohama carrying troops, she was sunk by the German submarine *U65* when 200 miles south-west of Malta.

WORCESTERSHIRE (1904–1917)

Bibby Line, Great Britain; Harland & Wolff, Belfast.
7,160 GRT, 452ft (137.7m) length, 54ft (16.5m) beam.
200 passengers in single class.
Quadruple expansion SR engines, twin screw, 15kts.
Date of disaster: 17 February 1917.

During a voyage from Rangoon to London and Liverpool on 17 February 1917, the liner *Worcestershire* struck a mine 12.5 miles south of the Colombo breakwater, Ceylon (Sri Lanka), and sank as a result of the damage she sustained. Two lives were lost. The *Worcestershire* had maintained the service from Great Britain to Burma with a sister ship, the *Herefordshire.*

MENDI (1905–1917)

British & African SN Co, Great Britain; Alexander Stephen, Glasgow.
4,230 GRT, 370ft (112.8m) length, 46ft (14.0m) beam.
170 passengers in two classes.
Triple expansion SR engine, single screw, 11.5kts.
Date of disaster: 21 February 1917.

The small Mendi, *the victim of a collision south of the Isle of Wight.* (National Maritime Museum, London)

Normally employed on African routes for Elder Dempster, the *Mendi* had been taken over for troop-carrying duties in the First World War. In January 1917 she joined a convoy with five other vessels, escorted by the cruiser HMS *Cornwall*, transporting Australian and South African troops to France from Cape Town. The *Mendi*'s troop complement comprised 806 officers and men of the South African Native Labour Contingent, which included Zulu, Pondo, Swazi, and Xhosa tribesmen. Following a close, but uneventful, encounter with the German raider *Wolf*, the convoy put into Plymouth prior to sailing for Le Havre on 20 February 1917 on the last leg of the voyage. The weather in the Channel was particularly thick and the convoy vessels had to pick their way through the fog as best they could, sounding their sirens but showing no navigation lights.

At 05.00 hrs on 21 February 1917, when south of the Isle of Wight, the *Mendi* collided with another ship of the convoy, the Royal Mail liner *Darro*, which struck the *Mendi* on her starboard side. The *Darro*'s bow smashed into the fore troop-deck, killing many of the native troops accommodated there. The *Mendi* began to list immediately, making it impossible to launch any of the lifeboats on the port side, and she sank no more than 20 minutes later, settling in 140ft of water. Before she disappeared beneath the surface, a large number of the black servicemen who were trapped on her deck were seen performing a warrior's dance as they submitted to their fate.

Due to the ever-present danger of enemy submarines, the *Darro* could not remain on the scene to render assistance. By the time other rescue vessels had arrived it was only possible to save 236 of those who had been aboard the *Mendi*. The casualties totalled 636, consisting of 599 black soldiers, eight white officers and NCOs, and 29 of the ship's 88 crewmen. Capt Henry Yardley was pulled from the water alive, but he had sustained head injuries when struck by the ship's foremast as the *Mendi* rolled over.

LACONIA (1911–1917)

Cunard Line, Great Britain; Swan, Hunter & Wigham Richardson, Newcastle.
18,099 GRT, 625ft (190.5m) LOA, 71ft (21.6m) beam.
2,850 passengers in three classes.
Quadruple expansion SR engines, twin screw, 17kts.
Date of disaster: 25 February 1917.

The sister ships *Laconia* and *Franconia* sailed between Liverpool and New York or Boston, with occasional cruise voyages in the low season. In October 1914, the *Laconia* was taken over by the Admiralty and converted into an auxiliary cruiser, but by the autumn of 1916 she had been returned to Cunard and resumed commercial sailings. On 25 February the following year she was sunk by the German submarine *U50* as she was returning to Liverpool from the United States, being hit by two torpedoes when 160 miles north-west of Fastnet. Both missiles struck her starboard side and she sank about one hour after the second explosion. The *Laconia* was carrying 75 passengers in addition to her crew of 217, and the attack claimed 12 lives, six of them crewmen.

DRINA (1913–1917)

Royal Mail Line, Great Britain; Harland & Wolff, Belfast.
11,483 GRT, 517ft (157.6m) LOA, 62ft (18.9m) beam.
995 passengers in three classes.
Quadruple expansion SR engines, twin screw, 13.5kts.
Date of disaster: 1 March 1917.

The *Drina* was the last of a class of five ships built for the service from Liverpool to the River Plate ports. Although owned exclusively by the Royal Mail Line, the *Drina* was registered under the Elder Dempster Group. At the outset of the First World War she became a hospital ship, but after only a year she returned to her normal duties. On 1 March 1917, while returning to her home port from Buenos Aires

The Laconia. *(World Ship Society)*

The Royal Mail Line's Drina *while serving as a hospital ship.* (Furness Withy Group)

with passengers and a cargo of coffee and meat, the *Drina* was torpedoed two miles west-south-west of the island of Skokholm, near the Pembrokeshire coast. Her assailant was the German submarine *UC65*. Fifteen lives were lost.

SAGAMORE (1892–1917)

Warren Line, Great Britain; Harland & Wolff, Belfast.
5,197 GRT, 430ft (131.1m) length, 46ft (14.0m) beam.
Triple expansion SR engine, single screw, 11kts.
Date of disaster: 3 March 1917.

While bound from Boston to Liverpool, the transatlantic steamship *Sagamore* was torpedoed and sunk by a German submarine 150 miles west-north-west of Fastnet on 3 March 1917. Her captain was among the 52 people who lost their lives.

VIGILANCIA (1893–1917)

Ward Line, USA; Delaware River Co, Chester, Pennsylvania.
4,115 GRT, 321ft (97.8m) length, 45ft (13.7m) beam.
Triple expansion SR engine, single screw, 14.5kts.
Date of disaster: 16 March 1917.

The Ward Line purchased the *Vigilancia* and her sister liner *Seguranca* from the New York and Brazil Mail SS Co in 1893. They were employed on the run from New York to Havana, Cuba. The *Vigilancia* was sunk by a German U-boat off Ushant on 16 March 1917, in the position 48°57'N–09°34'W. At the time she was bound from New York to Le Havre.

ANTONY (1907–1917)

Booth Line, Great Britain; Hawthorn Leslie, Newcastle.
6,446 GRT, 418ft (127.4m) length, 52ft (15.9m) beam.
572 passengers in two classes.
Triple expansion SR engines, twin screw, 14kts.
Date of disaster: 17 March 1917.

The Booth Line's *Antony* was one of a trio of ships, her sisters being the *Hilary* and *Lanfranc*. She was sunk on 17 March 1917 when a German submarine torpedoed her about 15 miles south-west of the Coningbeg light vessel, near the Saltee Islands, south of County Wexford, when she was bound from Pará (Belem), Brazil to Liverpool. Fifty five people were killed.

ALNWICK CASTLE (1901–1917)

Union Castle Line, Great Britain; William Beardmore, Glasgow.
5,893 GRT, 400ft (121.9m) length, 50ft (15.2m) beam.
540 passengers in three classes.
Triple expansion SR engines, twin screw, 12kts.
Date of disaster: 19 March 1917.

The *Alnwick Castle* was one of a group of five similar vessels employed on Union Castle's intermediate services to South Africa from Southampton. In September 1914 she was taken over as a troopship, but later was returned to her owners to resume commercial sailings. On 17 March 1917 she sailed from Plymouth bound for Cape Town and, one day out, stopped to pick up the survivors of the Hain Line steamer *Trevose*, which had been the victim of a U-boat attack. The following day, 19 March, when about 310 miles south-west of Bishop Rock lighthouse, in the position 47°38'N–13°24'W, she too was torpedoed. In deteriorating weather her lifeboats became separated, and two of them were never seen again. The remaining four drifted for between five and 10 days before being picked up. One was rescued by Spanish fishermen from Carino near Cape Ortegal, while another was picked up in mid-ocean by the Fabre liner *Venezia*. A number of people had died from exposure, while others had lost their sanity. In all, 40 of the *Alnwick Castle*'s complement of 139 perished, including three of those earlier rescued from the *Trevose*.

ROTORUA (1910–1917)

New Zealand Line, Great Britain; William Denny, Dumbarton.
11,130 GRT, 502ft (153.0m) LOA, 62ft (18.9m) beam.
534 passengers in three classes.
Triple expansion SR engines, triple screw, 14kts.
Date of disaster: 22 March 1917.

The liner *Rotorua* and her sister ship *Remuera* maintained their owner's service from London to Wellington. While returning from New Zealand on 22 March 1917, the *Rotorua* was torpedoed and sunk by the German submarine *UC17*, 24 miles east of Start Point, in the position 50°18′N–02°56′W. One life was lost.

MONTREAL ex-*HALIFAX* ex-*MINHO* (1896–1917)

French Line (CGT), France; Robert Napier, Glasgow.
3,342 GRT, 345ft (105.2m) length, 44ft (13.4m) beam.
Triple expansion SR engine, single screw, 12kts.
Date of disaster: 24 March 1917.

Commencing life under the Royal Mail Line flag with two sisters, the *Ebro* and *La Plata*, the *Minho* passed to the French Line with the *Ebro* in 1903 and they were renamed *Halifax* and *Quebec* respectively. The *Halifax* was further renamed *Montreal* in 1912. In spite of her name, she operated on the service to the West Indies. She was torpedoed by a German submarine in the Bay of Biscay on 24 March 1917 while she was outward bound to the Caribbean from Le Havre, sinking in the position 45°40′N–07°40′W.

CITY OF PARIS (1907–1917)

Ellerman Lines, Great Britain; Barclay Curle, Glasgow.
9,239 GRT, 493ft (150.3m) length, 57ft (17.4m) beam.
290 passengers in two classes.
Quadruple expansion SR engine, single screw, 15kts.
Date of disaster: 4 April 1917.

The *City of Paris* was torpedoed and sunk in the Mediterranean by the German submarine *U52*, south-east of Cap d'Antibes, in the position 42°47′N–07°56′E. The attack occurred on 4 April 1917, when the *City of Paris* was bound for Liverpool via Marseilles, having come from Karachi. She had been sailing a zigzag course after receiving warnings that enemy submarines were patrolling the area. It was reported that while the evacuation of the sinking ship was in progress the *U52* surfaced and began shelling her, later finishing her off with a second torpedo. No survivors were found when French warships reached the scene, all 122 people aboard having been killed.

RAVENNA (1901–1917)

Soc. de Navigazione a Vapore Italia, Italy; Odero, Genoa.
4,252 GRT, 363ft (110.6m) length, 43ft (13.1m) beam.
Triple expansion SR engine, single screw, 12kts.
Date of disaster: 4 April 1917.

The *Ravenna* served on the route from Italy to South America with a sister ship, the *Toscana*. She was torpedoed and sunk in the Mediterranean, on 4 April 1917, while returning to Genoa from Buenos Aires. The *Toscana* was also lost during the First World War.

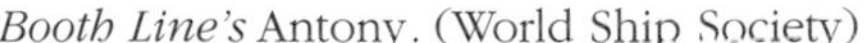

Booth Line's Antony. (World Ship Society)

TOP *Ellerman Lines'* City of Paris. (World Ship Society)

ABOVE *The French liner* Salta *struck an Allied mine while serving as a hospital ship.* (World Ship Society)

SALTA (1911–1917)

Soc. Générale des Transports Maritimes, France; Forges et Chantiers de la Mediterranée, La Seyne.
7,284 GRT, 449ft (136.9m) length, 53ft (16.2m) beam.
219 passengers in three classes.
Triple expansion SR engines, twin screw, 16kts.
Date of disaster: 10 April 1917.

The French steamship *Salta*, which normally operated between Marseilles and South America, was transferred to the Admiralty during the First World War for service as a hospital ship. On 10 April 1917, while bound from Southampton to Le Havre with hospital stores, she struck a mine half a mile north of the Whistle Buoy, in the Le Havre Roads. Although she was not carrying wounded there was still a heavy loss of life among the RAMC personnel and crew, with a total of 86 dead. It was a bitter irony that the minefield had been laid by friendly forces.

GANGE (1905–1917)

Messageries Maritimes, France; Messageries Maritimes, La Ciotat.
6,876 GRT, 447ft (136.2m) length, 53ft (16.2m) beam.
Triple expansion SR engines, twin screw, 12kts.
Date of disaster: 14 April 1917.

The French steamship *Gange* was the victim of a torpedo attack on 14 April 1917 while serving in a military capacity in the Mediterranean. She was outward bound from Marseilles, and the attack occurred as she was approaching the port of Bizerta. Some reports state that the *Gange* was sunk after striking a mine, but Lloyds' records indicate that a submarine was responsible. There is no information on casualties.

ARCADIAN ex-*ORTONA* (1899–1917)

Royal Mail Line, Great Britain; Vickers & Maxim, Barrow-in-Furness.
8,939 GRT, 500ft (152.4m) length, 55ft (16.8m) beam.
320 passengers in single class.
Triple expansion SR engines, twin screw, 18kts.
Date of disaster: 15 April 1917.

Before joining the Royal Mail Line in 1905, the *Arcadian* sailed for the Pacific Steam Navigation Co as the *Ortona*, and also spent some time employed in the Australia service for the Orient Line. Her days on the South American run ended with the outbreak of the First World War, when she was requisitioned for conversion into a troopship. In this employment, the *Arcadian* was sailing from Salonica to Alexandria on 15 April 1917, conveying 1,335 troops and crew, when she was attacked by a submarine in the position 36°50′N–24°50′E. The torpedo strike caused such widespread damage that the *Arcadian* sank in only five minutes, suddenly capsizing at the end. Fortuitously, the attack occurred almost immediately after a life-boat drill had been carried out, with the majority of the men still on deck. Consequently, a rapid but disciplined evacuation permitted 1,058 of those aboard to safely leave the ship and, had it not been for the *Arcadian* turning over as she went under, the number would have been higher. Of the 277 who died in the attack, 233 were army personnel (19 officers and 214 other ranks), 10 were naval ratings, and 34 were members of the *Arcadian*'s crew.

A dramatic photograph of the troopship Arcadian *sinking after being torpedoed.* (Imperial War Museum, Neg. SP813)

CAMERONIA (1911–1917)

Anchor Line, Great Britain; D. & W. Henderson, Glasgow.
10,963 GRT, 532ft (162.1m) LOA, 62ft (18.9m) beam.
1,700 passengers in three classes.
Triple expansion SR engines, twin screw, 17kts.
Date of disaster: 15 April 1917.

The Anchor liner *Cameronia*, which entered the Glasgow to New York service in September 1911, was later employed on a joint service in conjunction with Cunard, which included a call at Liverpool. In 1917 she was taken over for use as a troopship but only survived a few months, being torpedoed and sunk by the German submarine *U33*, 150 miles east of Malta, on 15 April. The *Cameronia* had been bound from Marseilles to Egypt with 2,630 troops. The sinking cost 129 lives, including one officer and 11 men from her crew. Some reports give a death toll of 210.

Anchor Line's Cameronia *sinking off Malta in 1917.* (Imperial War Museum, Neg. Q115414)

MASHOBRA (1914–1917)

British India Line, Great Britain; Barclay Curle, Glasgow.
8,174 GRT, 449ft (136.9m) length, 58ft (17.7m) beam.
129 passengers in two classes.
Triple expansion SR engines, twin screw, 13.5kts.
Date of disaster: 15 April 1917.

On the outbreak of the First World War, the India service liner *Mashobra* became a troop transport, performing in this capacity throughout the Gallipoli campaign. Following this she returned to her normal commercial duties. While returning to London from Calcutta on 15 April 1917 she was torpedoed and sunk by an Austrian submarine 140 miles south-west of Cape Matapan, in the position 35°34'N–20°40'E. The crew abandoned ship, after which she was sunk by shellfire from the submarine, which had surfaced following the torpedo attack. The *Mashobra*'s master, Capt H.J. Brooks, was taken prisoner. The loss of life amounted to eight members of the engine-room crew, killed by the explosion of the torpedo. The survivors were picked up by trawlers and taken to Malta, where they arrived the following day.

SONTAY (1907–1917)

Messageries Maritimes, France; Messageries Maritimes, La Ciotat.
7,247 GRT, 447ft (136.2m) length, 52ft (15.9m) beam.
Triple expansion SR engines, twin screw, 12kts.
Date of disaster: 16 April 1917.

One of a group of five vessels, the passenger liner *Sontay* operated on the service from France to the Far East via the Suez Canal. She was torpedoed and sunk on 16 April 1917 between Sardinia and Sicily while bound from Salonica to Marseilles, carrying 334 passengers and a crew of 81. She sank rapidly, taking many with her, including 45 passengers and her commander, Lt Mages, who, in the tradition of the sea, chose to go down with his ship. The death toll would have been higher but for the disciplined and prompt manner in which the *Sontay* was evacuated.

LANFRANC (1907–1917)

Booth Line, Great Britain; Caledon, Dundee.
6,287 GRT, 433ft (132.0m) LOA, 52ft (15.9m) beam.
571 passengers in two classes.
Triple expansion SR engines, twin screw, 14kts.
Date of disaster: 17 April 1917.

The steamship *Lanfranc* was one of a class of three vessels built for the service from Liverpool to Brazil. On the outbreak of the First World War, she was taken over by the Admiralty and operated as a hospital ship. In this capacity, while returning to Southampton from Le Havre on 17 April 1917 carrying both British and German wounded, she was torpedoed by a German submarine about 40 miles north-east of the French port, in the position 49°56'N–00°20'W. The *Lanfranc*'s full complement of 576 comprised 234 wounded British soldiers, 167 wounded German soldiers, a medical staff of 52, and a crew of 123. Of these, 29 of the military personnel died (14 British and 15 German), plus five crewmen. The survivors were picked up by escorting naval vessels.

ABOSSO (1912–1917)

Elder Dempster Line, Great Britain; Harland & Wolff, Belfast.
7,782 GRT, 425ft (129.5m) length, 57ft (17.4m) beam.
400 passengers in two classes.
Quadruple expansion SR engines, twin screw, 14kts.
Date of disaster: 24 April 1917.

Nearing the end of a voyage from Lagos to Liverpool, the *Abosso* was torpedoed and sunk by a German submarine on 24 April 1917, the attack taking place south-west of Ireland, about 180 miles from Fastnet in the position 50°50'N–15°00'W. Sixty-five people lost their lives. Before the First World War, the *Abosso* had been regularly engaged on the England to West Africa service.

The Booth Line's Lanfranc *was torpedoed while serving as a hospital ship.* (World Ship Society)

BALLARAT (1911–1917)

P&O Line, Great Britain; Caird, Greenock.
11,120 GRT, 515ft (157.0m) LOA, 62ft (18.9m) beam.
1,100 passengers in single class.
Quadruple expansion SR engines, twin screw, 14kts.
Date of disaster: 25 April 1917.

The *Ballarat* operated on the branch line service to Australia via Cape Town. When she first entered service she displayed on her funnel the blue anchor symbol of the William Lund Company, which had been recently absorbed by P&O. On 25 April 1917 she was sunk by the German submarine *UB32* near to the Scilly Isles as she was approaching the English Channel, in the position 49°33'N–05°36'W. She was on a voyage from Melbourne to London carrying troops and a cargo of bullion, copper, lead, and antimony ore. There were no casualties among the 1,752 people on board, all transferring safely to escorting destroyers.

Two views of the P&O liner Ballarat *sinking following a torpedo attack near the Scilly Isles.* (Imperial War Museum, Negs. Q50275 and Q50276)

MEDINA (1911–1917)

P&O Line, Great Britain; Caird, Greenock.
12,358 GRT, 570ft (173.7m) LOA, 62ft (18.9m) beam.
680 passengers in two classes.
Quadruple expansion SR engines, twin screw, 18kts.
Date of disaster: 28 April 1917.

The last vessel of the 'M' class, the *Medina* had the distinction of being selected as the Royal Yacht for King George V and Queen Mary's tour of India in 1912. Thereafter she commenced service on the London to Sydney route.

As she neared the end of a voyage from Sydney on 28 April 1917, having already called at Plymouth, the *Medina* was heading for London when the German submarine *UB31* attacked and sank her three miles east-north-east of Start

The Medina, *torpedoed and sunk after a brief but illustrious career which included duties as a Royal Yacht.* (A. Duncan)

Point. The torpedo struck her on the starboard side, flooding her engine-room and leaving her dead in the water, sinking fast. Distress calls were transmitted and the passengers and crew mustered in readiness to abandon ship. The *Medina* sank less than an hour after the attack, but by then the ship had been safely evacuated and the only lives lost were those of an engineer officer and five firemen killed by the initial explosion. Naval vessels took the lifeboats in tow to Dartmouth and Brixham.

TRANSYLVANIA (1914–1917)

Anchor Line, Great Britain; Scott's, Greenock.
14,315 GRT, 567ft (172.8m) LOA, 66ft (20.1m) beam.
2,420 passengers in three classes.
Steam turbines, twin screw, 16kts.
Date of disaster: 4 May 1917.

The Cunard Line ordered the *Transylvania* and her sister ship *Tuscania* for a joint Mediterranean to New York service with Anchor Line. In the event they both passed into Anchor Line ownership, sailing instead on the Glasgow to New York route. In May 1915 the *Transylvania* became a troopship, her military career extending for two years, supporting the campaign in the Balkans. Accompanied by the Japanese destroyers *Matsu* and *Sakaki*, the *Transylvania* sailed from Marseilles for Alexandria on 3 May 1917 with a full complement of 200 officers and 2,800 soldiers in addition to her crew. The day after her departure, as the ships were crossing the Gulf of Genoa, the German submarine *U63* torpedoed the *Transylvania* some 2.5 miles south of Cape Vado, hitting her on the port side in the engine compartments. Course was altered to head for the nearby coast, while the *Matsu* closed in on the stricken troopship to take off her passengers. Shortly after, a second torpedo struck the *Transylvania*, narrowly missing the *Matsu*, and she sank soon after in the position 44°15′N–08°30′E. Between them the *Matsu* and *Sakaki* picked up many survivors, but 414 lives were lost, among them the captain, Lt S. Brennel RNR, and 11 other crewmen.

GALICIA (1901–1917)

Pacific Steam Navigation Co, Great Britain; Wigham Richardson, Newcastle.
5,896 GRT, 400ft (121.9m) length, 50ft (15.2m) beam.
Triple expansion SR engines, twin screw, 14kts.
Date of disaster: 12 May 1917.

The *Galicia* was sunk three miles east of Teignmouth Pier on 12 May 1917 after she struck a mine. She was on a voyage from Liverpool to Valparaiso, the accident occurring after a call at Falmouth. The *Galicia* and her consort *Potosi* were employed on the run to South America.

HIGHLAND CORRIE (1910–1917)

Nelson Line, Great Britain; Russell, Port Glasgow.
7,583 GRT, 414ft (126.2m) length, 56ft (17.1m) beam.
120 passengers in two classes.
Triple expansion SR engine, single screw, 13kts.
Date of disaster: 16 May 1917.

The *Highland Corrie* was one of a large class of 10 cargo-passenger ships built for the service from London to South America. She was returning to her home port on 16 May 1917 with a small number of passengers and a cargo of frozen meat when she was attacked by a German submarine in the English Channel. She sank four miles south of the Owers light vessel, stationed off Selsey Bill. Five members of her crew were killed.

Cunard Line's Transylvania *was a torpedo loss.* (Tom Rayner)

Nelson Line's Highland Corrie. (World Ship Society)

HILARY (1908–1917)

Booth Line, Great Britain; Caledon, Dundee.
6,329 GRT, 433ft (132.0m) LOA, 52ft (15.9m) beam.
582 passengers in two classes.
Triple expansion SR engines, twin screw, 14kts.
Date of disaster: 25 May 1917.

The *Hilary* and her sisters, *Antony* and *Lanfranc*, operated between England and South America on a route which included a 1,000-mile-long passage up the River Amazon. All three ships were casualties of the First World War; indeed, all three were lost in 1917, in a period of just over two months. The *Hilary* was sunk on 25 May while serving as an armed merchant cruiser with the 10th Cruiser Squadron, being torpedoed by a German submarine during a patrol off the Shetland Islands.

DOVER CASTLE (1904–1917)

Union Castle Line, Great Britain; Barclay Curle, Glasgow.
8,271 GRT, 490ft (149.3m) LOA, 56ft (17.1m) beam.
220 passengers in single class.
Quadruple expansion SR engines, twin screw, 14kts.
Date of disaster: 26 May 1917.

Though built for the intermediate service, the *Dover Castle*, one of three sisters, was employed on the London to Cape Town and Mombasa service in the years before the First World War. She was lost on 26 May 1917 while serving as a hospital ship. During a voyage from Malta to Gibraltar in company with the hospital ship *Karapara* and the destroyers *Camelon* and *Nemesis*, the *Dover Castle* was torpedoed when about fifty miles north of Bona (Annaba), Algeria. The *Camelon* took off the wounded, the hospital staff, and most of the *Dover Castle*'s complement. A skeleton crew remained aboard under the captain in a bid to save the crippled ship, but all hope of achieving this was dashed when the *Dover Castle*'s attacker put another torpedo into

The hospital ship Dover Castle. (Imperial War Museum, Neg. Q22811)

her. She sank soon after. Seven engine-room crewmen were killed by the explosion of the first torpedo, but everyone else was saved.

C. DE EIZAGUIRRE ex-*LANDANA* ex-*LEOPOLDVILLE* (1904–1917)

Cia Transatlantica, Spain; Sir Raylton Dixon, Middlesborough.
4,629 GRT, 400ft (121.9m) length, 47ft (14.3m) beam.
Triple expansion SR engines, twin screw, 13.5kts.
Date of disaster: 27 May 1917.

The Spanish passenger ship *C. de Eizaguirre* operated in the North Atlantic service and in the West Indies and Central America trade. On 27 May 1917 during a voyage from Barcelona to Manila by way of the Cape of Good Hope, the *C. de Eizaguirre* struck a mine laid by the German raider *Wolf* off Robben Island, some 15 miles from Cape Town. The explosion broke her back and she sank within minutes, her bow and stern pointing skyward. She was carrying more than 150 passengers besides her crew, and most of these were asleep in their cabins at the time of the incident, which occurred in the early hours before daybreak. In the desperate race against time, only one lifeboat got waterborne, its 23 occupants and the chief engineer, who was picked up from a raft, being the only survivors.

YARRA (1883–1917)

Messageries Maritimes, France; Messageries Maritimes, La Ciotat.
4,142 GRT, 416ft (126.8m) length, 41ft (12.5m) beam.
Triple expansion SR engine, single screw, 13.5kts.
Date of disaster: 29 May 1917.

The French steamship *Yarra* was engaged on the service from Marseilles to ports east of Suez and Madagascar. She continued to make these voyages after the outbreak of war but was torpedoed and sunk in the eastern Mediterranean on 29 May 1917, while returning to France from Port Said and Madagascar with the Egyptian mails and 690 people aboard. Many of these were native passengers, some of whom lost their lives in the attack. In addition eight Arab stokers were killed, the total loss of life amounting to 56.

MIYAZAKI MARU (1909–1917)

Nippon Yusen Kaisha, Japan; Kawasaki, Kobe.
7,892 GRT, 465ft (141.7m) length, 54ft (16.5m) beam.
127 passengers in three classes.
Triple expansion SR engines, twin screw, 15.5kts.
Date of disaster: 31 May 1917.

The Japanese steamship *Miyazaki Maru*, which operated on the European service from Yokohama, was torpedoed and sunk by a German submarine on 31 May 1917. The attack occurred off Ushant, about 150 miles west of the Scilly Isles, as the *Miyazaki Maru* was proceeding to London with passengers. No information is recorded regarding casualties.

SOUTHLAND ex-*VADERLAND* (1900–1917)

White Star Line, Great Britain; John Brown, Clydebank.
12,018 GRT, 580ft (176.8m) LOA, 60ft (18.3m) beam.

The Miyazaki Maru, *another Japanese casualty of the First World War.* (Kawasaki Heavy Industries)

1,362 passengers in three classes.
Quadruple expansion SR engines, twin screw, 15kts.
Date of disaster: 4 June 1917.

The Red Star Line's *Vaderland* and *Zeeland* sailed between Antwerp and New York until 1914, when they were transferred to the White Star Line for the service from Liverpool. The following year they were renamed *Southland* and *Northland* respectively. After a spell on the service to Montreal, the *Southland* was taken over for troop carrying. On 4 June 1917, on a voyage from Liverpool to Philadelphia, she was sunk 140 miles north-west of Tory Island off the coast of County Donegal, Ireland, in the position 56°01'N–12°14'W, when the German submarine *U70* fired two torpedoes into her. Four of her crew were lost with her.

AOTEAROA as *AVENGER* (1916–1917)

Union SS Co of New Zealand, Great Britain; Fairfield, Glasgow.
14,744 GRT, 550ft (167.6m) LOA, 66ft (20.1m) beam.
600 passengers in three classes (designed).
Steam turbines, twin screw, 18kts.
Date of disaster: 14 June 1917.

The *Aotearoa* was laid down in 1913 for the Union Steamship Company of New Zealand, but at the outbreak of the First World War, when still incomplete, work on her was suspended. The Admiralty took her over on 21 June 1915 and ordered her completion as an auxiliary cruiser for the Royal Navy. She entered service as HMS *Avenger* in 1916. On 14 June 1917, while approaching Scapa Flow at the end of a patrol, she was torpedoed and sunk by the German submarine *U69* in the position 60°20'N–03°58'W. There was one fatality.

Below *The armed merchant cruiser HMS* Avenger, *conceived and ordered as the passenger liner* Aotearoa *for New Zealand services.* (Maritime Photo Library)

Bottom *HMS* Avenger *ex-*Aotearoa *sinking after a German torpedo attack.* (Maritime Photo Library)

CARTHAGINIAN (1884–1917)

Allan Line, Great Britain; Govan, Glasgow.
4,444 GRT, 386ft (117.6m) length, 45ft (13.7m) beam.
596 passengers in three classes.
Compound steam engine, single screw, 14kts.
Date of disaster: 14 June 1917.

Prior to the First World War, the *Carthaginian* served on various North Atlantic routes, normally based in Glasgow. On 14 June 1917 she was bound for Montreal from the River Clyde when she struck a mine 2.5 miles north-west of Inishtrahull, sinking as a result of the explosion.

HIMALAYA (1902–1917)

Messageries Maritimes, France; Messageries Maritimes, La Ciotat.
5,620 GRT, 428ft (130.5m) length, 47ft (14.3m) beam.
Triple expansion SR engines, twin screw, 13kts.
Date of disaster: 22 June 1917.

The French steamship *Himalaya* operated between France and the Far East via the Mediterranean and East African ports in the Red Sea. While sailing off the coast of Algeria on 22 June 1917, in the capacity of an auxiliary cruiser attached to the French Navy, the *Himalaya* was torpedoed and sunk by a German submarine with the loss of 28 lives.

MONGOLIA (1903–1917)

P&O Line, Great Britain; Caird, Greenock.
9,505 GRT, 540ft (164.6m) LOA, 58ft (17.7m) beam.
520 passengers in two classes.
Triple expansion SR engines, twin screw, 18kts.
Date of disaster: 23 June 1917.

Unlike her sister ship *Moldavia*, the *Mongolia* continued with her commercial sailings after the outbreak of the First World War. On 23 June 1917, when she was en route from London to Bombay, China, and Sydney with passengers, mail and cargo, she struck a mine laid by the raider *Wolf* in the approaches to Bombay, about 17 miles west of Jaujira. She remained afloat for only 13 minutes, but in this time it proved possible to launch her boats and get ashore all those who had survived the initial explosion, which killed three passengers and 20 crewmen.

ULTONIA (1898–1917)

Cunard Line, Great Britain; Swan & Hunter, Wallsend-on-Tyne.
8,845 GRT, 513ft (156.4m) LOA, 57ft (17.4m) beam.
Triple expansion SR engines, twin screw, 13kts.
Date of disaster: 27 June 1917.

The *Ultonia* was originally built as a livestock carrier but from 1903, after Cunard had concluded a 10-year contract to carry Hungarian emigrants to the New World, she operated between Fiume, Gibraltar, and New York, with steerage class accommodation only. Returning to London from New York, she was torpedoed and sunk on 27 June 1917 when the German submarine *U53* intercepted her 190 miles south-west of Fastnet, in the position 48°25′N–11°23′W. Two people were killed.

The P&O ship Mongolia*, a mine casualty.* (World Ship Society)

Messageries Maritimes' steamship Caledonien. (World Ship Society)

CALEDONIEN (1882–1917)

Messageries Maritimes, France; Messageries Maritimes, La Ciotat.
4,248 GRT, 413ft (125.9m), 41ft (12.5m) beam.
Triple expansion SR engine, single screw, 15kts.
Date of disaster: 30 June 1917.

The *Caledonien* was one of a class of seven sister ships built for the route from Marseilles, via the Suez Canal, to Australia and New Caledonia; hence her name. She was bound for Mauritius from Marseilles on 30 June 1917 when she struck a mine in the eastern Mediterranean and sank. There is no information on record regarding casualties.

MONGARA (1903–1917)

British India Line, Great Britain; Swan, Hunter & Wigham Richardson, Newcastle.
9,500 GRT, 540ft (164.6m) LOA, 58ft (17.7m) beam.
Triple expansion SR engines, twin screw, 13.5kts.
Date of disaster: 3 July 1917.

The *Mongara* served on the route from London to India via the Suez Canal. She had one sister, the *Morvada.* Although the *Mongara* continued in passenger service after the outbreak of war in August 1914, she often sailed on different routes from that of her normal service, as did many other passenger ships at that time. This resulted from the requirement to send ships wherever the needs of the moment dictated, and because it was difficult to maintain regular schedules under wartime conditions. Thus it was that the *Mongara* met her end during the return leg of a voyage from Sydney, Australia, on 3 July 1917. Having left Port Said she was approaching Messina, in company with an Italian destroyer and an armed trawler, when a German submarine torpedoed her about 1.5 miles from the harbour breakwater. Neither the destroyer nor the trawler, which had been on either side of the *Mongara,* were attacked. She sank within a few minutes, but all aboard her were rescued.

PEGU (1913–1917)

Henderson Line, Great Britain; William Denny, Dumbarton.
6,348 GRT, 445ft (135.6m) length, 55ft (16.8m) beam.
100 passengers in single class.
Triple expansion SR engine, single screw, 14kts.
Date of disaster: 8 July 1917.

The Henderson Line steamship *Pegu* served on the route from Glasgow and Liverpool to Rangoon. She was sunk on 8 July 1917 when she struck a mine seven miles south-east of Gatley Head, County Cork, while returning to Liverpool from Rangoon with a cargo of beans and rice.

SALSETTE (1909–1917)

P&O Line, Great Britain; Caird, Greenock.
5,842 GRT, 440ft (134.1m) length, 53ft (16.2m) beam.
220 passengers in two classes.
Quadruple expansion SR engines, twin screw, 20kts.
Date of disaster: 20 July 1917.

Constructed for the Aden to Bombay service, the *Salsette* was one of the earliest ships in the P&O fleet to have a white hull. From 1916–1917 she maintained the service from London to Sydney via Bombay, Colombo, and Melbourne. After leaving Tilbury outward bound on 19 July 1917, the *Salsette* was torpedoed in the English Channel the following day, 15 miles south-west of Portland Bill. The torpedo struck her forward on the starboard side, destroying many lifeboats and killing 15 members of the

crew. She sank after only five minutes, but in this time she was abandoned in an orderly fashion, the remaining lifeboats being launched without further loss of life. The survivors were taken to Weymouth.

OTWAY (1909–1917)

Orient Line, Great Britain; Fairfield, Glasgow.
12,077 GRT, 552ft (168.2m) LOA, 63ft (19.2m) beam.
1,100 passengers in two classes.
Quadruple expansion SR engines, twin screw, 18kts.
Date of disaster: 22 July 1917.

The Australian services liner *Otway* was a sister ship to the *Orsova*, *Osterley*, *Orvieto*, and *Orama*, and the *Otranto*, which later sank following a wartime collision with P&O Line's *Kashmir*. In December 1914 the *Otway* was commissioned by the Admiralty as an auxiliary cruiser, serving with the 10th Cruiser Squadron. She was sunk during a routine patrol north of the Hebrides on 22 July 1917, by a torpedo from the German submarine *UC49*. Ten naval ratings were killed in the explosion, but the remainder of her company were safely rescued.

MOOLTAN (1905–1917)

P&O Line, Great Britain; Caird, Greenock.
9,621 GRT, 520ft (158.5m) length, 58ft (17.7m) beam.

Above *The* Salsette, *another P&O war loss.* (World Ship Society)

Left *Orient Line's* Otway *saw auxiliary service with the 10th Cruiser Squadron before she was sunk by torpedo.* (P&O Group)

Below *The* Mooltan *was sunk by torpedo just one month after her sister ship, the* Mongolia. (World Ship Society)

514 passengers in two classes.
Quadruple expansion SR engines, twin screw, 18.5kts.
Date of disaster: 26 July 1917.

The liner *Mooltan* operated on the service from England to Australia via the Mediterranean and Suez. On 26 July 1917, while returning to London from Sydney with 554 people and a cargo of mails and meat, and escorted by the Japanese destroyers *Kusonoki* and *Ume*, the *Mooltan* was torpedoed without warning 53 miles north-north-west of Cape Serrat, Tunisia, in the position 37°56'N–08°34'E. All but two of those aboard were safely rescued by the escorting ships, which later unsuccessfully attempted to sink the German submarine. They were compelled to disengage for fear of leaving a second ship under their protection – Messageries Maritimes' *Lotus* – vulnerable to attack.

LETITIA (1912–1917)

Anchor-Donaldson Line, Great Britain; Scott's, Greenock.
8,991 GRT, 470ft (143.3m) length, 56ft (17.1m) beam.
1,300 passengers in two classes.
Triple expansion SR engines, twin screw, 14.5kts.
Date of disaster: 1 August 1917.

The *Letitia*, with her running-mate *Saturnia*, sailed in the Glasgow to Canada service. During the First World War the *Letitia* was taken over for conversion into a hospital ship, a role she continued to perform until 1 August 1917, when she was wrecked on the coast of Nova Scotia while bound from Liverpool to Quebec, repatriating wounded Canadian soldiers. She ran onto the rocks at Portuguese Cove, Chebucto Head, near Halifax.

CITY OF ATHENS (1901–1917)

Ellerman Lines, Great Britain; Workman Clark, Belfast.
5,594 GRT, 430ft (131.1m) length, 50ft (15.2m) beam.
96 passengers in two classes.
Triple expansion SR engine, single screw, 13.5kts.
Date of disaster: 10 August 1917.

The Ellerman Lines and its various associated companies maintained services between England and India, and East and South Africa. The *City of Athens* was sunk by a mine some 20 miles north-west of Green Point, Cape Town, on 10 August 1917, during a voyage from New York to India. The mine was one of a number laid by the German raider *Wolf* some months earlier. As well as setting fire to the *City of Athens*, the explosion felled the foremast and radio aerial, making it impossible to call for help. The lifeboats were launched, getting all 97 passengers and 115 crew safely away, but unfortunately one boat later capsized, drowning 15 passengers and four crewmen. Help for the remaining survivors arrived in the form of the tug *Ludwig Wiener*, which had been sent to the scene after the blazing *City of Athens* was sighted from the nearby African coast.

TURAKINA (1902–1917)

New Zealand Line, Great Britain; Hawthorn Leslie, Newcastle.
8,349 GRT, 473ft (144.2m) length, 59ft (18.0m) beam.
195 passengers in three classes.
Triple expansion SR engines, twin screw, 14kts.
Date of disaster: 13 August 1917.

The steamship *Turakina*, whose normal service was from

The Letitia *stranded on the rocks near Halifax, Nova Scotia, after conversion to a hospital ship.* (Imperial War Museum, Neg. Q61170)

The New Zealand Shipping Company's Turakina. (World Ship Society)

the United Kingdom to New Zealand, was sunk by torpedo 120 miles from Bishop Rock, in position 48°20'N–08°34'W, while sailing from London to New York on 13 August 1917. She was empty at the time of the attack, but two members of her crew were killed.

ATHENIA (1905–1917)

Anchor-Donaldson Line, Great Britain; Vickers & Maxim, Barrow-in-Furness.
9,080 GRT, 478ft (145.7m) length, 56ft (17.1m) beam.
500 passengers in two classes.
Triple expansion SR engines, twin screw, 13.5kts.
Date of disaster: 16 August 1917.

The ships of the Anchor-Donaldson Line operated between Glasgow and Canadian St Lawrence ports, and the *Athenia* joined this service in March 1905. Bound from Montreal to Glasgow, she fell victim to a German submarine on 16 August 1917, seven miles north-north-east of Inishtrahull Island, County Donegal. Fifteen members of her complement were killed.

DEVONIAN (1900–1917)

Leyland Line, Great Britain; Harland & Wolff, Belfast.
10,418 GRT, 571ft (174.0m) LOA, 59ft (18.0m) beam.
135 passengers in single class.
Triple expansion SR engine, single screw, 14kts.
Date of disaster: 21 August 1917.

The *Devonian* carried 135 first class passengers only on the

The Athenia. *Like her later namesake in the Second World War, she was a torpedo victim.* (World Ship Society)

The Verdi *of Lamport & Holt Line.* (World Ship Society)

route from Liverpool to Boston. On 21 August 1917, during a westbound crossing, she was torpedoed and sunk by the German submarine *U53* about 20 miles north-east of Tory Island, due north of the Bloody Foreland, County Donegal. Two people were killed.

VERDI (1907–1917)

Lamport & Holt Co, Great Britain; Workman Clark, Belfast.
7,120 GRT, 430ft (131.1m) length, 53ft (16.2m) beam.
Triple expansion SR engine, single screw, 14kts.
Date of disaster: 22 August 1917.

The *Verdi* sailed between Liverpool, Brazil, and ports on the River Plate. On 22 August 1917, during a voyage from New York to Liverpool, she was torpedoed by a German submarine 115 miles north-west of Eagle Island, County Mayo, and sank in the position 55°17′N–12°58′W. Six members of her crew lost their lives.

PARANA (1908–1917)

Soc. Génerale des Transports Maritimes, France; Forges et Chantiers de la Mediterranée, La Seyne.
6,248 GRT, 420ft (128.0m) length, 50ft (15.2m) beam.
171 passengers in three classes.
Triple expansion SR engines, twin screw, 14kts.
Date of disaster: 23 August 1917.

Consort to the *Pampa* on the service from France and Italy to South America, the *Parana* was the victim of a submarine attack in the Mediterranean during a voyage from Marseilles to Salonica. She was torpedoed off the Greek coast on 23 August 1917.

MALDA (1913–1917)

British India Line, Great Britain; Barclay Curle, Glasgow.
7,884 GRT, 450ft (137.2m) length, 58ft (17.7m) beam.
70 passengers in two classes.
Triple expansion SR engines, twin screw, 13.5kts.
Date of disaster: 25 August 1917.

The British India steamship *Malda* worked the route from England to India via the Suez Canal. Just after midday on 25 August 1917, while bound for London from Boston, she was attacked by a German submarine 136 miles south-west of the Scillies during a severe gale. While the lowering and filling of the lifeboats was under way, the U-boat surfaced and attempted to contact the survivors. Due to the ferocity of the weather this proved to be impossible, although the submarine was able to prevent efforts by the survivors to re-board the *Malda*, which remained afloat until the following morning. The boats set course for the Scillies but were soon scattered, landing at various places along the coast. One was picked up by another convoy ship bound for Milford Haven. It was believed at first that the loss of life was not too serious – no more than seven, four of whom had been killed by the exploding torpedo. However, official figures published later revealed that the death toll was actually 64.

ALESIA ex-*PRINCETOWN* ex-*PRINZ ADALBERT* (1902–1917)

Cie. Sud-Atlantique, France; Bremer Vulkan, Vegesack.
6,030 GRT, 403ft (122.8m) length, 49ft (14.9m) beam.
1,260 passengers in two classes.
Quadruple expansion SR engines, twin screw, 13kts.
Date of disaster: 6 September 1917.

The former German ship *Alesia* was built for Hamburg Amerika Line's Genoa and Naples to New York service. She passed to British owners in 1914 and then joined the Cie. Sud-Atlantique's service to Latin America in 1917. She was sunk by a German submarine off Ushant on 6 September 1917 when crossing from the River Tyne to Bordeaux.

The Malda. (P&O Group)

ELIZABETHVILLE (1910–1917)

Cie. Belge Maritime du Congo, Belgium; Alexander Stephen, Glasgow.
7,017 GRT, 415ft (126.5m) length, 55ft (16.8m) beam.
Quadruple expansion SR engines, twin screw, 14kts.
Date of disaster: 6 September 1917.

The *Elizabethville* and her sister ship *Albertville* were constructed for the service from Antwerp to Matadi for the company which was the forerunner of the Cie. Maritime Belge. The *Elizabethville* was sunk by a torpedo from a German submarine off Belle Isle, in the Bay of Biscay, on 6 September 1917, while bound for Falmouth from the Belgian Congo.

MINNEHAHA (1900–1917)

Atlantic Transport Line, Great Britain; Harland & Wolff, Belfast.
13,714 GRT, 616ft (187.8m) LOA, 65ft (19.8m) beam.
250 passengers in single class.
Quadruple expansion SR engines, twin screw, 16kts.
Date of disaster: 7 September 1917.

The second ship of the *Minneapolis* class, the *Minnehaha* was involved in two incidents in her 14 years of service prior to the First World War. In her maiden year she collided with and sank a tug in New York Harbour, while 10 years later she ran aground off the Scilly Isles and remained fast for almost a month. Though not engaged as a troopship, while bound for New York with passengers on 7 September 1917 she was torpedoed and sunk by the German submarine *U48* when 10 miles south of the Baltimore lighthouse, County Cork. She remained afloat for less than four minutes, and 43 people lost their lives in the attack.

VALPARAISO ex-*GERA* (1890–1917)

Lloyd de Pacifico, Italy; Fairfield, Glasgow.
4,930 GRT, 430ft (131.1m) length, 47ft (14.3m) beam.
Triple expansion SR engine, single screw, 13kts.
Date of disaster: 14 October 1917.

The former Norddeutscher Lloyd liner *Gera*, one of a class of six intermediate transatlantic steamships, passed to Italian owners in 1908 along with the *Weimar*. They were renamed *Valparaiso* and *Santiago* respectively and placed on the service from Italy to Chile. The *Valparaiso* was torpedoed and sunk in the Mediterranean on 14 October 1917.

OROPESA as *CHAMPAGNE* (1895–1917)

Pacific Steam Navigation Co, Great Britain; Harland & Wolff, Belfast.
5,364 GRT, 421ft (128.3m) length, 48ft (14.6m) beam.
Triple expansion SR engines, twin screw, 15kts.
Date of disaster: 15 October 1917.

On the outbreak of the First World War, the South American trade vessel *Oropesa* was taken over as an auxiliary cruiser, a unit of the 10th Cruiser Squadron under the command of Rear Admiral Sir Dudley de Chair. In 1917 she was loaned to the French Navy, although she retained her British crew. The French renamed her *Champagne*. She was torpedoed and sunk in the Irish Sea during a patrol on 15 October 1917, five officers and 51 ratings being killed. Earlier in the war, in March 1915, she had sunk a German submarine near Skerryvore.

CALIFORNIA (1902–1917)

Pacific Steam Navigation Co, Great Britain; Caird, Greenock.
5,629 GRT, 400ft (121.9m) length, 52ft (15.9m) beam.
Triple expansion SR engines, twin screw, 15kts.
Date of disaster: 17 October 1917.

The ships of the Pacific Steam Navigation Company served the ports on the Pacific coast of South America via Cape Horn. The sister liners *California* and *Mexico* entered the service in 1902. Fifteen years later, when bound from Liverpool to Callao on 17 October 1917, the *California* was the victim of a U-boat attack when she was torpedoed and sunk in the position 45°00′N–11°26′W.

ORAMA (1911–1917)

Orient Line, Great Britain; John Brown, Clydebank.
12,927 GRT, 569ft (173.4m) LOA, 64ft (19.5m) beam.
1,080 passengers in three classes.
Triple expansion SR engines with LP turbine, triple screw, 18kts.
Date of disaster: 19 October 1917.

There were six units in the pre-First World War *Orsova* class, built for the London to Brisbane service. The *Orama* was the last of the group, and had only been in service for three years when her commercial career was interrupted by the outbreak of war. She was converted into an auxiliary cruiser and engaged in convoy escort duties. In company with eight American destroyers, the *Orama* was escorting a large eastbound convoy across the Atlantic on 19 October 1917,

The Orient Line steamship Orama *in wartime grey paint scheme.* (P&O Group)

when she was torpedoed off the southern coast of Ireland by the submarine *U62*, under the command of Capt Ernst Hashagen. She remained afloat for almost four hours, during which time her crew was safely transferred to the destroyers, one of which – the USS *Conynham* – attempted, unsuccessfully, to ram the U-boat.

NAMUR (1907–1917)

P&O Line, Great Britain; Caird, Greenock.
6,694 GRT, 449ft (136.9m) length, 52ft (15.9m) beam.
94 passengers in two classes.
Quadruple expansion SR engines, twin screw, 14kts.
Date of disaster: 29 October 1917.

The *Namur* was one of a group of eight vessels introduced between 1906 and 1913 for employment on the service to Japan. She was sunk in the Mediterranean on 29 October 1917 while bound in convoy from Shanghai to London, being torpedoed without warning, approximately 55 miles east of Gibraltar, in the position 36°00′N–04°15′W. One life was lost.

HITACHI MARU (1906–1917)

Nippon Yusen Kaisha, Japan; Mitsubishi, Nagasaki.
6,557 GRT, 450ft (137.2m) length, 50ft (15.2m) beam.
Triple expansion SR engines, twin screw, 14kts.
Date of disaster: 7 November 1917.

The large group of liners which included the *Hitachi Maru* was employed initially on the Japan to Europe route, but later they were transferred to the Japan to Seattle service. As the *Hitachi Maru* was passing the southernmost point of the Maldive Islands on 26 September 1917, during a voyage from Yokohama to London, she was pursued by the German auxiliary cruiser *Wolf*. The *Hitachi Maru* attempted to drive off the raider with her single gun but the *Wolf* was better armed and soon overwhelmed her quarry. With 14 men dead, the liner's master, Capt Tominaga, surrendered his ship to

The Japanese steamship Hitachi Maru *served on Nippon Yusen Kaisha passenger routes to Europe.* (Kawasaki Heavy Industries)

Artist's impression of the encounter between the Hitachi Maru *and the German raider* Wolf. (W.Z. Bilddienst)

prevent further loss of life. The *Wolf* took the *Hitachi Maru* and her occupants to a lonely atoll where they remained for a month while the liner's cargo and coal were off-loaded. After the passengers and crew had also been transferred, the two ships put to sea again and headed for the Cargados Carajos Islands. During this time Capt Tominaga killed himself by jumping overboard. The *Hitachi Maru* was finally sunk by time bombs on 7 November. Prior to her capture, she had managed to radio for help and in response to her calls the Japanese and French cruisers *Tsushima* and *D'Estrees* searched the Indian Ocean for her, but to no avail.

ZIETEN as *TUNGUE* (1902–1917)

Norddeutscher Lloyd, Germany; F. Schichau, Danzig.
8,043 GRT, 449ft (136.9m) length, 55ft (16.8m) beam.
1,900 passengers in three classes.
Triple expansion SR engines, twin screw, 13.5kts.
Date of disaster: 27 November 1917.

The Norddeutscher Lloyd steamship *Zieten*, which operated between Germany and East Africa, was interned at Mozambique on 5 August 1914. The Portuguese Government requisitioned her in March 1916, renaming her *Tungue* and returning her to active service. A German submarine torpedoed and sunk her in the Mediterranean on 27 November 1917, while she was bound from Karachi to Milo Island, Greece.

APAPA (1914–1917)

Elder Dempster Line, Great Britain; Harland & Wolff, Belfast.
7,832 GRT, 426ft (129.8m) length, 57ft (17.4m) beam.
400 passengers in two classes.
Quadruple expansion SR engines, twin screw, 14kts.
Date of disaster: 28 November 1917.

The steamship *Apapa*, of the England to West Africa service, was torpedoed and sunk on 28 November 1917, apparently without warning, during a voyage from Lagos to Liverpool carrying 129 passengers and 120 crew. The German submarine attacked her about three miles north-east of Lynas Point, near Liverpool, the torpedo striking her amidships on the starboard side, causing her electric light system to fail. In spite of the extreme difficulty of organizing the evacuation in darkness, most of the lifeboats were successfully launched and filled. One boat, however, was struck by a second torpedo when the submarine resumed its attack, most of the occupants of this boat being killed or drowned. In all, 40 passengers and 37 crew lost their lives in the sinking of the *Apapa*. Her master, Capt Toft, had a lucky escape. He went down with his ship but later surfaced and was hauled from the sea, exhausted but alive, when rescue craft reached the scene.

Elder Dempster passenger ship Apapa. (A. Duncan)

IOANNINA ex-*HITTFIELD* ex-*ARCONIA* ex-*JULIETTE* ex-*DUNOLLY CASTLE* (1897–1917)

National Greek Line, Greece; Barclay Curle, Glasgow.
4,167 GRT, 368ft (112.2m) length, 47ft (14.3m) beam.
Triple expansion SR engine, single screw, 12.5kts.
Date of disaster: 15 December 1917.

The much-transferred passenger ship *Ioannina* started life as the Castle Line's *Dunolly Castle*. For her Greek owners she operated between Piraeus and New York. Bound for New York, she was torpedoed off the Azores by a German submarine on 15 December 1917, sinking in the approximate position 35°00′N–19°00′W.

ARAGON (1905–1917)

Royal Mail Line, Great Britain; Harland & Wolff, Belfast.
9,588 GRT, 530ft (161.5m) LOA, 60ft (18.3m) beam.
1,004 passengers in three classes.
Quadruple expansion SR engines, twin screw, 16kts.
Date of disaster: 30 December 1917.

A slightly smaller sister ship of the *Amazon*, *Araguaya*, and

The Aragon *was torpedoed and sunk with heavy loss of life.* (Tom Rayner)

The Aragon, *still afloat but gradually sinking, can be seen in the background almost concealed by rescue craft.* (Imperial War Museum, Neg. SP2054)

Avon, the *Aragon* joined them on the service from Southampton to South American Atlantic-coast ports. On the outbreak of the First World War she was taken over as a troop transport. During December 1917 she was employed carrying reinforcements to General Allenby's army fighting in Palestine, sailing in convoy from Marseilles. She arrived off Alexandria with around 2,500 troops on 30 December, but due to congestion in the port she was ordered to an anchorage outside the harbour, near the entrance to the mineswept channel, 11 miles north of GI Pass Beacon, in a position that was particularly exposed to submarine attack. Her vulnerability did not go unnoticed, and she was torpedoed later that day with the loss of 610 lives. Of these, 19 were from among her crew of 200, and included her commander, Capt F. Bateman.

Chapter Five

1918

THE U-BOAT OFFENSIVE CONTINUES

Though this was the final year of the war the submarine onslaught continued right up to the bitter end, with many more prestigious passenger ships falling victim to torpedoes before the cessation of hostilities on 11 November 1918 brought the carnage to an end. The very last passenger ship loss of the war was one of the worst, the *Surada* being torpedoed only nine days before the Armistice. The disaster which befell the Orient Line *Otranto*, barely a month earlier, was all the more tragic, resulting as it did from a collision between two convoy vessels bound for Europe, rather than from enemy action.

During the war's four years and three months of fighting, 173 passenger ships had been sunk, accounting for 13,441 known deaths. Of this total, just four vessels were German or Austrian, the remainder being either Allied or neutral ships. It is hardly surprising, therefore, that strenuous efforts were made to sequester all surviving German passenger vessels to make good the gaping holes left in the pre-war ranks of Allied liners. Yet while this enabled the Allies to restore revenue services with minimal delay, it was, perhaps, indirectly to Germany's advantage. While some of the victors' shipping companies, which had apparently gained from the exercise, nevertheless struggled to maintain balanced commercial schedules with the motley collection of outdated vessels at their disposal, Germany was able to restore its own fleet by the construction of modern, purpose-built passenger ships of the highest standard.

REGINA ELENA (1907–1918)

Navigazione Generale Italiana, Italy; Cantieri Liguria Ancon, Ancona.
7,940 GRT, 476ft (145.1m) length, 53ft (16.2m) beam.
1,424 passengers in three classes.
Quadruple expansion SR engines, twin screw, 16kts.
Date of disaster: 4 January 1918.

The *Regina Elena* was principally employed on the service to Latin America with three running mates, but she was also used for occasional voyages to New York. While bound for Tripoli from Massowah in East Africa, she fell victim to a torpedo attack in the Mediterranean on 4 January 1918.

REWA (1906–1918)

British India Line, Great Britain; William Denny, Dumbarton.
7,308 GRT, 456ft (139.0m) length, 56ft (17.1m) beam.
165 passengers in two classes.
Steam turbines, triple screw, 17kts.
Date of disaster: 4 January 1918.

The sister steamships *Rewa* and *Rohilla* were engaged in the service from London to India. During the First World War the *Rewa* was taken over for Admiralty service as a hospital ship. In this capacity she was attacked in the Bristol Channel, 19 miles from Hartland Point, by a German submarine, even though she was displaying clear identification of her status and was brightly illuminated. The attack occurred on 4 January 1918, when the *Rewa* was nearing the end of a voyage to Avonmouth from Salonica, having collected casualties at Malta and Gibraltar en route. In all, she was carrying 279 wounded, 80 medical staff, and

The Rewa *was another ship sunk while operating as a hospital ship.* (A. Duncan)

a crew of 207. The torpedo struck the *Rewa* amidships on her port side, causing an immediate list and making the launching of lifeboats difficult. Even so, as a result of good discipline and organization 14 boats were safely got away and, with the exception of three Lascar seamen, all aboard were safely rescued. The *Rewa* sank in the position 50°55′N–04°49′W. Her master, Capt J.E. Drake, kept the boats together, and by using flares attracted rescue vessels (two trawlers and a tanker) to the scene early the following morning.

ANDANIA (1913–1918)

Cunard Line, Great Britain; Scott's, Greenock.
13,404 GRT, 540ft (164.6m) LOA, 64ft (19.5m) beam.
2,140 passengers in two classes.
Quadruple expansion SR engines, twin screw, 16kts.
Date of disaster: 27 January 1918.

The *Andania* had completed only 15 months' commercial service when the First World War interrupted her employment on the run from London to Halifax and Boston or Montreal. Initially she was taken over as a troopship, but later resumed a partial route service activity between Liverpool and New York. Her career was ended on 27 January 1918 when the German submarine *U46* torpedoed and sunk her some two miles north-north-east of Rathlin Island lighthouse. Seven people were killed.

MINNETONKA (1902–1918)

Atlantic Transport Line, Great Britain; Harland & Wolff, Belfast.
13,440 GRT, 616ft (187.8m) LOA, 65ft (19.8m) beam.
250 passengers in single class.
Quadruple expansion SR engines, twin screw, 16kts.
Date of disaster: 30 January 1918.

The *Minnetonka* participated in the First World War in the role of armed auxiliary transport, guarding convoys as well as carrying troops. On 30 January 1918 the German submarine *U64*, commanded by Lt-Cdr Robert Moraht, encountered and sank her 40 miles north-west of Malta, in the position 36°12′N–14°55′E. The *Minnetonka* had been conveying the mails from Port Said to Marseilles, and was empty apart from her crew, four of whom were lost.

AURANIA (1917–1918)

Cunard Line, Great Britain; Swan, Hunter & Wigham Richardson, Wallsend-on-Tyne.
13,936 GRT, 540ft (164.6m) LOA, 64ft (19.5m) beam.
2,156 passengers in two classes (designed).
Steam turbines, twin screw, 16kts.
Date of disaster: 4 February 1918.

Planned for the London to Montreal or Boston service with sisters *Andania* and *Alaunia*, the *Aurania* in fact started her career as a troopship when she commenced her first voyage, from Newcastle to New York, on 28 March 1917. Less than a year later, on 4 February 1918, the *Aurania* was torpedoed by the German submarine *UB67*, approximately 15 miles north of Inishtrahull, when outward bound from Liverpool to New York. Eight people lost their lives. An attempt was made to tow the *Aurania* to port but she struck submerged rocks off Tobermory and became a total loss.

TUSCANIA (1915–1918)

Anchor Line, Great Britain; Alexander Stephen, Glasgow.
14,348 GRT, 576ft (175.6m) LOA, 66ft (20.1m) beam.
2,417 passengers in three classes.
Steam turbines, twin screw, 17kts.
Date of disaster: 5 February 1918.

Sister ship to the *Transylvania*, which commenced life with the Cunard Line, the *Tuscania* was an Anchor Line ship from the start. Like the *Transylvania*, she was lost in a torpedo attack during the First World War, when the submarine *UB77* attacked her on 5 February 1918, 13 miles north-west of Rathlin Island. The *Tuscania* was bound for

The Minnetonka. (World Ship Society)

The Cunard Ship Aurania. (World Ship Society)

Liverpool from New York with a total of 2,235 people on board, 2,030 of them American officers and troops. One hundred and sixty-six went down with the ship.

DUCA DI GENOVA (1907–1918)

La Veloce Line, Italy; Cantieri Navali Riuniti, La Spezia.
8,337 GRT, 476ft (145.1m) length, 53ft (16.2m) beam.
1,920 passengers in three classes.
Quadruple expansion SR engines, twin screw, 16.5kts.
Date of disaster: 6 February 1918.

The steamship *Duca di Genova*, originally built for the Navigazione Generale Italiana, was transferred to the La Veloce Line in 1913. She served in both the North American and South American trades from Genoa and Naples. She was sunk by torpedo, fired by *U64*, near Cape Canet in the Mediterranean on 6 February 1918, while returning to Genoa at the end of a voyage to New York. She foundered about a mile offshore.

The Anchor Line Tuscania. (World Ship Society)

GLENART CASTLE ex-*GALICIAN* (1900–1918)

Union Castle Line, Great Britain; Harland & Wolff, Belfast.
6,757 GRT, 440ft (134.1m) length, 53ft (16.2m) beam.
195 passengers in three classes.
Triple expansion SR engines, twin screw, 12kts.
Date of disaster: 26 February 1918.

The *Glenart Castle* was formerly the *Galician*, the sixth unit of a class of ships ordered by the Union Line prior to the merger with the Castle Line. While still under her original name she was very nearly a victim of the German armed merchant cruiser *Kaiser Wilhelm der Grosse* early in the First World War, when she was intercepted near Tenerife during a homeward bound voyage from Cape Town on 15 August 1914. After two military passengers had been seized, the *Galician* was permitted to proceed on her way. She was renamed *Glenart Castle* some days after this incident and thereafter was taken over by the Admiralty for service as a hospital ship. On 26 February 1918, while she was bound from Newport, South Wales, to Brest – where she was to take on wounded for return to England – she was torpedoed by the German submarine *UC56* and sank 20 miles west of Lundy Island. She was apparently clearly marked at the time of the attack, with all lights showing. Being outward bound, she was fortunately only carrying her crew and the medical staff, a total complement of 186 people. Nevertheless, 153 of these lost their lives, including the *Glenart Castle*'s master, Capt Burt, and 94 members of the crew.

CALGARIAN (1913–1918)

Canadian Pacific Line, Great Britain; Fairfield, Glasgow.
17,515 GRT, 600ft (182.9m) LOA, 72ft (21.9m) beam.
1,680 passengers in three classes.
Steam turbines, quadruple screw, 19.5kts.
Date of disaster: 1 March 1918.

The Allan liners *Calgarian* and *Alsatian* were introduced to the Liverpool to Halifax and St John's, Nova Scotia, route in 1913–1914. They passed to Canadian Pacific's ownership in July 1917, when this company absorbed the Allan Line, even though they were engaged in war duties at the time. The *Calgarian* never undertook commercial sailings for Canadian Pacific, for she was torpedoed by *U19* on 1 March 1918 while serving as a unit of the 9th Cruiser Squadron, sinking in a very short time with the loss of two officers and 47 ratings. The attack took place off Rathlin Head, Northern Ireland.

AMAZON (1906–1918)

Royal Mail Line, Great Britain; Harland & Wolff, Belfast.
10,037 GRT, 530ft (161.5m) LOA, 60ft (18.3m) beam.
870 passengers in three classes.
Quadruple expansion SR engines, twin screw, 15kts.
Date of disaster: 15 March 1918.

The *Amazon* was the first of five 'A' class steamers built between 1906 and 1912 for the Royal Mail Line's service from Southampton to La Plata ports. She was torpedoed and sunk by the submarine *U52* on 15 March 1918 when 30 miles north by west of Malin Head, Ireland. She was on a voyage from Liverpool to Buenos Aires at the time.

HIGHLAND BRIGADE (1901–1918)

Royal Mail Line, Great Britain; William Beardmore, Glasgow.
5,662 GRT, 384ft (117.0m) LOA, 50ft (15.2m) beam.
40 passengers in single class.
Triple expansion SR engine, single screw, 12.5kts.
Date of disaster: 7 April 1918.

The steamship *Highland Brigade* was bound from London to Buenos Aires when she was torpedoed without warning

The Allan liner Calgarian *was transferred to Canadian Pacific ownership in 1917 with her sister ship* Alsatian*, but never saw service for her new owners.* (World Ship Society)

Top *The Royal Mail liner* Amazon, *sister ship to the* Aragon *sunk in December 1917.* (World Ship Society)

Above *The* Highland Brigade. (World Ship Society)

and sunk on 7 April 1918. The attack occurred six miles south of St Catherine's Point, Isle of Wight, in the position 50°35′N–01°14′W.

POMERANIAN ex-*GRECIAN MONARCH* (1882–1918)

Canadian Pacific Line, Great Britain; Earle's, Hull.

4,365 GRT, 400ft (121.9m) LOA, 43ft (13.1m) beam.
1,100 passengers in three classes.
Compound steam engine, single screw, 12kts.
Date of disaster: 15 April 1918.

Allan Line bought the *Pomeranian* from the Monarch Line in September 1887 and placed her on the London to

The Allan Line steamship Pomeranian *berthed, with cavalry units on the quayside.* (Maritime Photo Library)

Montreal service. In 1893 she was severely damaged in a wild Atlantic storm and 12 people were killed. When she was repaired, two of her four masts were removed. On 15 April 1918, during a voyage from London to St John's, New Brunswick, the *Pomeranian* was sunk by a German submarine twelve miles south-west of Portland Bill. Fifty-five people, including the ship's master, were killed.

LAKE MICHIGAN (1901–1918)

Canadian Pacific Line, Great Britain; Swan & Hunter, Newcastle.
9,240 GRT, 469ft (142.9m) length, 56ft (17.1m) beam.
750 passengers in three classes.
Triple expansion SR engines, twin screw, 13kts.
Date of disaster: 16 April 1918.

The *Lake Michigan* was originally built with a sister ship, the *Lake Manitoba*, for the Elder Dempster Company's Beaver Line. In 1903 Canadian Pacific took over the Beaver Line fleet, and the *Lake Michigan* was placed on the service from Liverpool to Quebec and Montreal. On 16 April 1918 she fell victim to a submarine attack while bound from Liverpool and the River Clyde to St John's, New Brunswick, when she was torpedoed and sunk 93 miles north-west of Eagle Island, County Mayo, on Ireland's west coast. The *Lake Michigan* had earlier survived a mine explosion off Brest on 15 November 1916.

ORONSA (1906–1918)

Pacific Steam Navigation Co, Great Britain; Harland & Wolff, Belfast.
8,067 GRT, 465ft (141.7m) length, 56ft (17.1m) beam.
1,088 passengers in four classes.
Quadruple expansion SR engines, twin screw, 14kts.
Date of disaster: 28 April 1918.

The sister ships *Oriana*, *Oronsa*, and *Ortega* were introduced on the service to Pacific-coast ports of South America in 1906. Almost half of their passenger accommodation was in dormitories. Of the three, only the *Oronsa* did not survive the First World War. She was attacked by a German submarine twelve miles west of Bardsey Island, Wales, on 28 April 1918, while sailing in a convoy bound for Liverpool from the United States, having set out originally from Talcahuano, Chile. The torpedo struck the *Oronsa* aft, causing her boilers to blow up, and the devastation from the combined explosions resulted in her foundering after only 10 minutes. Even in this brief period a disciplined and well-organized evacuation operation made it possible to successfully launch all the lifeboats, and apart from four crew-members killed by the explosion there was no further loss of life. Escorting destroyers picked up the survivors.

SANT'ANNA (1910–1918)

Fabre Line, France; Forges et Chantiers de la Mediterranée, La Seyne.
9,350 GRT, 470ft (143.3m) length, 56ft (17.1m) beam.
1,970 passengers in three classes.
Triple expansion SR engines, twin screw, 16kts.
Date of disaster: 11 May 1918.

On 11 May 1918, during a voyage from Marseilles to Malta, the French passenger steamship *Sant'Anna* was torpedoed and sunk by an enemy submarine. Before the First World War, she had operated across the Atlantic between Marseilles and New York with a sister ship, the *Canada*.

VERONA (1908–1918)

Navigazione Generale Italiana, Italy; Workman Clark, Belfast.
8,886 GRT, 482ft (146.9m) length, 58ft (17.7m) beam.
Triple expansion SR engines, twin screw, 16kts.
Date of disaster: 11 May 1918.

The sister ships *Ancona*, *Taormina*, and *Verona* were built for the Soc. Anon. de Navigazione 'Italia' concern, transferring to the NGI in 1913. They were employed on both North Atlantic and South Atlantic routes. The *Verona* was sunk near Punta Pellaro, Italy, on 11 May 1918, after an enemy submarine torpedoed her. She had just called at Messina, having commenced her voyage at Genoa, but her intended destination and any casualties that may have resulted from the attack do not seem to be recorded.

OMRAH (1899–1918)

Orient Line, Great Britain; Fairfield, Glasgow.
8,291 GRT, 507ft (154.5m) LOA, 56ft (17.1m) beam.
823 passengers in three classes.
Triple expansion SR engines, twin screw, 17kts.
Date of disaster: 12 May 1918.

The *Omrah* entered the London to Melbourne and Sydney service, via the Suez Canal, in February 1899. Seventeen years later she was converted into a troopship for military duties in the First World War. After conveying units of the 52nd and 74th Divisions from Alexandria to Marseilles, in company with six other transports, the *Omrah* was torpedoed and sunk on 12 May 1918 on the return voyage. The attack occurred 60 miles south-west of Cape Spartivento, Sardinia. Fortunately, there was little loss of life for the *Omrah* was empty apart from her crew, and was only carrying mails.

MOLDAVIA (1903–1918)

P&O Line, Great Britain; Caird, Greenock.
9,505 GRT, 540ft (164.6m) LOA, 58ft (17.7m) beam.
514 passengers in two classes.
Triple expansion SR engines, twin screw, 18kts.
Date of disaster: 23 May 1918.

The *Moldavia* and her sister, the *Mongolia*, were employed on the route from London to Colombo, Melbourne, and Sydney. In 1915, the *Moldavia* was requisitioned for conversion to an auxiliary cruiser and was commissioned by the Admiralty. She continued in this role throughout the First World War, but after American entry into the conflict in 1917 she doubled as a troopship for the conveyance of soldiers from England to France. On 23 May 1918, while carrying a contingent of American troops, she was torpedoed in the English Channel, south of Brighton. With the exception of 56 soldiers drowned by the sudden inrush of water, all the remaining troops and crew were safely transferred to escorting destroyers.

VASILISSA SOPHIA as *LEASOWE CASTLE* (1917–1918)

National Steam Navigation Co, Greece; Cammell Laird, Birkenhead.
9,737 GRT, 488ft (148.7m) length, 58ft (17.7m) beam.
2,110 passengers in three classes (designed).
Quadruple expansion SR engines, twin screw, 17kts.
Date of disaster: 26 May 1918.

Ordered by a Greek company from the Cammell Laird shipyard at Birkenhead, this ship was not delivered to her owners on completion but was instead taken over by the British Government for war duties. The Controller of War Shipping placed her under the management of the Union Castle Line, and consequently she was renamed *Leasowe Castle*. Her career was short-lived, for on 26 May 1918, less then 18 months after commencing work as a troopship, she was sunk in the Mediterranean, some 150 miles west of Alexandria, while sailing in convoy from Egypt to Marseilles. In excess of 3,000 troops were aboard the *Leasowe Castle* in addition to her crew. Of these, a total of 92 people, including her master, Capt E.J. Hall, were killed.

The Orient liner Omrah *was sunk near Sardinia while serving as a troopship.* (P&O Group)

The former German liner President Lincoln *was sunk while operating as a troopship under the American flag.* (A. Duncan)

AUSONIA ex-*TORTONA* (1908–1918)

Cunard Line, Great Britain; Swan, Hunter & Wigham Richardson, Wallsend-on-Tyne.
8,153 GRT, 450ft (137.2m) length, 54ft (16.5m) beam.
1,050 passengers in two classes.
Triple expansion SR engine, single screw, 13kts.
Date of disaster: 30 May 1918.

The *Ausonia* was employed on the service from London and Southampton to Quebec and Montreal. She was sunk in the Atlantic by a German submarine on 30 May 1918 in the position 47°59′N–23°47′W, approximately 620 miles west of Fastnet. At the time she was bound from Liverpool to New York in ballast. There was a loss of 44 lives among those aboard, and the survivors spent eight days adrift in the lifeboats before they were picked up by the destroyer HMS *Zennia.*

PRESIDENT LINCOLN ex-*SCOTIAN* (1907–1918)

Hamburg Amerika Line, Germany; Harland & Wolff, Belfast.
18,168 GRT, 616ft (187.8m) LOA, 68ft (20.7m) beam.
3,350 passengers in three classes.
Quadruple expansion SR engines, twin screw, 14.5kts.
Date of disaster: 31 May 1918.

Ordered as the *Scotian* for the Furness Leyland Line along with a sister, the *Servian*, this ship was laid up incomplete after launching in October 1903, when her owners withdrew from the building contract. She was eventually completed as the *President Lincoln* for the Hamburg Amerika Line and spent seven years on the Atlantic run until she was interned in New York in August 1914. The American Government seized the liner in April 1917 and she was pressed into service as a troop transport under the same name controlled by the US War Shipping Administration. While returning to America from France on 31 May 1918, after taking a contingent of American troops to Europe, the *President Lincoln* was torpedoed by the submarine *U90* and sank in the position 47°57′N–15°11′W. Twenty six members of her crew were killed.

CAROLINA ex-*CITY OF SAVANNAH* ex-*LA GRANDE DUCHESSE* (1896–1918)

New York & Porto Rico Line, USA; Newport News Shipbuilding Co, Virginia.
5,093 GRT, 381ft (116.1m) length, 47ft (14.3m) beam.
Triple expansion SR engine, single screw, 15kts.
Date of disaster: 2 June 1918.

The American coastwise liner *Carolina* operated between New York and the West Indies, continuing sailings on this route after America's entry into the First World War in 1917. She was the victim of a U-boat attack on 2 June 1918, sinking 125 miles south-east of Sandy Hook while returning from San Juan, Puerto Rico, with passengers and a cargo of sugar.

PATIA (1913–1918)

Elders & Fyffes, Great Britain; Workman Clark, Belfast.
6,103 GRT, 417ft (127.1m) length, 53ft (16.2m) beam.
56 passengers in single class.
Triple expansion SR engines, twin screw, 14.5kts.
Date of disaster: 13 June 1918.

Like others of her fleetmates, the *Patia* was converted for war service as an auxiliary cruiser at the beginning of the First World War. On 13 June 1918, under the command of Capt W.G. Howard, she was torpedoed in the Bristol Channel by a German submarine, sinking with the loss of one officer and eight members of her crew and six military personnel.

DWINSK ex-*C.F. TIETGEN* ex-*ROTTERDAM* (1897–1918)

Russian American Line, Russia; Harland & Wolff, Belfast.
8,173 GRT, 469ft (142.9m) length, 53ft (16.2m) beam.

Triple expansion SR engines, twin screw, 15kts.
Date of disaster: 18 June 1918.

Built originally for the Holland Amerika service across the North Atlantic, the *Dwinsk* entered the Libau to New York service after joining the Russian American Line in 1913. Heading for New York from Brest in ballast, she was attacked by a German submarine on 18 June 1918 and sank 400 miles north-east of Bermuda in the position 39°10′N–63°01′W. Twenty-four members of her crew were killed.

ORISSA (1895–1918)

Pacific Steam Navigation Co, Great Britain; Harland & Wolff, Belfast.
5,360 GRT, 421ft (128.3m) length, 48ft (14.6m) beam.
Triple expansion SR engines, twin screw, 15.5kts.
Date of disaster: 25 June 1918.

The liner *Orissa* was one of a class of three ships, the others being the *Oravia* and *Oropesa*. During a voyage from Liverpool to Philadelphia on 25 June 1918, she was torpedoed by a German submarine when 20 miles south-west of Skerryvore. She sank in the position 56°20′N–07°02′W. Fortunately the *Orissa* had been in a light condition and was carrying no passengers, but six members of her crew were lost.

ABOVE *Elders & Fyffes'* Patia *shown sunk in shallow water, settled in an upright position. Her sister ship* Bayano *was an earlier casualty of the war.* (Maritime Photo Library)

BELOW *The Russian passenger ship* Dwinsk. (Edward Wilson)

Top *The Pacific Steam Navigation Company's* Orissa. (World Ship Society)

Above *The* Llandovery Castle. (World Ship Society)

LLANDOVERY CASTLE (1914–1918)

Union Castle Line, Great Britain; Barclay Curle, Glasgow.
11,423 GRT, 517ft (157.6m) LOA, 63ft (19.2m) beam.
429 passengers in three classes.
Quadruple expansion SR engines, twin screw, 15kts.
Date of disaster: 27 June 1918.

The *Llandovery Castle* had barely got into her stride on the service from London to West and East Africa when the outbreak of the First World War occurred. She continued commercial sailings, somewhat intermittently, until December 1915, when she was requisitioned for service as a troopship. In 1917 she was converted to a hospital ship and attached to the Canadian forces. On 27 June 1918, during a crossing from Halifax, Nova Scotia, to Liverpool with 258 people aboard, of whom 94 were nurses or medical officers from the Canadian Medical Service, the *Llandovery Castle* was torpedoed by the German submarine *U86*, under Capt Patzig, 116 miles south-west of Fastnet. The attack was launched without warning while the *Llandovery Castle* was displaying a brightly illuminated Red Cross sign. She sank inside 10 minutes, but having got all her lifeboats away it was hoped that casualties would be slight. This was not to be, however, for the *U86* surfaced and turned her guns on the helpless lifeboats. By the time rescue arrived only one boat, containing 24 people, remained afloat. After the war, two of the *U86*'s officers were tried for war crimes by the German Supreme Court. They were found guilty and imprisoned.

CINCINNATI as *COVINGTON* (1908–1918)

Hamburg Amerika Line, Germany; Blohm & Voss, Hamburg.
16,339 GRT, 600ft (182.9m) LOA, 65ft (19.8m) beam.
2,758 passengers in three classes.
Quadruple expansion SR engines, twin screw, 16kts.
Date of disaster: 1 July 1918.

The Hamburg Amerika liner *Cincinnati* was seized at Boston by the American authorities on 6 April 1917, on the entry of the United States into the war, having been interned there since 1914. She was commissioned as a Navy transport under the name *Covington*, managed by the US War Shipping Board, and employed to convey American troops to the battlefields of Flanders. On the return leg of one of these voyages, on 1 July 1918, the *Covington* was attacked by the German submarine *U86*, in the position 47°31′N–07°09′W. The empty troopship sank with the loss of six seamen.

SHIRALA (1901–1918)

British India Line, Great Britain; A. & J. Inglis, Glasgow.
5,306 GRT, 410ft (125.0m) length, 50ft (15.2m) beam.
1,446 passengers in three classes.
Triple expansion SR engine, single screw, 13kts.
Date of disaster: 2 July 1918.

British India Line's *Shirala* was employed in the service from London to Bombay via the Suez Canal and she continued with these duties, when circumstances permitted, throughout the First World War. The majority of her passengers, some 1,421, were accommodated on deck. She sailed from London bound for India on 30 June 1918 carrying cargo and passengers. After proceeding to Higham Bight and then to the Nore, where more cargo was loaded, she headed off down the Channel, only to be torpedoed by a German submarine approximately four miles north-east of the Owers light vessel on 2 July. The torpedo broke her back, and before she sank, taking eight of the crew with her, the bow and stern rose out of the water towards each other. A naval airship, patrolling overhead, witnessed the sinking and summoned help by radio, bringing naval craft to the aid of the survivors.

DJEMNAH (1875–1918)

Messageries Maritimes, France; Messageries Maritimes, La Ciotat.
3,785 GRT, 394ft (120.1m) length, 39ft (11.9m) beam.
Compound steam engine, single screw, 13.5kts.
Date of disaster: 15 July 1918.

The destruction of the passenger ship *Djemnah* during the

The American troopship Covington, *formerly Hamburg Amerika Line's* Cincinnati, *is seen on the left of this photograph taken on 25 May 1918, with another, unnamed troopship, possibly the* De Kalb *ex*-Prinz Eitel Friedrich, *on the right. They were units of the largest ever transatlantic convoy to Brest.* (United States National Archives)

Top *British India's* Shirala *in 'dazzle' camouflage, sinking with her back broken.* (World Ship Society)

Above *The French liner* Djemnah *was sunk by torpedo.* (World Ship Society)

night of 14–15 July 1918 was one of France's most serious maritime disasters of the First World War, the loss of life ranking only behind those experienced with the sinkings of the *Gallia*, *Provence II*, and *Amiral Magon*. She was carrying a large contingent of troops on an escorted convoy passage through the Mediterranean, bound from Marseilles to Madagascar, when a German submarine torpedoed her south of Crete. She sank with the loss of 442 lives.

CARPATHIA (1903–1918)

Cunard Line, Great Britain; Swan & Hunter, Newcastle.
13,603 GRT, 558ft (170.1m) LOA, 64ft (19.5m) beam.
1,704 passengers in two classes.
Quadruple expansion SR engines, twin screw, 14kts.
Date of disaster: 17 July 1918.

Whatever else is written about the *Carpathia*, she will always be best remembered as the ship whose mercy dash to the sinking *Titanic* resulted in the rescue of over 700 survivors. The *Carpathia*'s peacetime activities involved service to New York from both Liverpool and Trieste. She was torpedoed and sunk by the German submarine *U55* on 17 July 1918, 170 miles north-west of Bishop Rock during a voyage from Liverpool to Boston with passengers. There were five dead from the 220 crew but all 57 passengers were saved.

AUSTRALIEN (1889–1918)

Messageries Maritimes, France; Messageries Maritimes, La Ciotat.
6,377 GRT, 482ft (146.9m) length, 49ft (14.9m) beam.
Triple expansion SR engine, single screw, 17kts.
Date of disaster: 19 July 1918.

Below *The Cunard liner* Carpathia, *renowned for the assistance she rendered to the survivors of the* Titanic *disaster.* (World Ship Society)

Bottom *The Messageries Maritimes passenger vessel* Australien. (A. Duncan)

In consort with her sister ships *Armand Behic*, *Polynesien*, and *Ville de la Ciotat*, the *Australien* helped to establish Messageries Maritimes' services to Australia. A German submarine torpedoed and sank her in the Mediterranean on 19 July 1918 while she was sailing from Marseilles to Malta. She was carrying 951 passengers in addition to her normal crew, but a prompt and efficient evacuation of the sinking vessel permitted the safe rescue of all but 20 of her complement.

STATENDAM as *JUSTICIA* (1917–1918)

Holland Amerika Line, Netherlands; Harland & Wolff, Belfast.
32,234 GRT, 776ft (236.5m) LOA, 86ft (26.2m) beam.
3,430 passengers in three classes (designed).
Triple expansion SR engines with LP turbine, triple screw, 18.5kts.
Date of disaster: 20 July 1918.

Holland Amerika ordered a new liner for the North Atlantic run in the years immediately before the First World War. She was launched as the *Statendam* on 9 July 1914 but on the commencement of hostilities all work on her came to a halt. After negotiations between her intended owners and the British Government, the incomplete ship was requisitioned in 1917 for completion as a troopship. Renamed *Justicia*, denoting a future intention to make her available to the Cunard Line as a replacement for the *Lusitania*, she entered service in April 1917, but under White Star Line management.

She survived a torpedo attack in January 1918 but only lasted another seven months. On 19 July 1918, when 20 miles from the Skerryvore Rock, sailing in a convoy bound from Liverpool to New York, she was torpedoed by the

Below *Model of the Holland Amerika Line ship* Statendam, *which was sunk as the* Justicia *while in British war service.* (Harland & Wolff)

Bottom *The 'dazzle' camouflaged* Justicia. (Tom Rayner)

German submarine *UB64*. Due to damage that she had also received, the *UB64* broke off the attack and the damaged *Justicia* was taken in tow for Lough Swilly by tugs. Her fate was, however, sealed when the submarine *UB124* took up the offensive the following day. Two further torpedoes, bringing the total of hits she had received to five, finished her off, and she sank stern first at midday on 20 July, in the position 55°38'N–07°39'W. Sixteen members of the *Justicia*'s engine-room staff were killed by the explosions, but many hundreds of other crewmen escaped unharmed, to be picked up by escorting ships. The British destroyers HMS *Marne*, *Millbrook*, and *Pigeon*, that had arrived on the scene to render assistance, succeeded in sinking the *UB124*.

MONGOLIAN (1891–1918)

Canadian Pacific Line, Great Britain; D. & W. Henderson, Glasgow.
4,892 GRT, 400ft (121.9m) length, 45ft (13.7m) beam.
1,180 passengers in three classes.
Triple expansion SR engine, single screw, 13.5kts.
Date of disaster: 21 July 1918.

The Allan Line steamer *Mongolian* was employed on various North Atlantic routes, but primarily between Liverpool and Halifax, Portland and Boston, or Glasgow and Quebec or Montreal. Though engaged in war activities for the Admiralty, she passed, on paper, into Canadian Pacific ownership when they absorbed the Allan Line in 1917. She never sailed on a Canadian Pacific commercial voyage, however, for during a voyage from Middlesborough to London on 21 July 1918 she was torpedoed by a German submarine, sinking approximately five miles south-east of Filey Brig, Yorkshire, in the position 54°10'N–08°30'W. Thirty-six members of her crew lost their lives.

MARMORA (1903–1918)

P&O Line, Great Britain; Harland & Wolff, Belfast.
10,509 GRT, 546ft (166.4m) LOA, 60ft (18.3m) beam.
524 passengers in two classes.
Quadruple expansion SR engines, twin screw, 18.5kts.
Date of disaster: 23 July 1918.

This sister ship of the *Maloja* made several voyages to Bombay before joining the London to Sydney service in March 1904. She continued to operate on this route until August 1914, when the Admiralty took her over as an auxiliary cruiser in the 10th Cruiser Squadron. Many of her tours of duty took the *Marmora* to the South Atlantic, and she was involved in the hunt for the raider *Möwe*, in addition to escorting convoys bound for the Indian Ocean. On 23 July 1918 she was back in home waters and, while patrolling south of Ireland, was torpedoed by the German submarine *UB64*. She sank rapidly, but apart from 10 naval ratings killed by the exploding torpedo, the remainder of the *Marmora*'s complement were safely removed before she went down.

MAGELLAN (1893–1918)

Pacific Steam Navigation Co, Great Britain; Harland & Wolff, Belfast.
3,590 GRT, 360ft (109.7m) length, 43ft (13.1m) beam.
Triple expansion SR engine, single screw, 13.5kts.
Date of disaster: 25 July 1918.

The *Magellan* was attacked by a German U-boat on 25 July 1918 while bound for the United Kingdom from Malta. She sank in the position 38°06'N–09°08'E with the loss of one life. Before the First World War, she had served on the route to Pacific coast ports of South America with the sister ships *Antisiana*, *Inca*, and *Sarmiento*.

WARILDA (1914–1918)

Adelaide Steamship Co, Great Britain; William Beardmore, Glasgow.
7,713 GRT, 428ft (130.5m) LOA, 56ft (17.1m) beam.
430 passengers in three classes.
Quadruple expansion SR engines, twin screw, 16kts.
Date of disaster: 3 August 1918.

The Australian coastwise liner *Warilda* was taken over by the Admiralty shortly after completion, for service as a hospital ship. In this capacity she was the victim of a torpedo fired from a German submarine on 3 August 1918 while sailing from Le Havre to Southampton with 700 wounded servicemen. The attack was made in murky conditions, although the *Warilda* was conspicuously marked. She remained afloat for two hours or so, permitting the evacuation of 678 of those aboard, but 123 people went down with her when she sank in position 50°11'N–00°13'W.

POLYNESIEN (1890–1918)

Messageries Maritimes, France; Messageries Maritimes, La Ciotat.
6,363 GRT, 482ft (146.9m) length, 49ft (14.9m) beam.
Triple expansion SR engine, single screw, 17.5kts.
Date of disaster: 10 August 1918.

On 10 August 1918, during a voyage from Marseilles and Bizerta to Salonica, Greece, the steamship *Polynesien* was torpedoed and sunk by an enemy submarine near the entrance to Valetta Harbour, Malta. In peacetime the *Polynesien* had operated on the service from Marseilles to Australia via the Suez Canal with three sister ships, *Armand Behic*, *Australien*, and *Ville de la Ciotat*.

PAMPA (1906–1918)

Soc. Générale des Transports Maritimes, France; London & Glasgow SB Co, Glasgow.
4,471 GRT, 408ft (124.4m) length, 47ft (14.3m) beam.
171 passengers in three classes.
Triple expansion SR engines, twin screw, 14kts.
Date of disaster: 27 August 1918.

The French passenger ship *Pampa* served as a hospital ship during the First World War. On 27 August 1918, bound from

Top *The hospital ship* Warilda. (A. Duncan)

Above *The* Polynesien. (World Ship Society)

Marseilles and Bizerta to Salonica, she was torpedoed and sunk by an enemy submarine.

MESABA ex-*WINIFREDA* (1898–1918)

Atlantic Transport Line, Great Britain; Harland & Wolff, Belfast.
6,833 GRT, 482ft (146.9m) length, 52ft (15.9m) beam.
120 passengers in single class.
Triple expansion SR engine, single screw, 13kts.
Date of disaster: 1 September 1918.

The transatlantic steamship *Mesaba* was the victim of a torpedo attack on 1 September 1918. During a convoy voyage from Liverpool to Philadelphia in ballast, a German submarine sank her about 20 miles east of the Tuskar Rock off Greenore Point, County Wexford, in the position 52°17′N–05°38′W. Twenty lives were lost, including that of her commander.

MISSANABIE (1914–1918)

Canadian Pacific Line, Great Britain; Barclay Curle, Glasgow.
12,469 GRT, 520ft (158.5m) LOA, 64ft (19.5m) beam.
1,720 passengers in two classes.
Quadruple expansion SR engines, twin screw, 15.5kts.
Date of disaster: 9 September 1918.

The *Missanabie* and *Metagama* entered the Liverpool to St John's and Montreal service in the months immediately preceding the First World War. The *Missanabie* almost

RIGHT *The* Missanabie *was, with her sister ship* Metagama, *one of the first cabin-class ships built for the Canadian route across the Atlantic.* (World Ship Society)

BELOW *Union Castle's* Galway Castle. (World Ship Society)

survived the war, continuing throughout with her normal duties, but she succumbed to a torpedo attack from the German submarine *UB87* on 9 September 1918, while she was heading for New York from Liverpool in ballast. She sank approximately 52 miles south-east of Daunts Rock, near Cobh, County Cork. The attack claimed 45 lives.

GALWAY CASTLE (1911–1918)

Union Castle Line, Great Britain; Harland & Wolff, Belfast.
7,988 GRT, 452ft (137.8m) length, 56ft (17.1m) beam.
412 passengers in three classes.
Quadruple expansion SR engines, twin screw, 13.5kts.
Date of disaster: 12 September 1918.

The *Galway Castle* and her sister ships *Gloucester Castle* and *Guildford Castle* were employed on the intermediate service to South Africa in the years preceding the First World War. On the outbreak of war, the *Galway Castle* became a troopship and carried troops to fight in the campaign in German South-West Africa. On the completion of these duties she returned to her owners and resumed commercial sailings. Outward bound from Plymouth for Port Natal on 12 September 1918, she was torpedoed and sunk by the German submarine *U82*. The attack was made 160 miles south-west of Fastnet in the position 48°50'N–10°40'W. The explosion of the torpedo broke the *Galway Castle*'s back and it was feared that she would sink within minutes. It was also believed that the *U82* would resume the attack as long as the ship remained on the surface. Consequently, the boats were launched in haste and many of them were lost with their occupants as soon as they reached the water. Matters were made worse because communications between the two halves of the ship were unsatisfactory and great difficulty was experienced in accounting for all those aboard. Fortunately it was possible to radio for help, and destroyers were sent to the scene from Devonport, rescuing many survivors who would otherwise have drowned. Even so, 150 people were killed in the disaster, many in the unduly hurried evacuation. As it turned out, the wrecked *Galway Castle* remained afloat for three days.

MONTFORT (1899–1918)

Canadian Pacific Line, Great Britain; Palmer's, Newcastle.
7,087 GRT, 445ft (135.6m) length, 52ft (15.9m) beam.
1,230 passengers in two classes.
Triple expansion SR engine, single screw, 12.5kts.
Date of disaster: 1 October 1918.

The sister vessels *Monteagle* and *Montfort* were originally owned by Elder Dempster until Canadian Pacific Line acquired them in April 1903. They worked the route to Canada from Hong Kong. The *Montfort* was a First World War casualty, being sunk by the German submarine *U55* on 1 October 1918 while bound from London to Montreal. The attack took place approximately 170 miles south-west of Bishop Rock. Five of those aboard the *Montfort* were killed.

HIRANO MARU (1908–1918)

Nippon Yusen Kaisha, Japan; Mitsubishi, Nagasaki.
8,520 GRT, 474ft (144.5m) length, 54ft (16.5m) beam.
127 passengers in three classes.
Triple expansion SR engines, twin screw, 16kts.
Date of disaster: 4 October 1918.

The sinking of the *Hirano Maru* was the most serious Japanese merchant loss of the First World War. She was built for the route from Japan to Europe via the Suez Canal, maintaining the service with five sister ships. After the outbreak of war, she continued to make commercial sailings as normal until, on 4 October 1918, she was torpedoed and

The loss of the Hirano Maru *was the worst disaster involving a Japanese ship in the First World War.* (Mitsubishi Heavy Industries)

sunk 200 miles south of the Irish coast by a German submarine while bound from Liverpool to Yokohama. Although the *Hirano Maru*'s registered accommodation was for only 127 passengers, at the time of the attack she was carrying over 200, the total number of people aboard her amounting to 320. The weather conditions were severe, with strong winds and a rough sea, which made it almost impossible to lower the boats. In addition the *Hirano Maru* had sustained two torpedo hits, the second in her boiler-room, and was taking on water fast – so fast, in fact, that she only remained afloat for around seven minutes. Under such circumstances few people were able to escape from the ship, and 292 people perished with her when she sank, plunging almost vertically down, bow first. An American destroyer picked up the few survivors, only 11 of whom were passengers.

OTRANTO (1909–1918)

Orient Line, Great Britain; Workman Clark, Belfast.
12,124 GRT, 554ft (168.9m) LOA, 64ft (19.5m) beam.
1,300 passengers in two classes.
Quadruple expansion SR engines, twin screw, 18kts.
Date of disaster: 6 October 1918.

One of five similar ships on the Australia run via Suez, the *Otranto* was taken over at the beginning of the First World War for service as an auxiliary cruiser. Later she was tasked with the combined duties of convoy escort and troop transport. In this role, carrying American troops, she was nearing Great Britain at the end of a passage from New York on 6 October 1918, part of convoy HX50, the other vessels of which comprised the *Saxon*, *Briton*, *Kashmir*, *Oriana*, *Scotian*, *Plassey*, *Oxfordshire*, *City of York*, *Teucer*, *Rhesus*, *Orantes*, and *La Lorraine*. Three American destroyers were providing a screen, but only one, the USS *Dorsey*, was under instructions to proceed as far as the Irish coast, where British escort ships were expected to relieve her. Bad weather had been encountered from the outset, and the convoy ships struggled to maintain formation in high seas and poor visibility, conditions which also prevented the Royal Navy ships from rendezvousing as intended. Consequently when, on approaching the Irish Sea, the *Dorsey* detached herself as planned, the convoy was left entirely unprotected.

At this point HX50 appears to have lost its bearings. Capt

The Orient liner Otranto *before the First World War.* (P&O Group).

The Otranto *in war colours. She broke up on the shores of Islay after a collision with the P&O liner* Kashmir. (Maritime Photo Library)

Davidson, master of the *Otranto* and convoy commodore, ordered an alteration of course to port, believing that he was off the west coast of Ireland. His order was misinterpreted aboard the P&O vessel *Kashmir*, the next ship in line on her port beam, which was helmed, instead, to starboard. This put the two ships on converging courses. In spite of warning signals from the *Otranto*, and a last minute turn to starboard, a collision was unavoidable, and the *Kashmir* ploughed into the Orient ship's port side. The *Kashmir* suffered only superficial damage, but the *Otranto* was almost cut in two. Her stokehold and engine-room compartments swiftly flooded and, when the forward bulkheads collapsed under the pressure of water, the troopship began to settle rapidly at the head, listing to her port side.

Panic had set in among the American infantrymen aboard the *Otranto* – many of whom were deserters who had been drafted into Overseas Casual Companies for the crossing – and the chaos was significantly worsened when the boat-deck collapsed, hurling many would-be evacuees into the stormy seas. As the metalwork broke free, Capt Davidson was decapitated by flying debris, a further tragic blow at a time when his qualities of leadership were urgently needed.

The convoy's true position was, in fact, off the north coast of Islay, in the Irish Sea, and when land loomed into sight it was hoped that the helpless ship might drift ashore there and land her occupants before she broke in two, for no other form of rescue seemed possible. The *Otranto*'s wireless transmitter had been swept away before a distress call could be made, and her lifeboats had been pounded to splinters. Of the convoy's other vessels, only the *Kashmir* was aware of the *Otranto*'s predicament and she was already too far distant to be of any immediate assistance. At this point, the destroyer HMS *Mounsey* arrived on the scene, one of the eight convoy escorts expected from Lough Swilly, having pressed on alone in the appalling weather to locate the convoy. The *Mounsey* mounted an immediate rescue operation, but despite considerable efforts was only able to take off 367 people. The remaining 431 of the *Otranto*'s complement, 351 of them United States' servicemen, were drowned, many when the *Otranto* was finally washed ashore near Kilchiaran on Islay, where the heavy seas smashed her to pieces.

Note: Overseas Casual Companies were military units, with little or no training, which were specially assembled for a given purpose from a variety of sources, as distinct from a standing regiment.

SURADA (1902–1918)

British India Line, Great Britain; A. & J. Inglis, Glasgow.
5,324 GRT, 410ft (125.0m) length, 50ft (15.2m) beam.
Triple expansion SR engine, single screw, 10.5kts.
Date of disaster: 2 November 1918.

The passenger steamship *Surada* holds the dubious distinction of being the last passenger vessel to be sunk during the First World War, having been torpedoed on 2 November 1918, just nine days before the Armistice. Bound for the United Kingdom from Karachi, she was attacked in the swept channel outside Port Said. She had carried only a small number of passengers in a single class.

Chapter Six

1939

MAGNETIC MINE MENACE

Although the opening period of the Second World War was dubbed the 'Phoney War', because of the lack of any real evidence of conflict in Western Europe, attacks on passenger ships on the ocean highways commenced almost immediately. Indeed, the Anchor Donaldson liner *Athenia* was torpedoed and sunk without warning only the day after war was declared. Quite apart from the outrage this sinking aroused, it also invited criticism that Germany clearly intended to wage an unrestricted submarine war without regard for either civilian lives or international law. In fact this was not the case, and the regrettable incident was a serious embarrassment to the German Admiralty, which had not at this point intended to embark upon such a policy.

One of the principal causes of disasters to passenger ships at the beginning of the Second World War was the magnetic mine, which had been lain in large quantities in river estuaries by German ships and aircraft. It claimed numerous vessels, both Allied and neutral, and continued to present a serious hazard to shipping until about mid-1940, when 'de-gaussing' strips were developed. An interesting entry in the Lloyds War Loss Records for a sinking by magnetic mine is that of the Japanese passenger ship *Terukuni Maru* on 21 November 1939. The Lloyds' log was used only to record the sinking of Allied and neutral vessels. By the time the next Japanese passenger ship was sunk – the *Katori Maru* on 23 December 1941 – Britain, along with America, had declared war on Japan, so that the loss of the *Terukuni Maru* constitutes a unique entry in these official records.

Another major cause of losses in the opening months of the conflict was the deliberate scuttling of many German passenger ships. Caught overseas at the war's outbreak, or intercepted while trying to break through the British blockade as they attempted to make for German ports, they chose this option in preference to capture. Of the ships concerned, perhaps the most notorious and certainly the most graphically recorded incident was that involving the Norddeutscher Lloyd express steamer *Columbus*, destroyed by her crew in international waters close to the United States' Atlantic coast.

ATHENIA (1923–1939)

Anchor-Donaldson Line, Great Britain; Fairfield, Glasgow.
13,465 GRT, 538ft (164.0m) LOA, 66ft (20.1m) beam.
1,552 passengers in three classes.
Steam turbines, twin screw, 15.5kts.
Date of disaster: 3 September 1939.

The *Athenia* was the first submarine victim of the Second

The Anchor-Donaldson liner Athenia*, the first torpedo victim of the Second World War.* (World Ship Society)

World War. She was still involved in her peacetime business, bound from the Clyde and Liverpool for Montreal, when, only a matter of a few hours after war had been declared, she was attacked by *U30* on 3 September 1939, some 200 miles west of the Hebrides in the position 56°42'N–14°05'W. The *Athenia* was carrying 1,418 people, of whom 1,103 were passengers, including 311 Americans. The *Athenia* could not summon help, as her radio apparatus was destroyed when the submarine surfaced and shelled her. She carried sufficient lifeboats for all those aboard but, as the *Athenia* sank, she developed a severe list, making it difficult to launch them. Three boats were lost during the evacuation and the casualties from these accidents accounted for the majority of the 112 lives lost in the disaster (93 passengers and 19 crewmen). The *Athenia*'s master, Capt James Cook, survived the attack. The Germans denied responsibility for the sinking of the *Athenia* throughout the Second World War.

BRETAGNE ex-*FLANDRIA* (1922–1939)

French Line (CGT), France; Barclay Curle, Glasgow.
10,171 GRT, 472ft (143.9m) LOA, 59ft (18.0m) beam.
440 passengers in single class.
Steam turbines, twin screw, 14.5kts.
Date of disaster: 14 October 1939.

Formerly the *Flandria* of Royal Holland Lloyd, the *Bretagne* joined the French Line in 1936 and entered the service from St Nazaire or Le Havre to the West Indies. While bound for Le Havre from Cristobal, Panama, and Kingston, Jamaica, she was torpedoed and sunk by the submarine *U45* on 14 October 1939, 300 miles south-west of the Fastnet Rock, in the position 50°20'N–12°45'W. The submarine surfaced and shelled the sinking liner, hitting a lifeboat that was being lowered and killing some of the occupants. Only seven people were killed in all, but there were many seriously injured among the survivors, who were picked up by a British warship.

YORKSHIRE (1920–1939)

Bibby Line, Great Britain; Harland & Wolff, Belfast.
10,184 GRT, 499ft (152.1m) LOA, 58ft (17.7m) beam.
305 passengers in single class.
Steam turbines, twin screw, 15kts.
Date of disaster: 17 October 1939.

The turbine steamer *Yorkshire* was a lone ship built for the Liverpool to Rangoon service, which she entered in September 1920. She fell victim to a torpedo from the German submarine *U37* while returning to Liverpool on 17 October 1939, the attack taking place some 700 miles out into the Atlantic, north-west of Cape Finisterre, in the position 44°52'N–14°31'W. The *Yorkshire* was carrying 118 passengers and 160 crew, of whom 58 lost their lives, including her commander, Capt V.C.P. Smalley. The survivors were picked up by the *Independence Hall*, which had arrived on the scene in response to distress calls, and they were landed at Bordeaux on 20 October along with another group of survivors rescued from the *City of Mandalay*, an earlier U-boat kill.

The Bibby liner Yorkshire. (A. Duncan)

The motorship Canada. (East Asiatic Company)

CANADA (1935–1939)

East Asiatic Co, Denmark; Nakskov Skibs-Vaerft.
11,108 GRT, 493ft (150.3m) LOA, 64ft (19.5m) beam.
55 passengers in single class.
Diesel engine, single screw, 16kts.
Date of disaster: 4 November 1939.

The Danish motorship *Canada* was the last of a class of three similar ships operated on the route from Copenhagen to the west coast of North America via the Panama Canal. On 3 November 1939, during a voyage from Vancouver to Gothenburg and Copenhagen, via London and Hull, the *Canada* struck a mine about two nautical miles east of Holmpton, near Spurn Head. She sank the following day, her wreck lying in the position 53°42′N–00°07′E.

SIRDHANA (1925–1939)

British India Line, Great Britain; Swan, Hunter & Wigham Richardson, Newcastle.
7,745 GRT, 436ft (132.9m) length, 57ft (17.4m) beam.
122 passengers in two classes.
Triple expansion SR engines, twin screw, 13kts.
Date of disaster: 13 November 1939.

The Indian services steamship *Sirdhana* was one of a group of three ships, the other two being the *Santhia* and *Shirala*. She struck a mine on 13 November 1939 as she was leaving Singapore during a voyage from Rangoon to Hong Kong. On board were a great number of passengers, including 137 Chinese who had been deported from Singapore. The mine, which had been laid by a German raider, was some 3.5 miles offshore from the Fort Canning light. The *Sirdhana* sank with the loss of 20 passengers. Her wreck, which was lying in the position 01°15′N–103°53′E, was demolished from June 1952.

SIMON BOLIVAR (1927–1939)

Royal Netherlands SS Co, Netherlands; Rotterdamsche Droogdok, Rotterdam.
8,309 GRT, 420ft (128.0m) length, 59ft (18.0m) beam.
Quadruple expansion SR engine, single screw, 13.5kts.
Date of disaster: 18 November 1939.

The Dutch liner *Simon Bolivar* was engaged in the service from Amsterdam to the West Indies. She met her end on 18 November 1939, when, outward bound from Holland to Paramaribo, Surinam, she struck two mines, one on either side, off Harwich, in the position 51°49′N–01°41′E. The second mine exploded after an interval of a quarter of an hour. Tremendous devastation was caused by the violent explosions, numerous lifeboats were destroyed, and her masts were blown down. The liner immediately commenced to settle by the stern, which made the launching of the remaining lifeboats extremely difficult. As the explosion had wrecked the ship's radio equipment, it was also impossible to alert other ships to her plight, but other vessels nevertheless reached the scene in time to take off the survivors before the *Simon Bolivar* sank. Of the 400 or so passengers and crew aboard 84 were killed, including her master, Capt H. Voorspuiy.

TERUKUNI MARU (1930–1939)

Nippon Yusen Kaisha, Japan; Mitsubishi, Nagasaki.
11,930 GRT, 527ft (160.6m) LOA, 64ft (19.5m) beam.
249 passengers in three classes.
Diesel engines, twin screw, 17kts.
Date of disaster: 21 November 1939.

The *Terukuni Maru* was the first Japanese passenger ship casualty of the Second World War, but her loss occurred some time before Japan became involved in the conflict.

The Dutch liner Simon Bolivar, *a mine casualty off Harwich.* (L.L. von Münching)

With her sister ship *Yasukuni Maru*, she operated on the service from Yokohama to London, Rotterdam, and Hamburg. On 21 November 1939 she was nearing the end of a voyage to Europe when she struck a mine in the mouth of the River Thames, 1.5 miles from the Sunk lightship, in the position 51°50'N–01°30'E. The *Terukuni Maru* sank inside an hour, the explosion having opened up two of her holds. Eight lifeboats were launched, enabling all 206 people aboard to escape, including her master Capt Matsukura, the Trinity House pilot, and 28 passengers.

RAWALPINDI (1925–1939)

P&O Line, Great Britain; Harland & Wolff, Greenock.
16,619 GRT, 570ft (173.7m) LOA, 71ft (21.6m) beam.
600 passengers in two classes.
Quadruple expansion SR engines, twin screw, 17kts.
Date of disaster: 23 November 1939.

The *Rawalpindi* was one of a class of three ships introduced to the London, Bombay, and Far East service in 1925–1926, the others being the *Ranchi* and *Rajputana*. All three

The Nippon Yusen Kaisha ship Terukuni Maru *was sunk by a German mine in the River Thames.* (World Ship Society)

Top *The armed merchant cruiser* Rawalpindi, *seen in the brief interlude between her requisition on the outbreak of war and her loss in November 1939.* (Imperial War Museum, Neg. HU993)

Above *Listing and on fire, the auxiliary cruiser* Rawalpindi *is seen under attack from the battle-cruiser* Scharnhorst *in this painting by Norman Wilkinson. Her attacker, on the horizon to the right, is mistakenly portrayed as the pocket battleship* Deutschland. (P&O Group)

vessels were taken over as armed merchant cruisers in late-1939, at which time their second funnels were removed. However, the *Rawalpindi*, under the command of Capt E.C. Kennedy, father of the TV personality Ludovic Kennedy, was to survive for only two months.

On 23 November 1939, while patrolling between Iceland and the Faroes, she sighted the German battle-cruisers *Scharnhorst* and *Gneisenau*, returning to Germany from a commerce raiding sortie in the Atlantic. Realizing that he was hopelessly outmatched, Capt Kennedy attempted to escape behind a smoke-screen into a nearby fog bank. However, the *Scharnhorst* cut off his retreat and, after warning shots were ignored, opened fire on the virtually defenceless *Rawalpindi*. The *Gneisenau* then joined the fray, and after only five salvos the liner's guns had been silenced, her bridge and wireless-room destroyed, and she was heavily on fire amidships. She was at the mercy of the German capital ships and would no doubt have been finished off there and then but for the appearance of British naval units.

Three lifeboats had been lowered during a lull in the action and the occupants of two, 26 seamen, were picked up by the German battle-cruisers and taken prisoner. The 11 survivors in the third boat were rescued by the armed merchant cruiser *Chitral*, another converted P&O liner. The dead amounted to 275, including Capt Kennedy and 39 other officers. The blazing *Rawalpindi* drifted before the wind for three hours before she finally foundered.

The Polish motorship Pilsudski *was built in Italy.* (World Ship Society)

PILSUDSKI (1935–1939)

Gydnia America Line, Poland; Cantieri Riuniti Dell' Adriatico, Monfalcone.
14,294 GRT, 526ft (160.3m) LOA, 70ft (21.3m) beam.
759 passengers in two classes.
Diesel engines, twin screw, 20kts.
Date of disaster: 26 November 1939.

The sister ships *Pilsudski* and *Batory* were placed on the Gydnia to New York service in the mid-1930s. After the defeat of Poland they came under British control and were refitted as troopships. The *Pilsudski* survived for only two months, striking a mine in the mouth of the River Humber on 26 November 1939 and sinking in the position 53°15′N–00°30′E. She had been bound for Australia from Newcastle at the time, and 10 members of her crew were lost with her.

SPAARNDAM (1922–1939)

Holland Amerika Line, Netherlands; Nieuwe Waterweg Co, Schiedam.
8,857 GRT, 450ft (137.2m) length, 58ft (17.7m) beam.
988 passengers in three classes.
Steam turbine, single screw, 13kts.
Date of disaster: 27 November 1939.

On 27 November 1939, on a voyage from Tampico, New Orleans, and London to Antwerp and Rotterdam, the liner *Spaarndam* struck a magnetic mine in the Thames Estuary, three miles east-north-east of the Tongue light vessel. At the time she was being detained and inspected by British contraband control authorities. The explosion ripped her apart and she sank in shallow water in the position 51°35′N–01°24′E. Later she caught fire and burnt out, but a consignment of cotton which had formed a major part of her cargo was nevertheless salved in November 1952. Four crew-members and an elderly lady passenger lost their lives in the sinking. Before the war, in consort with the *Edam*, *Leerdam*, and *Maasdam*, the *Spaarndam* operated between Rotterdam and Cuba and Mexico, or Rotterdam and New York or Baltimore.

WATUSSI (1928–1939)

Woermann Line, Germany; Blohm & Voss, Hamburg.
9,552 GRT, 468ft (142.6m) length, 60ft (18.3m) beam.
300 passengers.
Steam turbine, single screw, 16kts.
Date of disaster: 2 December 1939.

The German liner *Watussi*, with her sister the *Ubena*, was employed in the South African service. During a voyage from Zanzibar and Mozambique to Hamburg, on 2 December 1939, the *Watussi* was identified 80 miles south of Cape Point by an Allied aeroplane. The plane radioed for a warship to intercept the German liner, but the *Watussi* was scuttled by her crew to prevent capture.

The Dutch liner Spaarndam, *submerged to her upper deck and broken in two behind the bridge after striking a mine in the Thames estuary in November 1939.* (L.L. von Münching)

The hospital ship Tairea *was sunk by the pocket battleship* Admiral Graf Spee. (World Ship Society)

TAIREA (1924–1939)

British India Line, Great Britain; Barclay Curle, Glasgow.
7,933 GRT, 465ft (141.7m) LOA, 60ft (18.3m) beam.
130 passengers.
Triple expansion SR engines, twin screw, 16kts.
Date of disaster: 3 December 1939.

One of three ships placed in the service from India to South Africa, the *Tairea* was sunk by the *Admiral Graf Spee* on 3 December 1939 after being intercepted off the coast of South-West Africa while bound from Brisbane and Durban for London. She sank in the position 20°20′S–03°05′E without loss of life.

USSUKUMA (1920–1939)

Deutsche Ost-Afrika Line, Germany; Blohm & Voss, Hamburg.
7,834 GRT, 418ft (127.4m) length, 56ft (17.1m) beam.
250 passengers.
Steam turbine, single screw, 14kts.
Date of disaster: 6 December 1939.

The steam passenger ship *Ussukuma*, employed on routes to East Africa, was another of the many German liners which chose self-destruction in favour of capture while making runs for safe havens in the early part of the Second World War. After she had been stopped by HMS *Ajax*, the *Ussukuma* was scuttled by her crew off Bahia, Brazil, on 6 December 1939.

COLUMBUS (1922–1939)

Norddeutscher Lloyd, Germany; Schichau, Danzig.
32,565 GRT, 775ft (236.2m) LOA, 83ft (25.3m) beam.
1,792 passengers in three classes.
Steam turbines, twin screw, 23kts.
Date of disaster: 19 December 1939.

In the years immediately prior to the First World War, Norddeutscher Lloyd laid down the hulls of two new giant liners for the transatlantic express service. The first ship, named *Columbus*, passed into British ownership under the Treaty of Versailles and was completed for the White Star Line. The second unlaunched hull, for which the name *Hindenburg* had been intended, adopted the name of her former sister, and finally entered service on the Bremerhaven to New York route in April 1924.

In August 1939, when the outbreak of the Second World War was imminent, the *Columbus* was on a Caribbean cruise. Because of the political situation her passengers were disembarked at Havana and she made for Vera Cruz, Mexico, in whose neutral waters she sought temporary sanctuary. During this time the *Columbus*' upperworks were darkened and the tops of her funnels painted back. That December her master, Capt Wilhelm Daehne, decided to make a run for home and attempt to break through the British naval blockade. The *Columbus* sailed on 14 December, her course set to take her along the United States' Atlantic coastline, then north-east past Iceland, before heading towards Murmansk or Oslo. It was hoped that, like her fleetmate *Bremen*, she would then be able to reach Germany by sailing close inshore as she passed Norway and Denmark. The voyage did not unfold as planned, however. Shadowed by American warships, first by a string of destroyers and later by the cruiser USS *Tuscaloosa*, the *Columbus* was intercepted on 19 December by the British destroyer HMS *Hyperion*, some 320 miles east of Cape Hatteras, Delaware. In part to avoid unnecessary risk to the

Top *The crew pull away in lifeboats from the sinking German liner* Columbus. (Capt Otto Giese)

Above *The* Columbus *on fire off Cape Hatteras, North Carolina, after being scuttled by her crew to prevent capture by the British destroyer HMS* Hyperion. (Imperial War Museum, Neg. OG245)

lives of his crew, and also to prevent capture by the British, Capt Daehne gave the order to scuttle, then to abandon ship, well rehearsed drills from the months of idleness in Mexico. Blazing from end to end and with her seacocks open, the *Columbus* sank just before midnight in the position 38°01′N–65°41′W. Two men died aboard her, who were thought to have mistakenly believed that it was another rehearsal and not the real thing. The *Tuscaloosa* picked up all 577 survivors and later landed them at New York. In contrast to the atrocities that were to be committed during the ensuing war, the *Columbus* incident reflected more humane attitudes, typified by the *Hyperion*'s concern for the well-being of the German crew and by the *Hyperion* and *Tuscaloosa* saluting the dying liner with their flags at half mast.

Chapter Seven

1940

WOLF PACKS AND SURFACE RAIDERS

Passenger ship losses during this, the first full year of the Second World War, resulted from a mixed bag of causes. The single dominant factor was that, for the most part, they were Allied rather than Axis vessels, a trend which was to continue for another two years or more.

Certain clusters of passenger ship losses were directly associated with a number of specific events and incidents. When the war began in earnest, for instance, the rapid German advance into the Low Countries and France resulted in many losses as passenger ships, trapped in ports or in river estuaries, were caught up in the fighting. Then shortly afterwards, during the emergency withdrawal of surviving British and French troops and refugees following the fall of France, many ships utilized in the evacuation were caught in the open by marauding German aircraft all along France's northern and western coasts. The terrible death-toll when the troopship *Lancastria* was bombed and sunk off St Nazaire remained the worst on record until almost the end of the war, when equally vulnerable German passenger vessels were similarly and mercilessly picked off while engaged in another frenetic relief operation.

One of the Union Castle's squat funnelled motorships of the inter-war years, the Dunbar Castle *is seen sunk in shallow waters in the Dover Straits after striking a mine.* (British & Commonwealth Shipping Co)

Italy's declaration of war in 1940 rendered the Mediterranean a war zone for the second time in 25 years, exposing ships there to the same dangers that existed in the Atlantic. Great Britain's capabilities, too, were now stretched to the limit as she was called on to wage war alone on a growing number of fronts. Out in the Atlantic, German raiders were already claiming their quota of victims, the armed merchantmen previously requisitioned for this work being supplemented by pocket battleships and larger warships. At the same time, the U-boat wolf packs were becoming increasingly active, aided by the establishment of support bases on France's western coast following her unexpected capitulation. Already, by July 1940, submarine bases had been constructed at Lorient and Brest in Brittany, allowing the rapid replenishment and return to sea of Germany's growing undersea armada.

DUNBAR CASTLE (1930–1940)

Union Castle Line, Great Britain; Harland & Wolff, Belfast.
10,002 GRT, 484ft (147.5m) LOA, 61ft (18.6m) beam.
460 passengers in two classes.
Diesel engines, twin screw, 14.5kts.
Date of disaster: 9 January 1940.

Between the World Wars, Union Castle were at the forefront of diesel propulsion development with their distinctive twin-funnelled motorships. Two of the smaller vessels built for the round-Africa service from London were the *Dunbar Castle* and *Llangibby Castle*. Sailing in a convoy outward bound from London to Beira, the *Dunbar Castle* sank on 9 January 1940 after striking a mine in the Straits of Dover two miles north-east of the North Goodwins, in the position 51°23′N–01°34′E. She was torn apart by the explosion, settling rapidly and foundering in shallow water within half an hour. There were nine men lost in the incident, including the master, Capt H.A. Causton, who was killed by the explosion. The 189 survivors were picked up by coastal patrol vessels. The wreck of the *Dunbar Castle*, which could be seen above the water, was broken up after the war.

RIO DE JANEIRO ex-*SANTA INES* (1914–1940)

Hamburg Sud Amerika Line, Germany; Bremer Vulkan, Vegesack.
5,261 GRT, 401ft (122.2m) length, 55ft (16.8m) beam.
Triple expansion SR engine, single screw.
Date of disaster: 9 April 1940.

The German liner *Rio de Janeiro* entered the South America service in 1914 and, apart from the interruption of the First World War, remained so engaged until the outbreak of the Second World War. She was renamed in 1921. On 9 April 1940, during the Norwegian campaign, she was intercepted by two Allied submarines – one British, the other Polish – while carrying troops and horses. When instructed to stop, she instead made off for Lillesand. Torpedoes were fired, and she sank rapidly, going down in the position 58°08′N–08°29′E. One hundred and fifty survivors made it to the Norwegian coast, but another 150 soldiers and 80 horses were drowned.

The Rio de Janeiro *was sunk off Norway by a Polish submarine.* (Hamburg Sud-Amerika Line)

AMASIS (1923–1940)

Hamburg Amerika Line, Germany; Bremer Vulkan, Vegesack.
7,129 GRT, 438ft (133.5m) length, 55ft (16.8m) beam.
Triple expansion SR engine, single screw, 12kts.
Date of disaster: 10 April 1940.

Kosmos Line ordered the construction of the cargo-passenger liner *Amasis* for service on their route to South America, which she entered in April 1923. In 1926 she was transferred to the Hamburg Amerika Line, continuing to operate on the same service but also working occasionally on other routes. She had accommodation for a small number of passengers in a single class. On the outbreak of the Second World War she was able to break through the British blockade, reaching her home port on 18 October 1939, but on 10 April the following year, while she was bound from Oslo to Lysekil, she was sunk in the Kattegat by the British submarine HMS *Sunfish*.

The German cargo-passenger liner Amasis. (Hapag-Lloyd)

LA CORUNA (1921–1940)

Hamburg Sud-Amerika Line, Germany; Reiherstieg Schiffswerke, Hamburg.
7,359 GRT, 414ft (126.2m) length, 55ft (16.8m) beam.
584 passengers in two classes.
Triple expansion SR engine, single screw, 12kts.
Date of disaster: 13 April 1940.

The German liner *La Coruna* served on the South American run from Hamburg with her sister ships *Espana* and *Vigo*. When returning to Germany from Rio de Janeiro on 13 April 1940 she was intercepted east of Iceland by the British armed merchant cruiser *Maloja*, a converted P&O liner. To avoid capture, the *La Coruna* was scuttled, sinking in the approximate position 64°00'N–11°00'W. Her complement was rescued by the *Maloja* and interned.

STATENDAM (1929–1940)

Holland Amerika Line, Netherlands; Harland & Wolff, Belfast.
29,511 GRT, 698ft (212.7m) LOA, 81ft (24.7m) beam.
1,654 passengers in four classes.
Steam turbines, twin screw, 19kts.
Date of disaster: 11 May 1940.

Until the emergence of the *Nieuw Amsterdam* in March 1938, the *Statendam* was the flagship of the Holland

Below *The newly-completed second* Statendam. (Harland & Wolff)

Bottom *The* Statendam *was trapped at her berth near the Wilhelminakade when German forces overran the port of Rotterdam in May 1940. The* Boschdyk *and* Veendam, *also casualties of the fighting, lie ahead of the burning* Statendam. (L.L. von Münching)

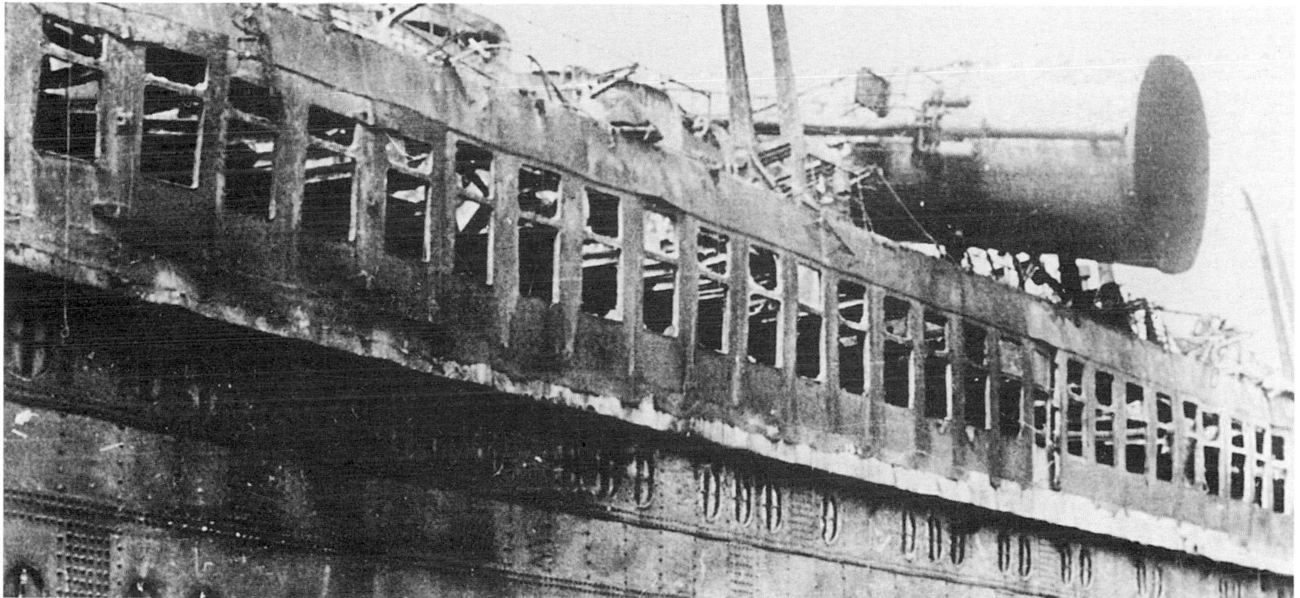

The damaged Statendam, *close-up views.* (L.L. von Münching)

Amerika Line, sailing between Rotterdam and New York. In December 1939 she was laid up at Rotterdam, where it was believed that Dutch neutrality would protect her. However, when Germany violated that neutrality in May 1940 and overran Holland the *Statendam*, along with the *Veendam* and *Boschdyk*, was bombed when fighting reached the dock area on 11 May. She caught fire and was completely burnt out over the next three days. The wrecked liner was subsequently towed to Hendrik Ido Ambacht that August and demolished.

VAN RENSSELAER (1920–1940)

Royal Netherlands SS Co, Netherlands; Nederlandsche Schps Maatschappij, Amsterdam.
4,299 GRT, 342ft (104.2m) length, 47ft (14.3m) beam.
Triple expansion SR engine, single screw, 12kts.
Date of disaster: 12 May 1940.

The Dutch passenger ship *Van Rensselaer* was sister to the *Crijnssen* and *Stuyvesant*, with which she operated on the service to Latin American ports. On 12 May 1940, after striking a mine laid inside the south pier at Ymuiden while outward bound from Amsterdam, she ran ashore and became a total wreck. There were 150 passengers aboard, many of them last minute evacuees who were fleeing from the advancing German Army, Holland having been invaded two days earlier. Five passengers and the captain were lost with her. Forty-three survivors managed to reach Ramsgate in lifeboats, but the others landed on the Dutch coast to face whatever future awaited them.

JAN PIETERZOON COEN (1915–1940)

Nederland Royal Mail Line, Netherlands; Nederlandsche Schps Maatschappij, Amsterdam.
11,140 GRT, 522ft (168.2m) LOA, 60ft (18.3m) beam.
412 passengers in three classes.
Triple expansion SR engines, twin screw, 15kts.
Date of disaster: 14 May 1940.

The Dutch liner *Jan Pieterzoon Coen* operated on the service from Amsterdam to the Dutch East Indies. After returning to Amsterdam from Genoa on 14 May 1940, she was deliberately sunk as a blockship between the pierheads at Ymuiden in an attempt to deny the Germans the use of the port. By 1945 the wreck had been almost cleared and was no longer an obstruction.

VILLE DE BRUGES ex-*PRESIDENT HARDING* ex-*PRESIDENT TAFT* ex-*LONE STAR STATE* (1922–1940)

Soc. Maritime Anversoise, Belgium; New York SB Corp, Camden, New Jersey.
13,869 GRT, 535ft (163.1m) LOA, 72ft (21.9m) beam.
625 passengers in two classes (as a United States ship).
Steam turbines, twin screw, 18kts.
Date of disaster: 14 May 1940.

The Antwerp registered *Ville de Bruges* was formerly one of the American Shipping Board's standard ships, constructed immediately after the First World War. Before joining her Belgian owners in 1940 she had spent 18 years under the

The Dutch steamer Jan Pieterzoon Coen. (World Ship Society)

management and ownership of United States Lines. On 14 May 1940 she was sunk by German bombers in the mouth of the River Scheldt, some 10 miles from Antwerp, while bound for New York with a complement of 117 crew and 34 refugees, three of whom were killed in the attack. The blazing liner was left beached and abandoned in the position 51°19'N–04°16'E. The wreck was removed in January 1952.

CHROBRY (1939–1940)

Gdynia Amerika Line, Poland; Nakskov Skibsvaerft, Nakskov.
11,442 GRT, 505ft (153.9m) LOA, 66ft (20.1m) beam.
1,167 passengers in three classes.
Diesel engines, twin screw, 17kts.
Date of disaster: 15 May 1940.

The new motorships *Chrobry* and *Sobieski* saw only limited service on the Gdynia to South America route before the outbreak of war interrupted their civilian careers. The *Chrobry*, which was in Brazil, sailed to Great Britain where she was fitted out as a troopship. During the Norwegian campaign the *Chrobry* carried troops from Leith to Smaaland, Bodo, and Harstad, but on 14 May 1940 she was bombed by German aircraft off Bodo and caught fire. Most of those aboard abandoned ship safely, but 11 of the 159 crew and an unknown number of troops were killed in the attack. The *Chrobry* was completely gutted, sinking the following day in the position 67°40'N–13°50'E.

MASHOBRA (1920–1940)

British India Line, Great Britain; Barclay Curle, Glasgow.
8,324 GRT, 465ft (141.7m) LOA, 58ft (17.7m) beam.
130 passengers in single class.
Triple expansion SR engines, twin screw, 13kts.
Date of disaster: 25 May 1940.

With her sister ship *Manela*, the liner *Mashobra* was employed in the service from London to Calcutta, making calls at Tangier, Port Said, Aden, Colombo, and Madras. Marseilles was added on the homeward run. Originally fitted with accommodation for up to 154 passengers in two classes, the pair were converted to one-class ships in the 1930s. On the outbreak of the Second World War, the *Mashobra* was taken over by the Fleet Air Arm and stationed at Scapa Flow as a depot ship. The following May she returned to active duties when she joined the force engaged in operations against Narvik. On 25 May 1940, 13 days after arriving off the Norwegian coast, the *Mashobra* was bombed by German aircraft and beached at Halstad in a badly damaged state. Her guns and stores were removed, and she was destroyed by naval units before they withdrew at the end of the Norwegian campaign.

BRAZZA ex-*CAMRANH* (1923–1940)

Chargéurs Reunis, France; Ateliers et Chantiers de la Loire, Nantes.
10,387 GRT, 492ft (150.0m) LOA, 59ft (18.0m) beam.
363 passengers in three classes.
Diesel engines, twin screw, 16kts.
Date of disaster: 28 May 1940.

Although built as a freighter, the *Camranh* was rebuilt as a passenger vessel at Nantes in 1927. She entered the Bordeaux to West Africa service under the name *Brazza* and was further rebuilt at Dunkerque in 1936. She continued with these duties after the outbreak of the Second World War and was torpedoed by *U37* on a south-bound voyage on 28 May 1940. She sank in the position 42°43'N–11°00'W, about 100 miles west of Oporto.

CARARE (1925–1940)

Elders & Fyffes, Great Britain; Cammell Laird, Birkenhead.
6,878 GRT, 425ft (129.5m) length, 55ft (16.8m) beam.
100 passengers.
Triple expansion SR engines, twin screw, 14kts.
Date of disaster: 28 May 1940.

The *Carare* was one of a class of six vessels employed on services to the West Indies. Her sisters were the *Ariguani, Bayano, Camito, Caronado,* and *Cavina.* On 28 May 1940, bound from Avonmouth to Santa Marta in ballast, carrying 97 crew and 29 passengers, she struck a mine in the Bristol Channel, in the position 51°17'N–03°44'W. Seven crew-members and three passengers were killed.

ORFORD (1928–1940)

Orient Line, Great Britain; Vickers, Barrow-in-Furness.
19,941 GRT, 659ft (200.9m) LOA, 75ft (22.9m) beam.
1,700 passengers in two classes.
Steam turbines, twin screw, 20kts.
Date of disaster: 1 June 1940.

The *Orford* was a sister ship of the *Orama.* Her other consorts in the London to Brisbane service were the *Oronsay, Otranto,* and *Orontes.* In 1939 she was requisitioned for trooping duties and the following summer she was drafted into the operation to evacuate the British Army from France, being directed to Marseilles from Mombasa. At the time the *Orford* was on loan to the French Government for the carriage of troops from Madagascar. German aircraft bombed her and set her on fire upon her arrival off Marseilles on 1 June 1940. She was beached and completely burnt out, 14 people being killed. The wreck was raised in 1947 and towed to Savona, Italy, for demolition.

CARINTHIA ex-*SERVIA* (1925–1940)

Cunard Line, Great Britain; Vickers Armstrong, Barrow-in-Furness.
20,277 GRT, 624ft (190.2m) LOA, 73ft (22.3m) beam.
1,650 passengers in three classes.
Steam turbines, twin screw, 18kts.
Date of disaster: 7 June 1940.

The *Carinthia* was one of a class of five ships built for Cunard Line's intermediate transatlantic service from

The Orient liner Orford, *the victim of an aerial attack.* (Maritime Photo Library)

Liverpool, the other four being the *Scythia*, *Samaria*, *Laconia*, and *Franconia*. During the Depression years, the *Carinthia* also went cruising. In September 1939 she became an armed merchant cruiser. She was torpedoed by the German submarine *U46* the following 7 June and sank off the Irish Coast in the position 53°13′N–10°40′W. The *Carinthia* remained afloat for some time, permitting the safe evacuation of all those aboard except for two officers and two ratings killed in the initial explosion.

ORAMA (1924–1940)

Orient Line, Great Britain; Vickers, Barrow-in-Furness.
19,840 GRT, 658ft (200.6m) LOA, 75ft (22.9m) beam.
1,836 passengers in two classes.
Steam turbines, twin screw, 19kts.
Date of disaster: 8 June 1940.

The five-ship class of liners of which the *Orama* was the first to be completed had been conceived for Orient Line's premier service from London to Brisbane, Australia. Only two of them survived the Second World War. In June 1940, six months after she was taken over as a troop transport, the *Orama* was attached to the task force conveying the British Expeditionary Force from Scapa Flow to Narvik during the Norwegian campaign. The *Orama*'s group included the destroyers HMS *Acasta* and *Ardent*, the aircraft carrier HMS *Glorious*, and the tanker *Oil Pioneer*. On 8 June they came

The Orama *sinking with the* Admiral Hipper *in attendance, a picture taken from the German destroyer* Hans Lody. (W.Z. Bilddienst)

under attack from the German naval vessels *Scharnhorst*, *Gneisenau*, and *Admiral Hipper*, accompanied by lighter craft, and all five British vessels were sunk. The *Orama* was bombarded by the heavy cruiser *Admiral Hipper* and was also torpedoed, sinking in the position 67°44′N–03°52′E with the loss of 19 lives. Fortunately the *Orama* was not carrying troops at the time, only a crew of 299, and the remainder of these, including her master, Capt F.G. Sherburne, were rescued by the *Admiral Hipper* and became prisoners-of-war.

ALBERTVILLE (1928–1940)

Cie. Belge Maritime, Belgium; Ateliers et Chantiers de la Loire, St Nazaire.
11,047 GRT, 537ft (163.7m) LOA, 62ft (18.9m) beam.
358 passengers in two classes.
Quadruple expansion SR engines with LP turbine, twin screw, 16.5kts.
Date of disaster: 11 June 1940.

The Belgian liner *Albertville* was ordered to sail from Bordeaux to Le Havre in June 1940 to assist in the evacuation of British and French troops retreating in the face of the German *Blitzkrieg*. After reaching the French port, the *Albertville* was attacked by German aircraft on 11 June and sank in the roadstead. Her sister ship *Leopoldville* was a torpedo loss in December 1944. Before the Second World War both liners had served on the Antwerp to Matadi, Congo (Zaire), route.

GENERAL METZINGER ex-*SOBRAL* ex-*CAP VILANO* (1906–1940)

Messageries Maritimes, France; Blohm & Voss, Hamburg.
9,467 GRT, 475ft (144.8m) length, 55ft (16.8m) beam.
Quadruple expansion SR engines, twin screw, 15kts.
Date of disaster: 11 June 1940.

The German liner *Cap Vilano* was seized by the Brazilian Government in 1917 and renamed *Sobral*. She was bought by Messageries Maritimes in 1924, for whom she sailed as the *General Metzinger*. She was sunk by German aircraft at Le Havre on 11 June 1940. The wreck was broken up for scrap in 1950.

PIRIAPOLIS (1938–1940)

Cie. Maritime Belge, Belgium; John Cockerill, Hoboken.
7,340 GRT, 459ft (139.9m) length, 61ft (18.6m) beam.
Diesel engine, single screw, 14kts.
Date of disaster: 11 June 1940.

The Belgian motor passenger ship *Piriapolis* and her sisters, *Copacabana* and *Mar del Plata*, were employed in the service from Europe to Latin America. When only two years old, the *Piriapolis* was sunk by German aircraft off Le Havre on 11 June 1940 while engaged in evacuating troops. She had been diverted to Le Havre and, earlier, La Pallice, while returning to Antwerp from Buenos Aires. It is not known whether there were any casualties.

The Orama *was lost during the Norwegian campaign.* (Author's collection)

VANDYCK (1921–1940)

Lamport & Holt Co, Great Britain; Workman Clark, Belfast.
13,233 GRT, 535ft (163.1m) LOA, 64ft (19.5m) beam.
680 passengers in three classes.
Steam turbines, twin screw, 14.5kts.
Date of disaster: 11 June 1940.

The *Vandyck* served on the run from New York to La Plata ports in partnership with her sister *Voltaire* until 1930. Both ships were then laid up, but their careers resumed from 1932 when they undertook a full time cruising service. In October 1939 the *Vandyck* was converted to a troopship. She was engaged in the Norwegian offensive in the summer of 1940, when Britain hoped in vain to stem German expansion in that direction. On 11 June she was bombed and sunk by German dive-bombers off the Norwegian coast. Two officers and five ratings were killed, and a further 161 were captured and made prisoners-of-war.

UMBRIA ex-*BAHIA BLANCA* (1912–1940)

Italian Government; Reiherstieg Schiffswerke, Hamburg.
9,349 GRT, 491ft (149.7m) length, 59ft (18.0m) beam.
Triple expansion SR engines, twin screw, 13kts.
Date of disaster: 12 June 1940.

This former Hamburg Sud-Amerika Line passenger steamship was sold to Argentine owners in 1918 and then to Italy in 1935 for troop-carrying service during the Abyssinian campaign. She was also employed on voyages to the Far East. On such a voyage from Genoa to Rangoon on 12 June 1940, the *Umbria*, as the Italians had renamed her, was scuttled off Port Sudan to prevent her falling into British hands. The wreck lay in the position 19°38′N–37°17′E until it was broken up for scrap.

Top *The* Vandyck *was another loss of the ill-fated Norwegian campaign.* (World Ship Society)

Above *The Anchor liner* Caledonia *was renamed* Scotstoun *for duties as an auxiliary cruiser.* (World Ship Society)

CALEDONIA as HMS *SCOTSTOUN* (1925–1940)

Anchor Line, Great Britain; Alexander Stephen, Glasgow.
17,046 GRT, 578ft (176.2m) LOA, 70ft (21.3m) beam.
1,342 passengers in three classes.
Steam turbines, twin screw, 17kts.
Date of disaster: 13 June 1940.

The transatlantic service passenger ship *Caledonia* was requisitioned for war duties as an armed merchant cruiser and commissioned under the name *Scotstoun* in September 1939. She was torpedoed and sunk by the German submarine *U25*, when 200 miles west of Inishtrahull in the position 57°00'N–09°57'W. Of her complement of 350 officers and ratings, six were killed.

ANDANIA (1922–1940)

Cunard Line, Great Britain; Hawthorn Leslie, Newcastle.
13,950 GRT, 538ft (164.0m) LOA, 65ft (19.8m) beam.
1,700 passengers in two classes.
Steam turbines, twin screw, 15kts.
Date of disaster: 16 June 1940.

Built for the Southampton to Montreal service, the *Andania* was switched to the Hamburg to New York route and later still to the service from Liverpool to Montreal. At the start of the Second World War, she was taken over by the Admiralty and converted into an armed merchant cruiser. She was torpedoed and sunk by the submarine *UA70* on 16 June 1940, 70 miles south-east of Reykjavik, Iceland, in the position 62°36'N–15°09'W. All aboard were saved as she remained afloat long enough to permit a full evacuation.

CHAMPLAIN (1932–1940)

French Line (CGT), France; Chantiers et Ateliers de St Nazaire (Penhoët).
28,124 GRT, 641ft (195.4m) LOA, 83ft (25.3m) beam.
1,053 passengers in three classes.
Steam turbines, twin screw, 20kts.
Date of disaster: 17 June 1940.

The cabin class liner *Champlain* sailed between Le Havre and New York from the time of her maiden voyage in June

Above *Rare photographs showing the* Champlain *sunk off the west coast of France after striking a magnetic mine. The* Champlain *appears to have had some form of disruptive colour scheme.* (L.L. von Münching *and* W.Z. Bilddienst)

Below *A peacetime view of the modernistic – for those days – cabin-class liner* Champlain, *showing her with heightened funnel.* (Cie. Générale Maritime)

1932. She was a striking vessel and, like many another French Line ship before her, she pioneered new trends in decor and appearance. On 17 June 1940 the *Champlain* was returning from New York with passengers. She had already called at St Nazaire when she struck a mine off the entrance to La Pallice, three miles west of La Rochelle, on the French Atlantic coast. Of the 381 crew and passengers still aboard, 11 crewmen were killed. Some reports state that 300 people lost their lives when the *Champlain* sank but this is incorrect. Her wreck remained in an upright position in shallow water throughout the war and demolition did not commence until the 1950s. By 1964 the last traces had been removed. Lloyds War Loss Records state that the *Champlain* was engaged on His Majesty's Service at the time of her loss but it has not been possible to either confirm or refute this.

LANCASTRIA ex-*TYRRHENIA* (1922–1940)

Cunard Line, Great Britain; William Beardmore, Glasgow.
16,243 GRT, 579ft (176.5m) LOA, 70ft (21.3m) beam.
1,785 passengers in three classes.
Steam turbines, twin screw, 16.5kts.
Date of disaster: 17 June 1940.

To the *Lancastria* goes the dubious distinction of being

Below *Cunard Line's* Lancastria *ex-*Tyrrhenia*, one of a class of four ships jointly operated with the Anchor Line.* (Author's collection)

Bottom *Viewed from a British destroyer, the* Lancastria *goes down off the French port of St Nazaire. Note the numerous men in the water swimming to safety.* (Imperial War Museum, Neg. HU2795)

the worst British merchant ship loss of the Second World War. She commenced duties as a troopship on 5 March 1940. That summer, when the fall of France was imminent, and the British Expeditionary Force had been pushed back to the beaches of Dunkerque, the *Lancastria* was drafted to St Nazaire to assist in the evacuation of British troops. On 17 June 1940 she embarked a large number of troops plus a small party of civilians. The precise number of her occupants does not seem to be known but, including the crew, it is variously given as 5,310 or 5,506. The Association of *Lancastria* Survivors believes that there may even have been as many as 9,000 on board. As she was about to weigh anchor, Charpentier Roads, in which the embarkation had taken place, came under attack from German bombers. In the third raid the *Lancastria* was hit by four bombs, one of which penetrated to her engine-room and exploded there. The doomed vessel assumed an immediate list and, in spite of great urgency in trying to launch the lifeboats, only two were successfully floated. After about 20 minutes, the *Lancastria* rolled over onto her port side before capsizing completely and sinking bow first. Small craft hurried to the scene and rescued many men from the water but, in spite of this, the death toll was extremely high. The official figures for the number of survivors was given as only 2,477, which meant that over 3,000 had perished, including 66 of the crew. The wreck, which was in the position 47°09′N–02°20′E, was broken up in September 1951.

MEXIQUE ex-*LAFAYETTE* ex-*ILE DE CUBA* (1915–1940)

French Line (CGT), France; Chantiers et Ateliers de Provence, Port du Bouc.
12,220 GRT, 563ft (171.6m) LOA, 64ft (19.5m) beam.
1,250 passengers in four classes.
Quadruple expansion SR engines with LP turbine, quadruple screw, 16kts.
Date of disaster: 19 June 1940.

Launched as the *Ile de Cuba* for CGT's West Indies service, a decision was made before she was completed to operate her instead on the New York route from Bordeaux. Hence she was renamed *Lafayette*. Her commercial career only commenced after the First World War had erupted in Europe, and after only one season it was interrupted when the *Lafayette* was taken over for use as a hospital ship. Following the Armistice the *Lafayette* resumed her transatlantic schedule until 1924, when she was switched to the Central American service. Four years later she was renamed *Mexique*.

The outbreak of the Second World War gave the old ship a new lease of life. After a series of mercy voyages, taking Jewish refugees to Mexico, she became a troopship. On 19 June 1940 the *Mexique* became another magnetic mine victim when she struck one at the entrance of Le Verdon harbour after arriving there from Oran. She sank and became a total loss, but her entire crew of 173 men was saved.

The victim of a magnetic mine, the Mexique *was sunk off Le Verdon.* (National Maritime Museum, London)

NIAGARA (1913–1940)

Canadian Australasian Line, Great Britain; John Brown, Clydebank.
13,415 GRT, 543ft (165.5m) LOA, 66ft (20.1m) beam.
704 passengers in three classes.
Triple expansion SR engines with LP turbine, triple screw, 18kts.
Date of disaster: 19 June 1940.

The steamship *Niagara* was originally built for the Union Steamship Company of New Zealand for service on the route from Sydney to Vancouver via New Zealand. In 1932, in the face of growing American and Japanese competition on the route, the Union SS Co formed a consortium with Canadian Pacific, called the Canadian Australasian Line, for the operation of the *Niagara* and her fleetmate *Aorangi*. On 17 June 1940 the *Niagara* left Auckland bound for Suva, Honolulu, and Vancouver, with 53 passengers and a valuable cargo of gold ingots valued at £2.5 million. She also had a considerable volume of small arms ammunition, ultimately destined for Great Britain. The following day, off Whangarei in the Hauraki Gulf, the *Niagara* struck a mine that had been laid some days earlier by the German raider *Orion*. The mine exploded adjacent to number two hold, causing the ship to settle by the head as the forepart flooded. The Huddart Parker liner *Wanganella* and the coaster *Kapiti* responded to her radio call for assistance, and between them they picked up all the passengers and the 201-man crew, including the master, Capt W. Martin. The *Niagara* sank in 75 fathoms in the position 35°53′S–174°54′E. Salvage operations to recover the gold bullion were immediately instigated and the majority of the

The Niagara, *owned by the Canadian Australasian Line.* (A. Duncan)

treasure (£2,379,000) had been lifted from the wreck by February 1942. The remainder of the gold bars were recovered in the spring and summer of 1953.

FOUCAULD ex-*HOEDIC* (1922–1940)

Chargéurs Reunis, France; Forges et Chantiers de la Mediterranée, La Seyne.
11,028 GRT, 501ft (152.7m) LOA, 58ft (17.7m) beam.
450 passengers.
Triple expansion SR engines, twin screw, 14kts.
Date of disaster: 20 June 1940.

The rebuilt passenger ship *Foucauld*, which had been renamed after a refit resulting from a capsizing accident at Le Havre in June 1928, was placed in the Le Havre to West Africa service. She also made cruises to the Azores, the Canaries, and the North Cape. She was bombed and burnt out during a German air raid on La Pallice on 20 June 1940. The wreck sank in shallow water and broke its back.

ARANDORA STAR ex-*ARANDORA* (1927–1940)

Blue Star Line, Great Britain; Cammell Laird, Birkenhead.
15,501 GRT, 535ft (163.1m) LOA, 68ft (20.7m) beam.
375 passengers in single class.
Steam turbines, twin screw, 16kts.
Date of disaster: 2 July 1940.

The *Arandora Star* joined her four sisters on the London to La Plata ports service in May 1927, but in 1928 she was

The cruise-ship Arandora Star, *a torpedo victim.* (Maritime Photo Library)

singled out for reconstruction into a luxury cruise liner. In this role she established a fine reputation for herself between 1929 and 1939, undergoing further extensive modification in 1936.

In May 1940 she was converted into a troopship, but was torpedoed and sunk in the Atlantic, 75 miles west of the Bloody Foreland, County Donegal, barely two months later, being attacked on 2 July by the German submarine *U47* while bound from Liverpool to Canada. Ironically, she had commenced her military career in an experimental role, assisting in the development of anti-torpedo nets. A further bitter irony was that she was carrying 1,178 German and Italian internees and prisoners-of-war, in addition to her crew of 174 and a military guard of 200 men. The torpedo struck the *Arandora Star* in her engine-room, and panic immediately broke out among the prisoners. This delayed the launching of life-saving apparatus, and also contributed directly to the death-toll, for many were forced overboard and drowned. The liner sank one hour after the attack, in the position 56°30'N–10°38'W, a total of 805 people losing their lives. Of the enemy aliens, 243 Germans and 470 Italians perished. In addition 37 soldiers and 55 members of the crew died, including her master, Capt E.W. Moulton. The *Arandora Star* had been proceeding without escort but, fortunately, the survivors were sighted by a Sunderland flying-boat, which directed the Canadian destroyer *St Laurent* to the scene.

It should be noted that the figures given in this account are from the Blue Star Line's records. The Lloyds War Loss Records give considerably different numbers in terms of the occupants of the *Arandora Star* as well as the casualties of the attack. These state that there were 176 crewmen, of whom 57 were lost, 254 military guardsmen, of whom 91 died, and 1,178 aliens and prisoners, of whom 143 Germans and 470 Italians perished.

AENEAS (1910–1940)

Blue Funnel Line, Great Britain; Workman Clark, Belfast.
10,058 GRT, 509ft (155.1m) LOA, 60ft (18.3m) beam.
288 passengers in single class.
Triple expansion SR engines, twin screw, 14kts.
Date of disaster: 4 July 1940.

Built for the service from Glasgow to Brisbane with two sisters, the *Aeneas* switched to the Far East route in 1925. In 1939 she was engaged on troop-carrying duties for the second time in her career, but she did not survive the Second World War, sinking on 4 July 1940, two days after German aircraft had bombed her 20 miles south of Plymouth. She had been sailing in convoy to London, and ultimately Glasgow, when the attack occurred, being hit a number of times. One bomb penetrated her port side and another exploded deep within her, blowing out her starboard side and killing many members of the engine-room staff. The ship caught fire and was abandoned. Of her crew of 122, 19 lost their lives. After drifting in the Channel for almost 48 hours, she finally foundered 11 miles from Portland Bill, in the approximate position 50°00'N–03°00'W.

KEMMENDINE (1924–1940)

Henderson Line, Great Britain; William Denny, Dumbarton.
7,837 GRT, 453ft (138.1m) length, 59ft (18.0m) beam.
150 passengers in single class.
Triple expansion SR engine, single screw, 14kts.
Date of disaster: 13 July 1940.

The *Kemmendine* was one of a group of five ships serving Rangoon from Glasgow and Liverpool. On 13 July 1940, during a voyage from the United Kingdom to Burma via Cape Town, she was sunk by the German raider *Atlantis* in the approximate position 04°00'S–82°00'E. The total number

The Henderson Line steamship Kemmendine *operated on the Glasgow to Rangoon service.* (World Ship Society)

The liner Meknès *was sunk in the English Channel while repatriating French servicemen after the fall of France.* (Arnold Kludas)

of personnel aboard her was 147, of whom 82 lost their lives, 57 being crew-members, 22 passengers, and three from a number of prisoners-of-war she was carrying. The *Atlantis* was herself sunk on 22 November 1941 by an aircraft from the cruiser HMS *Devonshire*.

MEKNÈS ex-*PUERTO RICO* (1913–1940)

French Line (CGT), France; Chantiers et Ateliers de St Nazaire.
6,127 GRT, 413ft (125.9m) length, 51ft (15.5m) beam.
Triple expansion SR engines with LP turbine, twin screw, 13kts.
Date of disaster: 24 July 1940.

The French steamship *Meknès* spent her entire career on the service from Bordeaux to Casablanca. Starting life as the *Puerto Rico*, she was renamed *Meknès* in 1929. After the fall of France in June 1940 she remained under Vichy control and was utilized for the repatriation of French servicemen who wished to return home. In this capacity, she left Southampton for Marseilles on 24 July 1940, carrying 1,079 naval officers and ratings in addition to her crew of 102. She was clearly marked with the French flag painted on her sides and was brightly illuminated. Nevertheless, a German E-boat which intercepted her some 35 miles south-east of Portland Bill, in the position either 50°04′N–02°15′W or 50°15′N–02°10′W, opened fire on her with machine-guns. The *Meknès* immediately signalled her name and nationality in response and, though not commanded to do so, she came to a dead stop in the water. Rather than accept her identification, or even investigate it, the E-boat's only reaction was to launch a torpedo into the heavily loaded ship, causing her to sink inside 10 minutes. There was great loss of life among those aboard, for although 898 survivors reached the English coast and others may have made it to the French side of the Channel, there were 383 people left unaccounted for. These figures may actually be on the low side, for Lloyds War Loss Records, compiled at the time of the sinking, state that the *Meknès* was carrying a total of 1,300 military personnel and that 402 of these, plus 33 members of the crew, were listed as missing. These higher casualty figures could possibly have been revised downward at a later date, when more information became available.

ACCRA (1926–1940)

Elder Dempster Line, Great Britain; Harland & Wolff, Belfast.
9,337 GRT, 450ft (137.2m) length, 62ft (18.9m) beam.
400 passengers.
Diesel engines, twin screw, 14.5kts.
Date of disaster: 26 July 1940.

The *Accra* and her sister, the *Apapa*, both Belfast-built motorships, were constructed for the West African cargo-passenger service from Liverpool. She was taken over for war service in September 1939, and on 26 July 1940 fell victim to a German submarine while sailing in convoy from Liverpool to Freetown and other West African ports. She sank in the position 55°40′N–16°28′W. Of the 499 passengers and crew on board the *Accra*, 24 were lost, many of these perishing when one of the lifeboats capsized in the choppy seas as it was being launched.

TRANSYLVANIA (1925–1940)

Anchor Line, Great Britain; Fairfield, Glasgow.
16,923 GRT, 552ft (168.2m) LOA, 70ft (21.3m) beam.
1,342 passengers in three classes.
Steam turbines, twin screw, 15.5kts.
Date of disaster: 10 August 1940.

The *Transylvania*, which spent 14 years on the Glasgow to New York run, was taken over as an armed merchant cruiser at the outbreak of the Second World War. While patrolling north of Ireland on 10 August 1940, she was torpedoed by the German submarine *U56* off Malin Head, in the position 55°50′N–08°03′W. She was taken in tow but foundered before reaching port. Due to rough seas the lifeboats could not be lowered, but trawlers came to the vessel's aid and rescued some 300 members of the crew, landing them on the west coast of Ireland. Another 48 lost their lives.

REMUERA (1911–1940)

New Zealand Line, Great Britain; William Denny, Dumbarton.
11,276 GRT, 502ft (153.0m) LOA, 62ft (18.9m) beam.
530 passengers in three classes.
Triple expansion SR engines, twin screw, 15kts.
Date of disaster: 26 August 1940.

Sister liner to the *Rotorua* (torpedoed in March 1917), the *Remuera* had operated in consort with her on the run from

The Anchor liner Transylvania. (A. Duncan)

London to Wellington. Returning from Wellington via the Panama Canal on 26 August 1940, the *Remuera* was attacked by German torpedo-bombers off Rattray Head, on the north-east coast of Scotland. She sank in the position 57°50′N–01°54′W, fortunately without any loss of life among her 94-strong crew.

DUNVEGAN CASTLE (1936–1940)

Union Castle Line, Great Britain; Harland & Wolff, Belfast.
15,050 GRT, 560ft (170.7m) LOA, 71ft (21.6m) beam.
508 passengers in two classes.
Diesel engines, twin screw, 16kts.
Date of disaster: 28 August 1940.

The sister ships *Dunvegan Castle* and *Dunnottar Castle* were built for the round-Africa service from London. The *Dunnottar Castle* survived the Second World War but the *Dunvegan Castle* did not, being torpedoed west of Ireland by *U46* on 27 August 1940 while serving as an armed

The Dunvegan Castle *operated on the London to Durban service prior to the Second World War.* (World Ship Society)

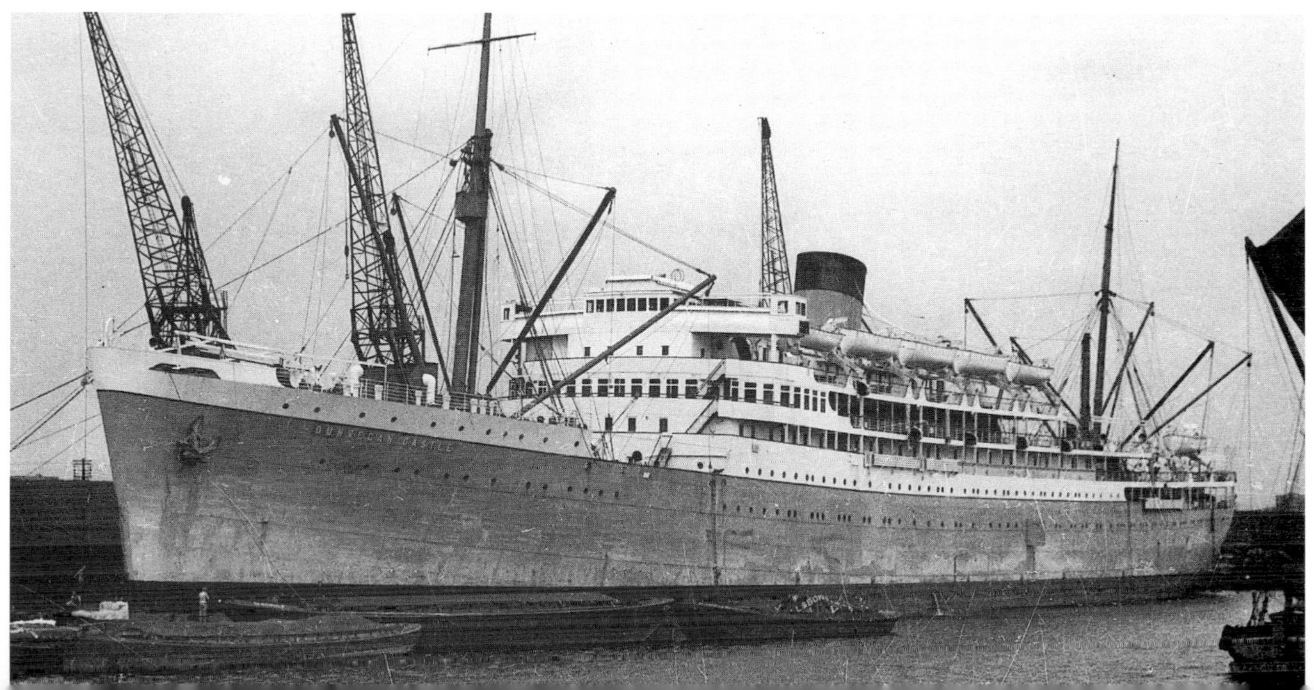

merchant cruiser. She sank the following day in the position 54°50′N–11°00′W. Four officers and 23 ratings were killed out of her complement of 277, her master, Capt H. Ardill, being among the survivors.

FLANDRE (1914–1940)

French Line (CGT), France; Chantiers de L'Atlantique, St Nazaire.
8,503 GRT, 480ft (146.3m) LOA, 57ft (17.4m) beam.
Compound steam engines with LP turbine, quadruple screw, 17kts.
Date of disaster: 14 September 1940.

French Line's *Flandre* served on the run to the West Indies and Central America. She was sunk by a magnetic mine at the mouth of the River Gironde on 14 September 1940. She was beached near La Coubre but broke apart as a result of the damage she had sustained and became a total loss.

ASKA (1939–1940)

British India Line, Great Britain; Swan, Hunter & Wigham Richardson, Newcastle.
8,323 GRT, 461ft (140.5m) LOA, 61ft (18.6m) beam.
2,636 passengers in four classes.
Steam turbines, twin screw, 17kts.
Date of disaster: 16 September 1940.

The liners *Amra*, *Aronda*, and *Aska* were built for the India to Africa service, the *Aska* commencing operations only a matter of months before the outbreak of the Second World War. Their accommodation provided for a very large element of deck passengers, by far the majority of the passengers carried. In September 1940 she sailed, independent of convoys, from Freetown and Bathurst bound for Liverpool, carrying 358 Free French troops in addition to her crew of 186. On 16 September she was near Rathlin Island, in the position 55°15′N–05°55′W, entering the Irish Sea by the North Channel when she was attacked by a German bomber which scored three hits, causing severe damage in the engine-room and forecastle. The order to abandon ship was given and the *Aska* was left ablaze and drifting in a north-westerly direction. She ran ashore on Cara Island the following day and became a constructive total loss. Nineteen French soldiers and 11 members of the crew lost their lives. The survivors were taken to Greenock after trawlers rescued them from the lifeboats.

CITY OF BENARES (1936–1940)

Ellerman Lines, Great Britain; Barclay Curle, Glasgow.
11,081 GRT, 509ft (155.1m) LOA, 62ft (18.9m) beam.
219 passengers in single class.
Steam turbines, twin screw, 15kts.
Date of disaster: 17 September 1940.

The Flandre *was yet another mine casualty.* (World Ship Society)

The Ellerman Lines flagship City of Benares, *whose loss by torpedo was all the more tragic as 77 evacuee children lost their lives in the disaster.* (Ellerman Lines)

The loss by torpedo of the Ellerman Lines flagship *City of Benares* on 17 September 1940 was one of the most tragic disasters of the Second World War, for she was engaged in carrying evacuee children to Canada. At that time British Government policy was to encourage the evacuation of juniors to the apparent safety of North America and South Africa for the duration, under a scheme managed on their behalf by the Children's Overseas Reception Board. The *City of Benares* departed Liverpool in convoy OB213 on 13 September 1940, bound for Montreal and Quebec. Aboard were 199 passengers, of whom 90 were children, and a crew of 209. Four days later, when she was about 600 miles out into the Atlantic, in the position 56°48'N–21°15'W, the *City of Benares* was torpedoed by the German submarine *U48* under the command of Capt Heinrich Bleichrodt. The attack occurred only a matter of hours after the convoy's Royal Navy escort had been withdrawn. The torpedo struck the *Benares* on the port side and she remained afloat for only a short period, during which time every effort was made to launch the boats. However, the weather was dirty and the seas very rough, some lifeboats capsizing and drowning their occupants. There followed a harrowing night on the open sea in freezing conditions, many of the survivors, particularly among the children, dying of exposure. Most of those rescued were picked up the following day by the destroyer HMS *Hurricane*, but one boat was not picked up until 10 days later, when it was sighted by a Sunderland flying-boat which directed a warship to its aid. In all, 258 of those aboard the *City of Benares* were killed, including 77 of the 90 children. In fact only 57 of her passengers survived the attack. Immediately after this tragedy the Government terminated the child evacuation programme to prevent similar disasters.

Before the war the *City of Benares* had sailed between Liverpool and Bombay via the Mediterranean, in conditions which were a far cry from those on the North Atlantic that had witnessed her destruction.

COMMISSAIRE RAMEL (1920–1940)

Messageries Maritimes, France; Soc. Provençale de Construction Navale, La Ciotat.
10,061 GRT, 500ft (152.4m) LOA, 59ft (18.0m) beam.
552 passengers in three classes.
Triple expansion SR engine with LP turbine, single screw, 14kts.
Date of disaster: 20 September 1940.

Completed in March 1920 as a cargo ship, the *Commissaire Ramel* was rebuilt as a passenger vessel in 1926, with accommodation for over 500 passengers. She sailed on the route from Marseilles to Sydney and Noumea, New Caledonia. In July 1940 she was seized in Australia and placed under the management of Shaw, Savill and Albion for the Ministry of War Transport, only to be intercepted in the Indian Ocean on 20 September, during a voyage from Sydney to the United Kingdom via South Africa, by the German auxiliary cruiser *Atlantis*. The troopship made an abortive attempt to radio for help, in response to which the *Atlantis* opened fire and set her alight. All but three of the 66 crew safely abandoned ship and were taken aboard the German vessel as prisoners. After sinking the *Commissaire*

The Commissaire Ramel. (A. Duncan)

Ramel in the position 28°25′S–74°23′E, some 1,000 miles south-east of Mauritius, the crew were landed in Italian Somaliland, where they were interned.

CITY OF SIMLA (1921–1940)

Ellerman Lines, Great Britain; W. Gray, West Hartlepool.
10,138 GRT, 476ft (145.1m) length, 58ft (17.7m) beam.
Steam turbines, twin screw, 13.5kts.
Date of disaster: 21 September 1940.

The steamship *City of Simla* was sunk by a German submarine on 21 September 1940 about 50 miles north-west of Malin Head, in the position 55°59′N–08°16′W. She was bound from London to Bombay via Cape Town with 167 passengers and a crew of 183. Three lives were lost.

Ellerman's City of Simla. (A. Duncan)

HIGHLAND PATRIOT (1932–1940)

Royal Mail Line, Great Britain; Harland & Wolff, Belfast.
14,137 GRT, 544ft (165.8m) LOA, 69ft (21.0m) beam.
701 passengers in three classes.
Diesel engines, twin screw, 16kts.
Date of disaster: 1 October 1940.

The *Highland Patriot* was the last of six ships built for the service from London to Buenos Aires. She was sunk on 1 October 1940 while returning to Glasgow from South America, when the German submarine *U38* torpedoed her about 500 miles west of the Bishop Rock. The position in which she sank is variously given as 52°20'N–19°04'W or 52°13'N–19°04'W. Three were lost out of her crew of 143.

EMPRESS OF BRITAIN (1931–1940)

Canadian Pacific Line, Great Britain; John Brown, Clydebank.
42,348 GRT, 758ft (231.0m) LOA, 97ft (29.6m) beam.
1,182 passengers in three classes.
Steam turbines, quadruple screw, 24kts.
Date of disaster: 26 October 1940.

The *Empress of Britain* was one of the largest liners to be placed on the Southampton to Quebec service, and a feature of her annual programme were her luxury cruises during the winter months. She was taken over as a troopship in late-November 1939. Almost a year later, on 26 October 1940, she was returning to the United Kingdom from Canada after a long voyage that had commenced in Cape Town, when a long-range German bomber attacked her about 100 miles north-west of the Irish coast in the position 54°53'N–10°49'W. She was hit by high explosive and incendiary bombs and left damaged and burning. She was abandoned by all but a small party of her complement of 643, the survivors being picked up by naval escorts. The Polish destroyer *Burza* took the *Empress of Britain* in tow,

Right *Dead in the water, the* Empress of Britain *on fire and listing after being attacked by enemy aircraft. Two days later she was finished off by torpedoes from a German submarine.* (Imperial War Museum, Neg. HU17754)

Below *The largest ship ever to be built for the Canadian passenger service across the Atlantic, the second* Empress of Britain. (Author's collection)

but on 28 October she was hit by two torpedoes from the German submarine *U32*, commanded by Lt Jaenisch. She blew up and sank in the position 55°16′N–09°50′W. The loss of life in the two separate attacks is variously put at 45 or 49. She was the largest British merchant ship lost in the Second World War.

LAURENTIC (1927–1940)

Cunard White Star Line, Great Britain; Harland & Wolff, Belfast.
18,724 GRT, 600ft (182.9m) LOA, 75ft (22.9m) beam.
1,500 passengers in three classes.
Triple expansion SR engines with LP turbine, triple screw, 17kts.
Date of disaster: 3 November 1940.

The outbreak of the Second World War led to a re-activation of the *Laurentic*'s career, for she had spent the previous three years laid up following a serious collision with the *Napier Star* in August 1935, and may otherwise have been destined for the breakers' yard. She now joined the Royal Navy as an armed merchant cruiser, patrolling the Western Approaches. On 3 November 1940, after she had gone to the aid of the sinking Elders & Fyffes ship *Casanare*, the *Laurentic* was torpedoed and sunk by the German submarine *U99*, off the Bloody Foreland, County Donegal, in the position 53°55′N–14°30′W. Three torpedoes sent her quickly to the bottom with the loss of 49 lives. Her master Capt E.P. Vivian, 51 officers, and 316 ratings were saved. The former Blue Funnel liner *Patroclus*, another auxiliary cruiser, was also sunk by *U99* as she was standing by to pick up survivors.

PATROCLUS (1923–1940)

Blue Funnel Line, Great Britain; Scott's, Greenock.
11,314 GRT, 530ft (161.5m) LOA, 62ft (18.9m) beam.
140 passengers in single class.
Steam turbines, twin screw, 15kts.
Date of disaster: 4 November 1940.

The *Patroclus* was engaged in the service from Liverpool to the Far East with three sister ships, *Sarpedon*, *Hector*, and *Antenor*. In September 1939 she was commissioned as an auxiliary cruiser. On 4 November the following year, the *Patroclus* was torpedoed off the west coast of Ireland by the German submarine *U99* while rendering assistance to the survivors of the former White Star liner *Laurentic*, another armed merchant cruiser which had been sunk earlier by the same U-boat. Despite the fact that her fore-part had totally disintegrated and fallen away, the *Patroclus* remained afloat for over five hours because her holds were filled with empty barrels, which gave her additional buoyancy. It consequently took five more torpedoes to finish her off. She finally sank in the position 53°43′N–14°41′W, taking 76 seamen with her. Her master Capt G.C. Wynter, 33 officers, and 230 ratings were rescued. The survivors were picked up the following morning by HMS *Achates* and another destroyer.

JERVIS BAY (1922–1940)

Aberdeen & Commonwealth Line, Great Britain; Vickers, Barrow-in-Furness.
14,129 GRT, 548ft (167.0) LOA, 68ft (20.7m) beam.
542 passengers in single class.
Steam turbines, twin screw, 16kts.
Date of disaster: 5 November 1940.

Cunard White Star's Laurentic *was laid up for an extended period following a collision prior to her recall to service for war duties.* (World Ship Society)

The Blue Funnel turbine steamship Patroclus. (World Ship Society)

When the *Jervis Bay* was sunk while defending a convoy against all the odds, a new chapter was written in the story of Britain's maritime heritage, for her courageous sacrifice permitted many other ships to escape. She was one of a group of five vessels built for the London to Brisbane service which was maintained under several owners, the last being the Aberdeen & Commonwealth Line from 1933. At the outbreak of the Second World War she was commissioned as an armed merchant cruiser and assigned to convoy escort duties.

On 5 November 1940 she was escorting the 38 ships of convoy HX84, bound for the United Kingdom from across the Atlantic, when it was attacked by the German pocket battleship *Admiral Scheer*. The convoy was by then some 1,000 miles east of Newfoundland, and apart from the *Jervis Bay* was totally unprotected. In order to give the other ships

The Aberdeen & Commonwealth cargo-passenger liner Jervis Bay. (Imperial War Museum, Neg. Q105811)

The Jervis Bay*'s courageous sacrifice in protecting her convoy from the* Admiral Scheer*, on the horizon to the right, is depicted in this painting of the famous incident.* (Furness Withy Group)

the opportunity to disperse, the *Jervis Bay* turned towards the enemy and steamed directly at her to engage. The hopelessly one-sided battle that ensued lasted for about one hour, the *Jervis Bay* taking the full brunt of the *Scheer*'s 11-inch guns while her own 6-inch pieces were largely ineffective against her adversary's armour. Nevertheless, her objective was achieved, in that by the time the *Jervis Bay* went down two hours later, night had fallen and the larger part of the convoy had made good its escape under cover of the darkness and smoke screens. Only six other vessels were sunk, namely the *Beaverford*, which had aided the *Jervis Bay* in defence of the convoy, and the *Maidan*, *Mopan*, *Fresno City*, *Kenbane Head*, and *Trewellard*, with a total loss of 168 officers and men. From the *Jervis Bay*, whose last position was 52°26′N–32°34′W, a further 34 officers and 156 seamen lost their lives, the 65 survivors of her crew being picked up by a Swedish vessel that had been crossing with the convoy.

ROMOLO (1926–1940)

Italia Line, Italy; Stabilimento Tecnico Triestino, Trieste.
9,780 GRT, 506ft (154.2m) LOA, 62ft (18.9m) beam.
Diesel engines, twin screw, 14kts.
Date of disaster: 6 November 1940.

The sister ships *Romolo* and *Remo* were engaged in the Italy to Australia service via the Suez Canal. Built for Lloyd Triestino, they passed to the Italia Line in the 1930s. When the *Romolo* was approached in mid-Pacific by the Australian armed merchant cruiser *Manoora* on 6 November 1940, the crew scuttled their ship to prevent her from being captured.

APAPA (1927–1940)

Elder Dempster Line, Great Britain; Harland & Wolff, Belfast.
9,333 GRT, 451ft (137.5m) length, 62ft (18.9m) beam.
400 passengers.
Diesel engines, twin screw, 14.5kts.
Date of disaster: 15 November 1940.

The motor liner *Apapa* served on the route from Liverpool to West Africa with her sister ship *Accra*. On 15 November 1940, during a voyage from Lagos to her home port, she was bombed and sunk by German aircraft 200 miles west of County Mayo, Ireland. The position was stated to be 54°34′N–16°47′W according to her master, Capt Vaughan Davies, but is also recorded as 54°31′N–16°34′W or 53°50′N–16°23′W. She was carrying 95 passengers and a crew of 158 at the time, of whom five and 18 respectively lost their lives.

PATRIA (1914–1940)

Messageries Maritimes, France; Chantiers de la Mediterranée, La Seyne.
11,885 GRT, 512ft (156.1m) LOA, 59ft (18.0m) beam.
2,240 passengers in three classes.
Triple expansion SR engines, twin screw, 16kts.
Date of disaster: 25 November 1940.

Though built for the Marseilles to New York service of Fabre Line, from 1932 the *Patria* was operated under charter by Messageries Maritimes between Marseilles and ports in the eastern Mediterranean. In January 1940 she was

Dramatic views of the Elder Dempster motorship Apapa *ablaze and sinking after she was attacked and bombed by German aircraft.* (Maritime Photo Library)

purchased outright by Messageries Maritimes but, with the capitulation of France that June, she was laid up at Haifa. The British authorities took her over for duties transporting illegal Jewish immigrants out of Palestine to British colonies. The first voyage, scheduled for late-November, was to have been to Mauritius. On 23 November the *Patria*

The loss of the Patria *was to occur as the result of sabotage while engaged on exceptional wartime service for the British Government.* (World Ship Society)

embarked 1,903 illegal emigrants and 116 Palestinian Police. Her departure was, however, indefinitely delayed, and she remained at her moorings with her large complement of passengers for two days, awaiting instructions. Early on 25 November, an explosion on the *Patria*'s starboard side, below the waterline, caused her to list, then capsize and sink. The ship submerged after only a brief interval, the flooding having been accelerated by the rapid egress of water through numerous open portholes on the starboard side. Harbour craft rescued many of those on board but there was still a heavy loss of life, amounting to 279 people. Of these, 25 were known to have drowned, while the remainder were unaccounted for and presumed dead. The rescued were taken to detention centres ashore with the exception of 25 refugees who were hospitalized, 13 of whom later escaped. The *Patria* had been the victim of an act of sabotage but the perpetrators of the atrocity were never identified. Underwriters advised against salvage as the ship was of no further commercial value. It lay on its side in about six fathoms until 1952, when it was broken up and removed.

RANGITANE (1929–1940)

New Zealand Line, Great Britain; John Brown, Clydebank.
16,712 GRT, 553ft (168.5m) LOA, 70ft (21.3m) beam.
595 passengers in three classes.
Diesel engines, twin screw, 15kts.
Date of disaster: 27 November 1940.

The New Zealand Line placed three twin-funnelled motorships – the *Rangitiki*, *Rangitata*, and *Rangitane* – in the Southampton to Wellington service in 1929. Highly successful liners, the first two survived until 1962, but the *Rangitane* was a casualty of the Second World War. While returning to the United Kingdom from Auckland via the Panama Canal route, she was intercepted on 27 November 1940 by the German raiders *Komet* and *Orion*, some 320 miles north of East Cape, New Zealand. Both cruisers shelled the liner and the unexpected attack left her a burning shambles. The crew and passengers, totalling 312 people, nevertheless abandoned ship in a disciplined fashion. The *Rangitane* was then finished off with a torpedo, sinking in the position 36°58′S–175°22′W. Six passengers and 10 members of the crew lost their lives. The survivors were picked up by the *Komet* and *Orion* (the latter operating under the alias *Nanyo Maru*), and, after being kept aboard for several weeks, they were landed on the island of Emirau, in the Bismarck Archipelago, on 21 December 1940. There they joined a large number of captives from other victims of the raiders *Komet*, *Orion*, *Kulmerland*, and *Narvik*. All 500 or more prisoners were subsequently rescued.

OSLOFJORD (1938–1940)

Norwegian Amerika Line, Norway; Deschimag AG Weser, Bremen.
18,673 GRT, 590ft (179.8m) LOA, 73ft (22.3m) beam.
860 passengers in three classes.
Diesel engines, twin screw, 19kts.
Date of disaster: 1 December 1940.

Newest ship in the Norwegian Amerika Line fleet, the twin-funnelled *Oslofjord* had only completed two seasons in the North Atlantic service when the eruption of war in Europe put an end to her civilian career. Initially laid up at New York, she was taken over as a troopship in October 1940 and converted at Halifax, Nova Scotia. Only two months later, on 1 December, she struck a mine laid by German aircraft in the Tyne estuary as she was nearing the end of the voyage from Halifax to Newcastle via Liverpool. She was beached south of the Tyne Pier, near South Shields, but on the night of 21–22 December she broke her back. Her fore-end capsized and she was abandoned as a constructive total loss.

Survivors of the capture and sinking of the Rangitane *were abandoned on a Pacific island.* (National Maritime Museum, London)

The Oslofjord *struck a mine and sank soon after she had been requisitioned for war service.* (Bjorn Pederson)

MONTROSE as HMS *FORFAR* (1922–1940)

Canadian Pacific Line, Great Britain; Fairfield, Glasgow.
16,402 GRT, 576ft (175.6m) LOA, 70ft (21.3m) beam.
1,810 passengers in two classes.
Steam turbines, twin screw, 17kts.
Date of disaster: 2 December 1940.

The Canadian Pacific liners *Montcalm* and *Montrose* were taken over as the armed merchant cruisers *Wolfe* and *Forfar* respectively on the outbreak of the Second World War. Although built for the Montreal service they had spent much of the 1930s engaged on cruises. The *Wolfe* survived the war, remaining in Admiralty service thereafter until she was scrapped. The *Forfar*, however, was torpedoed by the German submarine *U99* on 1 December 1940, 500 miles west of Ireland. She sank the following day in the position 54°23′N–20°11′W, with the loss of her commander, Capt N.A.C. Hardy, 36 officers, and 136 ratings. Just 21 survivors (three officers and 18 ratings) were picked up by the destroyer HMS *Thames*.

CALABRIA ex-*WERRA* (1922–1940)

Italia Line, Italy; Deschimag AG Weser, Bremen.
9,476 GRT, 480ft (146.3m) LOA, 57ft (17.4m) beam.
Triple expansion SR engines.
Date of disaster: 8 December 1940.

The Norddeutscher Lloyd transatlantic steamship *Werra* was sold to Italy in 1935. Renamed *Calabria*, she served as a troop-carrier under the management of Italia Line until captured by the British while dry-docked at Calcutta on 11 June 1940. She was taken over by the Ministry of War Shipping under the management of British India Line. On 8 December 1940, when she was nearing the end of a voyage from Calcutta and Freetown to the River Clyde, a German submarine torpedoed and sank her in the position 52°43′N–18°07′W. Her entire complement of 230 Indian passengers and 130 crewmen was lost.

The Canadian Pacific liner Montrose *was sunk under the name HMS* Forfar *while serving as an auxiliary cruiser.* (World Ship Society)

RHEIN (1925–1940)

Hamburg Amerika Line, Germany; Deschimage AG Weser, Bremen.
6,013 GRT, 453ft (138.1m) length, 58ft (17.7m) beam.
Diesel engine, single screw.
Date of disaster: 11 December 1940.

The motorship *Rhein* was built for the Hugo Stinnes Line, only to be acquired from them by Hamburg Amerika Line in 1926. She sailed for both companies between Germany and the West Indies. She was scuttled in the Gulf of Mexico on 11 December 1940 to avoid capture by the Dutch cruiser *Van Kinsbergen*, which had intercepted her.

ROTORUA ex-*SHROPSHIRE* (1911–1940)

Federal SN Co, Great Britain; John Brown, Clydebank.
10,890 GRT, 544ft (165.8m) LOA, 61ft (18.6m) beam.
671 passengers in three classes.
Quadruple expansion SR engines, twin screw, 14kts.
Date of disaster: 11 December 1940.

The New Zealand Line acquired this replacement *Rotorua* in 1922 by taking over the former Federal Line's *Shropshire*, which had been laid up following a serious fire. They had her fully rebuilt and converted to oil-firing before she made her first voyage from Southampton to Wellington in March 1923. Although refurbished at their expense and operated by the New Zealand Line under the name *Rotorua*, the ship remained registered under the ownership of Federal SN Co.

From September 1939 the *Rotorua* operated as a troopship, only to be sunk on 11 December 1940 after being torpedoed by the German submarine *U96*, 110 miles west of St Kilda, Scotland, in the position 58°56'N–11°20'W. She was returning to Avonmouth from Lyttleton and Halifax, and had on board 27 service personnel, a Chinese prisoner, and a crew of 122. Of these three servicemen and 18 crewmen lost their lives, including the *Rotorua*'s master, Capt E.R. Kemp. A further two crewmen were taken prisoner.

WESTERN PRINCE (1929–1940)

Furness Withy, Great Britain; Napier & Miller, Glasgow.
10,926 GRT, 516ft (157.3m) LOA, 64ft (19.5m) beam.
102 passengers in single class.
Diesel engines, twin screw, 16kts.
Date of disaster: 14 December 1940.

The four Furness *Prince* liners were built for the service from New York to La Plata ports, South America. The *Western Prince* was sunk during a voyage from New York to Liverpool on 14 December 1940, when, 500 miles west of the Orkney Islands, in the position 59°32'N–17°47'W, the German submarine *U96* torpedoed her twice. She sank with

The New Zealand Shipping Company's Rotorua, *formerly the* Shropshire. (World Ship Society)

The Italian passenger ship Sardegna, *originally the* Sierra Ventana. (World Ship Society)

the loss of 16 lives, including that of her captain. Another 154 people (55 passengers and 99 crew) were rescued.

BADEN (1922–1940)

Hamburg Amerika Line, Germany; Bremer Vulkan, Vegesack.
8,803 GRT, 468ft (142.6m) length, 58ft (17.7m) beam.
90 passengers.
Triple expansion SR engine, single screw, 12.5kts.
Date of disaster: 26 December 1940.

The *Baden*, which had two sister ships, the *Bayern* and *Wurttemburg*, operated on the service from Germany to South America. On 26 December 1940 she was intercepted by British warships in mid-Atlantic, west of Portugal, in the position 43°00'N–27°45'W. To avoid capture she was scuttled by her crew. After she had been abandoned and her crew picked up, the *Baden* was finished off by gunfire.

SARDEGNA ex-*SIERRA VENTANA* (1923–1940)

Lloyd Triestino, Italy; Bremer Vulkan, Vegesack.
11,452 GRT, 511ft (155.7m) LOA, 61ft (18.6m) beam.
1,113 passengers in three classes (as a German ship).
Triple expansion SR engines, twin screw, 14kts.
Date of disaster: 29 December 1940.

The former Hamburg-Sud Amerika liner *Sierra Ventana* passed to the Italia Line in 1935. Renamed *Sardegna*, she made commercial voyages to South America as well as trooping voyages to Tripoli. In 1937 she was sold to Lloyd Triestino without a further change of name. On 29 December 1940, while carrying troops from Bari to Valona (Vlore), Albania, she was torpedoed by the Greek submarine *Proteus*, and sank off the Albanian coast in the position 40°31'N–19°02'E. The survivors were picked up by escorting vessels, one of which – the torpedo boat *Antares* – rammed and sank the submarine.

Chapter Eight

1941

CONVOY CASUALTIES AS THE WAR WIDENS

For all the waste of men and materials in the First World War, a number of vital lessons had been learned from the experience, and these were applied to good effect from virtually day one of the new global conflict. An Allied naval blockade of the Western Approaches, the North Sea, and the entrance to the Baltic had, of course, been instituted immediately after the outbreak of hostilities. Similarly, the convoy system was adopted straight away for all troop-carrying and supply shipping movements, although it took a little while to get it organized and fully operative. Convoy movements became a notable feature of the naval war from 1941 and, consequently, so did casualties to passenger ships attacked while performing escort duties, some 56 large and fast merchant passenger vessels having been taken over for such duties.

During the year, convoys to Malta commenced in a bid to relieve the besieged island fortress; so too did Arctic convoys to Murmansk and Archangel in support of the Soviet Union, which had joined the Allied cause from June 1941, after Adolf Hitler had launched his offensive against Russia, Operation Barbarossa. As the campaign in North Africa intensified, troop convoys were also required to ferry fighting men to this theatre. Those of Axis origin crossed the Mediterranean, while some Allied convoys made their way to the Middle East round the Cape. These varied movements all exposed vessels to attack and destruction by aircraft, surface raiders, mines and, of course, submarines. Suffice to say that, as was the case for almost the entire war, torpedo attacks accounted for the majority of ships sunk during this 12-month period.

A hint of relief for Great Britain came in August 1941, when the Atlantic Charter was signed with the United States, and just four months later America became an ally following the Japanese attack on Pearl Harbor. Now the war had extended to truly global proportions, to embrace the vast expanse of the Pacific Ocean.

The Oropesa. (A. Duncan)

OROPESA (1920–1941)

Pacific Steam Navigation Co, Great Britain; Cammell Laird, Birkenhead.
14,075 GRT, 552ft (168.2m) LOA, 66ft (20.1m) beam.
632 passengers in three classes.
Steam turbines, twin screw, 14kts.
Date of disaster: 16 January 1941.

The *Oropesa* was built for the service from Liverpool to Valparaiso but she also spent long periods under charter to the Royal Mail Line on the route from Hamburg to New York, and for six years she was laid up at Dartmouth. During the Second World War she served as a troopship until she was sunk on 16 January 1941, when the German submarine *U96* hit her with three torpedoes 100 miles north-west of the Bloody Foreland, County Donegal. She was heading for the United Kingdom from Mombasa with 39 passengers and a crew of 210. She sank in the position 56°30′N–11°40′W, taking 113 of those on board with her, including her commander, Capt H.E.H. Croft.

ALMEDA STAR ex-*ALMEDA* (1926–1941)

Blue Star Line, Great Britain; Cammell Laird, Birkenhead.
14,935 GRT, 597ft (182.0m) LOA, 68ft (20.7m) beam.
150 passengers in single class.
Steam turbines, twin screw, 16kts.
Date of disaster: 17 January 1941.

The Almeda Star *ashore on 27 May 1937, two miles north of Boulogne.* (Tom Rayner)

Along with her consorts, the *Almeda Star*, the lead ship of her class, was lengthened and increased in size during 1935, after eight years of service. She operated on the route from London to the La Plata ports, South America, until the beginning of the Second World War. On 17 January 1941, during an unescorted wartime voyage from Liverpool to the River Plate, she was torpedoed by the German submarine *U96* when 350 miles west of the Hebrides. She sank in the position 58°40′N–13°38′W, about 35 miles north of Rockall. The weather was very bad at the time, and the sea extremely rough. In these conditions, the crippled ship was probably completely overwhelmed, sinking to a depth of over 1,200ft. There were no survivors from the 194 passengers, 137 crewmen, and 29 gunners she was carrying. Her master, Capt H.C. Howard, was the Commodore of the Blue Star fleet.

LIGURIA ex-*MELITA* (1918–1941)

Lloyd Triestino, Italy; Harland & Wolff, Belfast.
15,183 GRT, 546ft (166.4m) LOA, 67ft (20.4m) beam.
1,750 passengers in two classes (as a British ship).
Triple expansion SR engines with LP turbine, triple screw, 16kts.
Date of disaster: 22 January 1941.

The Canadian Pacific liners *Melita* and *Minnedosa* were sold for breaking up in Italy in April 1935 but were immediately resold to the Italian Government for service as troopships. They were managed by Italia Line at first, but came under Lloyd Triestino control from 1937. The *Liguria* was hit and seriously damaged by an aerial torpedo while at Tobruk on 6 July 1940. Laid up, she was hit by a bomb during a later air raid on 22 January 1941, and burnt out and capsized. British salvage teams raised the ship in 1950 and she was towed to Savona for scrapping, arriving there on 31 August 1950.

WAHEHE as *EMPIRE CITIZEN* (1922–1941)

Woermann Line, Germany; Reiherstieg Schiffswerke, Hamburg.
4,709 GRT, 361ft (110.0m) length, 50ft (15.2m) beam.
250 passengers.
Quadruple expansion SR engine, single screw, 11kts.
Date of disaster: 2 February 1941.

The German steamship *Wahehe* was operated by the Woermann Line between Germany and Africa with a sister ship, the *Wadai*. In spite of attempts to scuttle her, the *Wahehe* was captured by British warships off Vigo on 21 February 1940 and taken over for war transportation duties. Renamed *Empire Citizen*, she was sunk by a German submarine in the North Atlantic on 2 February 1941, in the

The German Wahehe *was taken over for British war service as the* Empire Citizen *after her capture in 1940.* (World Ship Society)

position 58°12'N–23°22'W, when en route to Rangoon from Liverpool. She was carrying 12 passengers in addition to her crew of 71. Every passenger and all but five members of the crew were lost, including the ship's master, Capt Hughes.

ANCHISES (1911–1941)

Blue Funnel Line, Great Britain; Workman Clark, Belfast.
10,046 GRT, 509ft (155.1m) LOA, 60ft (18.3m) beam.
288 passengers in single class.
Triple expansion SR engines, twin screw, 13.5kts.
Date of disaster: 28 February 1941.

The *Anchises* was a sister ship to the *Aeneas* and *Ascanius*. Apart from war service in both the First and Second World Wars, she spent her entire career on the Glasgow to Brisbane run. She was sunk on 28 February 1940 after repeated bomb attacks by German aircraft off the coast of Ireland, in the position 55°14'N–13°17'W. The attacks had commenced on 27 February as the *Anchises* was nearing the end of a voyage to Liverpool from Hong Kong carrying 39 passengers and a crew of 146. She went down 140 miles west of the Bloody Foreland, County Donegal, taking 16 people with her – Capt D.W. James, her commander, three passengers, and 12 crewmen.

PO ex-*VIENNA* ex-*WIEN* (1911–1941)

Lloyd Triestino, Italy; Lloyd Austriaco, Trieste.
7,367 GRT, 454ft (138.4m) LOA, 53ft (16.2m) beam.
Quadruple expansion SR engines, twin screw, 18kts.
Date of disaster: 15 March 1941.

The Italian steamship *Po* was formerly the Lloyd Austriaco company's *Wien*, forfeited after the First World War, when Austria lost her Adriatic coastal boundary. Lloyd Triestino renamed her first *Vienna* and later, from 1937, the *Po*. She sailed in the Far East service, via Suez. She was sunk by British aircraft off Valona on 14–15 March 1941 while serving as a hospital ship, going down about a mile offshore in 16 fathoms of water.

BREMEN (1929–1941)

Norddeutscher Lloyd, Germany; Deschimag AG Weser, Bremen.
51,656 GRT, 938ft (285.9m) LOA, 101ft (30.8m) beam.
2,000 passengers in four classes.
Steam turbines, quadruple screw, 28.5kts.
Date of disaster: 16 March 1941.

The *Bremen* was the famous Atlantic record-breaker which had wrested the Blue Riband from Cunard's *Mauretania* on her maiden voyage in May 1929. Following the outbreak of the Second World War she was taken over by the German Navy for conversion to a troopship for Operation Sealion, the planned invasion of Great Britain. On the cancellation of this operation she was laid up at Bremerhaven. It was during the period of enforced idleness which followed that, on 16 March 1941, the great liner was apparently deliberately set alight by one of her crew and completely destroyed. It was claimed that this action had been precipitated by a reprimand over a relatively trivial matter, but some reports state that the fire was an act of anti-Nazi sabotage. Whatever the cause, no lives were lost in the disaster, and the wrecked remains of the *Bremen* were broken up locally.

The loss of the *Bremen* has been included because it resulted in part from her circumstances having been created by the general state of hostilities; also because, if sabotage was the cause of her loss, this constituted a deliberate act of political opposition to the Third Reich.

BRITANNIA (1926–1941)

Anchor Line, Great Britain; Alexander Stephen, Glasgow.
6,525 GRT, 465ft (141.7m) length, 59ft (18.0m) beam.
300 passengers.
Quadruple expansion SR engine, single screw, 13kts.
Date of disaster: 25 March 1941.

The *Britannia* operated between the United Kingdom and India. During a voyage from Glasgow and Liverpool to Cape Town and Bombay on 25 March 1941, after conversion to an

Below *Lloyd Triestino's steamship* Po. (World Ship Society)

Bottom *Norddeutscher Lloyd's record-breaking* Bremen. (Hapag-Lloyd)

The Britannia *was sunk by the raider* Thor. (World Ship Society)

armed troopship (single gun), she was intercepted by the German commerce raider *Thor*, south-west of Freetown, in the position 07°24'N–24°03'W. The two vessels opened fire on each other, but after an hour the hopelessly outgunned *Britannia* was forced to concede. After her boats had been lowered so that the 281 passengers and 203 crew-members could make good their escape, the *Thor* continued to fire on her until she sank. No assistance was given to the survivors and when, later, it was possible to complete a head-count, 127 passengers and 122 crew were found to be missing and were never subsequently accounted for. One boat with 63 of the survivors was picked up by a Spanish ship, the *Bachi*. Another, containing 38 survivors, reached the coast of Brazil on 17 April 1941.

Earlier the *Thor* had come up against two other British liners and on both occasions managed to escape. The first encounter, on 28 July 1940, was with the 14-year-old *Alcantara*, a 22,209 GRT Royal Mail liner serving as an armed merchant cruiser. In an hour-long battle both ships received extensive damage but the *Thor* was luckily able to reduce the *Alcantara*'s speed with one hit and used the opportunity to escape into the mist. Her master, Capt O. Kahler, was anxious to avoid a major confrontation at this time since he had only left Kiel early the previous month. As for the *Alcantara*, she was compelled to enter Rio de Janeiro to obtain repairs. On 5 December the same year the *Thor* was engaged by the Union Castle liner *Carnarvon Castle*, also serving in an auxiliary cruiser role, 700 miles north-east of Montevideo, in the position 31°00'S–43°15'W. This action also lasted about an hour, at the end of which time the British vessel had received the greater punishment. Six of her complement were dead and urgent repairs had to be carried out in Montevideo. The *Thor* escaped to fight another day. Four months later she sank the armed merchant cruiser *Voltaire*, and during her short but dramatic career she destroyed a total of 150,000 tons of Allied shipping. She herself was sunk in Yokohama on 30 November 1942, when the tanker *Uckermark*, lying alongside her, exploded.

NORTHERN PRINCE (1929–1941)

Furness Withy, Great Britain; Lithgows, Port Glasgow.
10,917 GRT, 516ft (157.3m) LOA, 64ft (19.5m) beam.
101 passengers in single class.
Diesel engines, twin screw, 16kts.
Date of disaster: 3 April 1941.

The four 'compass-point' *Prince* liners sailed between New York and the River Plate carrying cargo and just over 100 first-class passengers each. In 1941 the *Northern Prince* left Liverpool in convoy bound for Piraeus via Cape Town and Port Said. On 3 April she was nearing the end of this long voyage, passing through the Antikithera Channel, Greece, when she was bombed and sunk by German aircraft, going down in the position 35°34'N–23°23'E. Fortunately, there was no loss of life among the 110-strong crew.

VOLTAIRE (1923–1941)

Lamport & Holt Co, Great Britain; Workman Clark, Belfast.
13,248 GRT, 535ft (163.1m) LOA, 64ft (19.5m) beam.
680 passengers in three classes.
Quadruple expansion SR engines, twin screw, 14.5kts.
Date of disaster: 4 April 1941.

Like her earlier namesake, sunk by the German raider *Möwe* in the Atlantic on 2 December 1916, the replacement *Voltaire*, which entered service in August 1923, also fell victim to a German auxiliary cruiser. On 4 April 1941, while serving as an armed merchant cruiser bound from Trinidad to Freetown, she encountered the raider *Thor* some 700 miles west-south-west of the Cape Verde Islands. She engaged the *Thor* but with her lighter, less powerful armament she was outmatched. After an hour of intense action the *Voltaire* was unmanoeuvrable and ablaze, and

Fleetmate of the Vestris, *the* Voltaire *was another victim of the German commerce raider* Thor. (Author's collection)

half an hour later she sank in the position 14°30′N–40°30′W, the action having claimed the lives of 13 of her officers and 62 ratings. Her master, Capt J.A.P. Blackburn, 21 other officers, and 173 ratings were picked up by the *Thor* and imprisoned for the duration. It was believed initially that the death-toll was higher, 266 casualties being reported, while her adversary was mistakenly identified as the *Santa Cruz*.

COMORIN (1925–1941)

P&O Line, Great Britain; Barclay Curle, Glasgow.
15,132 GRT, 545ft (166.1m) LOA, 70ft (21.3m) beam.
306 passengers in two classes.
Quadruple expansion SR engines, twin screw, 16kts.
Date of disaster: 6 April 1941.

In the mid-1920s, P&O built three new intermediate liners for the London to Sydney service, the *Cathay*, *Chitral*, and *Comorin*. While serving as an auxiliary cruiser during the Second World War, the *Comorin* caught fire and sank in mid-Atlantic on 6 April 1941. Assistance to the crew-members abandoning ship was rendered by the British destroyers HMS *Brooke* and *Lincoln*, the *Lincoln* drifting floats and rafts towards the blazing ship to aid in the

P&O's Comorin, *lost after she was engulfed in a mid-ocean fire.* (A. Duncan)

evacuation. Even so, 20 lives were lost. The following day, the derelict hulk of the *Comorin* was torpedoed and sunk by the *Brooke.*

NAZARIO SAURO (1921–1941)

Lloyd Triestino, Italy; Ansaldo, Genoa.
8,150 GRT, 447ft (136.2m) length, 52ft (15.9m) beam.
Steam turbines, twin screw, 14kts.
Date of disaster: 6 April 1941.

The liners *Ammiraglio Bettolo* and *Nazario Sauro* were introduced to the Italy to South America service by the Transatlantica Italiana Company, their original owners. Later they passed into the Lloyd Triestino fleet. The *Nazario Sauro* was at Massowah (Massawa), Eritrea, when it fell to British forces in April 1941, and on 6 April, five days after British Army units took Asmara, the colony's capital, the crew of the *Nazario Sauro* scuttled their ship to prevent her from falling into British hands. The wreck was condemned in the London prize court on 8 November 1949.

COLOMBO ex-*SAN GENNARO* (1917–1941)

Lloyd Triestino, Italy; Palmers, Newcastle.
12,003 GRT, 536ft (163.4m) LOA, 64ft (19.5m) beam.
2,800 in three classes.
Quadruple expansion SR engines, twin screw, 17kts.
Date of disaster: 8 April 1941.

Originally a cargo ship operated by the Transoceanica Company, a subsidiary of Navigazione Generale Italiana, the *San Gennaro* was reconstructed as the passenger liner *Colombo* in August 1921. Thereafter she sailed in the Naples to New York or Genoa to Valparaiso services until transferred to Italia Line in 1932. A further move in 1937 took her to Lloyd Triestino for the Genoa to Massowah and Djibouti service. On 8 April 1941, the *Colombo* was docked in the port of Massowah, Eritrea, when it fell to British forces. To prevent the ship from being captured, her crew deliberately sank her by detonating explosive charges. The wreck was raised by the British after the war and in 1951 it was broken up for scrap.

SANNIO ex-*GENERAL MITRE* ex-*ARTUS* (1921–1941)

Lloyd Triestino, Italy; Bremer Vulkan, Vegesack.
9,834 GRT, 485ft (147.8m) LOA, 58ft (17.7m) beam.
Triple expansion SR engines with LP turbine, single screw.
Date of disaster: 10 April 1941.

The former Hamburg Amerika Line steamer *General Mitre* was sold to Lloyd Triestino in 1935 after brief spells with the Hugo Stinnes Line and AG für Seeschiffe. Lloyd Triestino operated the renamed *Sannio* in the service to East Africa. She was scuttled at Massowah on 10 April 1941 to avoid capture by the British after the fall of Eritrea.

The Italian passenger vessel Colombo *was scuttled to avoid seizure by the British.* (World Ship Society)

RAJPUTANA (1925–1941)

P&O Line, Great Britain; Harland & Wolff, Belfast.
16,644 GRT, 568ft (173.1m) LOA, 71ft (21.6m) beam.
595 passengers in two classes.
Quadruple expansion SR engines, twin screw, 17kts.
Date of disaster: 13 April 1941.

With her sister ships *Ranchi* and the celebrated *Rawalpindi*, the *Rajputana* maintained the service from London to Bombay between the wars. In September 1939 she was taken over, like the *Rawalpindi*, for duties as an armed merchant cruiser, and her second funnel was removed as part of the conversion. In this role, escorting Atlantic convoys, the *Rajputana* was torpedoed and sunk by the German submarine *U108* on 13 April 1941. The attack took place west of Ireland, in the position 64°50′N–27°25′W. She was struck twice over a period of two hours but remained afloat long enough to enable most of those aboard to be evacuated. Rescue ships were swiftly guided to the scene of the disaster by Allied patrol aircraft. Nevertheless, six officers and 35 ratings lost their lives. The *Rajputana*'s master, Capt F.H. Taylor, was among those rescued.

ZAMZAM ex-*BRITISH EXHIBITOR* ex-*LEICESTERSHIRE* (1909–1941)

Soc. Misr. de Navigation Maritime, Egypt; Harland & Wolff, Belfast.
8,299 GRT, 467ft (142.3m) length, 54ft (16.5m) beam.
Quadruple expansion SR engines, twin screw, 14kts.
Date of disaster: 17 April 1941.

The Egyptian liner *Zamzam*, formerly the Bibby Line's

Top *The armed merchant cruiser* Rajputana, *one of the sister ships of the* Rawalpindi. *Like the* Rawalpindi, *her funnels were reduced from two to one for naval service.* (P&O Group)

Above *The* Rajputana *sinking, a picture which conveys all the horrors of a ship going down in mid-ocean after a submarine attack. Men struggle in the water to reach the rescue vessel in the foreground.* (Associated Press)

Leicestershire, was shelled and sunk by a German submarine on 17 April 1941 while bound from Pernambuco and New York to Table Bay and Suez. She went down in the position 27°41′S–08°08′W, her 120 crew and 200 passengers being picked up by the German ship *Dresden* and later landed at St Jean de Luz, France, near the Spanish border.

PENNLAND ex-*PITTSBURGH* (1922–1941)

Holland Amerika Line, Netherlands; Harland & Wolff, Belfast.
16,322 GRT, 601ft (183.2m) LOA, 67ft (20.4m) beam.
538 passengers in single class.
Triple expansion SR engines with LP turbine, triple screw, 16kts.
Date of disaster: 25 April 1941.

The Dominion Line's *Pittsburgh* and *Regina*, constructed for the transatlantic service from Liverpool, were separated for four years from 1925, but were later reunited under the Red Star Line houseflag, when they were renamed *Pennland* and *Westernland*. They retained these names when they passed to Holland Amerika Line ownership in June 1939. The *Pennland* became a troopship in 1940 under the control of the British Ministry of War Transport. She was bombed and sunk by German aircraft on 25 April 1941 while bound from Alexandria to Athens to evacuate British and Australian soldiers, many of whom she had only recently conveyed to the Balkans in her previous two trips. She was hit by no less than eight bombs with many more near misses, and sank shortly after. The survivors from her 251 crew and 100 troops were picked up by HMS *Griffin* and landed at Crete the next day. Four men lost their lives in the attack, all engine-room staff killed when a bomb penetrated the engine compartments and exploded. There seems to be some uncertainty as to precisely where the *Pennland* went down. Some accounts say she was bombed in the Gulf of Athens, others off Suda Bay, Crete. Lloyds records state that she was sunk off Bela Pouli, near the San Giorgio Islands.

The Holland Amerika Line's Pennland, *which sank off Crete after being attacked by German aircraft.* (L.L. von Münching)

COSTA RICA ex-*PRINSES JULIANA* (1910–1941)

Royal Netherlands SS Co, Netherlands; Nederlandsche Schps Maatschappij, Amsterdam.
8,672 GRT, 455ft (138.7m) length, 55ft (16.8m) beam.
Quadruple expansion SR engines, twin screw, 22kts.
Date of disaster: 27 April 1941.

Formerly a cargo vessel, the *Costa Rica* operated between the Netherlands and Dutch Guiana (Surinam). On 27 April 1941, while bound for the southern shores of the Mediterranean from Kalamata, Greece, she was sunk in an air-attack in the position 35°54′N–23°49′E. She was transporting troops at the time, but luckily her entire complement, including the 178-strong crew, was saved.

SLAMAT (1924–1941)

Rotterdam Lloyd, Netherlands; Kon Maatschappij de Schelde, Vlissingen.
11,636 GRT, 530ft (161.5m) LOA, 62ft (18.9m) beam.
420 passengers in three classes.
Steam turbines, twin screw, 15kts.
Date of disaster: 27 April 1941.

The Dutch liner *Slamat* was normally engaged on the service from Rotterdam to Batavia (Djakarta). In 1940, after the Netherlands had fallen to German forces, she came under British control and was converted into a troopship. During the evacuation of British troops from Greece, on 27 April 1941, the *Slamat* was bombed by German aircraft and sank in the Gulf of Nauplia, Peloponnesus, in the position 37°01′N–23°10′E. On board were a large number of troops that had been embarked at Crete the previous day, making a total complement of some 900 men with the crew, of whom 193 were drowned when the *Slamat* went down. The survivors were picked up by the British destroyers HMS *Wryneck* and *Diamond*, but in continuing air attacks these two warships were also sunk by dive-bombers, with the result that another 650 of the *Slamat*'s survivors lost their lives. When the casualties of the *Wryneck* and *Diamond* are added to the list, the total number killed in the three disasters amounted to 1,096, including the masters of all three ships.

CITY OF NAGPUR (1922–1941)

Ellerman Lines, Great Britain; Workman Clark, Belfast.
10,146 GRT, 490ft (149.3m) LOA, 59ft (18.0m) beam.
318 passengers in two classes.
Quadruple expansion SR engine, single screw, 14kts.
Date of disaster: 29 April 1941.

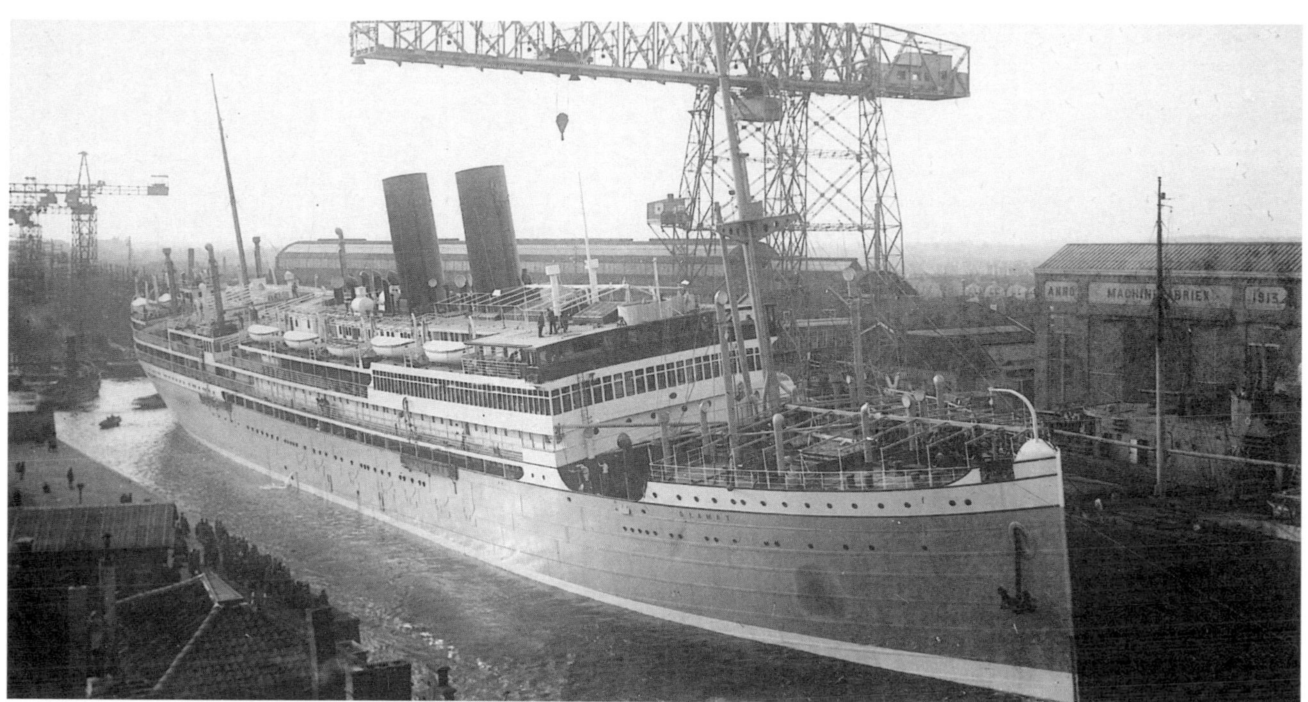

Top *Rotterdam Lloyd's* Slamat, *seen in her builder's yard at Vlissingen on 2 April 1924.* (Royal Schelde Group)

Above *The Ellerman Lines vessel* City of Nagpur. (A. Duncan)

The *City of Nagpur* spent the first 12 years of her life on the route from Glasgow to Bombay. From that time onwards she reverted to the London to Africa service, with a season of cruises each summer. At the outset of the Second World War she was taken over for military duties and in this capacity was torpedoed and sunk by the German submarine *U75* on 29 April 1941, about 700 miles west of Fastnet, in the position 52°30'N–26°00'W. She had been bound from

Glasgow to Freetown, Natal, Bombay, and Karachi with 274 service passengers and a crew of 204. Fortunately the majority of this large complement was saved, the casualties amounting to 16.

NERISSA (1926–1941)

Furness Bermuda Line, Great Britain; W. Hamilton, Glasgow.
5,583 GRT, 349ft (106.4m) length, 54ft (16.5m) beam.
162+ passengers in two classes.
Triple expansion SR engine, single screw, 14kts.
Date of disaster: 30 April 1941.

On 30 April 1941, during a voyage to Liverpool from Halifax, Nova Scotia, and St John's, Newfoundland, the steamship *Nerissa* was attacked by a German submarine about 200 miles west of Inishtrahull. She sank in the position 55°57′N–10°08′W with 175 passengers and a crew of 112 on board, of whom 124 passengers and 83 crew-members lost their lives. The *Nerissa*'s peacetime employment had been on the route from New York to Bermuda and the West Indies.

EUROPA (1931–1941)

East Asiatic Co, Denmark; Burmeister & Wain, Copenhagen.
10,224 GRT, 484ft (147.5m) LOA, 62ft (18.9m) beam.
64 passengers in single class.
Diesel engine, single screw, 15kts.
Date of disaster: 3 May 1941.

The motorship *Europa* was built for the East Asiatic Company's service from Copenhagen to Portland, Oregon, and Vancouver in partnership with the *Canada* and *Amerika*. Following the German occupation of Denmark, she undertook war duties in support of the Allies under the management of Canadian National Steamships, Montreal. On 3 May 1941, the *Europa* was berthed at Liverpool when a German air raid took place. She was bombed and extensively damaged in the air attack and burnt out, being later beached as a constructive total loss. All of her crew of 45 were saved. After the war, she was broken up at New Ferry on the River Mersey.

IXION (1912–1941)

Blue Funnel Line, Great Britain; Scott's, Greenock.
10,221 GRT, 518ft (157.9m) LOA, 60ft (18.3m) beam.
600 passengers in single class.
Triple expansion SR engines, twin screw, 13.5kts.
Date of disaster: 8 May 1941.

The *Ixion* and six sisters joined the Blue Funnel Line services from Glasgow and Liverpool to Brisbane and the Far East between 1910 and 1913, some of them offering a limited accommodation for first-class passengers. The *Ixion* carried 600 emigrants in steerage class. Having survived the

Furness Bermuda West Indies Line's small Nerissa *operated the routes to the Caribbean from New York.* (World Ship Society)

The Danish motorship Europa. (East Asiatic Company)

First World War, she was lost on 8 May 1941, the day after the German submarine *U94* torpedoed her 200 miles south of Reykjavik, in the position 61°29′N–22°40′W. The *Ixion* had been bound from Glasgow to New York at the time of the sinking. There were no casualties among her crew of 105.

SHROPSHIRE as HMS *SALOPIAN* (1926–1941)

Bibby Line, Great Britain; Fairfield, Glasgow.
10,549 GRT, 502ft (153.0m) LOA, 60ft (18.3m) beam.
275 passengers in single class.
Diesel engines, twin screw, 15.5kts.
Date of disaster: 13 May 1941.

The 'County' class of Bibby Line consisted of the *Shropshire*, *Cheshire*, *Staffordshire*, and *Worcestershire*, employed on the service from Liverpool to Rangoon. On the outbreak of the Second World War, the *Shropshire* was taken over by the Admiralty and commissioned as an armed merchant cruiser, being renamed *Salopian* because there was another Royal Navy ship already named *Shropshire*. The *Salopian* was torpedoed and sunk 400 miles south-east of Cape Farewell, Greenland, in the position 56°43′N–38°57′W, on 13 May

The Bibby Line's Shropshire *was renamed* Salopian *for naval service.* (World Ship Society)

1941. She was apparently hit twice after three other torpedoes had already missed her. The *Salopian* remained afloat for two hours and 278 survivors were picked up. Her former sisters, *Cheshire* and *Worcestershire*, both survived torpedo attacks.

CONTE ROSSO (1922–1941)

Lloyd Triestino, Italy; William Beardmore, Glasgow.
17,856 GRT, 591ft (180.1m) LOA, 74ft (22.6m) beam.
2,276 passengers in three classes.
Steam turbines, twin screw, 18.5kts.
Date of disaster: 24 May 1941.

In her 17 years as a commercial passenger liner, the *Conte Rosso* served three companies on three different routes. Between the years 1922 and 1932 she operated between Genoa and New York or Buenos Aires for Lloyd Sabaudo. She then joined the new Italia Line fleet on the reorganization of the Italian merchant marine, switching to the Trieste to Shanghai service. Later the same year she transferred to Lloyd Triestino working as a troopship, mainly transporting soldiers between Italy and North Africa. On 24 May 1941 she was torpedoed and sunk by the British submarine HMS *Upholder*, under the command of Lt-Cdr M.D. Wanklyn, about 15 miles east of Syracuse in the position 36°57′N–15°34′E. The *Conte Rosso* was bound for Tripoli in convoy, carrying 2,500 troops, over 800 losing their lives in the sinking. The *Upholder* later sank the Italia Line sister ships *Neptunia* and *Oceania*. Lt-Cdr Wanklyn was lost with the submarine HMS *Upholder* on 14 April 1942. He was awarded the Victoria Cross for sinking the *Conte Rosso* on 24 May 1941.

ADDA (1922–1941)

Elder Dempster Line, Great Britain; Harland & Wolff, Greenock.
7,816 GRT, 435ft (132.6m) length, 57ft (17.4m) beam.
Diesel engines, twin screw, 14kts.
Date of disaster: 8 June 1941.

The *Adda* was introduced to the England to West Africa service shortly after the First World War as part of her owner's programme for replacing fleet losses. She met her end in the Second World War when she was torpedoed and sunk by a submarine on 8 June 1941 about 80 miles west of Freetown, during a voyage from Liverpool to Freetown, Takoradi, Accra, and Lagos. She was carrying 154 crew, of whom eight were killed, and 260 passengers, two of these also losing their lives. The attack took place in the position 08°30′N–14°39′W.

The Italia Line steamer Conte Rosso, *one of three troopships torpedoed and sunk by the submarine* Upholder *under the command of Lt-Cdr M.D. Wanklyn, who was awarded the Victoria Cross.* (World Ship Society)

VIGRID (1923–1941)

Gdynia America Line, Poland; Deutsche Werft, Hamburg.
4,765 GRT, 400ft (121.9m) length, 54ft (16.5m) beam.
Diesel engines, twin screw.
Date of disaster: 24 June 1941.

The Gdynia America Line chartered the Norwegian motorship *Vigrid* for service on the route from Poland to the West Indies and Central America. She was still in their employ when the Second World War started and was consequently drafted into the service of the Allied cause. During a voyage from New Orleans to Belfast and Manchester, on 24 June 1941, she was torpedoed and sunk 400 miles south-east of Cape Farewell, in the position 54°30′N–41°30′W. Aboard her were 10 passengers and 37 crew, of whom 26 lost their lives.

Holland Amerika Line's Maasdam. (L.L. von Münching)

MAASDAM (1921–1941)

Holland Amerika Line, Netherlands; Maatschappij Fijenoord, Rotterdam.
8,812 GRT, 450ft (137.2m) length, 58ft (17.7m) beam.
90 passengers in two classes.
Steam turbine, single screw, 13kts.
Date of disaster: 26 June 1941.

The Dutch steamship *Maasdam* was one of a class of four ships, the others being the *Edam*, *Leerdam*, and *Spaarndam*. She was principally employed on the route from Rotterdam to Cuba and Mexico but also made occasional voyages to New York and Baltimore. On 26 June 1941 she was torpedoed and sunk by a German submarine with the loss of two lives, both American Red Cross nurses. The attack took place on the North Atlantic, in the position 60°00′N–30°35′W, while the *Maasdam* was bound in convoy from New York and Halifax, Nova Scotia, to Liverpool, under the command of Capt Jan Boshoff. She sank rapidly, her condition worsened by the blast of an exploding ammunition ship on her port side, the *Malaya*, which had been hit in the same attack. The steamer *Ronda* and the Norwegian tanker *Havprins* between them picked up the survivors, 34 of whom were landed at Reykjavik, Iceland, and 44 at Avonmouth. Third Engineer Eugene Plouvier was awarded the Bronze Medal for Lifesaving by Queen Wilhelmina in recognition of his attempts to save one of the nurses, who ultimately succumbed to exhaustion. Before he could receive the medal, Plouvier was himself killed when the *Zaandam* was sunk in November 1942.

ANSELM (1935–1941)

Booth Line, Great Britain; William Denny, Dumbarton.
5,954 GRT, 412ft (125.6m) length, 55ft (16.7m) beam.
Steam turbine, single screw, 14kts.
Date of disaster: 5 July 1941.

The Booth Line operated a cargo and passenger service to South America from Liverpool, the *Anselm* participating in this trade until the beginning of the Second World War, when she was taken over for service as an auxiliary transport. She was lost on 5 July 1941 when a German submarine torpedoed and sank her during a convoy trooping voyage from Gourock to Freetown. The attack took place in a position variously given as 44°25′N–28°35′W or 44°20′N–28°20′W, about 300 miles north of the Azores, when the *Anselm* was carrying 98 crew and 1,210 troops. Of these, four crewmen and around 250 soldiers were killed.

LADY SOMERS (1929–1941)

Canadian National Line, Canada; Cammell Laird, Birkenhead.
8,194 GRT, 420ft (128.0m) length, 59ft (18.0m) beam.
Steam turbines, twin screw, 14kts.
Date of disaster: 15 July 1941.

The five vessels of the *Lady* class were the *Lady Drake*, *Lady Hawkins*, *Lady Rodney*, *Lady Somers*, and the *Lady*

The Booth liner Anselm *was sunk by torpedo.* (National Maritime Museum, London)

Nelson. The *Lady Somers* was another torpedo victim, being attacked by a German submarine in the Atlantic on 15 July 1941, in the position 37°12′N–20°32′W, while she was serving as an auxiliary cruiser under Cdr G.L. Dunbar. Of her total complement, 138 were taken to neutral Spanish ports while it was believed, at the time, that the remaining 37 men had perished. However, they were later reported to be safe, so no lives were lost in the sinking. Information on the loss of the *Lady Somers* was classified as confidential for some time. The effect of this was to lead to erroneous reports on the circumstances of the ship's sinking, and it was mistakenly believed that she went down in the Caribbean, six days after the actual date, with the loss of 250 passengers.

CALIFORNIA ex-*ALBANIA* (1920–1941)

Lloyd Triestino, Italy; Scott's, Greenock.
13,060 GRT, 539ft (164.3m) LOA, 64ft (19.5m) beam.
150 passengers in two classes.
Steam turbines, twin screw, 15.5kts.
Date of disaster: 11 August 1941.

Completion of the Cunard Line's *Albania*, the fourth ship of the pre-First World War 'A' class, was delayed by hostilities until 1920, when she emerged in a somewhat different configuration to that of her intended partners. Because she did not fit into a balanced schedule she was laid up in 1925. Navigazione Libera Triestina of Italy bought her in January 1930 and placed her in their service to Seattle under the name *California*. Five years later she became a hospital ship and two years later still, on the reorganization of the Italian merchant marine, she passed to Lloyd Triestino. British torpedo-bombers sank her at Syracuse, Sicily, on 11 August 1941. She was still in a sunken state in January 1949 but was subsequently raised and scrapped.

The Hamburg Sud-Amerika Line vessel Bahia Laura, *settling in the water after the attack on her convoy which also sank the smaller* Donau. (W.Z. Bilddienst)

ESPERIA (1921–1941)

Adriatica Line, Italy; Soc. Ersercicio Bacini, Riva Trigoso.
11,398 GRT, 528ft (160.9m) LOA, 62ft (18.9m) beam.
479 passengers in four classes.
Steam turbines, twin screw, 18kts.
Date of disaster: 20 August 1941.

The *Esperia* and a sister ship, the *Ausonia*, were ordered by Soc. Italiano di Servizi Maritime before the First World War, the latter from a German shipyard. The effects of the war, high inflation, and shortages of materials combined to delay the construction of the two ships and the *Ausonia* was finally broken up incomplete. The *Esperia* entered the Genoa to Alexandria service, with the return leg to Venice, and remained so engaged until the Second World War, even though she transferred to Lloyd Triestino in 1932 and to Adriatica in 1937. She was then taken over as a troopship, carrying reinforcements to the Italian armies fighting in North Africa. On 20 August 1941 she was sailing in a convoy to Libya when she was torpedoed and sunk by the British submarine HMS *Unique* 11 miles north-west of Tripoli. Thirty one people were killed.

BAHIA LAURA (1918–1941)

Hamburg Sud-Amerika Line; Germany, Palmers, Newcastle.
8,561 GRT, 448ft (136.5m) length, 57ft (17.4m) beam.
Quadruple expansion SR engines.
Date of disaster: 30 August 1941.

The *Bahia Laura* has only a marginal qualification for inclusion in this book in terms of her type and normal role, but it was considered that she merited an entry by virtue of the gravity of the disaster which befell her while ferrying troops. She was torpedoed and sunk by a British submarine west of Seloen Island, Norway, on 30 August 1941. The *Bahia Laura* was in a troop convoy at the time of the attack, another victim being the small steamship *Donau*, which had been in the service of the Flensburger Dampfer Co prior to the war. All of the convoy vessels were carrying full complements of troops and the *Bahia Laura* and *Donau* were no exceptions. Despite vigorous efforts to save those aboard the stricken troopships, some 1,700 German soldiers lost their lives.

NEPTUNIA (1932–1941)

Italia Line, Italy; Cantieri Riuniti Dell'Adriatico, Monfalcone.
19,475 GRT, 590ft (179.8m) LOA, 76ft (23.2m) beam.
1,532 passengers in three classes.
Diesel engines, twin screw, 19kts.
Date of disaster: 18 September 1941.

See next entry.

TOP *The Italia liner* Neptunia *was sunk on the same day as her sister ship* Oceania, *18 September 1941. The British submarine HMS* Upholder *was responsible.* (Italia Line)

ABOVE *The Italia liner* Oceania. *She and her sister* Neptunia *were among the most attractive of the pre-war motorships.* (Italia Line)

OCEANIA (1932–1941)

Italia Line, Italy; Cantieri Riuniti Dell'Adriatico, Monfalcone.
19,507 GRT, 589ft (179.5m) LOA, 76ft (23.2m) beam.
1,385 passengers in three classes.
Diesel engines, quadruple screw, 19kts.
Date of disaster: 18 September 1941.

The sister ships *Neptunia* and *Oceania* were ordered by and built for the Cosulich Line. In January 1937 they became Italia ships when Cosulich became the last unit to officially amalgamate with the Italia Flotta Riunite combine. The first three years of their careers were spent on the run from Trieste and Naples to Brazil, Uruguay, and Argentina, but from February 1935 they were switched to the service from Genoa to Bombay and Shanghai via Suez.

In 1940 the *Neptunia* and *Oceania* both became Italian Navy troop transports and, together to the end, they were both sunk on 18 September 1941 while sailing in convoy from Taranto to Tripoli along with the *Saturnia*, another Italia Line vessel, and protected by five Italian destroyers. About 60 miles from Tripoli, the convoy was attacked by British submarines, HMS *Upholder* achieving two hits on the

The Soviet passenger liner Dnyepr *was originally the Ybarra Line's* Cabo San Augustin, *seen here.* (Edward Wilson)

Neptunia, which foundered shortly afterwards. Later the same day the *Oceania* was hit by another of the *Upholder*'s torpedoes and was seriously disabled. She was taken in tow by two of the destroyers but later, after receiving two more hits, she too sank. Casualty figures from the sinkings vary considerably from source to source, with some reports

The French motorship Theophile Gautier, *seen here displaying neutrality markings, was sunk by a British submarine.* (World Ship Society)

claiming that 5,000 men were drowned out of the total of 7,000 soldiers and crewmen aboard the two ships. However, Italian records state that 384 lost their lives as a result of the attack. Earlier in 1941 the *Upholder* had also sunk the liner *Conte Rosso*. Her captain, Lt-Cdr M.D. Wanklyn, received the Victoria Cross, DSO and two bars for his exploits.

DNYEPR ex-*CABO SAN AGUSTIN* (1931–1941)

Sovtorgflot, USSR; Soc. Espanola de Construccion Naval, Bilbao.
12,589 GRT, 500ft (152.4m) LOA, 63ft (19.2m) beam.
512 passengers in two classes (as a Spanish ship).
Diesel engines, twin screw, 16kts.
Date of disaster: 3 October 1941.

Having survived the Spanish Civil War, in which she performed troop-carrying duties for the Republican forces, the *Cabo San Agustin*, sister liner to the *Cabo San Antonio*, was laid up at Feodosiya on the Black Sea, where she was seized by the Russians. Renamed *Dnyepr*, she was placed in Soviet passenger service based on Odessa. On 3 October 1941 she was torpedoed by a German aircraft off Anapa, south of the Straits of Kerch, while bound from Novorossiysk to Odessa to evacuate Russian troops trapped by the German army's push on Stalingrad (Volgograd). There is some dispute as to the precise date of the sinking. Lloyds' records contain no reference to the disaster.

THEOPHILE GAUTIER (1926–1941)

Messageries Maritimes, France; Chantiers et Ateliers de France, Dunkerque.
8,194 GRT, 445ft (135.6m) LOA, 56ft (17.1m) beam.
280 passengers.
Diesel engines, twin screw, 12.5kts.
Date of disaster: 4 October 1941.

The French passenger motorship *Theophile Gautier* remained under the control of the Vichy regime following the armistice agreed between France and Germany in 1940. She was therefore looked upon as an enemy vessel and a legitimate target when she was encountered in the Aegean Sea by a British submarine on 4 October 1941, and was torpedoed as she was passing Euboea Island. She sank soon after with the loss of 20 lives. At the time the *Theophile Gautier* had been returning to Marseilles from Thessaloniki.

MADRID ex-*SIERRA NEVADA* (1922–1941)

Norddeutscher Lloyd, Germany; Vulkan Werke, Stettin.
8,753 GRT, 439ft (133.8m) length, 56ft (17.1m) beam.
Triple expansion SR engines, twin screw, 13.5kts.
Date of disaster: 9 December 1941.

Built for Norddeutscher Lloyd's services to South America, the *Sierra Nevada* also made occasional crossings to New York from Bremerhaven. Renamed *Madrid* in 1925, she was bombed and sunk in a British air-raid on Ymuiden on 9 December 1941.

Nippon Yusen Kaisha's Katori Maru *was the victim of a Dutch submarine.* (Mitsubishi Heavy Industries)

KATORI MARU (1913–1941)

Nippon Yusen Kaisha, Japan; Mitsubishi, Nagasaki.
9,834 GRT, 520ft (158.5m) LOA, 59ft (18.0m) beam.
Triple expansion SR engines with LP turbine, triple screw, 15.5kts.
Date of disaster: 23 December 1941.

Sister ship to the *Kashima Maru*, the *Katori Maru* met a like fate, as did the three other ships of the same class. The *Katori Maru*'s end came on 23 December 1941, only days after war had been declared between Japan and the United States of America, making her Japan's first Second World War passenger ship loss after becoming a participant in the conflict. She was sunk by a Dutch submarine off Kuching, Sarawak, in the position 02°30′N–110°00′E.

RUTH ALEXANDER ex-*CALLAO* ex-*SIERRA CORDOBA* (1913–1941)

Dollar Line, USA; Vulkan Werke, Stettin.
8,226 GRT, 439ft (133.8m) length, 56ft (17.1m) beam.
Triple expansion SR engines, twin screw, 14kts.
Date of disaster: 31 December 1941.

The *Sierra Cordoba*, one of four vessels built for the Norddeutscher Lloyd service from Germany to South America, was interned in Peru in the First World War. The Peruvian Government seized her in 1917, renaming her *Callao*. Later she passed to the United States and was operated by Dollar Line as the *Ruth Alexander*, under which name she became the first American passenger ship to be lost in the Second World War. She was bombed and sunk by Japanese aircraft off the north-west coast of Borneo on 31 December 1941, during a voyage from Manila to Balik Papan. One member of her crew was killed.

Chapter Nine

1942

AMPHIBIOUS LANDINGS EVERYWHERE

In contrast to 1941, the year that followed was one of greater cheer for the Allied cause and, in retrospect, was probably the turning point of the war. To paraphrase a famous wartime quotation, it may not have been the beginning of the end but it was certainly the end of the beginning. The reverses suffered at Dunkerque, Pearl Harbor, and even the Coral Sea, now gave way to the successes of Midway, El Alamein, and Stalingrad. The Allies turned to the offensive, engaging Axis forces in all theatres of the war. At sea, this positive turn of events re-introduced passenger ships to an aspect of naval warfare that was now to be employed on a hitherto unimagined scale – amphibious landings.

In order to recover lands occupied by the Germans in Africa, the Mediterranean and Europe, and by the Japanese throughout the Pacific, it was necessary to land invasion forces from the sea. Passenger ships formed the back-bone of the troop transportation effort involved in such operations and, as a consequence, they were rendered acutely vulnerable to attack, especially at the point of disembarkation. The destruction of the *Sir Galahad* at Bluff Cove in the Falkland Islands some 40 years later merely underlines the acute peril in which exposed and temporarily immobile vessels have always been placed when landing troops.

The Lady Hawkins, *owned by Canadian National Line.* (Maritime Photo Library)

The amphibious assaults of the Second World War commenced during 1942 with landings on the Solomon Islands in August, and at Guadalcanal and in Tunisia that November. The latter campaign, known as Operation Torch, amplified the potentially costly down-side of such operations as far as passenger ship losses were concerned. From the assembly of the invasion force at the beginning of the month to the dispersal of the transportation fleet after the landings had been completed, 'Torch' was the greatest disaster to Allied passenger shipping of the whole war, a total of 17 vessels having been sunk during or in connection with the operation.

LADY HAWKINS (1929–1942)

Canadian National Line, Canada; Cammell Laird, Birkenhead.
7,988 GRT, 419ft (127.7m) length, 59ft (18.0m) beam.
Steam turbines, twin screw, 14kts.
Date of disaster: 19 January 1942.

The *Lady Hawkins*, one of the *Lady* class, was the victim of a torpedo attack on 19 January 1942 when bound from Halifax and Boston to Bermuda. She was attacked by a German submarine when 150 miles from Cape Hatteras, in the approximate position 35°00′N–72°30′W, two torpedoes striking her forward holds and engine-room. The *Lady Hawkins* was carrying 210 passengers and 112 crew, of whom only 71 were saved, these being in the single lifeboat recovered of the three known to have been launched. The survivors were picked up by the New York and Porto Rico Line ship *Coamo* and taken to San Juan.

GANDIA ex-*KONIGSTEIN* ex-*ARAWA* (1907–1942)

Cie. Maritime Belge, Belgium; Swan, Hunter & Wigham Richardson, Newcastle.
9,626 GRT, 459ft (139.9m) length, 59ft (18.0m) beam.
Triple expansion SR engines, twin screw, 14kts.
Date of disaster: 22 January 1942.

The Bernstein Line bought the *Arawa* from Shaw Savill & Albion in 1928 for service across the Atlantic and had her passenger accommodation extended in 1931. Renamed *Konigstein*, she maintained these duties until 1940 when she was transferred to Cie. Maritime Belge. As the *Gandia* she was intended for the West African service from Antwerp, but the outbreak of the Second World War interfered with these plans. The *Gandia* was utilized thereafter in the Allied war effort, but was lost during a convoy voyage from Liverpool to St John, New Brunswick, on 22 January 1942. The *Gandia* had experienced considerable difficulty in maintaining her position, and shortly after becoming separated from the rest of the convoy she was torpedoed by a German submarine. The position was roughly 45°00'N–41°00'W, some 420 miles south of Cape Race. Of her crew of 88 men, 42 went down with her and a further 24 died in the lifeboats before they could be rescued.

VICTORIA (1931–1942)

Lloyd Triestino, Italy; Cantieri Riuniti Dell'Adriatico, Trieste.
13,062 GRT, 540ft (164.6m) LOA, 68ft (20.7m) beam.
600 passengers.
Diesel engines, quadruple screw, 22kts.
Date of disaster: 24 January 1942.

The twin-funnelled *Victoria* was a nicely-proportioned liner and the fastest motorship in the world until the advent of the Dutch *Oranje*. Her career began on the service from Trieste to Alexandria, but later she switched to the Bombay run from Genoa, with an extension to Shanghai from October 1936. In 1940 she became a troop transport, attached to the Italian Navy. She was sunk in the Gulf of Sirte (Sidri), Libya, by torpedoes dropped by British aircraft during a voyage from Taranto to Tripoli on 24 January 1942. She went down in the position 33°40'N–17°45'E.

SPREEWALD ex-*ANUBIS* ex-*SPREEWALD* (1922–1942)

Hamburg Amerika Line, Germany; Deutsche Werft, Hamburg.
5,083 GRT, 399ft (121.6m) length, 54ft (16.5m) beam.
Diesel engines, twin screw, 12.5kts.
Date of disaster: 31 January 1942.

In spite of claims in some reports that a British submarine was responsible for her destruction, the German liner *Spreewald* was accidentally sunk by her own forces on 31 January 1942. Having left Yokohama in November 1941, she was making for the refuge of a port in German-controlled territory when she was mistakenly identified by *U333* and torpedoed 450 miles north of the Azores, in the position 45°17'N–24°50'W. The *Spreewald* had aboard, in addition to her own crew, the surviving crew members of the Australian ship *Mareeba*, which had been sunk by a commerce raider,

The Spreewald *was a victim of 'friendly fire', being sunk by a German U-boat.* (Hapag-Lloyd)

probably the *Kormoran*, north-west of the Nicobar Islands on 26 June 1941. Twenty three of these men were killed and just one survived to become a prisoner-of-war. It is believed that many of the *Spreewald*'s own crew also lost their lives. From 1922 to 1939 the *Spreewald* had operated between Germany and the West Indies.

EMPRESS OF ASIA (1913–1942)

Canadian Pacific Line, Great Britain; Fairfield, Govan.
16,909 GRT, 592ft (180.4m) LOA, 68ft (20.7m) beam.
1,238 passengers in four classes.
Steam turbines, quadruple screw, 20kts.
Date of disaster: 5 February 1942.

The sister ships *Empress of Asia* and *Empress of Russia* were the first large passenger liners to have cruiser sterns. They sailed in the Vancouver to Yokohama service. From 1941 the *Empress of Asia* served as a troopship, and it was in the course of these duties that she arrived at Singapore, from Bombay, on 5 February 1942 with some 2,235 reinforcements for the British garrison there. About six miles from her destination the *Empress* was attacked by a large number of Japanese dive-bombers, sustaining five direct hits. Four bombs exploded in the vicinity of her bridge, while a fifth penetrated within the vessel. She caught fire, and the Australian sloop *Yarra* came alongside to assist in her evacuation. Various casualty figures are given but Lloyds' records state that 15 troops were killed and one member of the 416-strong deck and engine-room crew died later in hospital. A further 147 catering staff were all saved. A large number of the survivors were taken prisoner by the Japanese when they captured Singapore just 10 days after the attack. The abandoned *Empress of Asia* drifted ashore near the Sultan Shoal, west of Keppel Harbour, and was completely burnt out over the next two days. The wreck was scrapped from 1952 on, with work still in progress as late as March 1960.

Canadian Pacific Line's Empress of Asia *operated with her sister* Empress of Russia *between Vancouver and Yokohama.* (World Ship Society)

NORMANDIE as USS *LAFAYETTE* (1935–1942)

French Line (CGT), France; Chantiers et Ateliers de St Nazaire (Penhoët).
83,423 GRT, 1,029ft (313.6m) LOA, 118ft (36.0m) beam.
1,972 passengers in three classes.
Turbo-electric propulsion, quadruple screw, 30kts.
Date of disaster: 9 February 1942.

The classic French Line transatlantic record-breaker *Normandie* was laid up at New York at the outbreak of the Second World War. When the United States entered the war, she was seized by the US War Shipping Administration and transferred to the US Navy. Conversion into a troopship was immediately undertaken but in a somewhat hasty and ill-organized fashion.

While structural alterations were still being executed, stores and provisions for trooping activities were brought aboard, including highly inflammable kapok life-preservers, hampering the workmen and creating a potential fire risk. On 9 February 1942 some of the life-preservers were accidentally ignited by workmen cutting away stanchions in the ship's main saloon. Due to the ship's condition, ship-to-shore communications were only partially established, while the hydrant and hose connections were in the process of conversion from French to American fittings. These mechanical and communication delays allowed the fire to firmly establish itself. Activity ashore was little better co-ordinated, and there was significant additional delay before the New York Fire Department was alerted. It took another four hours for the fire to be brought under control, by which time the vast quantities of water pumped aboard, much of it frozen in her upper superstructure, had caused the *Lafayette* to list to port. As the tide rose in the River Hudson the list increased until, at 2.45 a.m. on 10 February, the *Lafayette* rolled over on her side to rest half-submerged at her berth. The fire had resulted in one death.

It took until September 1943 for the ship to be salvaged but by this time she had been cut down to the promenade deck, and the huge amounts of money spent on the

Above *The spectacular French Line record-breaker* Normandie *in New York harbour before the outbreak of war.* (Author's collection)

Below *Fighting the fire aboard the blazing* Lafayette, *which is already beginning to list to port.* (United States National Archives)

Left *The wreck of the* Lafayette *lying between the New York piers is in an advanced state of clearance at the time of this photograph. To her left is the* Mauretania *and to her right the* Queen Elizabeth. (United States National Archives)

The Dollar Line passenger ship President Taylor *is shown here under her original name,* President Polk. (American President Lines)

operation precluded any further expense on refurbishing her for an active role. Consequently the remains of the ex-*Normandie* were sold for scrapping in October 1946. In spite of the fire-prone reputations of pre-war French liners, numerous fire prevention features had been incorporated into the *Normandie*'s design, including fire-retarding paints,

The five Monte *ships of Hamburg Sud-Amerika Line were an unlucky class. The* Monte Cervantes *foundered in January 1930; the* Monte Rosa, *as the* Empire Windrush, *was destroyed by fire in March 1954; and the other three ships were all war losses. This is the* Monte Sarmiento. (Hamburg Sud-Amerika Line)

fire-proof screens above the watertight bulkheads, and an abundant supply of hydrants.

PRESIDENT TAYLOR ex-*PRESIDENT POLK* ex-*GRANITE STATE* (1921–1942)

American President Line, USA; New York SB Corp, Camden, New Jersey.
10,508 GRT, 522ft (159.1m) LOA, 62ft (18.9m) beam.
78 passengers in single class.
Triple expansion SR engines, twin screw, 14kts.
Date of disaster: 14 February 1942.

The former *President Polk* was renamed in 1938 when she became an American President Line ship. As the *President Taylor* she continued in the round-the-world service that she had maintained for 14 years for the Dollar Line. The United States Army took her over in December 1941 and converted her into a transport. On 14 February 1942 the following year, the *President Taylor* ran aground at Canton Island, in the Phoenix Group, in the approximate position 03°00′S–172°00′W. Her entire civilian crew was repatriated and US Navy craft endeavoured to salvage her. No progress had been made by 3 May and, due to the transport's exposed position and the urgent need for the salvage equipment elsewhere, the *President Taylor* was abandoned. The wreck was later destroyed by Japanese warplanes.

MONTE SARMIENTO (1924–1942)

Hamburg Sud-Amerika Line, Germany; Blohm & Voss, Hamburg.
13,625 GRT, 524ft (159.7m) LOA, 65ft (19.8m) beam.
2,470 passengers in two classes.
Diesel engines, twin screw, 14.5kts.
Date of disaster: 26 February 1942.

First ship of the *Monte* class, the *Monte Sarmiento* was taken over after the outbreak of war for service as an accommodation ship, stationed at Kiel, where she was bombed and sunk during an Allied air raid on 26 February 1942. The wrecked ship was raised in 1943 and towed to Hamburg, where it was broken up.

HORAI MARU ex-*PAYS DE WAES* ex-*INDARRO* (1912–1942)

Osaka Shosen Kaisha, Japan; William Denny, Dumbarton.
9,204 GRT, 451ft (137.5m) length, 60ft (18.3m) beam.
Quadruple expansion SR engines, twin screw, 15kts.
Date of disaster: 1 March 1942.

The passenger steamship *Horai Maru* was previously the *Pays de Waes* of Lloyd Belge Royal, and spent much of her life in the African trade, from both Europe and Japan. She was sunk in the Sunda Strait on 1 March 1942, in the position 05°56′S–106°12′E, by a combination of aircraft bombs and gunfire from Allied warships. The wreck was raised on 10 December 1946 and beached at Siglap, to be broken up in 1948.

TJIKARANG (1922–1942)

Royal Interocean Lines, Netherlands; Nederlandsche Schps Maatschappij, Amsterdam.
9,505 GRT, 483ft (147.2m) length, 60ft (18.3m) beam.
Triple expansion SR engines, twin screw, 12.5kts.
Date of disaster: 2 March 1942.

The steamship *Tjikarang* operated between the Dutch East Indies and ports on the Chinese mainland, in the main carrying deck passengers. On 2 March 1942, she was scuttled at Sourabaya, Java, following the Japanese capture of Indonesia. The wreck, lying in the position 07°11′S–112°43′E, was removed after the war.

YOKOHAMA MARU (1912–1942)

Nippon Yusen Kaisha, Japan; Kawasaki, Kobe.
6,147 GRT, 406ft (123.7m) length, 49ft (14.9m) beam.
Triple expansion SR engines, twin screw, 14kts.
Date of disaster: 10 March 1942.

The *Yokohama Maru* and her sister ship, the *Shidzuoka Maru*, were built for the Japan to Seattle transpacific service and were also used on a South Sea Islands route. The *Yokohama Maru*'s long life was ended on 10 March 1942 when American land-based and carrier-based aircraft attacked her off Lae, New Guinea. She sank in the position 07°01′S–147°07′E. It is not known whether the sinking claimed any lives.

KITANO MARU (1909–1942)

Nippon Yusen Kaisha, Japan; Mitsubishi, Nagasaki.
8,512 GRT, 473ft (144.2m) length, 54ft (16.5m) beam.
127 passengers in three classes.
Triple expansion SR engines, twin screw, 15kts.
Date of disaster: 27 March 1942.

The *Kitano Maru* was a unit of the six-strong *Hirano Maru* class built for the Japan to Europe service. Five of the ships were war victims, the name-ship during the First World War, the others during the Second World War. The *Kitano Maru* struck a mine near Lingayen in the Philippines on 27 March 1942, and sank in the position 16°10′N–120°24′E.

The Tjikarang *was operated by the Java-China-Japan Line, later restyled as Royal Interocean Lines.* (World Ship Society)

CITY OF NEW YORK (1930–1942)

American South African Line, USA; Sun SB & Drydock Co, Chester, Pennsylvania.
8,272 GRT, 470ft (143.3m) LOA, 61ft (18.6m) beam.
Diesel engines, twin screw, 14kts.
Date of disaster: 29 March 1942.

The *City of New York* was a pioneer vessel on the route from New York to South Africa, her owners being the predecessors of the Farrell Line. On 29 March 1942, during a voyage from Lourenco Marques (Maputo) to New York, she was torpedoed and sunk in the position 35°16′N–74°25′W, 30 miles east of Cape Hatteras. Of her complement of 144, which included 47 passengers, three were killed, 23 were missing, and 118 were saved, her master, Capt G.T. Sullivan, being among the survivors. The *City of New York* had not been sailing in a convoy. The position of the loss is also given as 35°00′N–74°40′W.

HECTOR (1924–1942)

Blue Funnel Line, Great Britain; Scott's, Greenock.
11,198 GRT, 530ft (161.5m) LOA, 62ft (18.9m) beam.
175 passengers in single class.
Steam turbines, twin screw, 15kts.
Date of disaster: 5 April 1942.

The *Hector* was the third ship of a quartet built for the Far East service from Liverpool. Accommodation was provided for 175 first-class passengers, later increased. She was taken

The American-South African Line passenger ship City of New York, *a pioneer vessel on the route from New York to Cape Town.* (World Ship Society)

over as an armed merchant cruiser early in the Second World War, operating in home waters until after Japan entered the conflict, when she transferred to the Indian Ocean. On 5 April 1942 she was in the harbour at Colombo, Ceylon (Sri Lanka), when it was attacked by Japanese aircraft from a carrier task force. She received several hits, caught fire, and sank. Her wreck was raised in 1946 and beached at Uswetakeiyawa, five miles north of Colombo, prior to being scrapped on the spot. The same Japanese naval force sank the aircraft-carrier HMS *Hermes* three days later.

MALDA (1922–1942)

British India Line, Great Britain; Barclay Curle, Glasgow.
9,066 GRT, 465ft (141.7m) length, 58ft (17.7m) beam.
175 passengers.
Steam turbines, twin screw, 13kts.
Date of disaster: 6 April 1942.

The *Malda* was one of a class of six ships employed in the service from England to Calcutta via the Suez Canal. During a voyage from Calcutta to Colombo on 6 April 1942, the *Malda* came under attack from Japanese aircraft and received bomb damage, and was subsequently sunk by gunfire from Japanese cruisers. The attack took place off Gopalpore, in the position 19°45′N–86°27′E. Out of her crew of 179, 25 lost their lives.

SAGAING (1925–1942)

Henderson Line, Great Britain; William Denny, Dumbarton.
7,994 GRT, 454ft (138.4m) length, 61ft (18.6m) beam.
150 passengers in single class.
Triple expansion SR engine, single screw, 14kts.
Date of disaster: 9 April 1942.

The *Sagaing* was sister ship to the *Kemmendine* and *Yoma*, both also lost during the Second World War. Along with the *Amarapoora* and *Pegu* they made up a class of five ships used in the service from Glasgow and Liverpool to Rangoon. On 9 April 1942, while disembarking passengers at Trincomalee, the *Sagaing* was bombed by Japanese aircraft. She caught fire and was beached. Two members of the crew of 138 were killed. The *Sagaing* was later refloated, but as she was a constructive total loss she was sunk again deliberately in August 1943, in a dredged berth where, less her upperworks, she was utilized as a pier.

ULYSSES (1913–1942)

Blue Funnel Line, Great Britain; Workman Clark, Belfast.
14,499 GRT, 580ft (176.8m) LOA, 68ft (20.7m) beam.
250 passengers in single class.
Triple expansion SR engines, twin screw, 14kts.
Date of disaster: 11 April 1942.

The *Ulysses* was the last vessel of the Blue Funnel's seven-ship *Aeneas* class. She operated between Liverpool or Glasgow and Brisbane. On 11 April 1942, on a voyage from Sydney to Liverpool via the Panama Canal and Halifax, Nova Scotia, the *Ulysses* was sunk by the German submarine *U160*, which attacked her off Palm Beach, on the coast of North Carolina, in the position 34°23′N–75°35′W. All the passengers and crew, including her master, Capt J.A. Russell, were saved.

TOP *British India Line's second* Malda *and the second ship of the name to fall victim to the war at sea.* (World Ship Society)

ABOVE *The Blue Funnel Line's* Ulysses. (A. Duncan)

SAN JACINTO (1903–1942)

New York & Porto Rico Line, USA; Delaware River SB Co, Chester, Pennsylvania.
6,069 GRT, 380ft (115.8m) length, 53ft (16.2m) beam.
Triple expansion SR engines, twin screw, 15.5kts.
Date of disaster: 22 April 1942.

The passenger steamship *San Jacinto*, originally owned by the Mallory Line, worked between New York and Havana

The San Jacinto, *a New York & Porto Rico Steamship Company vessel.* (World Ship Society)

and San Juan. On a voyage from Puerto Rico to New York on 22 April 1942, she was torpedoed and sunk by a German submarine 300 miles south-west of Bermuda, in the position 31°10'N–70°45'W. On board were 104 passengers in addition to a crew of 79, nine passengers and five crew-members losing their lives.

LADY DRAKE (1929–1942)

Canadian National Line, Canada; Cammell Laird, Birkenhead.
7,985 GRT, 419ft (127.7m) length, 59ft (18.0m) beam.
Steam turbines, twin screw, 14kts.
Date of disaster: 5 May 1942.

Ships of the *Lady* class of the Canadian National Line sailed between St Lawrence ports, Newfoundland, and Nova Scotia to South America. On 5 May 1942 the *Lady Drake* was returning from Demerara and Bermuda to St John, New Brunswick, when she was torpedoed and sunk by a German submarine north of Bermuda, in the position 35°43'N–64°43'W. There were 12 casualties – six crew and six passengers – among the 272 people that she was carrying. Her master at the time was Capt Percy Kelly.

TAIYO MARU ex-*CAP FINISTERRE* (1911–1942)

Nippon Yusen Kaisha, Japan; Blohm & Voss, Hamburg.
14,457 GRT, 591ft (180.1m) LOA, 65ft (19.8m) beam.
1,389 passengers in three classes (as a German ship).
Quadruple expansion SR engines, twin screw, 16kts.
Date of disaster: 8 May 1942.

The Hamburg Sud Amerika liner *Cap Finisterre* was a war prize from the First World War, ceded to the Japanese after a brief interlude as an American flag troopship. Toyo Kisen Kaisha placed her in the Pacific service from Yokohama to San Francisco, renaming her *Taiyo Maru*. In 1926 she passed to Nippon Yusen Kaisha when the two companies merged. Fifteen years later she was taken under Japanese Government control when war broke out in the Pacific. On 8 May 1942 the *Taiyo Maru* was bound for south-east Asian ports with about 300 crewmen and 700 industrialists and mechanics from the Mitsui organization, who were to establish industrial and manufacturing facilities in Japanese-occupied countries. South-west of the island of Kyushu, in the position 30°40'N–127°54'E, the *Taiyo Maru* was torpedoed and sunk by the submarine USS *Grenadier*. Of the approximately 1,000 people aboard the ship, 780 lost their lives.

ATSUTA (ATUTA) MARU (1909–1942)

Nippon Yusen Kaisha, Japan; Mitsubishi, Nagasaki.
7,983 GRT, 473ft (144.2m) length, 54ft (16.5m) beam.
Triple expansion SR engines, twin screw, 15kts.
Date of disaster: 30 May 1942.

One of a class of six ships, throughout her career the *Atsuta Maru* alternated between the Japan to Europe route and the transpacific service. She met her end on 30 May 1942 while employed as a naval transport, when the American submarine USS *Pompano* torpedoed and sank her in the East China Sea in the position 26°07'N–129°06'E. Casualty figures are not known.

ELYSIA (1908–1942)

Anchor Line, Great Britain; D. & W. Henderson, Glasgow.
6,757 GRT, 440ft (134.1m) length, 53ft (16.2m) beam.
100 passengers in single class.
Triple expansion SR engine, single screw, 12.5kts.
Date of disaster: 5 June 1942.

Anchor Line introduced the steamship *Elysia* and her sister ship *Castalia* to the England to India service in the early years of the twentieth century. Both vessels had long and uneventful lives until the *Elysia* was torpedoed by two Japanese surface raiders on 5 June 1942 about 350 miles from Durban, in the position 27°15'S–36°24'E. She had been

When the Taiyo Maru, *originally Hamburg Sud-Amerika Line's* Cap Finisterre, *was torpedoed, she sank with heavy loss of life.* (Author's collection)

on a voyage from Glasgow to Aden and Bombay via the Cape.

CRIJNSSEN (1919–1942)

Royal Netherlands SS Co, Netherlands; Maatschappij Fijenoord, Rotterdam.
4,298 GRT, 342ft (104.2m) length, 47ft (14.3m) beam.
203 passengers in two classes.
Triple expansion SR engine, single screw, 12.5kts.
Date of disaster: 10 June 1942.

The *Crijnssen* and her sisters *Stuyvesant* and *Van Rensselaer* served on the route from the Netherlands to the northern coast of South America. On a voyage from Demerara and Curacoa to New Orleans on 10 June 1942, the *Crijnssen* was torpedoed and sunk in the position 18°14′N–85°11′W. From her complement of 66 crew and 27 passengers only one crewman was never accounted for. Of the survivors, 49 were picked up by the American steamship *Lebore*, only to become casualties when this ship was sunk six days later.

JAGERSFONTEIN (1934–1942)

Holland Afrika Line, Netherlands; Nederlandsche Schps Maatschappij, Amsterdam.
10,083 GRT, 487ft (148.4m) LOA, 63ft (19.2m) beam.
113 passengers in two classes
Diesel engines, twin screw, 17kts.
Date of disaster: 26 June 1942.

Ships of the Holland Afrika Line operated between Hamburg, Rotterdam, and Lourenco Marques (Maputo). The sister liners *Bloemfontein* and *Jagersfontein* joined the service in 1934. When Germany occupied the Netherlands in 1940, the *Jagersfontein* switched to the Dutch East Indies and was re-registered at Batavia. On 26 June 1942, during a voyage to Liverpool from Galveston, Texas, the *Jagersfontein* was torpedoed by the German submarine *U107* when 500 miles east of Bermuda. She sank in the position 32°02′N–54°53′W without loss of life to the 67 crew and 98 passengers she carried.

AVILA STAR ex-*AVILA* (1927–1942)

Blue Star Line, Great Britain; John Brown, Clydebank.
14,443 GRT, 569ft (173.4m) LOA, 68ft (20.7m) beam.
150 passengers in single class.
Steam turbines, twin screw, 16kts.
Date of disaster: 5 July 1942.

The third of Blue Star Line's five-ship class of passenger-cargo liners completed for the South American trade from London in the 1920s, the *Avila Star* was the fourth of the quintet to be sunk in the Second World War. Returning to Liverpool from Buenos Aires and Freetown on 5 July 1942, under the command of Capt John Fisher, she was torpedoed by the submarine *U201* north-east of the Azores, sinking in the position 38°04′N–22°45′W. One lifeboat was destroyed by a second torpedo explosion soon after it had been lowered. Another got caught up in the falls, spilling its occupants into the sea.

For the occupants of the five remaining lifeboats, the aftermath of the sinking was an epic struggle for survival on the open ocean, in which was demonstrated the highest

The United Netherlands Line's Jagersfontein. (World Ship Society)

order of gallantry in saving life at sea. The lifeboats made for the Portuguese coast as best they could, at first in a group, but becoming separated as time passed. The occupants of the boats included many sick and injured who required medical attention and reassurance. The survivors aboard three of the boats – numbers 1, 4 and 8 – were rescued by the Portuguese destroyer *Lima* on 8–9 July and taken to Ponta Delgada. The remaining two lifeboats – numbers 2 and 6 – managed to keep together until 11 July, when they lost contact with each other, after which lifeboat number 6 was never seen again. Fortunately the limited food and water aboard lifeboat number 2 had been carefully rationed from the outset, a vital factor in keeping many of its occupants alive until they were picked up on 25 July by the Portuguese sloop *Pedro Nunes*, which conveyed them to Lisbon. Of the 25 passengers and 171 crew members who had been aboard the *Avila Star*, 17 and 45 respectively were lost. Many had died in the lifeboats, mostly from injuries sustained in the torpedo attack but also from exposure and illness. Others lost their sanity, and one passenger jumped overboard from lifeboat number 2 in a state of delirium, and could not be saved.

The Avila Star, *fourth vessel of her class to be sunk during the Second World War. None of the five 'A'* Stars *survived the war.* (World Ship Society)

The Blue Star officers and crewmen had displayed outstanding courage, seamanship, and fortitude throughout the ordeal, a fitting tribute to the traditions of their service. Four officers were awarded the OBE in recognition of their bravery and leadership: Chief Officer Eric Pearce, First Officer Michael Tallack, Second Officer John Anson, and Third Officer R.T. Clarke. Chief Officer Pearce also received the Lloyd's War Medal for Bravery at Sea. Among many other commendations, a female passenger, Maria Elizabeth Ferguson, and Boatswain John Gray were also individually recognized, receiving the British Empire Medal.

HARUNA MARU (1922–1942)

Nippon Yusen Kaisha, Japan; Mitsubishi, Nagasaki.
10,421 GRT, 520ft (158.5m) LOA, 62ft (18.9m) beam.
175 passengers in single class.
Steam turbines, twin screw, 15.5kts.
Date of disaster: 7 July 1942.

The four liners *Hakone Maru*, *Haruna Maru*, *Hakozaki Maru*, and *Hakusan Maru* sailed in the Yokohama to Hamburg service via the Suez Canal. All four were casualties of the Second World War, only the *Haruna Maru*'s loss being not directly attributable to enemy action. On 7 July 1942, while engaged on military duties, she had stranded off Suruga Wan, 50 miles south-west of Yokohama, and became a total loss.

The Haruna Maru. (Mitsubishi Heavy Industries)

UMTATA (1935–1942)

Natal Line, Great Britain; Swan, Hunter & Wigham Richardson, Newcastle.
8,137 GRT, 468ft (142.6m) LOA, 61ft (18.6m) beam.
100 passengers.
Triple expansion SR engines with LP turbine, twin screw, 15kts.
Date of disaster: 7 July 1942.

The ships of the Natal Line, owned by Bullard, King & Co, operated between England and South Africa until 1957, when taken over by Elder Dempster Lines. The *Umtata* and her sisters *Umgeni* and *Umtali* were the newest and largest ships in the service at the outbreak of the Second World War, each providing accommodation for 100 passengers. Having sustained torpedo damage on 9 March 1942, the *Umtata* was under tow of the tug *Edmund J. Moranon* on 7 July, bound from the island of St Lucia to Port Everglades, Florida, for repairs. Near Key West, in the position 25°35′N–80°02′W, she was rocked by an explosion caused by a torpedo or a mine, the definite cause never being determined. The already damaged liner sank soon after, but all 90 members of her crew were saved.

DOMALA as *EMPIRE ATTENDANT* (1921–1942)

British India Line, Great Britain; Barclay Curle, Glasgow.
8,441 GRT, 450ft (137.2m) length, 58ft (17.7m) beam.
130 passengers.
Diesel engines, twin screw, 13kts.
Date of disaster: 15 July 1942.

The *Domala*, sister ship to the *Dumana*, was normally

The Empire Attendant, *rebuilt from the seriously war-damaged British India motorship* Domala, *was sunk by a torpedo off Spanish West Africa.* (World Ship Society)

engaged on her owner's Indian services. She was bound from London and Antwerp to Calcutta on 2 March 1940 when she was attacked by a Heinkel bomber in the English Channel, 20 miles from St Catherine's Point. On board, apart from her crew, were 143 Indians who had been repatriated by the Germans, her total complement being 295. Four bombs struck the *Domala*, causing heavy casualties, and the German aircraft then strafed her with its machine-guns. Her master, Capt Fitt, was killed, along with 36 members of his crew and 63 of the Indian passengers. The *Domala* was taken in tow for Cowes while the Dutch steamship *Jonge Willem*, a Royal Navy destroyer and boats from the shore, picked up survivors from the water and the few lifeboats and rafts that had been launched. The *Jonge Willem* too became a target for the lone German marauder but suffered no damage or casualties.

The *Domala* was eventually taken to Southampton, where she was repaired on the personal instructions of Winston Churchill, then First Lord of the Admiralty, 'in the plainest way for the roughest work'. Renamed *Empire Attendant*, she was taken over by the Ministry of Supply, under the management of Andrew Weir & Company. On 15 July 1942, when bound for Durban and Karachi from the River Mersey, she was torpedoed off Rio de Oro, Spanish West Africa, by the German submarine *U582*, all of her crew of 59 being lost. She sank in the position 23°38′N–21°51′W.

The Gloucester Castle *sailing from her home port of Southampton in the 1930s.* (British & Commonwealth Shipping Co)

GLOUCESTER CASTLE (1911–1942)

Union Castle Line, Great Britain; Fairfield, Glasgow.
7,999 GRT, 452ft (137.8m) length, 56ft (17.1m) beam.
300 passengers.
Quadruple expansion SR engines, twin screw, 13.5kts.
Date of disaster: 15 July 1942.

The *Gloucester Castle* and her sister ships, *Galway Castle* and *Guildford Castle*, were employed in the intermediate service to Africa. The *Gloucester Castle* was laid up at Netley, in Southampton Water, in early-1939, but she was reactivated on the outbreak of war. On 15 July 1942, during a voyage from Birkenhead to Cape Town, East London, and Simonstown, she was attacked at night near Ascension Island by the German raider *Michel*, in the approximate position 08°00′S–01°00′E. The raider destroyed the *Gloucester Castle*'s wireless transmitter and all the starboard side lifeboats before finishing her off inside 10 minutes. Her master, Capt H.H. Rose, was among 93 people killed from the ship's complement of 142 crew and 12 passengers (the latter all women and children). The 61 survivors escaped in two port-side lifeboats and were picked up by the *Michel*, later being transferred to the supply tanker *Charlotte Schliemann*. Landed at Yokohama, Japan, they were interned for the remainder of the war, their whereabouts and movements only revealed near the war's end, by which time two of the survivors had died.

TJINEGARA (1931–1942)

Royal Interocean Lines, Netherlands; Nederlandsche Schps Maatschappij, Amsterdam.
9,227 GRT, 440ft (134.1m) length, 62ft (18.9m) beam.
2,000 passengers.
Diesel engine, single screw, 15kts.
Date of disaster: 26 July 1942.

The motorship *Tjinegara* could carry up to 2,000 passengers on the service from Java and Sumatra to Malaya, Indo-China, and China, many of them accommodated on deck. She was torpedoed and sunk by a Japanese submarine on 26 July 1942, while bound from Brisbane to Noumea, New Caledonia. The attack took place about 80 miles from her destination and she went down in the position 23°10′S–165°00′E, without loss of life.

BRAZIL MARU (1939–1942)

Osaka Shosen Kaisha, Japan; Mitsubishi, Nagasaki.
12,752 GRT, 549ft (167.3m) LOA, 68ft (20.7m) beam.
901 passengers in three classes.
Diesel engines, twin screw, 21.5kts.
Date of disaster: 5 August 1942.

The *Brazil Maru* was built for the service between Japan and South America. Following the outbreak of war in the Pacific the Imperial Japanese Navy had originally planned to convert her into an aircraft carrier, like her sister ship *Argentina Maru*, but these plans were abandoned and she instead served as a troopship. She was torpedoed by the

Osaka Shosen Kaisha's pre-war Brazil Maru. *Her sinking ranks as one of the worst Japanese losses of the Second World War.* (*Mitsui-OSK Lines*)

American submarine USS *Greenling* on 5 August 1942, midway between the Pacific islands of Guam and Truk, in the position 09°51′N–150°38′E. She had aboard 400 soldiers and 200 passengers, besides her crew, and there were heavy casualties.

CITY OF LOS ANGELES ex-*CITY OF HAVRE* ex-*VICTORIOUS* as *GEORGE F ELLIOT* (1918–1942)

Baltimore Mail Line, USA; Bethlehem SB Corp, Alameda, California.
8,378 GRT, 486ft (148.1m) length, 56ft (17.1m) beam.
Steam turbine, single screw, 16kts.
Date of disaster: 8 August 1942.

The Baltimore Mail Line's transatlantic steamship *City of Los Angeles* was taken over as a transport by the United States Government in the Second World War under the name *George F Elliot*. Japanese aircraft attacked and sunk her off Guadalcanal on 8 August 1942.

BAEPENDY ex-*TIJUCA* (1899–1942)

Lloyd Brasileiro, Brazil; Blohm & Voss, Hamburg.
4,801 GRT, 375ft (114.3m) length, 46ft (14.0m) beam.
Quadruple expansion SR engine, single screw, 12.5kts.
Date of disaster: 15 August 1942.

The *Baependy* sailed between Santos and Hamburg and other European ports. Originally a unit of the Hamburg Sud-Amerika Line fleet, she had been seized by Brazil in 1917 and transferred to Lloyd Brasileiro. Sailing in consort with other Brazilian vessels, including the coast-wise liner *Araquara*, she was attacked by a German U-boat on 15 August 1942 during a voyage from Rio de Janeiro and Bahia to Manaos, in the position 11°50′S–37°00′W. The *Baependy*, was carrying 246 passengers and troops and 74 crew to Fernando Noronha. Of these, only 36 were saved. The *Araquara* was also sunk with the loss of 12 lives. When the attack occurred Brazil was not at war with Germany although diplomatic relations had been cut, but the sinking provoked such a public outcry, with crowds demonstrating

The Lloyd Brasileiro steamship Baependy. *Her loss was the worst disaster to befall a Brazilian registered passenger ship.* (National Maritime Museum, London)

in the streets, that war was declared within a matter of seven days.

ARNO ex-*CESAREA* ex-*FORT ST GEORGE* ex-*WANDILLA* (1912–1942)

Lloyd Triestino, Italy; William Beardmore, Glasgow.
8,024 GRT, 428ft (130.5m) LOA, 56ft (17.1m) beam.
Quadruple expansion SR engines, twin screw, 16kts.
Date of disaster: 10 September 1942.

First built for the Adelaide Steamship Company, this ship transferred to the Furness Bermuda Line after First World War service as a British hospital ship. In 1935 she was sold to Lloyd Triestino. As the *Arno*, she was attacked by a British torpedo-bomber 40 miles north of Tobruk on 10 September 1942. A total of 27 lives were lost in the sinking, the Italians claiming that the *Arno* was being used as a hospital ship.

LACONIA (1922–1942)

Cunard Line, Great Britain; Swan, Hunter & Wigham Richardson, Newcastle.
19,680 GRT, 623ft (189.9m) LOA, 73ft (22.3m) beam.
2,200 passengers in three classes.
Steam turbines, twin screw, 16.5kts.
Date of disaster: 12 September 1942.

Third vessel of the *Scythia* class, the *Laconia* made her maiden voyage to New York in May 1922. She was based at Liverpool, although she also made crossings from Hamburg and Southampton. From September 1939 she served as an armed merchant cruiser under Royal Navy control until, in 1940, she was converted to a troopship.

The *Laconia* was sunk in the South Atlantic on 12 September 1942 by the German submarine *U156*. The attack occurred when the *Laconia*, which was bound from Suez to England via the Cape of Good Hope, was about 800 miles south-west of Freetown, in the position 05°05′S–11°38′W. She was carrying a total of 3,254 people, including 1,793 Italian prisoners-of-war and a crew of 692; the remaining 769 were listed as passengers but included Polish guards responsible for the prisoners.

On surfacing following the attack, the commander of *U156*, Capt Werner Hartenstein, approached the sinking vessel to take prisoners whereupon he discovered the nature of the *Laconia*'s occupants. At this, he summoned other nearby submarines to come to the aid of the survivors and his calls were answered by the *U506*, the *U507*, and the Italian submarine *Capellini*. All four vessels took lifeboats in tow, while further radio messages requested help from surface vessels, to which the Vichy French naval ships *Gloire*, *Dumont d'Urville*, and *Annamite* sailed from Casablanca in response. During 16 and 17 September the surfaced submarines, which were flying Red Cross flags, were attacked by Allied aircraft, and the *U156* was damaged. The rescue operation proceeded regardless until, with the

Britain's second-costliest shipping loss of the Second World War was that of the Laconia. *Her casualties were mainly Italian prisoners-of-war.* (Tom Rayner)

The Blue Star liner Andalucia Star. (World Ship Society)

arrival of the French warships late on 17 September, the survivors were trans-shipped for return to Casablanca. Only then did the submarines resume their normal duties.

Whether the *U156* would have instituted such a conscientious rescue operation had the *Laconia*'s complement not included Italian prisoners-of-war is open to debate, but it nevertheless amounted to a brave and humanitarian act in the face of considerable danger, saving many lives which would otherwise have been lost. Admiral Karl Donitz's order, following the *Laconia* incident, that in future U-boats should not attempt to rescue survivors was one of the 'war crimes' of which he was accused at the Nüremburg trials in 1946, but the international military court acquitted him of this particular charge.

The death-toll from the sinking of the *Laconia* was high despite the concerted rescue efforts. Lloyds records state that only 975 people were saved, 400 of whom were Italians. Other sources put the figure for survivors higher, at around 1,110. Among the dead was the *Laconia*'s commander, Capt R. Sharpe, who, just over two years earlier, had survived the sinking of the *Lancastria* off St Nazaire.

ANDALUCIA STAR ex-*ANDALUCIA* (1927–1942)

Blue Star Line, Great Britain; Cammell Laird, Birkenhead.
14,943 GRT, 597ft (182.0m) LOA, 68ft (20.7m) beam.
150 passengers in single class.
Steam turbines, twin screw, 16kts.
Date of disaster: 6 October 1942.

The *Andalucia Star* was the second of the group of five vessels constructed for Blue Star's passenger-cargo service from London to South America, the others being the *Almeda Star*, *Avila Star*, *Avelona Star*, and *Arandora Star*. On 6 October 1942, under the command of Capt J. Hall, she was sunk by the German submarine *U107* while bound from Buenos Aires and Freetown to Liverpool, three torpedoes in total hitting her. The attack took place in the position 06°38'N–15°46'W, about 400 miles west of Monrovia, Liberia. There were four casualties out of 246 people on board, three of them crew-members and the other a passenger. The survivors were picked up by the corvette HMS *Petunia* two days after the attack and taken to Freetown.

ORONSAY (1925–1942)

Orient Line, Great Britain; John Brown, Clydebank.
20,043 GRT, 659ft (200.9m) LOA, 75ft (22.9m) beam.
1,836 passengers in two classes.
Steam turbines, twin screw, 19kts.
Date of disaster: 9 October 1942.

Due to the loss of three of the *Orsova*-class ships during the First World War, the Orient Line implemented a vigorous rebuilding programme which added five new 20,000 GRT vessels to the fleet between 1924 and 1929. The second ship of the new class to be completed was the *Oronsay*, which spent the 14 years from February 1925 operating on the run from London to Brisbane. On the outbreak of the Second World War, she was requisitioned for duties as a troop transport, many of her wartime voyages being in waters familiar from her peacetime service. On 9 October 1942, while bound from Cape Town to Freetown in convoy, the *Oronsay* was torpedoed and sunk by the Italian submarine *Archimede* some 800 miles west-south-west of Monrovia, in

The Orient Line express mail steamer Oronsay. (Maritime Photo Library)

the position 04°29′N–20°52′W. She was carrying 130 passengers and a crew of 346, five of whom were killed when a second torpedo was fired at the ship as the boats were being lowered. With her engine and boiler rooms wrecked, the *Oronsay* foundered soon after she had been abandoned. A group of 288 survivors were rescued by a British warship, others being picked up by the Vichy French warship *Dumont d'Urville* and a French merchantman and taken to Dakar, where 63 were interned as prisoners-of-war. The *Oronsay's* master, Capt Norman Savage, was later awarded the CBE.

DUCHESS OF ATHOLL (1928–1942)

Canadian Pacific Line, Great Britain; William Beardmore, Glasgow.
20,119 GRT, 601ft (183.2m) LOA, 75ft (22.9m) beam.
1,570 passengers in three classes.
Steam turbines, twin screw, 21kts.
Date of disaster: 10 October 1942.

Canadian Pacific introduced the *Duchess* ships to the Liverpool to Montreal service between 1928 and 1929. The *Duchess of Atholl*, lead ship of the class, became a troopship

The Duchess of Atholl *was sunk while returning to England from a troop-carrying voyage to the Middle East.* (World Ship Society)

in December 1939. Her military career lasted until 10 October 1942, when, 200 miles east of Ascension Island, in the position 07°03′S–11°12′W, she was sunk by the German submarine *U178* while sailing in convoy from Cape Town to the United Kingdom via Freetown. She was carrying 534 passengers and 296 crew, of whom four were killed, the survivors being picked up by other ships in the convoy.

ORCADES (1937–1942)

Orient Line, Great Britain; Harland & Wolff, Belfast.
23,456 GRT, 664ft (202.4m) LOA, 82ft (25.0m) beam.
1,068 passengers in two classes.
Steam turbines, twin screw, 21kts.
Date of disaster: 10 October 1942.

The liners *Orion* and *Orcades*, introduced to Orient Line's Australian service in the mid-1930s, marked a dramatic change to modern styling in the Orient fleet. They were the company's largest liners, and it was with them that the characteristic biscuit-coloured hull was introduced, which was to become a distinguishing feature of all Orient Line ships thereafter. In October 1939 the *Orcades* was taken over as a troopship.

Three years later, while bound from Cape Town to the United Kingdom on 10 October 1942, she was hit by two torpedoes from the German submarine *U172*, the attack taking place 300 miles west-south-west of the Cape of Good Hope. Despite a brave attempt by a volunteer crew of 55 men to get the severely damaged vessel back to Cape Town, her steering gear failed, and after three more torpedoes struck her she had to be abandoned. The *Orcades* eventually sank in the position 31°51′S–14°40′E. She had been carrying 352 crew and 712 passengers, 30 and 18 respectively losing their lives, some in an accident when the boats were being lowered. The survivors were picked up by the Polish steamship *Narwik*. The *Orcades*' master, Capt Charles Fox, was later decorated with the CBE and the Lloyds War Medal for outstanding bravery at sea.

VILLE DE VERDUN as *TEISON MARU* (1921–1942)

Messageries Maritimes, France; North of Ireland SB Co, Londonderry.
7,209 GRT, 411ft (125.3m) length, 53ft (16.2m) beam.
Triple expansion SR engine, single screw.
Date of disaster: 14 October 1942.

The sister ships *Ville de Verdun* and *Ville d'Amiens* were purchased from the Cie. Havraise de Navigation in 1928 for employment on the service from France to Tahiti and the New Hebrides via the Panama Canal, carrying passengers and cargo. Captured by the Japanese and renamed *Teison Maru*, the former *Ville de Verdun* was torpedoed and sunk 100 miles west of Keelung, Formosa (Taiwan), on 14 October 1942, in the position 25°22′N–121°15′E. The submarine responsible was the American USS *Finback*.

The Orcades *was a sister to the* Orion. *These mid-1930s Orient Line fleet additions heralded the change into modern styling.* (Vickers Limited)

AFRICA MARU (1918–1942)

Osaka Shosen Kaisha, Japan; Mitsubishi, Nagasaki.
9,476 GRT, 475ft (144.8m) length, 61ft (18.6m) beam.
Triple expansion SR engines, twin screw, 13kts.
Date of disaster: 20 October 1942.

The *Africa Maru* was one of a class of five vessels built for operation on various transpacific routes after the First World War. She was sunk by the American submarine USS *Finback* on 20 October 1942 in the Straits of Formosa, in the position 24°26′N–120°26′E. Casualties are unknown.

PRESIDENT COOLIDGE (1931–1942)

American President Line, USA; Newport News SB & Drydock Co, Virginia.
21,936 GRT, 654ft (199.3m) LOA, 81ft (24.7m) beam.
990 passengers in four classes.
Turbo-electric propulsion, twin screw, 21kts.
Date of disaster: 26 October 1942.

The turbo-electric passenger liners *President Coolidge* and *President Hoover* were built for the transpacific service from San Francisco to China and Japan. They represented a major achievement for the Dollar Line, their original owners, for the company had only been operating on the route since February 1924. After 1938, when Dollar Line fell on harder times, the fleet and services were reorganized by the American Government under the American President Line banner. After the United States entered the Second World

Top *The transpacific turbo-electric liner* President Coolidge. *In this photograph she is carrying the insignia of American President Lines on her funnels, after having passed into their ownership in 1938.* (American President Lines)

Above *Survivors witness the* President Coolidge*'s last moments as she slips from the reef upon which her captain had driven her after she struck a mine at Espiritu Santo.* (Associated Press)

War, the *President Coolidge* was converted into an Army troop transport.

On 26 October 1942, while she was proceeding from Noumea, New Caledonia, to Luganville Bay, New Hebrides (Vanuatu), under the command of Capt Henry Nelson, the *President Coolidge* struck an American mine while approaching the volcanic island of Espiritu Santo. On board were some 5,050 troops. The ship was beached, and remained on an even keel, albeit with a gradually increasing list to port. Thanks to prompt action and exemplary discipline it was possible to evacuate the entire ship with the loss of only three lives, an Army captain and two members of the crew. The operation was completed in the very nick of time, for just after she had been abandoned, the *President Coolidge*, by now on her beam ends, slipped off the reef on which she had settled and sank in deep water. The bow came to rest in 70ft of water, while the stern section, which broke away as she went under, went even deeper, to 270ft. With the aid of small craft the survivors made it to nearby beaches, wet but safe. The wreck of the *President Coolidge*, popular with aqua divers, was declared an underwater national park in 1984.

The Elder Dempster liner Abosso *was a torpedo loss.* (Tom Rayner)

ABOSSO (1935–1942)

Elder Dempster Line, Great Britain; Cammell Laird, Birkenhead.
11,330 GRT, 481ft (146.6m) LOA, 65ft (19.8m) beam.
550 passengers in two classes.
Diesel engines, twin screw, 15kts.
Date of disaster: 29 October 1942.

From June 1935, when she entered service, until the outbreak of the Second World War, the *Abosso* served on the Liverpool to Apapa route. Thereafter she served as a troopship. On 29 October 1942 she was attacked and sunk by the German submarine *U575* during a voyage from Cape Town to Liverpool, in the position 48°30′N–28°50′W. Lloyds records state that out of a complement of 371, including 161 crew and 189 passengers, there were only 31 survivors, of whom only 17 were passengers, her master, Capt Tate, being among those killed. Other reports state that the loss of life amounted to either 168 or 137, in the latter case presumably adjusting for the occupants of the one lifeboat that managed to get away.

PRESIDENT DOUMER (1933–1942)

Messageries Maritimes, France; Soc. Provençale des Constructions Navals, La Ciotat.
11,898 GRT, 492ft (150.0m) LOA, 64ft (19.5m) beam.
903 passengers in four classes.
Diesel engines, twin screw, 18kts.
Date of disaster: 30 October 1942.

At a time when most new Messageries Maritimes' vessels were emerging with the distinctive square funnels that were

The Messageries Maritimes motorship President Doumer *was torpedoed off Freetown while in convoy.* (World Ship Society)

introduced in the inter-war years, the designers uncharacteristically reverted to a conventional funnel-style for the *President Doumer*. She was engaged in the service from Marseilles to Madagascar and the Far East until she became a troopship with the French Navy on the outbreak of the Second World War. After the fall of France in 1940, she was seized by the British at Port Said and placed under the management of Bibby Line, based at Aden. The *President Doumer* was torpedoed and sunk by the German submarine *U604* in the position 35°08′N–16°44′W, some distance north-east of Madeira, on 30 October 1942. She was carrying 63 passengers and 282 crew, bound from Freetown to the United Kingdom. There were only 85 survivors, all from among the crew.

MENDOZA (1920–1942)

Soc. Générale des Transports Maritimes, France; Swan, Hunter & Wigham Richardson, Newcastle.
8,199 GRT, 460ft (140.2m) length, 58ft (17.7m) beam.
248 passengers in three classes.
Steam turbines, twin screw, 15kts.
Date of disaster: 1 November 1942.

Before the war, the steamship *Mendoza* operated on the South American service. Following the occupation of France by German forces in the summer of 1940, the *Mendoza*, which had been away from her home port, was seized by the British and placed under the control of the Ministry of War Transport, managed for them by Alfred Holt & Co (Blue Funnel Line). She was sunk by a German submarine on 1 November 1942 about 100 miles west of Durban, in the position 29°20′S–32°14′E. She had been on a voyage from Mombasa to Durban and was carrying 253 military and naval personnel plus a 153-strong crew. Of these, 23 crew-members were killed, including the master, Capt B.T. Batho, as well as a small number of the passengers.

ZAANDAM (1939–1942)

Holland Amerika Line, Netherlands; Wilton Fijenoord, Rotterdam.
10,909 GRT, 501ft (152.7m) LOA, 64ft (19.5m) beam.
160 passengers in single class.
Diesel engines, twin screw, 18kts.
Date of disaster: 2 November 1942.

The *Zaandam* and *Noordam* entered the service from Rotterdam to New York in the months preceding the Second World War and completed only a small number of round voyages before hostilities interrupted their transatlantic schedules. From May 1940 they were placed initially under the control of the British Ministry of War Transport, but were later allocated to the US War Shipping Administration for war service in the Pacific and Far Eastern theatres.

Various voyages were undertaken by the *Zaandam*, to

The Dutch passenger ship Zaandam, *torpedoed in November 1942.* (L.L. von Münching)

New Zealand, Australia, Sumatra, Java, Chile, South Africa, and Ismailia, until on 21 October 1942 she left Cape Town for New York on what was to turn out to be her last trip, carrying a cargo of ore, flax, and hemp, and a complement of 299, comprising 130 crew and 169 passengers. Among the latter were survivors from the sunken vessels *Examelia, Swiftsure, Coloradan*, and *Chickasaw City*. On 2 November, when some 300 miles off the coast of Brazil, north-east of Cape San Roque, the *Zaandam* was hit by two torpedoes from the *U174* and sank inside 10 minutes. The position is variously given as 01°23′S–36°22′W, 02°40′N–39°50′W, or 01°17′N–36°40′W. Only the starboard boats could be launched, those on the port side having been destroyed by the explosions. It was ultimately established that 130 of those aboard were killed as a result of the attack, including 69 of the survivors from the ships sunk previously, but these figures were only arrived at after some considerable passage of time.

The first group of survivors, a total of 106 men in two lifeboats, under the charge of Second Officer K. Karssen, were picked up by the American tanker *Gulf State* five days after the sinking. They were taken to Port of Spain, Trinidad. A second party, numbering 60, under Second Officer W. Broekhof, landed on a remote part of the Brazilian coast on 10 November; that they had come safely through the ordeal only became known when the officers rode on horseback to Barreirinhas and had the chief of police there advise the British consul. For the final three survivors there was a harrowing test of human endurance, an epic story of 83 days adrift on the open ocean on a flimsy raft, one of the longest such experiences on record. At the outset there had been five men on the raft but two Americans, George Beasley and James Maddox, died on the 66th and 77th days respectively. The remaining three castaways, two Dutchmen, Cornelis Van der Slot and Nicko Hoogendam, and an American, Basil Izzi, kept themselves alive on rainwater and the occasional snared fish or seabird. They were picked up by a United States Navy patrol craft on 24 January 1943, in the position 09°14′N–58°45′W, having drifted almost 2,000 miles. Their survival was a tribute to both their fortitude and determination.

Two of Holland's most experienced shipmasters perished with the *Zaandam*, Capt Jacob M. Stamperius, the ship's commander, and Capt Jan Pieter Wepster of the *Volendam*, who was travelling as a passenger.

CITY OF CAIRO (1915–1942)

Ellerman & Bucknall Line, Great Britain; Earle's, Hull.
8,034 GRT, 465ft (141.7m) LOA, 55ft (16.8m) beam.
Quadruple expansion SR engine, single screw, 13.5kts.
Date of disaster: 6 November 1942.

The *City of Cairo* was sunk by a torpedo on 6 November 1942 while sailing from Bombay and Cape Town to Pernambuco (Recife), Brazil, en route to the United Kingdom. The attack took place in the position 23°30′S–05°30′W, 82 crew-members and 22 passengers being killed. Two of the survivors, the third officer and a female passenger, were picked up by a Brazilian minelayer

The City of Cairo. (World Ship Society)

on 27 December 1942 after 51 days on the open sea – another of the great examples of endurance at sea. Three other survivors were taken aboard the German blockade runner *Rhakotis* but two were killed later when she was sunk by British warships, 200 miles north-west of Cape Finisterre on 1 January 1943.

PRESIDENT VAN BUREN as *THOMAS R STONE* (1941–1942)

American President Line, USA; Newport News SB & Drydock Co, Virginia.
9,260 GRT, 465ft (141.7m) length, 69ft (21.0m) beam.
96 passengers in single class.
Steam turbine, single screw, 16.5kts.
Date of disaster: 7 November 1942.

The almost new *President Van Buren*, one of a sextet built for the transpacific service, was lost while sailing as a transport under the name *Thomas R Stone*. On 7 November 1942 she was torpedoed and sunk 120 miles north-west of Algiers while under tow. All aboard her were saved. The wreck, which lay in shallow water, was subjected to salvage attempts, but when these failed it was broken up in 1949.

PORTHOS (1914–1942)

Messageries Maritimes, France; Ateliers et Chantiers de la Gironde, Bordeaux.
12,692 GRT, 528ft (160.9m) LOA, 61ft (18.6m) beam.
1,598 passengers in four classes.
Triple expansion SR engines, twin screw, 14kts.
Date of disaster: 8 November 1942.

Messageries Maritimes' Porthos, *one of the many Allied passenger ship losses which occurred during the North African landings.* (World Ship Society)

The *Porthos*, a sister ship to the liner *Athos*, which had been sunk by a torpedo in February 1917, was herself a casualty of the Second World War, capsizing after being bombed during the Allied landings at Casablanca on 8 November 1942. Two years earlier, on 24 September 1940, she had been damaged at Dakar when British warships bombarded the French naval base there. Salvage of the *Porthos* commenced in November 1944 and she was raised the following May. However, she never resumed commercial service, for in a gale in 1946 the still-damaged wreck was driven on the rocks and sank for a second time. After she had been refloated once more, the *Porthos* was broken up, the work being complete by 15 January 1951.

SAVOIE ex-*KRALJICA MARIJA* ex-*ARAGUAYA* (1906–1942)

French Line (CGT), France; Workman Clark, Belfast.
10,196 GRT, 532ft (162.1m) LOA, 61ft (18.6m) beam.
365 passengers in single class (as a British ship).
Quadruple expansion SR engines, twin screw, 16kts.
Date of disaster: 8 November 1942.

The Royal Mail liner *Araguaya*, a veteran of the La Plata service and hospital-ship duties in the First World War, was sold to Jugoslavenska Lloyd in November 1930 and renamed *Kraljica Marija*. In 1940 she was resold to the French Government, managed for them by the French Line. She was rechristened *Savoie*, with a view to her being placed in the South American service once more but these plans were frustrated by the fall of France in June 1940. On 8 November 1942, at the time of the North African landings, the *Savoie* was sunk by Allied gunfire while she was anchored in the harbour at Casablanca. Subsequently refloated, she was towed outside the harbour and beached, to be broken up where she lay at a later date.

SANTA LUCIA as *LEEDSTOWN* (1933–1942)

Grace Line, USA; Federal SB Co, Kearny, New Jersey.
9,135 GRT, 484ft (147.5m) length, 72ft (21.9m) beam.
Steam turbines, twin screw, 20kts.
Date of disaster: 9 November 1942.

Passenger vessels of the Grace Line operated between New York and ports on the west coast of South America. The *Santa Lucia* was one of a quartet of modern two-funnelled liners added to the service between 1932 and 1933. In the Second World War she was taken over for Government service as a troopship, under the name *Leedstown*. Allied forces suffered heavy troopship losses during the invasion of North Africa, the *Leedstown* being the first American ship to be sunk during the operation. After being subjected to aerial bombardment by German aircraft, she was torpedoed and sunk off Algiers just after midday on 9 November 1942.

AWATEA (1936–1942)

Union SS Co of New Zealand, Great Britain; Vickers Armstrong, Barrow-in-Furness.
13,482 GRT, 545ft (166.1m) LOA, 74ft (22.6m) beam.
566 passengers in three classes.
Steam turbines, twin screw, 22kts.
Date of disaster: 11 November 1942.

One of the largest liners to serve a New Zealand shipping

One of the largest vessels to be operated by the Union Steamship Company of New Zealand, the Awatea *was sunk during the North African campaign.* (Author's collection)

company, the *Awatea* operated between Sydney and Auckland, with some voyages extended as far as Vancouver from 1940. In September 1941 she entered service as a troopship and she was employed transporting commandos to North Africa during Operation Torch in November 1942. On 11 November the *Awatea* was attacked only one mile from the port breakwater by six German bomber aircraft as she was leaving Bougie (Bejaia), bound for Gibraltar. Though two of the bombers were shot down by her anti-aircraft guns, the aerial attack inflicted widespread damage on the *Awatea*, setting her on fire and compelling the crew to abandon ship. The drifting derelict eventually sank near Cape Carbon. There were no deaths, though four of her complement were wounded.

CATHAY (1925–1942)

P&O Line, Great Britain; Barclay Curle, Glasgow.
15,225 GRT, 545ft (166.1m) LOA, 70ft (21.3m) beam.
306 passengers in two classes.
Quadruple expansion SR engines, twin screw, 16kts.
Date of disaster: 11 November 1942.

The liner *Cathay*, with her sisters *Comorin* and *Chitral*,

The P&O liner Cathay *as built, with black colouring and twin funnels.* (A. Duncan)

The troopship Cathay *on fire and sinking following German air attacks off Bougie, Algeria.* (Imperial War Museum, Neg. A12834)

was built for the Australian service from London. She spent the first three years of the Second World War employed as an auxiliary cruiser but was converted to a troopship in 1942. She took part in the North African landings the same year. Arriving off Bougie from Glasgow on 11 November, she was unloading her troops when German aircraft bombed her. An unexploded bomb, lodged between the decks above one of her canteens, detonated spectacularly during the night, sealing her fate. Ablaze from end to end, she sank the following day in the position 36°44'N–05°07'E, with the loss of one life.

EXCALIBUR as *JOSEPH HEWES* (1930–1942)

American Export Line, USA; New York SB Corp, Camden, New Jersey.
9,359 GRT, 474ft (144.5m) LOA, 61ft (18.6m) beam.
125 passengers in single class.
Steam turbine, single screw, 16kts.
Date of disaster: 11 November 1942.

The American Export Line's steamship *Excalibur* operated with three sisters on the transatlantic service from New York to Mediterranean ports. She was taken over for war service as a troop transport in 1941, when she was renamed *Joseph Hewes.* In consort with a number of other converted American liners, the *Joseph Hewes* took part in the Allied landings in North Africa in November 1942, when she was just one of five American troopships accounted for by submarine attacks. While lying in Fedalah Roads, near Rabat, on 11 November, she was torpedoed and sunk by the German submarine *U173*. In excess of 100 American officers and men died in the sinking of the transports. Many more were injured.

The Excalibur *in her peacetime American Export Line colours, before being renamed the* Joseph Hewes. (World Ship Society)

The Hokoku Maru, *seen here, and her sister* Aikoku Maru *were employed as auxiliary cruisers during the war.* (Mitsui-OSK Lines)

HOKOKU MARU (1940–1942)

Osaka Shosen Kaisha, Japan; Tama SB Co., Tama.
10,438 GRT, 537ft (163.7m) LOA, 66ft (20.1m) beam.
400 passengers in three classes.
Diesel engines, twin screw, 17kts.
Date of disaster: 11 November 1942.

After only 18 months in the Japan to Europe service, the *Hokoku Maru* was refitted for the Japanese Navy as an auxiliary cruiser, being commissioned on 10 March 1942. Eight months later, on 11 November, while operating in the Indian Ocean with her sister ship *Aikoku Maru*, she intercepted the Dutch tanker *Ondina* in the position 19°45′S–92°40′E, escorted by the Indian minesweeper *Bengal*. The Japanese vessels opened fire with their 6-inch guns at 3,500 yds as they closed in, but although they were the heavier-armed, the *Bengal* returned their fire most effectively, hitting the *Hokoku Maru* with a number of shells and causing an explosion which set her on fire. The *Ondina* also joined the fray and scored hits on both Japanese ships, but was struck in reply by shells and torpedoes. Capt W. Horsman, her master, was killed, and after their ammunition was exhausted and the *Ondina* had been abandoned, other members of her crew lost their lives in the boats.

By this time the four ships had been separated. The *Hokoku Maru* sank in the approximate position 20°00′S–93°00′E following a second explosion, while the *Aikoku Maru* withdrew, believing that the *Bengal* and *Ondina* had both been sunk, a belief shared by the Allied vessels of each other. In fact, both survived the exchange: the badly-damaged *Bengal* limped back to Colombo, while the *Ondina*'s crew reboarded her and succeeded in reaching Freemantle.

LIPARI (1922–1942)

Chargéurs Reunis, France; Ateliers et Chantiers de la Loire, St Nazaire.
9,954 GRT, 478ft (145.7m) length, 59ft (18.0m) beam.
225 passengers in three classes.
Steam turbines, twin screw, 13.5kts.
Date of disaster: 11 November 1942.

Sister ship to the *Hoedic*, which capsized at Le Havre in November 1928 and was rebuilt as the *Foucauld*, the *Lipari* was sunk in the harbour at Casablanca after catching fire and breaking in two when Allied warships shelled the port from 8 to 11 November 1942. Before the Second World War she had been engaged in the South American service from France.

NIEUW ZEELAND (1928–1942)

Koninklijke Paketvaart Maatschappij, Netherlands; Rotterdamsche Droogdok Maatschappij, Rotterdam.
11,069 GRT, 527ft (160.6m) LOA, 62ft (18.9m) beam.
155 passengers in single class.
Steam turbines, twin screw, 15kts.
Date of disaster: 11 November 1942.

The *Nieuw Zeeland* and her sister liner, *Nieuw Holland*, were engaged in the service from Java to Australia. In 1940 both ships became troopships under British management on behalf of the Dutch Government in exile. The *Nieuw Zeeland* was involved in the transportation of troops for the North Africa landings in 1942 when, on 11 November, while returning to the United Kingdom, she was torpedoed and sunk off the African coast by the German submarine *U407* in the position 35°59′N–03°45′W. Fifteen members of her crew of 243 were killed, but a small group of 13 passengers were all saved.

The Dutch passenger ship Nieuw Zeeland, *owned by the Royal Packet Navigation Company.* (World Ship Society)

The Viceroy of India *introduced turbo-electric propulsion to the P&O line fleet.* (Maritime Photo Library)

VICEROY OF INDIA (1929–1942)

P&O Line, Great Britain; Alexander Stephen, Glasgow.
19,627 GRT, 612ft (186.5m) LOA, 76ft (23.2m) beam.
673 passengers in two classes.
Turbo-electric propulsion, twin screw, 20kts.
Date of disaster: 11 November 1942.

One of the first large turbo-electric liners to be built, the *Viceroy of India* entered the London to Bombay service in February 1929 and remained so employed until September 1939, when she was converted into a troopship. The *Viceroy of India* was another casualty of the North African landings in November 1942. After disembarking her troops at Algiers she set sail for Gibraltar and the United Kingdom on 11 November, only to be torpedoed by the German submarine *U407* 35 miles from Oran, in the position 36°24′N–00°35′W. Although the *Viceroy of India* was by then empty of troops, there were 22 passengers aboard as well as a crew of 432, of whom four lost their lives. The remainder were picked up by the destroyer HMS *Boadicea.*

EXETER as *EDWARD RUTLEDGE* (1931–1942)

American Export Line, USA; New York SB Corp, Camden, New Jersey.
9,360 GRT, 450ft (137.2m) length, 61ft (18.6m) beam.
147 passengers in single class.
Steam turbine, single screw, 16kts.
Date of disaster: 12 November 1942.

The North Atlantic steamship *Exeter* was renamed *Edward*

Rutledge in late-1941 after she was taken over as a naval transport by the United States Navy. In consort with her sister ship, the former *Excalibur*, and other requisitioned American passenger ships, she was involved in the Allied landings at Casablanca, Morocco, in November 1942. On 12 November, while approaching the beaches off Fedalah, the *Edward Rutledge* was torpedoed and sunk by the German submarine *U130*.

KARANJA (1931–1942)

British India Line, Great Britain; Alexander Stephen, Glasgow.
9,891 GRT, 486ft (148.1m) LOA, 64ft (19.5m) beam.
250 passengers.
Steam turbines, twin screw, 18kts.
Date of disaster: 12 November 1942.

The liners *Karanja* and *Kenya*, partners in the East African service, were taken over for naval and military duties during the Second World War, the *Karanja* in the role of a transport. She participated in the North African landings, but was bombed and sunk by German aircraft off Bougie (Bejaia) on 12 November 1942.

PRESIDENT CLEVELAND ex-*GOLDEN STATE* as *TASKER H BLISS* (1921–1942)

American President Line, USA; Newport News SB & Drydock Co, Virginia.
14,123 GRT, 539ft (164.3m) LOA, 72ft (21.9m) beam.
560 passengers in two classes
Steam turbines, twin screw, 17kts.
Date of disaster: 12 November 1942.

This liner spent 20 years on the San Francisco to Far East service, four of them with the Pacific Mail Line, another 13 with the Dollar Line, and the final three with the American President Line. She was renamed *President Cleveland* in 1922. In June 1941 she became the United States Army transport *Tasker H Bliss*, later transferring to the Navy. The *Tasker H Bliss* was another of the casualties of the North African campaign, being torpedoed and sunk by the *U130* off Fedalah, Casablanca, on 12 November 1942.

PRESIDENT PIERCE ex-*HAWKEYE STATE* ex-*BERRIEN* as *HUGH L SCOTT* (1921–1942)

American President Line, USA; Bethlehem SB Corp, Sparrows Point, Maryland.
12,579 GRT, 535ft (163.1m) LOA, 72ft (21.9m) beam.
561 passengers in two classes.
Steam turbines, twin screw, 17kts.
Date of disaster: 12 November 1942.

One of a large class of standard ships designed for the United States Shipping Board, the *President Pierce* served in turn the Pacific Mail Line, the Dollar Line, and its successor the American President Line, serving the transpacific trade. Prior to 1922 she had been operated by Matson Line. In July 1941 she was taken over for military service with the United States Navy under the name *Hugh L Scott*, and was one of the five American naval transports lost on or about 12 November 1942 during the Allied landings in North Africa. Torpedoed and sunk while anchored off Fedalah, near Casablanca, the *Hugh L Scott* was another victim of the *U130*, which had penetrated a minefield and a destroyer screen to carry out the attack.

British India's Karanja *was sunk in the same attack which claimed the P&O ship* Cathay. (World Ship Society)

The Arizona Maru. (A. Duncan)

ARIZONA MARU (1920–1942)

Osaka Shosen Kaisha, Japan; Mitsubishi, Nagasaki.
9,684 GRT, 475ft (144.8m) length, 61ft (18.6m) beam.
Triple expansion SR engines, twin screw, 13kts.
Date of disaster: 14 November 1942.

The *Arizona Maru* was the last vessel of a five-ship class built for transpacific operations. Her four sisters were lost in torpedo attacks during the Second World War, but the *Arizona Maru* was sunk in an aerial attack. On 14 November 1942 she was attacked by American land and carrier-based aircraft near the Solomon Islands, and went down in the position 08°30'S–158°45'E.

NARKUNDA (1920–1942)

P&O Line, Great Britain; Harland & Wolff, Belfast.
16,632 GRT, 606ft (184.7m) LOA, 69ft (21.0m) beam.
673 passengers in two classes.
Quadruple expansion SR engines, twin screw, 17.5kts.
Date of disaster: 14 November 1942.

The *Narkunda* and her sister *Naldera* were building during the First World War, and consequently there were various plans to complete them as warships, including auxiliary cruisers and aircraft carriers, rather than as passenger ships. However, the pair finally entered the London to Sydney service as originally planned. The *Naldera* was scrapped in

The Narkunda *was lost off Bougie, P&O suffering a total of four losses during Operation Torch.* (A. Duncan)

1938 but, remarkably, the *Narkunda* was given a new lease of life when, simultaneously, she was converted to oil-firing. In May 1940 she was taken over as a troopship. She participated in the invasion of North Africa in November 1942, but was sunk soon after landing her troops at the Bougie (Bejaia) beachhead. She had already been damaged as she approached the landing zone on 13 November, when the Italian submarine *Platino* succeeded in torpedoing her. As she departed for Algiers the following evening, after the disembarkation, German aircraft bombed and sank her in the position 36°49′N–05°01′E. Thirty one members of her crew lost their lives.

SADO MARU (1898–1942)

Nippon Yusen Kaisha, Japan; Workman Clark, Belfast.
6,227 GRT, 445ft (135.6m) length, 49ft (14.9m) beam.
213 passengers in three classes.
Triple expansion SR engines, twin screw, 14kts.
Date of disaster: 14 November 1942.

The *Sado Maru* was one of a group of 12 similar ships that had been employed on various sea routes from Japan throughout prolonged careers. The *Sado Maru* operated on the service to Europe via the Red Sea and the Mediterranean. She was sunk near the Solomon Islands on 14 November 1942 by a combination of United States' land and carrier-based warplanes. The position was 08°30′S–158°45′E.

WARWICK CASTLE (1931–1942)

Union Castle Line, Great Britain; Harland & Wolff, Belfast.
20,107 GRT, 677ft (206.3m) LOA, 75ft (22.9m) beam.
699 passengers in three classes.
Diesel engines, twin screw, 17kts.
Date of disaster: 14 November 1942.

In what amounted to a revolutionary change of policy in new construction for their fleet, Union Castle had ordered three large motorships for the express service to the Cape from Southampton. The *Warwick Castle* was the last of the class to enter service. In 1938 the three liners were rebuilt. More powerful engines were installed and their twin funnels were replaced with a single, more modern one. The *Warwick Castle* was employed as a troopship during the Second World War, and was attacked by the German submarine *U413*, on 14 November 1942, in similar circumstances to the *Viceroy of India*, as she was returning from landing invasion troops in French North Africa. The attack took place 200 miles off the coast of Portugal, in the position 39°16′N–13°25′W, while the *Warwick Castle* was en route from Gibraltar to the River Clyde. On board were 165 passengers and a crew of 263, of whom 63 were killed including the commander, Capt H.L. Shaw.

ETTRICK (1938–1942)

P&O Line, Great Britain; Barclay Curle, Glasgow.
11,279 GRT, 517ft (157.6m) LOA, 63ft (19.2m) beam.
194 passengers in two classes.
Diesel engines, twin screw, 17kts.
Date of disaster: 15 November 1942.

In the late 1930s a class of four troop-carrying passenger motorships were built to the order of the Ministry of Transport. They were the *Dilwara* and *Dunera*, owned by the British India Line, P&O's *Ettrick*, and Bibby Line's *Devonshire*. When not engaged in trooping activities they reverted to relatively inexpensive cruise voyages. During the Second World War the four near sisters became full-time troopships, all but the *Ettrick* surviving the hostilities

The Union Castle mail ship Warwick Castle. (World Ship Society)

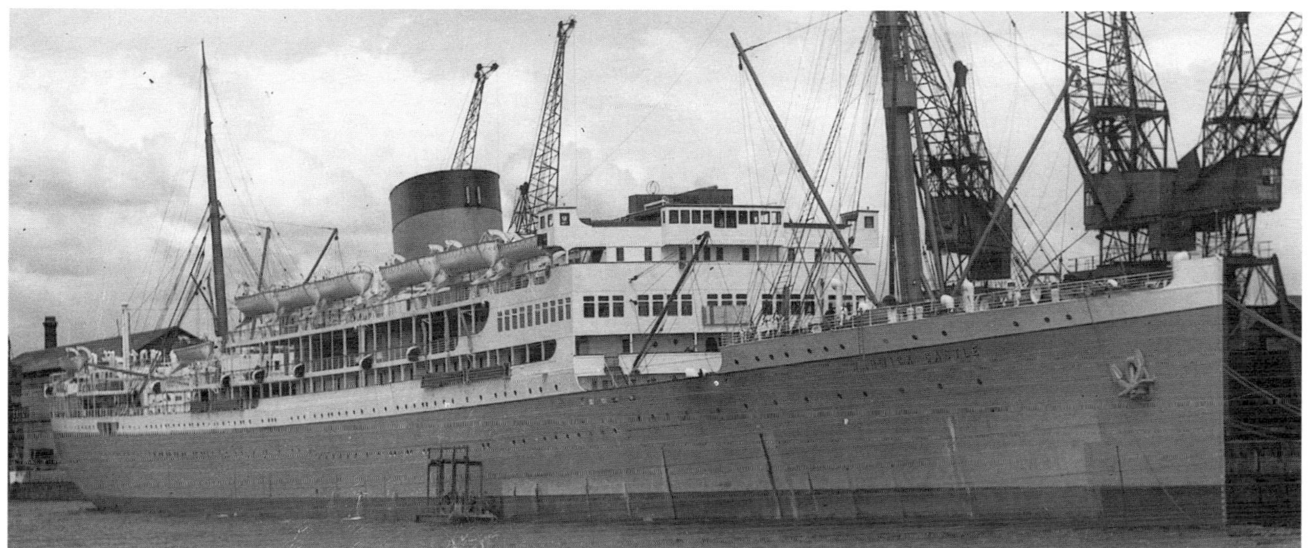

The Ettrick *was also employed as a Ministry of Transport troopship prior to the Second World War, though with a lower troop capacity.* (World Ship Society)

unscathed. The *Ettrick* was enlisted for support and transport duties during the Allied operations in French North Africa in November 1942. While returning to the United Kingdom on 15 November, after the landings were completed, she was torpedoed and sunk by the German submarine *U155* 150 miles west of Gibraltar, in the position 36°13′N–07°54′W. The *Ettrick* had been heading for the River Clyde to disembark a small number of military personnel she was carrying in addition to her crew of 209. There were 25 casualties in all, 18 of them naval ratings and seven Indian crew members.

TILAWA (1924–1942)

British India Line, Great Britain; Hawthorn Leslie, Newcastle.
10,006 GRT, 471ft (143.6m) LOA, 59ft (18.0m) beam.
1,135 passengers.
Quadruple expansion SR engine, single screw, 12kts.
Date of disaster: 23 November 1942.

The British India steamships *Talma* and *Tilawa* maintained the service from Calcutta to Japan, offering accommodation for 1,000 Asiatic passengers in steerage class in addition to other grades. During a voyage from Bombay to Mombasa and Durban on 23 November 1942, the *Tilawa* was attacked by the Japanese submarine *I29*. The first torpedo struck her when she was in the position 07°35′N–61°06′E and, although the damage was not critical, it set off a panic among the 732 native passengers. They rushed the boats and many accidents were caused in their desperation to get off the ship. Some were crushed by falling boats which were lowered incorrectly, others were drowned when overcrowded boats capsized. After the evacuation had been satisfactorily and more orderly concluded the *Tilawa*'s master, Capt F. Robinson, had the boats and rafts re-assembled around the ship with a view to re-boarding her, as it was evident that she was not going to sink. At this point, however, the *I29* fired a second torpedo and the *Tilawa* rolled over and soon disappeared beneath the surface.

Apart from her passengers, she had also been carrying a crew of 226, of whom 28 were killed. The death-toll among the natives amounted to 252, an unnecessarily high figure due almost entirely to their undisciplined behaviour when the Tilawa was abandoned.

The British India passenger vessel Tilawa. (P&O Group)

ALASKAN (1918–1942)

American Hawaiian SS Co, USA; Bethlehem SB Corp, Sparrows Point, Maryland.
5,364 GRT, 415ft (126.5m) length, 54ft (16.5m) beam.
Triple expansion SR engines, 10.5kts.
Date of disaster: 28 November 1942.

The *Alaskan* was torpedoed by a German submarine 600 miles north-east of Natal, Brazil, during a voyage from Port Said and Table Bay for Paramaribo and the United States. She was not sailing in convoy. She sank on 28 November 1942 in the position 03°58′N–26°19′W with the loss of five lives out of her crew of 46. Her master, Capt E.E. Greenlaw, was among the survivors.

NOVA SCOTIA (1926–1942)

Furness Warren Line, Great Britain; Vickers Armstrong, Barrow-in-Furness.
6,796 GRT, 423ft (128.9m) LOA, 55ft (16.8m) beam.
185 passengers in two classes.
Quadruple expansion SR engines, twin screw, 15kts.
Date of disaster: 28 November 1942.

The *Nova Scotia* and her sister *Newfoundland* were engaged on the passenger-cargo service from Liverpool to St John's, Newfoundland, Halifax, and Boston. After the outbreak of the Second World War, the *Nova Scotia* came under the control of the Ministry of War Shipping and served as a troopship on other, less familiar ocean routes. On 28 November 1942 she was sailing from Aden to Durban with a full complement comprising 127 crew, 12 service personnel, six non-military passengers, and 780 Italian prisoners-of-war under the guard of 130 South African troops. Off the African coast, near Lourenco Marques (Maputo), in the position 28°30′S–33°00′E, she was torpedoed by a German

The heavy loss of life suffered when the Furness Warren Line passenger liner Nova Scotia *was torpedoed made it one of the worst British maritime disasters of the Second World War.* (Furness Withy Group)

submarine and sank rapidly with a heavy loss of life. Of the 1,055 people aboard, 863 reportedly lost their lives. Only 16 of the crew survived, while the largest number of casualties was among the Italian prisoners-of-war, of whom 650 perished. There were 42 survivors among the South African guards. In some accounts the total casualties are put at 768, but this figure cannot be substantiated.

LLANDAFF CASTLE (1926–1942)

Union Castle Line, Great Britain; Workman Clark, Belfast.
10,786 GRT, 490ft (149.3m) LOA, 61ft (18.6m) beam.
390 passengers.
Quadruple expansion SR engines, twin screw, 14kts.
Date of disaster: 30 November 1942.

On the round-Africa service from London, the *Llandaff Castle* ran in consort with the *Llandovery Castle*, the second ship to bear the name. In 1940, the *Llandaff Castle* became a troopship and on 30 November 1942, while serving in this role, she was torpedoed by the German submarine *U177* while bound from Mombasa and Dar-es-Salaam to Durban, following the Allied landings in Madagascar. The attack took place about 100 miles south-east of Lourenco Marques (Maputo), in the position 27°20′S–33°40′E. On board were 150 passengers and 163 crew, three of the latter losing their lives.

NANKIN as *LEUTHEN* (1912–1942)

Eastern & Australian SS Co, Great Britain; Caird, Greenock.
7,131 GRT, 449ft (136.9m) length, 52ft (15.9m) beam.
Quadruple expansion SR engines, twin screw, 14kts.
Date of disaster: 30 November 1942.

The *Nankin* had served with three other P&O classmates – the *Nagoya*, *Nellore*, and *Novara* – until her sale to the Eastern & Australian company in September 1932. She became a victim of the German auxiliary cruiser *Thor*, which captured her in the Indian Ocean, about 1,000 miles from Australia, on 10 May 1942. The *Thor* took her to Yokohama, where her crew was interned along with prisoners from other ships the raider had captured or sunk. The intention was to use the *Nankin* as a supply ship to support the *Thor*'s raiding activities, and she was renamed *Leuthen* with this in mind. However, when the tanker *Uckermark* exploded in Yokohama on 30 November 1942, destroying the nearby *Thor*, the *Leuthen* was also wrecked by the blast.

COAMO (1925–1942)

New York & Porto Rico Line, USA; Newport News SB & Drydock Co, Virginia.
7,057 GRT, 429ft (130.8m) length, 59ft (18.0m) beam.
Steam turbine, single screw, 16.5kts.
Date of disaster: ? December 1942.

The American liner *Coamo*, built for the Atlantic coast run to the West Indies, became a troopship during the Second World War. In autumn 1942 the Allies were preparing for the invasion of North Africa and a large convoy was mustered to support the landings, the *Coamo* finding herself joined by certain of her peacetime contemporaries, notably the Clyde Mallory liners *Iriquois* and *Shawnee*. After unloading their troops, the *Coamo* and *Shawnee* returned to Gibraltar, where they formed part of an England-bound convoy that sailed on 26 November 1942. One day out, the *Coamo*, which was carrying neither passengers nor cargo, was ordered to sail independently to Norfolk, Virginia. She headed off across the Atlantic unescorted, and was last seen on 1 December in the position 53°00′N–13°19′W. The *Coamo* never arrived at Norfolk, and because no

Top *The P&O liner* Nankin, *later captured in the Pacific by the raider* Thor. (World Ship Society)

Above *The American liner* Coamo *disappeared without trace during a voyage across the Atlantic in December 1942, one of only three such incidents involving passenger ships since 1910.* (Frank Braynard)

information was ever received as to the cause of her disappearance she was ultimately assumed as lost with all hands, the precise cause of the loss unknown. Although it has been speculated that she was torpedoed this is unlikely, for it would have come to light after the war when the enemy's records were surrendered.

CERAMIC (1913–1942)

Shaw Savill & Albion, Great Britain; Harland & Wolff, Belfast.
18,713 GRT, 679ft (207.0m) LOA, 69ft (21.0m) beam.
340 passengers in single class.
Triple expansion SR engines with LP turbine, triple screw, 16kts.
Date of disaster: 6 December 1942.

The *Ceramic* was constructed for the White Star Line's Australia service, serving Sydney from Liverpool for almost 21 years. She was then sold to Shaw Savill & Albion in 1934, from which time Brisbane became her terminus port in Australia. In February 1940 she was converted into a troopship, but her contribution to the war effort lasted only until 6 December 1942, when she was torpedoed west of the Azores, in the position 40°30′N–40°20′W, by the German submarine *U515* under the command of Capt-Lt W. Henke. The *Ceramic* had been bound from Liverpool to St Helena, Durban, and Sydney, carrying 378 passengers and 278 crew. The *U515*'s torpedoes struck her with such devastating impact that she foundered before distress calls could be made. There was only one survivor, Sapper A.E. Munday, who was picked up by another U-boat the following day, after a gale had capsized the lifeboat he had been in.

The Shaw Savill & Albion liner Ceramic. (Furness Withy Group)

STRATHALLAN (1938–1942)

P&O Line, Great Britain; Vickers Armstrong, Barrow-in-Furness.
23,722 GRT, 664ft (202.4m) LOA, 82ft (25.0m) beam.
1,011 passengers in two classes.
Steam turbines, twin screw, 21kts.
Date of disaster: 21 December 1942.

The *Strathallan* was the third ship of the second group of *Strath* liners introduced to the London to Sydney service in the 1930s. Eighteen months after entering service, the *Strathallan* was taken over as a troopship. She became one of the large number of Allied troopships lost at or around the time of the landings in North Africa. Most of the American losses were off Casablanca, while the British casualties were predominantly in the area north of Algeria. The *Strathallan* sailed from Glasgow to the Mediterranean in convoy on 11 December 1942, with a total complement of 5,122, including 4,408 troops, 248 nurses, and a crew of 431. On 21 December, when about 40 miles north of Oran (Ouahran), the German submarine *U562* torpedoed her, starting a fire in the engine-room which spread to a cargo hold containing ammunition. The *Strathallan* was immediately abandoned due to the risk of further explosions, and all but 11 people, six of whom were crew-members, were picked up safely by other ships. The *Strathallan* was taken in tow by a salvage tug but sank the following morning in the position 30°01′N–00°30′W, only 12 miles from port.

P&O's express turbine steamer Strathallan *in the service from London to India and Australia.* (World Ship Society)

Chapter Ten

1943

ENIGMA BREAKS THE U-BOAT CIPHERS

Amphibious operations continued throughout 1943, with landings in Sicily, Calabria and Salerno in the Mediterranean, and at Bougainville in the Solomon Islands. However, the focus of attention during the year once more fell on the submarine war in the Atlantic Ocean. With the build-up for the invasion of Europe beginning to get under way Atlantic traffic became increasingly heavier. Consequently U-boat activity was at its most intensive. The carefully orchestrated attacks of the massed 'wolf packs' were at their most effective in the mid-ocean 'air gap', where they were out of range of shore-based aircraft operating from bases in the USA and Canada on the one side, and Britain and Northern Ireland on the other. March 1943 was the Allies' worst month in the Atlantic, with 43 vessels sunk in the first 20 days. So bad did the situation get that the convoy system was pushed very close to the brink of collapse.

As is so often the case, however, the darkest hour came just before the dawn. The Allies already had at their disposal growing numbers of escort carriers to provide mid-ocean air cover, and quantities of new hunter-killer anti-submarine escorts were leaving the shipyards. Nevertheless, the effectiveness of the latter was limited by their inability to pinpoint the U-boats, which waited until darkness to launch their attacks. The breakthrough came in spring 1943, at the height of the crisis, when 'boffins' at Bletchley Park (predecessor of GCHQ), with their Enigma machines and Colossus computers, broke the Lorenz ciphers by which U-boats were directed to positions in the paths of oncoming convoys. Now it was the turn of the hunters to become the hunted. To say the change in fortunes was dramatic is to be guilty of gross understatement. Hard on the heels of the worst statistics of the war, there followed a period (May to September 1943) during which extremely few Allied ships fell victim to U-boats in the Atlantic.

HEIYO MARU (1930–1943)

Nippon Yusen Kaisha, Japan, Osaka Iron Works, Osaka.
9,816 GRT, 460ft (140.2m) length, 60ft (18.3m) beam.
Diesel engine, single screw, 16kts.
Date of disaster: 17 January 1943.

The motorship *Heiyo Maru* entered service between Kobe and the west coast ports of the United States and South America in 1930. Taken over for military purposes when war broke out between Japan and America, she was torpedoed and sunk near the Marshall Islands on 17 January 1943, in the position 10°13'N–151°25'E.

TEVERE ex-*GABLONZ* (1912–1943)

Lloyd Triestino, Italy; Cantieri San Rocco, Trieste.
8,448 GRT, 452ft (137.8m) length, 56ft (17.1m) beam.
240 passengers.
Quadruple expansion SR engines, twin screw, 16kts.
Date of disaster: 20 January 1943.

The three Lloyd Austriaco sister ships *Helouan*, *Gablonz*, and *Wien* passed into Lloyd Triestino ownership after the First World War, the *Gablonz* being renamed *Tevere*. She was operated in the service from Italy to the Far East until 1940, when she was taken over as a hospital ship with the Italian Navy. She was damaged on 22 February 1941 when she struck a mine in the approaches to Tripoli. On 21 April 1941, while undergoing repairs at Tripoli, she was further damaged during an air raid, and later still, on 20 January 1943, the still not fully-restored *Tevere* was scuttled by Italian forces to deny the Allies access to the port. She was not refloated until 16 January 1950. On 6 May of the same year she was towed to Savona, where she was scrapped.

VIMINALE (1925–1943)

Italia Line, Italy; Cantieri San Rocco, Trieste.
8,657 GRT, 467ft (142.3m) LOA, 57ft (17.4m) beam.
400 passengers.
Diesel engines, twin screw, 13kts.
Date of disaster: 23 January 1943.

The motorship *Viminale* and her sister ship *Esquilino* served on the route from Italy to Australia via Suez, originally under the Lloyd Triestino houseflag but from 1931 for the Italia Flotte Riunite. Like many of the Danish East Asiatic Company's motor vessels, these ships also had no funnels. The *Viminale* was seriously damaged at Palermo on 3 January 1943 by what was described as a 'human torpedo' (probably the 'Chariot', a propeller-driven explosive charge ridden into position by a pair of divers). She was taken in tow for Taranto but was struck by a second projectile on 23

The Tevere *was serving as a hospital ship when her crew deliberately scuttled her at Tripoli.* (World Ship Society)

January and ran aground at Port Salvo, Melito. Refloated soon after, she was towed to Messina instead, where she arrived on 28 January. Inspection of the ship revealed that she was so extensively damaged that repair was unrealistic, so the *Viminale* was abandoned as a total loss.

FUSHIMI (HUSIMI) MARU (1914–1943)

Nippon Yusen Kaisha, Japan; Mitsubishi, Nagasaki.
10,936 GRT, 525ft (160.0m) LOA, 63ft (19.2m) beam.
512 passengers in three classes.
Triple expansion SR engines, twin screw, 15.5kts.
Date of disaster: 1 February 1943.

The *Fushimi Maru* was fourth of a group of five ships built for the European trade, although she spent four-and a-half years (from September 1917) on the service across the Pacific. She was another of the many Japanese losses in the Second World War, sunk by the American submarine USS *Tarpon* off the coast of Honshu on 1 February 1943, in the position 34°16′N–138°17′E.

TATSUTA (TATUTA) MARU (1930–1943)

Nippon Yusen Kaisha, Japan; Mitsubishi, Nagasaki.
16,975 GRT, 583ft (177.7m) LOA, 72ft (21.9m) beam.
820 passengers in three classes.
Diesel engines, quadruple screw, 19kts.
Date of disaster: 8 February 1943.

Sister ship to the *Asama Maru*, the *Tatsuta Maru* operated with her consort on the service from Yokohama to San

Nippon Yusen Kaisha's Tatsuta Maru, *one of three new ships introduced to the Yokohama to San Francisco service in the early 1930s.* (Mitsubishi Heavy Industries)

Francisco. In 1941 she was taken over by the Japanese Navy for trooping duties, in which capacity she was torpedoed and sunk on 8 February 1943 by the US submarine *Tarpon* in the position 33°45'N–140°25'E, about 50 miles south-east of Mikura Jima, off the eastern coast of Honshu.

TAINUI as *EMPIRE TRADER* (1908–1943)

Shaw, Savill & Albion, Great Britain; Workman Clark, Belfast.
9,957 GRT, 477ft (145.4m) length, 61ft (18.6m) beam.
414 passengers in three classes.
Triple expansion SR engines, twin screw, 15kts.
Date of disaster: 21 February 1943.

The Shaw Savill steamship *Tainui* operated on the run to New Zealand with her sister *Arawa*, initially via Cape Horn and later through the Panama Canal. In 1940 she passed to Government ownership under the name *Empire Trader*, although Shaw Savill retained management of her. On 21 February she was torpedoed while crossing to New York from Newport and Belfast, being last sighted in the position 47°40'N–28°46'W. All 106 people aboard were saved, being picked up from her lifeboats some time later.

COLOMBIA (1930–1943)

Royal Netherlands Steamship Co, Netherlands; P. Smit Jr, Rotterdam.
10,782 GRT, 457ft (139.3m) LOA, 61ft (18.6m) beam.
309 passengers in three classes.
Diesel engines, twin screw, 15kts.
Date of disaster: 27 February 1943.

The largest passenger vessel ever to join the Royal Netherlands Steamship Company's fleet, the *Colombia* operated on the route from Amsterdam to Central America. In 1940, after the Netherlands had been overrun by German forces, the *Colombia* was commissioned into the Royal Dutch Navy as a submarine depot ship. While on a voyage from East London to Simonstown on 27 February 1943, she was sunk in the position 33°36'S–27°29'E by the German submarine *U516*. Eight members of her crew were killed.

The first Empress of Canada, *seen in her wartime livery.* (Imperial War Museum, Neg. H13559)

TEIYO MARU ex-*SAARLAND* (1924–1943)

Teikoku Senpaku Kaisha, Japan; Blohm & Voss, Hamburg.
6,863 GRT, 449ft (136.9m) length, 58ft (17.7m) beam.
Steam turbine, single screw, 12.5kts.
Date of disaster: 3 March 1943.

The Hamburg Amerika Line's *Saarland* was employed on the route from Germany to the West Indies. She was transferred to Japanese owners in 1940, though whether this was a normal, commercial transaction or an arrangement necessitated by wartime circumstances is not known. On 3 March 1943 the *Teiyo Maru*, as she had been renamed, was sunk by American and Australian land-based aircraft in the Macassar Straits, going down in the position 07°15'S–148°30'E.

EMPRESS OF CANADA (1922–1943)

Canadian Pacific Line, Great Britain; Fairfield, Glasgow.
21,517 GRT, 653ft (199.0m) LOA, 77ft (23.5m) beam.
1,758 passengers in four classes.
Steam turbines, twin screw, 20kts.
Date of disaster: 14 March 1943.

The *Empress of Canada* was the first major unit to join the Canadian Pacific fleet after the First World War, spending most of her life in the transpacific service between Vancouver and Yokohama. Her accommodation included a large number of spaces for Asiatic steerage passengers. Following the outbreak of war in September 1939, the *Empress of Canada* was converted into a troopship. She was torpedoed by the Italian submarine *Leonardo da Vinci* on 14 March 1943, about 400 miles south of Cape Palmas in the position 01°13'S–09°57'W. She was heading for Takoradi, having left Durban some days earlier, and was carrying about 1,400 Greek and Polish refugees in addition to a contingent of Italian prisoners-of-war. About an hour after the first torpedo attack, the submarine fired a second torpedo. Even though the *Empress of Canada* remained afloat barely 20 minutes after being struck by this, a remarkably large number of people were got safely off the ship. Nevertheless, the death-toll was heavy, with no less than 340 people being killed, including many of the Italian prisoners, 44 members of the crew of 318, and eight gunners. The *Empress of Canada*'s master, Capt G. Goold, was amongst the survivors.

TAKACHIHO (TAKATIHO) MARU (1934–1943)

Osaka Shosen Kaisha, Japan; Mitsubishi, Nagasaki.
8,154 GRT, 473ft (144.2m) LOA, 59ft (18.0m) beam.
785 passengers.
Steam turbines, twin screw, 16.5kts.
Date of disaster: 19 March 1943.

The Japanese liner *Takachiho Maru* served in the Japan to South America trade from 1934 to 1941. Thereafter she was diverted to war duties with the Japanese military forces until 19 March 1943, when she was torpedoed and sunk by the American submarine USS *Kingfish* about 150 miles east of Foochow, in the position 26°00′N–122°18′E.

WINDSOR CASTLE (1922–1943)

Union Castle Line, Great Britain; John Brown, Clydebank.
19,141 GRT, 686ft (209.1m) LOA, 75ft (22.9m) beam.
604 passengers in three classes.
Steam turbines, twin screw, 19kts.
Date of disaster: 23 March 1943.

The *Windsor Castle* and *Arundel Castle* were the first new express liners placed on the South African mail service after the First World War. Completed with four funnels, a refit and modernization in 1937 reduced the number to two, while other refinements included a raked bow which added 25ft to their length. With the commencement of hostilities in September 1939, the *Windsor Castle* was converted into a troopship. She was lost on 23 March 1943 when German aircraft torpedoed her 110 miles north-west of Algiers, in the

Below *The Cape mail ship* Windsor Castle *seen after reconstruction had reduced her funnels from four to two and extended her bow with a modern rake.* (British & Commonwealth Shipping Co)

Bottom *The last moments of the* Windsor Castle, *viewed from an escorting naval ship. The launch has just assisted in the recovery of survivors.* (British & Commonwealth Shipping Co)

position 37°27'N–00°54'E according to her master, though Lloyds record the position as 37°28'N–01°10'E. The *Windsor Castle* was sailing in a convoy that had left Greenock some days earlier, and she had 290 crew and 2,699 troops aboard. Fortunately she remained afloat for 13 hours after the attack, enabling other convoy ships and escorts to take off her entire complement, apart from one crewman who was killed. She finally sank by the stern while rescue vessels were still gathered about her.

SUWA MARU (1914–1943)

Nippon Yusen Kaisha, Japan; Mitsubishi, Nagasaki.
10,672 GRT, 521ft (158.8m) LOA, 62ft (18.9m) beam.
511 passengers in three classes.
Triple expansion SR engines, twin screw, 15.5kts.
Date of disaster: 28 March 1943.

The troop transport *Suwa Maru* was torpedoed south-west of Wake Island on 28 March 1943 by the American submarine USS *Tunny*. She was run aground, and it was hoped that she might be refloated later and repaired. However, this was not to be, for on 5 April two more US submarines, the *Seadragon* and *Finback*, finished her off. Her wreck lay in the position 19°13'N–166°34'E.

The *Suwa Maru* came from an unlucky class, all four of her sister ships also being lost as a result of hostile action. Apart from short periods working in the Pacific, the entire class had operated on the service between Japan and Europe.

CITY OF BARODA (1918–1943)

Ellerman Lines, Great Britain; Barclay Curle, Glasgow.
7,129 GRT, 433ft (132.0m) length, 57ft (17.4m) beam.
Triple expansion SR engine, single screw, 12kts.
Date of disaster: 2 April 1943.

The steamship *City of Baroda* was bound for Durban, Colombo, and Calcutta from London and Trinidad, with 143 passengers and 160 crew, when she was torpedoed and sunk by a German submarine on 2 April 1943. The attack occurred near Luderitz, South Africa, in a position variously given as 26°56'S–15°21'E and 27°56'S–15°21'E, shortly after the *City of Baroda* had left Walvis Bay, Namibia. One member of the crew and 13 passengers lost their lives. The ship broke in two after grounding in the position 27°20'S–15°06'E, and by 26 April the wreck had disappeared altogether.

LA PLATA ex-*SACHSEN* (1922–1943)

Hamburg Sud-Amerika Line, Germany; Bremer Vulkan, Vegesack.
8,109 GRT, 468ft (142.6m) length, 58ft (17.7m) beam.
20 passengers in single class.
Triple expansion SR engine, single screw, 12.5kts.
Date of disaster: 4 April 1943.

The South American service steamship *La Plata* was destroyed by United States aircraft when they attacked shipping off the Norwegian port of Bodo on 4 April 1943.

The Suwa Maru *commenced her operational life on the Japan to Europe service until the submarine danger compelled her owners to transfer her to a Pacific route in September 1917.* (World Ship Society)

The Lloyd Triestino Francesco Crispi *in Transatlantica Italiana colours.* (Tom Rayner)

Set on fire, she ran aground near Rodoy, in the position 66°39'N–13°06'E. The wreck was further damaged in an air raid on 26 April 1944, so that when salvage was later undertaken only the after part was raised. This was towed to Stavanger for scrapping.

LOMBARDIA ex-*RESOLUTE* ex-*BRABANTIA* ex- *WILLIAM O'SWALD* (1920–1943)

Lloyd Triestino, Italy; Deschimag AG Weser, Bremen.
20,006 GRT, 616ft (187.8m) LOA, 72ft (21.9m) beam.
103 passengers plus 4,420 troops.
Triple expansion SR engines with LP turbine, triple screw, 17kts.
Date of disaster: 4 April 1943.

After a varied career, commencing as the centre of a reparations dispute at the end of the First World War, followed by 15 years' service on various routes for three different owners, this liner was sold to the Italian Government in August 1935 for conversion into a troopship, being managed for them by Lloyd Triestino. Prior to this her longest spell in one company's ownership – nine years from 1926 – had been with the Hamburg Amerika Line, serving on the North Atlantic run with her sister ship *Reliance*. While serving as a troopship, the *Lombardia* was caught in an air raid on Naples on 4 April 1943, bomb hits leaving her flooded and grounded. Four months later to the day, she was hit in a second strike, when she caught fire, burnt out, and sank. Her wreck was raised in the winter of 1946–1947, and on 1 June 1947 was towed to La Spezia, where it was broken up.

WAROONGA ex-*HORORATA* (1914–1943)

British India Line, Great Britain; William Denny, Dumbarton.
9,365 GRT, 511ft (155.7m) length, 64ft (19.5m) beam.
Quadruple expansion SR engines, twin screw, 14kts.
Date of disaster: 6 April 1943.

Formerly the *Hororata* of the New Zealand Line, the *Waroonga* was torpedoed by a German submarine while sailing in convoy from New York to Liverpool on 6 April 1943, her voyage having commenced at Sydney. The attack took place 500 miles south-east of Cape Farewell, Greenland, in the position 57°10'N–35°30'W. Out of 132 people aboard, 19 were lost, six of them passengers.

FRANCESCO CRISPI (1925–1943)

Lloyd Triestino, Italy; Ansaldo San Giorgio, Muggiano.
7,464 GRT, 447ft (136.2m) LOA, 52ft (15.9m) beam.
Steam turbines, twin screw, 14.5kts.
Date of disaster: 19 April 1943.

The *Francesco Crispi* and her sister ship, *Giuseppe Mazzini*, were originally built for the Transatlantic Italiana Company, passing to Lloyd Triestino in the early 1930s. Both ships operated between Italy and Latin America. The *Francesco Crispi* was torpedoed and sunk by a British submarine on 19 April 1943 with the loss of over 800 lives. She was attacked about 18 miles from Cape Le Serre, Elba, in the position 42°46'N–09°46'E.

AMERIKA (1930–1943)

East Asiatic Co, Denmark; Burmeister & Wain, Copenhagen.
10,218 GRT, 484ft (147.5m) LOA, 62ft (18.9m) beam.
52 passengers in single class.
Diesel engine, single screw, 14kts.
Date of disaster: 22 April 1943.

Following the German occupation of Denmark in April 1940, the motorship *Amerika* came under the British flag, managed for the Ministry of War Shipping by the United Baltic Corporation but remaining under the command of her Danish master, Capt Chr. Nielsen. On 22 April 1943, while bound in convoy from Halifax, Nova Scotia, to Liverpool with a general cargo, the *Amerika* was torpedoed by the German submarine *U306*. She sank in the position

The Amerika, *third of East Asiatic's distinctive motor vessels to be sunk in the Second World War.* (East Asiatic Company)

57°30′N–42°50′W. Besides her cargo, the *Amerika* had 72 crew, 53 passengers, and 15 gunners aboard. Of these 86 lost their lives, comprising 42 of the crew, 37 passengers, and seven of the gunners, Capt Nielsen being among the dead. The *Amerika* had commenced her working life on a route to Siam, later switching to the North American west coast service from Copenhagen.

SICILIA ex-*COBLENZ* (1923–1943)

Lloyd Triestino, Italy; Deschimag AG Weser, Bremen.
9,646 GRT, 479ft (146.0m) LOA, 57ft (17.4m) beam.
Steam turbines, twin screw, 11kts.
Date of disaster: 23 April 1943.

Built as the *Coblenz* for Norddeutscher Lloyd, one of a class of six steamers for the North Atlantic service, this ship was renamed *Sicilia* when she was purchased by the Italia Line in August 1935. She was transferred to Lloyd Triestino some time later. In the Second World War, the *Sicilia* was taken over as a naval hospital ship. While berthed at Naples on 23 April 1943, she was destroyed during an Allied air raid. Demolition of the wreck, which was raised after the war, was completed by the end of March 1949.

KAMAKARU MARU ex-*CHICHIBU* (*TITIBU*) *MARU* (1930–1943)

Nippon Yusen Kaisha, Japan; Yokohama Dock Co, Yokohama.
17,526 GRT, 584ft (178.0m) LOA, 74ft (22.6m) beam.
817 passengers in three classes.
Diesel engines, twin screw, 19kts.
Date of disaster: 28 April 1943.

The *Chichibu Maru*, named after Crown Prince Chichibu, entered the Yokohama to San Francisco service in April 1930. When the new system of transliteration, introduced in 1937, led to the ship's name being re-spelt *Titibu* it led to a certain amount of innuendo among American travellers, to the embarrassment of NYK officials. Consequently the company prudently renamed the vessel *Kamakura Maru*. On the outbreak of war in the Pacific, the *Kamakura Maru* became a Japanese Navy transport with occasional voyages as a hospital ship. During a voyage from Manila to Singapore on 28 April 1943, she was torpedoed and sunk by the United States submarine *Gudgeon* east of Palawan, in the Sulu Sea, in the position 10°18′N–121°44′E.

GNEISENAU (1935–1943)

Norddeutscher Lloyd, Germany; Deschimag AG Weser, Bremen.
18,160 GRT, 652ft (198.7m) LOA, 74ft (22.6m) beam.
293 passengers in two classes.
Steam turbines, twin screw, 21kts.
Date of disaster: 2 May 1943.

Norddeutscher Lloyd introduced the sister ships *Gneisenau* and *Scharnhorst* on the run from Hamburg to the Far East in the mid-1930s, the former steam-turbine driven, the latter powered by turbo-electric engines. They were distinctive in having Maier-formed bows. In 1940 the *Gneisenau* became a naval accommodation ship. Consideration was given to converting her into an aircraft-carrier in similar fashion to her sister, which was commissioned into the Imperial Japanese Navy in December 1943. Before this could be proceeded with, however, she was lost on 2 May 1943 during a voyage carrying troops from Hamburg to Norway via the Kiel Canal, when she struck a mine laid by a British aircraft west of Gedser, on the Island of Lolland in the Baltic, in the position 54°38′N–12°26′E. Though beached, she became a total wreck. In 1946 the Danish Government purchased the damaged hulk for breaking up, and by December 1956 the last traces of the *Gneisenau* had been removed.

VOGTLAND as *BERAKIT* (1924–1943)

Hamburg Amerika Line, Germany; Blohm & Voss, Hamburg.
7,106 GRT, 449ft (136.9m) length, 58ft (17.7m) beam.
Diesel engines, twin screw, 12kts.
Date of disaster: 7 May 1943.

The Hamburg-Amerika Line's *Vogtland*, which was normally engaged in the service from Germany to the West Indies and Central America, was seized at Batavia by the Dutch authorities when the Netherlands was invaded by Germany in 1940. Renamed *Berakit* and utilized in a military role, she was torpedoed and sunk in the Indian Ocean by a Japanese submarine on 7 May 1943, in the position 03°04'N–75°20'E. She had been bound from Colombo and Calcutta to Durban and the West Indies when the attack occurred. Of the 80 people she was carrying, three were killed and her master was taken prisoner.

CENTAUR (1924–1943)

Ocean SS Co (Alfred Holt & Co), Great Britain; Scott's, Greenock.
3,222 GRT, 316ft (96.3m) length, 48ft (14.6m) beam.
Diesel engines, 14kts.
Date of disaster: 14 May 1943.

During the Second World War, the cargo-passenger ship *Centaur* was loaned to the Australian Government for service as a hospital ship. In this capacity she was attacked and sunk by a Japanese submarine on 14 May 1943, 43 miles east of Brisbane in the position 27°17'S–154°05'E. The *Centaur*, which was burning her lights and clearly marked in Red Cross colours, was bound from Sydney to Cairns and New Guinea at the time, carrying a crew of 74 and 257 service and hospital personnel. There were only 63

The Maier-bowed Gneisenau *capsized after striking a mine in the Baltic.* (Hapag-Lloyd)

The Blue Funnel liner Centaur. (World Ship Society)

The Henderson Line steamer Yoma. (National Maritime Museum, London)

survivors from this complement, 45 members of the crew perishing as well as 223 nurses, doctors, and orderlies. No boats were launched, as the ship foundered in under three minutes. The submarine surfaced, seemingly to observe the *Centaur*'s last moments, but offered no assistance to those struggling in the water.

MIN ex-*JAVA* as *CONEGLIANO* (1913–1943)

Messageries Maritimes, France; Bremer Vulkan, Vegesack.
7,997 GRT, 484ft (147.5m) length, 62ft (18.9m) beam.
Quadruple expansion SR engine, single screw.
Date of disaster: 6 June 1943.

The Messageries Maritimes steamship *Min* served on the run to the Far East until the outbreak of the Second World War. She was seized by the Germans at Bizerta, Tunisia, in November 1942 and was passed to the Italians soon after, who renamed her *Conegliano*. On 6 June 1943, while at Olbia, Sardinia, the *Conegliano* was sunk in an air-attack. She had been scheduled to join a convoy bound for North Africa through the Sicilian Channel.

YOMA (1928–1943)

Henderson Line, Great Britain; William Denny, Dumbarton.
8,139 GRT, 460ft (140.2m) length, 61ft (18.6m) beam.
150 passengers in single class.
Quadruple expansion SR engine, single screw, 14kts.
Date of disaster: 17 June 1943.

The *Yoma* served on the route from Great Britain to Rangoon, via the Suez Canal, with four sisters, *Amarapoora*, *Kemmendine*, *Pegu*, and *Sagaing*. On 17 June 1943 she was sailing in convoy to Port Said, with 1,670 troops in addition to her crew of 175, when a German submarine torpedoed her off Benghazi, in the position 33°03′N–22°04′E. The *Yoma* sank in 500 fathoms, taking her master, Capt George Patterson, 32 members of the crew, and 451 troops with her.

CITY OF VENICE (1924–1943)

Ellerman Lines, Great Britain; Workman Clark, Belfast.
8,308 GRT, 473ft (144.2m) LOA, 58ft (17.7m) beam.
Quadruple expansion SR engine, single screw, 13kts.
Date of disaster: 4 July 1943.

Another Second World War casualty for the Ellerman Lines was the *City of Venice*, which was sunk by a German submarine in the Mediterranean on 4 July 1943 when she was carrying troops and munitions from the River Clyde to

Ellerman Lines' City of Venice. (A. Duncan)

Sicily. She sank in the position 36°44′N–01°31′E. Eleven of the 180-strong crew lost their lives, and there were also fatalities among the troops, though no figures are available.

DE LA SALLE (1924–1943)

French Line (CGT), France; Barclay Curle, Glasgow.
8,400 GRT, 440ft (134.1m) length, 56ft (17.1m) beam.
Triple expansion SR engines, twin screw, 14kts.
Date of disaster: 9 July 1943.

Although French Line's *De la Salle* was one of a pair of ships, her sister *Sinaia* was, unusually, owned by the Fabre Line. The French Line employed the *De la Salle* mainly on the West Indies and Central America services. During a voyage from Liverpool to Freetown, Walvis Bay, and East London on 9 July 1943, she was torpedoed and sunk by a German submarine in the Gulf of Benin, in the position 05°50′N–02°22′E. She was carrying 150 crew and 99 passengers, of whom eight crew-members and two passengers were lost.

TALAMBA (1924–1943)

British India Line, Great Britain; Hawthorn Leslie, Newcastle.
8,018 GRT, 466ft (142.0m) LOA, 60ft (18.3m) beam.
130 passengers.
Triple expansion, twin screw, 16kts.
Date of disaster: 10 July 1943.

The *Talamba* was sister ship to the *Tairea* and the *Takliwa*,

Below *The* De la Salle. (World Ship Society)

Bottom *The* Talamba *was bombed and sunk while serving as a hospital ship.* (World Ship Society)

the latter of which was wrecked in 1945. During the Second World War the *Talamba* served as a hospital ship, and while so employed she was bombed and sunk three miles off Avola, Sicily, on 10 July 1943. In addition to her crew of 168, she had embarked 400 wounded just prior to the attack, which occurred late in the evening. Her status was clearly evident as she was brightly illuminated, but this did not deter the German aircraft from attacking. The wounded were removed by other ships, as were all but five of the crew, the only casualties. Early the following day the *Talamba* foundered in the position 36°55′N–15°14′E.

DUCHESS OF YORK (1929–1943)

Canadian Pacific Line, Great Britain; John Brown, Clydebank.
20,021 GRT, 601ft (183.2m) LOA, 75ft (22.9m) beam.
1,570 passengers in three classes.
Steam turbines, twin screw, 18kts.
Date of disaster: 11 July 1943.

The *Duchess of York* was the last vessel of a class of four ships built for the Canada run from Liverpool. Serving as a troopship, she was sunk by German long range bombers on 11 July 1943, west of Oporto, Portugal, while bound from Glasgow to Freetown with 607 troops and a crew of 281. Set on fire in the attack, she had to be abandoned, the destroyers *Douglas* and *Iroquois* and the frigate *Moyola* rescuing all but 11 crewmen and 23 troops. The blazing wreck was torpedoed by one of the convoy escorts the following day and sank in the position 41°18′N–15°24′W.

CALIFORNIA (1923–1943)

Anchor Line, Great Britain; Alexander Stephen, Glasgow.
16,792 GRT, 575ft (175.3m) LOA, 70ft (21.3m) beam.
1,785 passengers in three classes.
Steam turbines, twin screw, 16kts.
Date of disaster: 12 July 1943.

The *California* was the last ship of the *Cameronia* class, four vessels engaged in the transatlantic service from Glasgow or London. Following the outbreak of the Second World War, she spent three years as an armed merchant cruiser, reverting to a troopship role in 1942. Early on 12 July 1943 she was proceeding in a convoy west of Portugal, bound for Freetown from the River Clyde, when she came under attack from German aircraft. Hit a number of times, the *California* caught fire and had to be abandoned by her 449 passengers and crew of 318, of whom 72 lost their lives according to Lloyds' records, the casualties being three officers, 43 ratings, and 26 passengers. The *California* was finally sunk in the position 41°15′N–15°24′W by shell fire from naval escorts.

The Duchess of York *was sunk by bombs dropped from Focke-Wulf warplanes.* (World Ship Society)

GENERAL ARTIGAS ex-*WESTPHALIA* (1923–1943)

Hamburg Sud-Amerika Line, Germany; Howaldtswerke, Kiel.
11,254 GRT, 495ft (150.9m) LOA, 60ft (18.3m) beam.
802 passengers in two classes.
Steam turbine, single screw, 12.5kts.
Date of disaster: 25 July 1943.

The Hamburg Amerika liners *Thuringia* and *Westphalia* were engaged in the Hamburg to New York service until 1930, when they were refitted for the South American service and renamed *General San Martin* and *General Artigas* respectively. They passed into Hamburg Sud-Amerika Line ownership as part of the reorganization of German merchant shipping in the mid-1930s. From January 1939 the *General Artigas* was used as a naval accommodation ship based at Hamburg. She was sunk in Kuhwerder Harbour during a British air-raid on 25 July 1943, the incomplete Hamburg Amerika express passenger liner *Vaterland* being destroyed during the same attack. The *General Artigas*, which was a total loss, was raised and scrapped in 1946.

VATERLAND (1943)

Hamburg Amerika Line, Germany; Blohm & Voss, Hamburg.
ca. 41,000 GRT, 827ft (252.1m) LOA, 98ft (29.9m) beam.

The Anchor liner California *was bombed and sunk while sailing in convoy.* (A. Duncan)

1,322 passengers in three classes (designed).
Turbo-electric propulsion, twin screw, 23.5kts.
Date of disaster: 25 July 1943.

In the late 1930s, Hamburg Amerika planned to construct

This model gives an impression of the intended appearance of the turbo-electric liner Vaterland. (Hapag-Lloyd)

The Vaterland *never saw passenger service. Allied bombers destroyed her while she was still incomplete, her gaping foredeck being testimony to the destructive power of their high explosive bombs.* (Imperial War Museum, Neg. A29698 *and* L.L. von Münching)

three new express liners for their North Atlantic service. The first of these, yard number 523, unofficially named *Vaterland*, was laid down at the Blohm & Voss shipyard in 1938. By the time she was launched on 24 August 1940, Germany was at war. As the *Vaterland* could not enter scheduled service she was laid up incomplete. There were also problems with the supply of materials, priority being given to naval vessels. The hull was secured in Kuhwerder Harbour and utilized as a floating store, in which capacity it was bombed and critically damaged on 25 July 1943. The decks were blown out and the wooden material stored aboard caught fire. The gutted wreck of the *Vaterland* was surrendered in May 1945, but being fit only for scrap she was broken up in a local breaker's yard during 1948.

BAGÉ ex-*SIERRA NEVADA* (1912–1943)

Lloyd Brasileiro, Brazil; Vulkan Werke, Stettin.
8,235 GRT, 439ft (133.8m) length, 56ft (17.1m) beam.
Triple expansion SR engines, twin screw, 13kts.
Date of disaster: 1 August 1943.

The former Hamburg Sud-Amerika liner *Sierra Nevada* passed to Lloyd Brasileiro in 1917 and was engaged in the service from Santos to Hamburg. During a voyage from Pernambuco to Bahia on 1 August 1943 she was torpedoed by a German submarine in the position 11°29'S–36°58'W, off the Brazilian coast. The submarine then surfaced and shelled the vessel, sinking her. Of 28 passengers and 107 crew, 87 were saved.

PIEMONTE ex-*MINNEDOSA* (1918–1943)

Lloyd Triestino, Italy; Barclay Curle, Glasgow.
15,186 GRT, 546ft (166.4m) LOA, 67ft (20.4m) beam.
1,341 passengers in three classes (as a British ship).
Triple expansion SR engines with LP turbine, triple screw, 16.5kts.
Date of disaster: 15 August 1943.

The *Minnedosa* entered the Canadian Pacific's Dominion service from Liverpool in 1919 and, with her sister ship *Melita*, continued in this employment for the next 12 years. Both ships had been laid down for the Hamburg-Amerika Line, but Canadian Pacific took over the building contracts in March 1915. After intermittent spells laid up in the early 1930s both ships were sold to be scrapped at Turin, but instead found themselves re-commissioned under the Italian flag as troopships. The *Minnedosa* was renamed *Piemonte* while the *Melita* became the *Liguria*. The *Piemonte*'s usefulness during the Second World War was curtailed following a torpedo attack on 17 November 1942, when she was hit while two miles from Capo Rasocolmo near Messina, Sicily. She nevertheless succeeded in reaching Sparta, where she was patched up, and from there she made for Messina to obtain full repairs. However, these were not carried out and she was laid up. On 10 July 1943 she received additional slight damage in an air-raid, and then in a subsequent raid, on 15 August, sustained a number of bomb hits and capsized. The wreck was refloated in 1949 and on 24 July the same year was towed to La Spezia to be broken up.

BALOERAN as *STRASSBURG* (1930–1943)

Rotterdam Lloyd, Netherlands; Maatschappij Fijenoord, Rotterdam.
16,981 GRT, 574ft (174.9m) LOA, 70ft (21.3m) beam.
634 passengers in four classes.
Diesel engines, twin screw, 18kts.
Date of disaster: 1 September 1943.

The *Baloeran* was a sister ship to the *Dempo* and was employed with her in the service from Rotterdam to the Dutch East Indies. When the Netherlands fell in the summer of 1940 the German Navy seized the *Baloeran*, which was berthed at Rotterdam, and had her converted to the hospital ship *Strassburg* at the Wilton Fijenoord shipyard. On completion of the refit, in July 1941, she was placed under the management of the Hamburg Amerika Line. Two years later, on 1 September 1943, the *Strassburg* struck a mine 10

The Lloyd Brasileiro passenger ship Bagé. (World Ship Society)

The wreck of the German hospital ship Strassburg, *formerly the Rotterdam Lloyd motor passenger vessel* Baloeran, *near Ymuiden.* (W.Z. Bilddienst)

to 15 miles north of Ymuiden, while sailing to Hamburg from Rotterdam. The badly holed ship was taken in tow in an attempt to get her to port but she was beached in the position 52°29′N–04°32′E when it was feared that she would sink. Subsequent attempts to salvage the *Strassburg* were unsuccessful and she was finally destroyed completely when attacked by British MTBs on 20 September 1943. The wreck was further subjected to bombing during an RAF raid on 19 October.

The stylish Conte di Savoia. *Of all the Italian ships built between the wars she was eclipsed only by the* Rex. (Italcantieri SpA)

CONTE DI SAVOIA (1932–1943)

Italia Line, Italy; Cantieri Riuniti Dell'Adriatico, Trieste.
48,502 GRT, 860ft (262.1m) LOA, 96ft (29.3m) beam.
2,200 passengers in four classes.
Steam turbines, quadruple screw, 28kts.
Date of disaster: 11 September 1943.

Ordered by Lloyd Sabaudo, the *Conte di Savoia* served on the Atlantic route alongside the *Rex*, Italy's only Blue Riband holder, in the combined Italia Line fleet. The two big liners, considered too large and vulnerable for military service in the Mediterranean, were laid up on the outbreak of the Second World War, the *Conte di Savoia* at Malamocco, near Venice. While lying there, she was attacked by United States fighter-bombers on 11 September 1943 and set on fire. The blazing liner gradually keeled over and sank in the shallow waters of the lagoon. The wreck was raised on 16 October 1945 and at first consideration was given to rebuilding the once beautiful ship. However, as this would have proved too expensive, on 24 April 1950 she was finally towed to Monfalcone, Trieste, for scrapping.

NEWFOUNDLAND (1925–1943)

Furness Warren Line, Great Britain; Vickers Armstrong, Newcastle.
6,791 GRT, 423ft (128.9m) LOA, 55ft (16.8m) beam.
185 passengers in two classes.
Quadruple expansion SR engines, twin screw, 15kts.
Date of disaster: 13 September 1943.

The steamship *Newfoundland* was engaged in the service from Liverpool to St John's, Newfoundland, Halifax, Nova Scotia, and Boston, with her sister liner *Nova Scotia.* Neither ship survived the Second World War. The *Newfoundland* was taken over as a hospital ship and in this capacity she participated in the Allied landings at Salerno, Italy, in September 1943. After arriving from Bizerta, she anchored off the beaches where, on

The refloated hull of the Conte di Savoia *seen after the Second World War. The funnel uptakes from her engine-room salients can be seen above the burned and partially scrapped decks.* (L.L. von Münching)

13 September, she was bombed and set on fire by German aircraft. The ship burned out of control for two days until Allied warships sunk her with their guns. The wreck lay in the position 40°14'N–13°20'E. At the time of the attack the *Newfoundland* had aboard her a total of 315 people of which, fortunately, only two were medical cases. Of her total complement, 21 lost their lives, comprising five doctors, six nurses, six Army medical staff, and four members of the crew.

YAMATO MARU ex-*GIUSEPPE VERDI* (1915–1943)

Nippon Yusen Kaisha, Japan; Soc. Esercizio Bacini, Riva Trigoso.
9,760 GRT, 505ft (153.9m) length, 59ft (18.0m) beam.
Quadruple expansion SR engines, twin screw, 16.5kts.
Date of disaster: 13 September 1943.

The Transatlantica Italiana steamship *Giuseppe Verdi* was sold to Nippon Yusen Kaisha in 1927, along with her consort, the *Dante Alighieri.* Renamed *Yamato Maru* and serving as a troop transport, she was torpedoed and sunk by the American submarine USS *Snook* on 13 September 1943. The attack took place 200 miles south-east of Shanghai, in the position 30°06'N 123°33'E, when the *Yamato Maru* was carrying 1,092 passengers and crew, of whom 1,065 were saved.

The Furness Warren liner Newfoundland, *bombed and sunk off Salerno while serving as a hospital ship.* (World Ship Society)

EXCAMBION as *JOHN PENN* (1931–1943)

American Export Line, USA; New York SB Corp, Camden, New Jersey.
9,360 GRT, 450ft (137.2m) length, 61ft (18.6m) beam.
147 passengers in single class.
Steam turbine, single screw, 16kts.
Date of disaster: 23 September 1943.

The *Excambion* was one of a group of pre-war passenger ships known as the 'Four Aces' employed in the transatlantic service from New York to the Mediterranean. The other three were the *Excalibur*, *Exeter* and *Exochorda*. The United States Navy took the *Excambion* over in 1941 for service as a transport under the name *John Penn*. She was bombed and sunk near Guadalcanal, on 23 September 1943, by Japanese dive-bombers and torpedo-bombers.

KASHIMA (KASIMA) MARU (1913–1943)

Nippon Yusen Kaisha, Japan; Kawasaki, Kobe.
9,908 GRT, 522ft (159.1m) LOA, 59ft (18.0m) beam.
380 passengers in three classes.
Triple expansion SR engines, twin screw, 14.5kts.
Date of disaster: 27 September 1943.

The *Kashima Maru* was the second ship of a class of five vessels for the Japan to Europe service. Apart from a brief interlude on the transpacific service between 1917 and 1922 she continued working this route for 28 years. The *Kashima Maru* was sunk by torpedoes from the American submarine USS *Bonefish* on 27 September 1943. She was attacked 200 miles east of Saigon, in the position 10°14′N–109°45′E.

STUTTGART (1923–1943)

Deutsche Arbeitsfront, Germany; Vulkan Werke, Stettin.
13,387 GRT, 551ft (167.9) LOA, 65ft (19.8m) beam.
990 passengers in single class.
Triple expansion SR engines, twin screw, 16kts.
Date of disaster: 9 October 1943.

Formerly employed on the North Atlantic service from Bremerhaven to New York, the *Stuttgart* was sold to the Deutsche Arbeitsfront in 1938 and used full-time for workers' cruises under the management of her original owners, Norddeutscher Lloyd. She was sister ship to the *Munchen*, rebuilt in 1930 as the *General Von Steuben*. In 1939 the *Stuttgart* was transferred to the German Navy and converted into a hospital ship. She was bombed and set on fire by American aircraft on 9 October 1943, during the first Allied air-raid on the port of Gotenhafen (Gdynia). The *Stuttgart* was packed with wounded servicemen at the time, very few of whom could be rescued as the fire spread rapidly out of control. Blazing from end to end, the wrecked ship was towed outside the harbour and there sunk by gunfire with the bodies of the 80 to 100 victims still on board.

BERNADIN DE SAINT PIERRE as *TEIBI MARU* (1925–1943)

Messageries Maritimes, France; J.C. Tecklenborg, Wesermünde.
10,085 GRT, 476ft (145.1m) LOA, 60ft (18.3m) beam.
299 passengers in three classes.
Steam turbines, twin screw, 16kts.
Date of disaster: 10 October 1943.

A number of French passenger liners were seized by the Japanese in Far East ports during the Second World War, the *Bernadin de Saint Pierre*, which operated for much of her life on the service from Marseilles to Madagascar, being one of those captured at Saigon. She was passed into Japanese Government transport service as the *Teibi Maru* but survived only until 10 October 1943, when she was

The Norddeutscher Lloyd liner Stuttgart *prior to her transfer to the Deutsche Arbeitsfront for full-time cruising.* (Author's collection)

The German hospital ship Stuttgart, *bombed at Gdynia and later intentionally sunk outside the port as being damaged beyond repair.* (W.Z. Bilddienst)

torpedoed off the coast of Vietnam by the American submarine USS *Bonefish*, sinking in the position 14°44'N–110°19'E.

CHICAGO MARU (1910–1943)

Osaka Shosen Kaisha, Japan; Kawasaki, Kobe.
5,866 GRT, 410ft (125.0m) length, 49ft (14.9m) beam.
Triple expansion SR engines, twin screw, 13kts.
Date of disaster: 15 October 1943.

The sister ships *Chicago Maru*, *Seattle Maru*, and *Tacoma Maru* plied the transpacific route between Osaka and Tacoma, Washington. All three were sunk during the Second World War. The *Chicago Maru* was torpedoed by the American submarine USS *Tullibee* on 15 October 1943, sinking off the west coast of Formosa (Taiwan) in the position 24°35'N–120°31'E.

FUJI (HUZI) MARU (1937–1943)

Nippon Yusen Kaisha, Japan; Mitsubishi, Nagasaki.
9,138 GRT, 453ft (138.1m) length, 60ft (18.3m) beam.
Steam turbines, twin screw, 18kts.
Date of disaster: 27 October 1943.

The Fuji Maru, *built for Nippon Yusen Kaisha.* (World Ship Society)

On 27 October 1943 the *Fuji Maru*, a steamship employed on the service to Europe via the Suez Canal, was torpedoed north-west of the Ryukyu Islands by the American submarines *Shad* and *Grayback*. She sank in the position 28°25′N–128°04′E.

TJISAROEA as *CHIHAYA MARU* (1926–1943)

Royal Interocean Line, Netherlands; Nederlandsche Schps Maatschappij, Amsterdam.
7,089 GRT, 420ft (128.0m) length, 55ft (16.8m) beam.
Steam turbine, single screw, 12.5kts.
Date of disaster: 2 November 1943.

Fleetmate of the *Tjinegara*, the turbine steamer *Tjisaroea* operated on Royal Interocean Line's South-East Asian service until the outbreak of war in the Pacific. She was captured by Japanese forces south of the Lombok Islands, in the Indian Ocean, on 4 March 1942, when she was en route from Cochin to Fremantle, having last departed Tandjong Priok two days earlier. The ship was condemned by the Yokosuka Prize Court on 29 August 1942 and thereafter she was pressed into Japanese service as the *Chihaya Maru*. She was torpedoed by the American submarine USS *Seahorse* 300 miles east of the Ryukyu Islands on 2 November 1943, sinking in the approximate position 29°00′N–134°00′E.

TANGANJIKA (1922–1943)

Hamburg Amerika Line, Germany; Blohm & Voss, Hamburg.
8,540 GRT, 449ft (136.9m) length, 58ft (17.7m) beam.
250 passengers.
Steam turbine, single screw, 14kts.
Date of disaster: 4 November 1943.

Originally owned by the Woermann Line, the steamship *Tanganjika* was employed in the African service, sailing in consort with the sister ships *Njassa* and *Usambara*. She was bombed and sunk at Wilhelmshaven during an Allied air-raid on 4 November 1943, being salvaged and broken up after the war.

MARNIX VAN SINT ALDEGONDE (1930–1943)

Nederland Line, Netherlands; Nederlandsche Schps Maatschappij, Amsterdam.
19,355 GRT, 608ft (185.3m) LOA, 74ft (22.6m) beam.
771 passengers in four classes.
Diesel engines, twin screw, 18kts.
Date of disaster: 6 November 1943.

The *Marnix van Sint Aldegonde* was the sister ship of the *Johan van Oldenbarnevelt*, which was destroyed by fire as the *Lakonia* in December 1963. Like her sister, the *Marnix van Sint Aldegonde* operated between Amsterdam and the Dutch East Indies. In September 1939 she was laid up at Surabaya but in 1940 she was converted into a troopship in support of the Allied cause. On 6 November 1943, bound in convoy from Liverpool to the Mediterranean with 2,924 troops, she was torpedoed by a German aircraft off the Algerian coast, in the position 37°12′N–06°16′E. The severely-damaged ship was evacuated by all but a skeleton crew and was then taken in tow for Philippeville (Skikola) by naval vessels and the transport *Santa Elena*. Efforts to save the stricken troopship were in vain, however, and she foundered before port could be reached, about six miles from Cape Bougaroin Lighthouse. In addition the *Santa Elena* received damage for her troubles, somehow managing to collide with the *Marnix van Sint Aldegonde* during the towing manoeuvre. There was no loss of life among either the troops aboard the *Marnix*, or her 311-man crew. The *Santa Elena* was sunk later the same day during further air-raids.

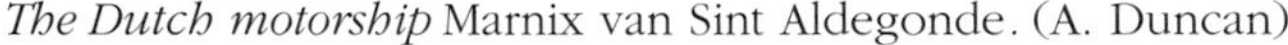

The Dutch motorship Marnix van Sint Aldegonde. (A. Duncan)

SANTA ELENA (1933–1943)

Grace Line, USA; Federal SB & Drydock Co, Kearny, New Jersey.
9,135 GRT, 484ft (147.5m) length, 72ft (21.9m) beam.
Steam turbines, twin screw, 19kts.
Date of disaster: 6 November 1943.

The Grace Line introduced a quartet of twin-funnelled liners to the service from New York to Pacific coast ports of South America in the 1930s, namely the *Santa Elena*, *Santa Lucia*, *Santa Paula*, and *Santa Rosa*. The first two were lost in torpedo attacks, the *Santa Lucia* under the name *Leedstown*. In November 1943 the troopship *Santa Elena* sailed from Liverpool to Naples with 1,889 Canadian troops, 44 guardsmen, 101 nurses and a crew of 133. On 6 November she was attacked by German aircraft off Bougie (Bejaia), Algeria, in the position 37°12'N–06°16'E, being torpedoed and sunk after rendering assistance to the already stricken *Marnix van Sint Aldegonde*. Only four crewmen lost their lives out of the *Santa Elena*'s vast complement, the Matson liner *Monterey* taking off the survivors.

TANGO MARU (1905–1943)

Nippon Yusen Kaisha, Japan; Mitsubishi, Nagasaki.
7,475 GRT, 456ft (139.0m) length, 52ft (15.9m) beam.
Triple expansion SR engines, twin screw, 14kts.
Date of disaster: 13 November 1943.

The *Tango Maru* sailed almost uninterruptedly between Japan and Europe for almost 35 years, allowing for the sporadic nature of the service she maintained during the First World War. She was sunk in the East China Sea on 13 November 1943, but the precise circumstances of her loss, though stated to be as a result of a cause connected with the war, are not recorded.

HIYE (HIE) MARU (1930–1943)

Nippon Yusen Kaisha, Japan; Yokohama Dock Co, Yokohama.
11,622 GRT, 536ft (163.4m) LOA, 66ft (20.1m) beam.
330 passengers in three classes.
Diesel engines, twin screw, 18kts.
Date of disaster: 17 November 1943.

The *Hiye Maru* entered the Hong Kong and Kobe to Seattle service in August 1930, remaining so engaged until 1941 when she was taken over as a submarine tender for the Japanese Navy. Later she became a supply ship carrying vital stores and materials to the far-flung outposts of the Japanese Empire. On 17 November 1943 she was torpedoed and sunk by the American submarine USS *Drum* about 300 miles north-west of New Ireland in the position 01°48'N–148°24'E.

BELLE ISLE (1918–1943)

Chargéurs Reunis, France; Forges et Chantiers de la Mediterrannée, La Seyne.
9,589 GRT, 479ft (146.0m) length, 58ft (17.7m) beam.

The Marnix van Sint Aldegonde, *seen during Operation Torch, just prior to her loss.* (L.L. von Münching)

184 passengers in three classes.
Triple expansion SR engines, twin screw, 13kts.
Date of disaster: 24 November 1943.

The *Belle Isle*, one of a large group of similar ships, entered the service from France to South America in early 1918. On 24 November 1943 she was in dry dock at Toulon when the port came under attack from Allied warplanes. The *Belle Isle* was hit by several bombs and set on fire. Her completely burnt out shell was scrapped after the end of the war.

ROHNA (1926–1943)

British India Line, Great Britain; Hawthorn Leslie, Newcastle.
8,602 GRT, 461ft (140.5m) length, 61ft (18.6m) beam.
5,216 passengers in four classes.
Quadruple expansion SR engines, twin screw, 13kts.
Date of disaster: 26 November 1943.

Some 40 years before the sinking of the container ship *Atlantic Conveyer* by an Exocet missile off the Falkland Islands, the liner *Rohna*, serving as a troopship, was one of the first merchant ships to fall victim to this method of attack. On 26 November 1943 she was bound from Oran to India in convoy, carrying 2,232 people of whom 2,014 were troops, the majority American. Off Djidjelli, Algeria, in a position variously given as 37°10'N–05°20'E and 36°56'N–05°20'E, the convoy came under attack from German aircraft, one of which launched a glider bomb at the *Rohna* which struck her amidships on the port side. Extensive damage was caused by the explosion and the aft end of the ship was engulfed in flames. It was impossible to launch any of the port side boats and many of those from the starboard side capsized through overcrowding. The *Rohna* sank by the stern after an hour-and-a-half, her

The British India Line passenger ship Rohna *was the victim of a German pilot-less glider bomb, one of the first attacks of its kind.* (P&O Group)

engines and boilers breaking free and bursting through the hull plating. The loss of life was very heavy, a total of 1,149 people perishing in the disaster, 1,015 of them American troops while a further 133 were crewmen. For British merchant shipping losses during the Second World War, these figures were only exceeded by the sinkings of the *Lancastria* and *Laconia*. Fourteen British soldiers who had been aboard managed to escape. Prior to the war, the *Rohna* had served on the Far East service with her sister, the *Rajula*. They carried a huge number of passengers for their quite small size, but 5,064 of the total complement were accommodated on deck.

BUENOS AIRES MARU (1930–1943)

Osaka Shosen Kaisha, Japan; Mitsubishi, Nagasaki.
9,626 GRT, 473ft (144.2m) LOA, 62ft (18.9m) beam.
Diesel engines, twin screw, 17kts.
Date of disaster: 27 November 1943.

The *Buenos Aires Maru* and her sister ship the *Rio de Janeiro Maru* were employed on a round-the-world service via South America. From 1942 the *Buenos Aires Maru* served as a Japanese Navy hospital ship. On 25 November 1943 she was damaged in a torpedo attack in the South China Sea. Two days later, while limping home for repairs, she came under attack from United States aircraft off the coast of the island of St Matthias and was sunk in the position 02°44′S–149°15′E.

HAKONE MARU (1921–1943)

Nippon Yusen Kaisha, Japan; Mitsubishi, Nagasaki.
10,420 GRT, 520ft (158.5m) LOA, 62ft (18.9m) beam.
175 passengers in single class.
Steam turbines, twin screw, 16kts.
Date of disaster: 27 November 1943.

The first unit of Nippon Yusen Kaisha's 'H' class of European service steamships, the *Hakone Maru* became a war loss on 27 November 1943. She was attacked in the Straits of Formosa by aircraft of the United States Army Air Force, and sank in the position 25°20′N–120°00′E.

NITTA MARU as *CHUYO* (1940–1943)

Nippon Yusen Kaisha, Japan; Mitsubishi, Nagasaki.
17,150 GRT, 590ft (179.8m) LOA, 73ft (22.3m) beam.
285 passengers in three classes.
Steam turbines, twin screw, 22kts.
Date of disaster: 4 December 1943.

Many of the passenger liners under construction for Japanese companies in the 1930s were designed with a view to conversion to aircraft-carriers in time of national emergency. Among the vessels included in this scheme were the Nippon Yusen Kaisha sisters *Nitta Maru*, *Kasuga Maru*, and *Yawata Maru*, three new ships planned for the Yokohama to Hamburg service. Due to the outbreak of war in Europe the *Nitta Maru* instead entered the Yokohama to San Francisco service when she was completed in March 1940. Her commercial career lasted only two years. In May 1942 she was taken in hand for conversion into an escort aircraft-carrier at Kure shipyard. On 25 November that year she was commissioned as the *Chuyo*, entering the Pacific fray immediately thereafter. She was torpedoed and sunk by the American submarine USS *Sailfish* on 4 December 1943 in the position 32°37′N–143°39′E, about 275 miles south-east of Honshu.

Right *The Osaka Shosen Kaisha passenger ship* Buenos Aires Maru. (A. Duncan)

Below *The* Hakone Maru *was employed on the Japan to Europe service.* (Maritime Photo Library)

Bottom *The* Nitta Maru *was subsequently converted into the aircraft-carrier* Chuyo. (Nippon Yusen Kaisha)

The Dumana. (World Ship Society)

CAP PADARAN ex-*D'IBERVILLE* (1922–1943)

Chargéurs Reunis, France; Ateliers et Chantiers de la Loire, St Nazaire.
8,169 GRT, 417ft (127.1m) length, 55ft (16.8m) beam.
850 passengers.
Steam turbine, single screw, 12kts.
Date of disaster: 9 December 1943.

Prior to the Second World War, the *Cap Padaran* served on the France to Far East service. She was torpedoed by a submarine on 9 December 1943 during a voyage from Taranto to Augusta, Sicily, the attack taking place east of Crotone, Calabria, in the position 39°15'N–17°30'E. The stricken ship was taken in tow but the line parted. Her back broken, she sank soon after. She had been carrying a crew of 195 which included 13 gunners, and five of this complement were killed.

AQUILEJA ex-*PRINS DER NEDERLANDEN* (1914–1943)

Lloyd Triestino, Italy; Nederlandsche Schps Maatschappij, Amsterdam.
9,448 GRT, 498ft (151.8m) LOA, 57ft (17.4m) beam.
Quadruple expansion SR engines, twin screw, 15kts.
Date of disaster: 14 December 1943.

The former Nederland Line ship *Prins der Nederlanden* was transferred to Lloyd Triestino in 1935, renamed *Aquileja*, and employed in the service from Trieste to East Africa via Suez. The *Aquileja* was damaged and set on fire during an air-raid on Marseilles on 14 December 1943, while being used as a hospital ship with the Italian Navy. The wrecked former liner was scuttled there in June 1944.

GINYO MARU (1921–1943)

Nippon Yusen Kaisha, Japan; Asano SB Co, Tsurumi.
8,613 GRT, 445ft (135.6m) length, 58ft (17.7m) beam.
Steam turbines, twin screw, 12kts.
Date of disaster: 16 December 1943.

The steamship *Ginyo Maru* was originally built for Toyo Kisen Kaisha and transferred to Nippon Yusen Kaisha ownership in 1926, sailing between Japan and South America via ports on the west coast of the United States. She was sunk on 16 December 1943 by the American submarine USS *Flying Fish*, foundering off Kaohsiung, Formosa (Taiwan), in the position 22°27'N–120°08'E.

DUMANA (1923–1943)

British India Line, Great Britain; Barclay Curle, Glasgow.
8,427 GRT, 450ft (137.2m) length, 58ft (17.7m) beam.
130 passengers.
Diesel engines, twin screw, 13kts.
Date of disaster: 24 December 1943.

The motorship *Dumana* was torpedoed and sunk by a submarine on 24 December 1943 in the position 04°27'N–06°58'W, near to Monrovia, during a coastal voyage from Port Etienne, Mauritania, to Takoradi, Gold Coast (Ghana). The torpedo struck the *Dumana* on her port side and the damage was so extensive that she sank quickly and there was insufficient time to launch all her boats. She was carrying 21 RAF personnel and a crew of 148 at the time, many of whom were Lascars. There were 31 deaths, 24 crewmen and seven service personnel. A memorial to the *Dumana*'s casualties was later constructed at Sassandra, Ivory Coast.

Chapter Eleven

1944

AIRCRAFT DOMINATE AS 'OVERLORD' IS LAUNCHED

As the war entered its penultimate year, all the signs continued to indicate a deterioration in the position of the Axis forces, the year's unfolding events further underlining this decline. This trend was even borne out by the passenger ships losses recorded during the year: for every Allied passenger ship that was sunk, there were three German, Italian, or Japanese losses. As German forces in Europe retreated, the passenger vessels that they had earlier commandeered were deliberately sabotaged to deny the advancing Allies the use of port facilities and anchorages. At the same time American and British warplanes, encountering less and less opposition in the skies over southern Europe, were able to pick off lone vessels seeking refuge in the coastal waters of the Adriatic and Aegean seas.

However, the freedom of movement enjoyed by Allied air forces in Europe was as nothing compared to that increasingly enjoyed by American naval and air force units in the Pacific. United States' submarines acquired a reputation as fearsome as ever the German U-boats had earned, with a success rate that threatened the virtual elimination of the Japanese Navy and merchant marine alike. And what little the submarines missed was accounted for by American warplanes. The American air attack on the Japanese base at Truk in the Caroline Islands on 17 and 18 February 1944 is a case in point. The base and numerous ships in the harbour were destroyed by a carrier task force which dropped 30 times more high explosive bombs than the Japanese had on Pearl Harbor three years previously.

The most important milestones in the war in Europe during 1944 were the landings at Anzio in January, in Southern France in August, and, most significant of all, as a signal that the war was approaching its climax, in Normandy in June, when Operation Overlord was set in motion. In the Pacific, meanwhile, the string of islands that fell to the American Marines was seemingly endless: Kwajalein, Eniwetok, Saipan, Guam, and Tinian, to name but a few. By the year's end, General Douglas MacArthur was able to fulfil his promise of 1941 that he would return, with the first landings being made in the Philippine Islands in October.

SPHINX as *SUBIACO* (1914–1944)

Messageries Maritimes, France; Ateliers et Chantiers de la Loire, St Nazaire.
11,375 GRT, 503ft (153.3m) LOA, 60ft (18.3m) beam.
384 passengers in three classes.
Triple expansion SR engines, twin screw, 14kts.
Date of disaster: 5 January 1944.

Messageries Maritimes' passenger ship Sphinx *in her guise as a French Navy hospital ship. She was later captured by the Italians and renamed* Subiaco. (World Ship Society)

The Tacoma Maru. (Mitsui-OSK Lines)

The Messageries Maritimes' steamship *Sphinx*, which was normally engaged in the service from Marseilles to the Far East, became a French Navy hospital ship in 1939. In June of the following year she was seized at Marseilles by the Italians, who renamed her *Subiaco*. The *Subiaco* was sunk at Genoa on 5 January 1944 in an Allied air-raid, her wreck being broken up after the war.

PANAMA MARU (1910–1944)

Osaka Shosen Kaisha, Japan; Mitsubishi, Nagasaki.
5,287 GRT, 407ft (124.1m) length, 51ft (15.5m) beam.
Triple expansion SR engines, twin screw, 13kts.
Date of disaster: 23 January 1944.

The *Panama Maru* was one of a group of seven similar passenger vessels employed on routes to South America from Japan. She was bombed by Chinese warplanes off Santuao, China, on 23 January 1944 and sank in the position 27°08'N–120°30'E.

The Monte Pascoal *was damaged beyond all repair in an air-raid on Hamburg.* (Hamburg Sud-Amerika Line)

YASUKUNI MARU (1930–1944)

Nippon Yusen Kaisha, Japan; Mitsubishi, Nagasaki.
11,930 GRT, 527ft (160.6m) LOA, 64ft (19.5m) beam.
249 passengers in three classes.
Diesel engines, twin screw, 18kts.
Date of disaster: 31 January 1944.

The *Yasukuni Maru* spent almost 10 years on the Yokohama to Hamburg service. She was sister ship to the *Terukuni Maru* which sank in November 1939 after striking a mine in the River Thames. The *Yasukuni Maru* was a war casualty herself, torpedoed and sunk on 31 January 1944 north-west of the island of Truk, in the position 09°21'N–147°02'E. Her assailant was the US submarine *Trigger*.

TACOMA MARU (1909–1944)

Osaka Shosen Maru, Japan; Kawasaki, Kobe.
6,178 GRT, 419ft (127.7m) length, 49ft (14.9m) beam.
Triple expansion SR engines, twin screw, 13kts.
Date of disaster: 1 February 1944.

Sister ship to the *Chicago Maru* and *Seattle Maru*, the *Tacoma Maru* was also engaged on the transpacific service from Japan to the USA. The American submarine USS *Hake* torpedoed and sank the *Tacoma Maru* on 1 February 1944 off the island of Halmahera in the Moluccas Group, in the position 01°35'N–128°58'E.

MONTE PASCOAL (1931–1944)

Hamburg Sud-Amerika Line, Germany; Bremer Vulkan, Vegesack.
13,870 GRT, 524ft (159.7m) LOA, 65ft (19.8m) beam.

2,408 passengers in two classes.
Diesel engines, twin screw, 14.5kts.
Date of disaster: 3 February 1944.

The liner *Monte Pascoal* served as an accommodation ship for the workers at the Wilhelmshaven naval dockyard from January 1940 until 3 February 1944, when she was hit during an air-raid. The ship was completely gutted by fire and sank. After being sealed, she was pumped out and refloated on 12 May 1944, but no attempt was made to restore the seriously damaged vessel, and the following May she was seized in this condition as a British war prize. Because she was beyond economic recovery, she was loaded with materials used in the manufacture of chemical warfare weapons, towed out into the Skagerrak, and deliberately sunk there on 31 December 1946.

AIKOKU MARU (1940–1944)

Osaka Shosen Kaisha, Japan; Tama SB Co., Tama.
10,437 GRT, 537ft (163.7m) LOA, 66ft (20.1m) beam.
400 passengers in three classes.
Diesel engines, twin screw, 17kts.
Date of disaster: 17 February 1944.

The *Aikoku Maru* operated in the service from Japan to Europe for just over 12 months before being taken over for conversion to an auxiliary cruiser in August 1941. She was commissioned into the Japanese Navy the following March. On 11 November 1942 she was involved in an action in the Indian Ocean in consort with her sister ship *Hokoku Maru*. The *Hokoku Maru* was sunk by the frigate *Bengal*, while the damaged *Aikoku Maru* withdrew from the indecisive exchange and returned to base for repairs. A year later, in October 1943, she reverted to the role of transport. She survived for a further three months until 17 February 1944, when American carrier-based aircraft sank her in the harbour at Truk Atoll, in the position 07°22′N–151°54′E.

HEIAN MARU (1930–1944)

Nippon Yusen Kaisha, Japan; Osaka Iron Works, Osaka.
11,616 GRT, 536ft (163.4m) LOA, 66ft (20.1m) beam.
330 passengers in three classes.
Diesel engines, twin screw, 18kts.
Date of disaster: 17 February 1944.

The *Heian Maru* sailed in the Hong Kong and Kobe to Seattle service with two sister liners. On 15 December 1941 she was taken over as a submarine tender with the Imperial Japanese Navy. She sank on 17 February 1944 in the position 07°23′N–151°51′E, near the island of Truk in the Carolines, after she had been attacked by aircraft from American carriers.

RIO DE JANEIRO MARU (1930–1944)

Osaka Shosen Kaisha, Japan; Mitsubishi, Nagasaki.
9,627 GRT, 461ft (140.5m) length, 62ft (18.9m) beam.
Diesel engines, twin screw, 17kts.
Date of disaster: 17 February 1944.

Sister ship of the *Buenos Aires Maru*, the motorship *Rio de Janeiro Maru* operated a round-the-world service via South America. In the Second World War she was converted to a submarine tender, serving with the Japanese Navy. She was

The Aikoku Maru *saw war service as an armed merchant cruiser.* (Mitsui-OSK Lines)

Above *The Nippon Yusen Kaisha passenger ship* Heian Maru. (World Ship Society)

Below *The* Rio de Janeiro Maru *was converted into a submarine tender during the war.* (A. Duncan)

attacked near the Caroline Islands on 17 February 1944 by aircraft from American carriers, sinking in the position 07°20′N–151°53′E.

D'ARTAGNAN as *TEIKO MARU* (1925–1944)

Messageries Maritimes, France; Ateliers et Chantiers de la Gironde, Bordeaux.
15,105 GRT, 565ft (172.2m) LOA, 65ft (19.8m) beam.
420 passengers in three classes.
Triple expansion SR engines, twin screw, 14kts.
Date of disaster: 22 February 1944.

Messageries Maritimes' *D'Artagnan* was another passenger vessel taken over by the Japanese in the Second World War. In her case it followed destruction by fire at Shanghai in October 1941. She was refloated by the Japanese Navy and, following repairs, was renamed *Teiko Maru*, the Japanese operating her on a charter arrangement concluded with the Vichy Government in France. She was employed as a troopship until 22 February 1944, when she was torpedoed and sunk off the Natuna Islands in the position 03°03′N–109°16′E. Her attacker was the American submarine USS *Puffer*.

PRESIDENT GRANT ex-*PRESIDENT ADAMS* ex-*CENTENNIAL STATE* (1921–1944)

American President Line, USA; New York SB Corp, Camden, New Jersey.
10,533 GRT, 516ft (157.3m) LOA, 62ft (18.9m) beam.
78 passengers in single class
Triple expansion SR engines, twin screw, 14kts.
Date of disaster: 26 February 1944.

Sixth of the US Shipping Board's class of 502ft standard design vessels, the *Centennial State* joined the United States Line in August 1921 after a brief period with the US Mail Line. She was renamed *President Adams*. Two years later she was sold to the Dollar Line for service on the round-the-world route from New York via Hawaii, the Far East, and the Mediterranean. She was renamed again in 1938, when the Dollar Line was restructured as the American President Line, becoming the *President Grant*. She was taken over as an Army transport in November 1941 and in this capacity she stranded on underwater rocks off Ulma Reef, 70 miles from Milne Bay, New Guinea, on 26 February 1944. The prospects for successful salvage were considered to be most unfavourable and she was therefore abandoned as a constructive total loss.

AMERICA MARU (1898–1944)

Osaka Shosen Kaisha, Japan; Swan & Hunter, Newcastle.
6,307 GRT, 423ft (128.9m) length, 51ft (15.5m) beam.
Triple expansion SR engines, twin screw, 17kts.
Date of disaster: 6 March 1944.

The original owners of the elderly liner *America Maru* and her sister ships, *Hongkong Maru* and *Nippon Maru*, were Toyo Kisen Kaisha. She was acquired by the OSK Line in the 1920s, serving on transpacific routes between the World Wars. After the outbreak of war in the Pacific in 1941 the *America Maru* was converted to a troop transport. She was lost on 6 March 1944, when she was torpedoed by the submarine USS *Nautilus*. The attack took place between Iwo Jima and the Ladrone Islands, in the Marianas Group, in the position 21°50′N–143°54′E. The loss of life is not recorded.

VIGO as *SPERRBRECHER 10* (1922–1944)

Hamburg Sud-Amerika Line, Germany; Howaldtswerke, Hamburg.
7,418 GRT, 413ft (125.9m) length, 55ft (16.8m) beam.
600 passengers.
Triple expansion SR engine, single screw, 12kts.
Date of disaster: 7 March 1944.

The liners *Espana*, *La Coruna*, and *Vigo* operated between Hamburg and La Plata ports, each having accommodation for around 600 passengers. The last-named was rechristened *Sperrbrecher 10* (*Sperrbrecher* meaning 'blockade runner') after she had passed into the control of the German Navy for military service. According to some reports she was sunk on 7 April 1943 when she struck a mine in Danish waters. However, the sinking actually occurred on 7 March 1944 in the River Weser.

DEMPO (1931–1944)

Rotterdam Lloyd, Netherlands; Kon. Maatschappi de Schelde, Vlissingen.
17,024 GRT, 574ft (174.9m) LOA, 70ft (21.3m) beam.
634 passengers in four classes.
Diesel engines, twin screw, 18kts.
Date of disaster: 17 March 1944.

The sister ships *Baloeran* and *Dempo* joined the service from Rotterdam to the Dutch East Indies in 1930 and 1931 respectively. On the outbreak of the Second World War their careers abruptly diverged, with the captured *Baloeran* serving the Axis powers, while the *Dempo* joined the Allies as a troopship. While sailing from Naples to Oran, North Africa, on 17 March 1944, as a unit of convoy SNF17, the *Dempo* was torpedoed and sunk without loss of life by the German submarine *U371*. The attack occurred between Algiers and Philippeville in the position 37°08′N–05°27′E.

MIIKE MARU (1941–1944)

Nippon Yusen Kaisha, Japan; Mitsubishi, Nagasaki.
11,739 GRT, 535ft (163.1m) LOA, 66ft (20.1m) beam.
236 passengers in two classes (designed).
Diesel engines, twin screw, 20kts.
Date of disaster: 21 April 1944.

The *Miike Maru* was intended for the service from Kobe to Vancouver and Seattle, but due to the outbreak of war between Japan and the United States and Great Britain while she was still under construction, she was fitted out instead as a troopship immediately following completion. She was torpedoed and sunk by the American submarine USS *Trigger*

Hamburg Sud-Amerika's Vigo. (Hamburg Sud-Amerika Line)

on 21 April 1944, the attack taking place south-west of Yap, at the north-eastern tip of the Caroline Islands, in the position 08°20′N–134°53′E. The sinking claimed 18 lives.

ASIE as *ROSSANO* (1914–1944)

Chargéurs Reunis, France; Ateliers et Chantiers de France, Dunkerque.
8,561 GRT, 439ft (133.8m) length, 55ft (16.8m) beam.
Triple expansion SR engines, twin screw, 14.5kts.
Date of disaster: 10 May 1944.

The Sperrbrecher 10 *ex-*Vigo *was sunk by a mine. Note the striking camouflage.* (W.Z. Bilddienst)

The former Chargéurs Reunis liner *Asie*, which had been engaged in the service from Bordeaux to West Africa until 1939, was seized by the Germans at Marseilles on 13 March 1943. The Germans did not retain her, however, transferring her to the Italians on 4 May the same year, who renamed her *Rossano*. She was burnt out and sunk on 10 May 1944 when Allied aircraft bombed the port of Genoa.

MARCO POLO ex-*GANGE* ex-*PRESIDENTE WILSON* ex-*GENERALE DIAZ* ex-*KAISER FRANZ JOSEF I* (1912–1944)

Adriatica Line, Italy; Cantieri Navale Triestino, Monfalcone.
12,588 GRT, 500ft (152.4m) LOA, 62ft (18.9m) beam.
374 passengers in three classes.
Quadruple expansion SR engines, twin screw, 18kts.
Date of disaster: 12 May 1944.

The steamship *Kaiser Franz Josef I* was the largest passenger ship ever to operate under the Austrian national flag, her original owners being Unione Austriaca. After the First World War she was ceded to Italy and over the course of the next 20 years she served three companies under four names on three different routes. The years 1919 to 1929 saw her under the Cosulich Line houseflag, more or less her former owners restructured under Italian nationality. From 1929 to 1937 she was operated by Lloyd Triestino, and from then until the Second World War she sailed between Venice and Alexandria as the Adriatica Line's *Marco Polo*. In September 1943, after the armistice between Italy and the Allies, she was placed under the management of a German company, Mediterranean Reederei GmbH. On 12 May 1944 she was scuttled by the Germans at La Spezia to deny use of the harbour to the advancing Allies. The wreck was raised in 1949 and sold for breaking up.

The Lloyd Triestino passenger liner Marco Polo. *Her varied career lasted 32 years.* (World Ship Society)

HAKUSAN MARU (1923–1944)

Nippon Yusen Kaisha, Japan; Mitsubishi, Nagasaki.
10,380 GRT, 520ft (158.5m) LOA, 62ft (18.9m) beam.
175 passengers in single class.
Steam turbines, twin screw, 15.5kts.
Date of disaster: 4 June 1944.

Sister ship to the *Hakozaki Maru*, the *Hakusan Maru* was another torpedo victim. Also taken over as a troop transport with the Japanese Navy, she was sunk by the American submarine USS *Flier* on 4 June 1944, 400 miles south-west of Iwo Jima in the position 22°55′N–136°44′E.

SANTA CLARA as *SUSAN B. ANTHONY* (1930–1944)

Grace Line, USA; New York SB Corp, Camden, New Jersey.
8,183 GRT, 483ft (147.2m) length, 63ft (19.2m) beam.
150 passengers.
Turbo-electric propulsion, twin screw, 16.5kts.
Date of disaster: 7 June 1944.

The former Grace Line turbo-electric liner *Santa Clara*, which served on the route from New York to South America, was renamed *Susan B. Anthony* when she became a troopship in the Second World War. She was sunk on 7 June 1944, during the Operation Overlord landings in Normandy, when she struck a mine off the French coast. There was no loss of life among the large contingent of troops she had brought from the Bristol Channel, all being taken off safely by landing craft. The wreck of the *Susan B. Anthony* lay in the position 49°33′N–00°47′W until it was cleared after the war.

GAROET (1917–1944)

Rotterdam Lloyd, Netherlands; Kon. Maatschappij de Schelde, Vlissingen.
7,133 GRT, 446ft (135.9m) length, 54ft (16.5m) beam.
Steam turbine, single screw, 14kts.
Date of disaster: 19 June 1944.

The troopship Susan B Anthony, *formerly the Grace Line turbo-electric passenger ship* Santa Clara, *is seen here painted in US Navy Measure 22 protective colours. This photograph was taken at the Norfolk Navy Yard on 13 May 1943.* (United States National Archives)

The Dutch steamship Garoet *was a victim of the submarine war.* (L.L. von Münching)

The Dutch turbine steamship *Garoet*, which served on the route to the Dutch East Indies via Africa, became a torpedo victim on 19 June 1944, while on a voyage from Bombay and Mormugas to Durban. She was attacked by the German submarine *U181* some 500 miles north-east of Mauritius and sank in the position 12°30'S–64°00'E. The *Garoet* was not carrying passengers at the time, but there were only 10 survivors from her crew of 98, five of these being picked up from rafts on 30 June and a further five on 4 July.

IZUMO MARU as *HIYO* (1942–1944)

Nippon Yusen Kaisha, Japan; Kawasaki, Kobe.
27,700 GRT, 722ft (220.1m) LOA, 88ft (26.8m) beam.
890 passengers in three classes (designed).
Steam turbines, twin screw, 24kts.
Date of disaster: 20 June 1944.

In 1938 Nippon Yusen Kaisha ordered two large express passenger liners for the transpacific trade from Yokohama to San Francisco. Completion was scheduled for 1940, the year that the Olympic Games were to be held in Tokyo. The two vessels, named *Izumo Maru* and *Kashiwara Maru*, were partly financed by the Japanese Government on the understanding that they would be available for conversion to aircraft-carriers in a national emergency, the vessels' design reflecting these contingency plans.

Hardly a year after construction had begun, though long before Pearl Harbor, the Japanese Government decided to exercise its option to convert the ships into aircraft-carriers, and it was in this form that they were eventually completed in May and June 1942, by then bearing not the slightest resemblance to passenger liners. Their naval names were *Hiyo* and *Junyo* respectively. Prior to their construction, all Japanese aircraft-carriers could be truly described as 'flat-tops', for it was only with the *Hiyo* and *Junyo* that the island superstructure with super-imposed funnel was introduced, a

The Izumo Maru *was completed as the fleet carrier* Hiyo, *here seen at sea with, in the distance, her sister ship* Junyo *ex-* Kashiwara Maru. (Sekai No Kansen)

The Hiyo *during the Battle of the Philippine Sea, frame from cine film shot at the time.* (Pathé Cinema)

style continued in later ships. The *Hiyo*'s brief life was packed with incident. In August 1942, along with her sister, she took part in the Battle of the Eastern Solomons, followed two months later by the Battle of Santa Cruz. Further battle honours were earned in the Guadalcanal campaign and the Battle of Tassafaronga. She was damaged in a torpedo attack on 11 June 1943 when the American submarine USS *Trigger* hit her when she was south of Tokyo Bay. With the aid of a cruiser she made it to Yokosuka, where she was repaired.

A year later, in partnership again with the *Junyo*, she took part in the Battle of the Philippine Sea, during which, on the afternoon of 20 June 1944, dive-bombers and torpedo-bombers from the American carrier USS *Bellau Wood* concentrated their attacks on her, hitting her repeatedly. Though she survived the onslaught the *Hiyo* had been mortally wounded, for petroleum vapour was leaking from her fuel tanks, and when this ignited she was shaken by a series of massive explosions, which few of her crew survived. Blazing from end to end, the *Hiyo* finally rolled over and sank 450 miles north-east of Yap in the position 15°30′N–133°50′E.

NELLORE (1913–1944)

Eastern & Australian SS Co, Great Britain; Caird, Greenock.
6,942 GRT, 450ft (137.2m) length, 52ft (15.9m) beam.
94 passengers in two classes.
Quadruple expansion SR engines, twin screw, 13kts.
Date of disaster: 29 June 1944.

Formerly a P&O vessel, one of a quartet built for the Australian service, the *Nellore* passed to new owners in 1929. She was torpedoed and sunk by a Japanese submarine on 29 June 1944 during a voyage from Bombay to Fremantle, Melbourne, and Sydney. The attack took place about 400 miles east of the Chagos Archipelago, in the Indian Ocean, in the position 07°51′S–75°20′E. The *Nellore* was carrying 341 people, 209 of them passengers. Of these, 79 were killed and 11 others were taken prisoner. Thirty-eight of the dead were from a lifeboat containing 47 survivors which, following the sinking, endured 28 days adrift, during which time it covered over 2,500 miles of ocean. When the boat eventually reached land at Madagascar only nine of its occupants remained alive.

VIRGILIO (1927–1944)

Italia Line, Italy; Cantieri Officine Meridionali, Baia.
11,718 GRT, 506ft (154.2m) LOA, 62ft (18.9m) beam.
640 passengers in three classes.
Diesel engines, twin screw, 14kts.
Date of disaster: ? June 1944.

The *Virgilio*, sister liner to the *Orazio* which was destroyed by fire off the French coast in January 1940, operated in the Genoa to Valparaiso service. From June 1940 she was employed as a naval hospital ship, but when Italy sued for peace in September 1943 the Germans seized the ship at La

The Eastern & Australian Steamship Company's Nellore, *seen here in her original P&O colours.* (World Ship Society)

Spezia. On 6 December 1943 she was damaged in a torpedo attack in the Gulf of Genoa. Taken to Toulon, she was deliberately blown up by the Germans before they withdrew from the area at the end of June 1944. Her wreck was broken up after the war.

KAMO MARU (1908–1944)

Nippon Yusen Kaisha, Japan; Mitsubishi, Nagasaki.
8,524 GRT, 465ft (141.7m) length, 54ft (16.5m) beam.
Triple expansion SR engines, twin screw, 15kts.
Date of disaster: 3 July 1944.

The *Kamo Maru* was employed on the service from Japan to Europe via Suez ports, with a brief interlude spent on the transpacific run. She was torpedoed and sunk some 100 miles west of Kagoshima, Japan, on 3 July 1944, in the position 32°24′N–138°46′E. Her attacker was the American submarine USS *Tinosa*. The *Kamo Maru* had previously been damaged by a torpedo on 27 October 1943, when she was attacked in the East China Sea.

ITALIA (1905–1944)

Lloyd Triestino, Italy; N. Odero & Co, Genoa.
5,203 GRT, 393ft (119.8m) length, 47ft (14.3m) beam.
Triple expansion SR engines, twin screw, 15kts.
Date of disaster: 6 July 1944.

The passenger liner *Italia* was transferred between four Italian shipping lines in her 39-year career: La Veloce, Navigazione Generale Italiana, Soc. Italiana di Servizi Marittimi, and Lloyd Triestino. The *Italia* was attacked by British aircraft in an inlet west of Brovigne, near Trieste, on 6 July 1944. Hit by rockets, she was shaken by an internal explosion and caught fire, subsequently keeling over and sinking. Attempts to salvage her on 18 September 1944 were unsuccessful.

STOCKHOLM as *SABAUDIA* (1941–1944)

Swedish Amerika Line, Sweden; Cantieri Riuniti Dell'Adriatico, Trieste.
29,307 GRT, 675ft (205.7m) LOA, 83ft (25.3m) beam.
1,350 passengers in three classes on scheduled service or 640 passengers in single class when cruising (designed).
Diesel engines, triple screw, 19kts.
Date of disaster: 6 July 1944.

After the liner *Stockholm* had been destroyed by fire on 19 December 1938, while fitting out at Monfalcone, a second, identical ship was ordered to replace her. Given the same name when launched on 10 March 1940, the second *Stockholm* was completed in October 1941, only to find herself blockaded by the war that had erupted during the period of her delayed construction. As her owners, Swedish Amerika Line, could not take delivery of the vessel she was sold to the Italian Government, which planned to use her as a troop transport. Even though it is claimed that the *Sabaudia*, as she was renamed, made a limited number of trooping voyages, there is no evidence

The Swedish Amerika Line's new flagship Stockholm *seen undergoing sea trials in October 1941.* (Italcantieri SpA)

The Sabaudia*'s wreck lying half-submerged at Vallone de Zaule. The gaping hole in her side and other damage was caused by bombs.* (A. Duncan *and* A. Kludas)

to support this. The fact that she had still not received a full complement of lifeboats when she was towed to Vallone de Zaule, Muggia, for laying up in 1944 suggests otherwise. She was, however, employed as a German barracks ship for a while after the Italian capitulation in September 1943. There may have been some resistance to the Germans' acquisition of the *Sabaudia*, for Lloyd's records show that prior to a British air-raid on 6 July, in which she was bombed and set on fire, she had already been sunk by unknown causes. It is not apparent whether she had been raised after this first incident, but the air-raid certainly left her in a gutted and partially sunk condition. Lying near the sunken liners *Duilio* and *Giulio Cesare*, the *Sabaudia* was further damaged in air raids in early 1945. She was refloated in 1949 and broken up locally, ending a very brief and unproductive career.

DUILIO (1923–1944)

Lloyd Triestino, Italy; Ansaldo, Sestri Ponente.
24,281 GRT, 635ft (193.5m) LOA, 76ft (23.2m) beam.
757 passengers in three classes.
Steam turbines, quadruple screw, 19kts.
Date of disaster: 10 July 1944.

The liners *Duilio* and *Giulio Cesare* were the first large passenger vessels to fly the Italian flag. They first entered service on the New York run from Genoa and Naples for their original owners, Navigazione Generale Italiana. After 1928 they sailed on the South American service until 1932 when, following absorption into the Italia Line fleet, they switched to the African service from Genoa to Cape Town. A further move in their chequered careers took them to Lloyd Triestino ownership in 1937. This saw the only break in their partnership for, while the *Duilio* continued in the African passenger service, the *Giulio Cesare* was operated between Italy and the Far East. In 1940 the pair were reunited when they were laid up together at Trieste. They were briefly re-activated in the spring of 1942 when, painted in the colours of the International Red Cross, they were chartered for a few repatriation voyages from East Africa. Once these were completed, they returned to lay-up at Vallone di Zaule, near Trieste, where both ships were scuttled by their crews in September 1943 when Italy surrendered. They were raised by the Germans, only to be sunk again in Allied air-raids, the *Duilio* on 10 July 1944. The capsized ships sustained further damage in another raid on 11 September. When the Allies took Trieste and the surrounding area they discovered the ships still in this condition. Ending their lives in unison, both the *Duilio* and her sister were raised and scrapped in 1948.

TANDA ex-*MADRAS* ex-*TANDA* (1914–1944)

Eastern & Australian SS Co, Great Britain; Alexander Stephen, Glasgow.
7,174 GRT, 430ft (131.1m) length, 58ft (17.7m) beam.
Triple expansion SR engines, twin screw, 13kts.
Date of disaster: 15 July 1944.

Originally in British India Line service, the *Tanda* later joined the Eastern & Australian Steamship Company, working between Australia, Malaysia, and India. During a voyage from Melbourne to Colombo and Bombay on 15 July 1944 the *Tanda* was sunk by a Japanese submarine east of the Laccadive Islands, in a position variously given as 13°22′N–74°09′E or 13°26′N–74°14′E. Out of 216 people aboard, 19 lost their lives.

SEATTLE MARU (1909–1944)

Osaka Shosen Kaisha, Japan; Kawasaki, Kobe.
6,182 GRT, 419ft (127.7m) length, 49ft (14.9m) beam.
Triple expansion SR engines, twin screw, 13kts.
Date of disaster: 16 July 1944.

The *Seattle Maru* was one of the pioneer vessels of Osaka Shosen Kaisha on the route from Osaka to Tacoma, Washington, a service which she maintained with her sister liners *Chicago Maru* and *Tacoma Maru*. The American submarine USS *Piranha* torpedoed and sunk the *Seattle Maru* on 16 July 1944, 100 miles north-west of Luzon, Philippine Islands, in the position 19°26′N–120°18′E.

AKI MARU ex-*MISHIMA MARU* (1942–1944)

Nippon Yusen Kaisha, Japan; Mitsubishi, Nagasaki.
11,409 GRT, 535ft (163.1m) LOA, 66ft (20.1m) beam.
137 passengers in single class (designed).
Diesel engines, twin screw, 20kts.
Date of disaster: 26 July 1944.

The *Aki Maru* was originally conceived for the Kobe to Seattle service, the plans being later revised for her to operate on the Australia route. However, when she entered service in May 1942 it was as a naval troop transport. It was

The Italian ship Duilio *sank at her anchorage at Vallone di Zaule, near Trieste. In the background is the sunken hull of the* Sabaudia *ex*-Stockholm. (Maj Aldo Fraccaroli)

The Eastern & Australian Steamship Company liner Tanda, *formerly P&O's* Madras. (World Ship Society)

while performing these duties that she was torpedoed west of Luzon, Philippine Islands, by the USS *Crevalle* on 26 July 1944, sinking in position 18°28′N–117°59′E. The attack claimed 41 lives.

FUSO (HUSO) MARU ex-*LATVIA* ex-*RUSS* ex-*ROSSIJA* ex-*RUSSIA* (1908–1944)

Osaka Shosen Kaisha, Japan; Barclay Curle, Glasgow.
8,596 GRT, 475ft (144.8m) length, 57ft (17.4m) beam.
1,291 passengers in two classes (as a Polish ship).
Triple expansion SR engines, twin screw, 14kts.
Date of disaster: 31 July 1944.

This much-transferred and renamed liner commenced life as the *Russia* of the Russian American Line. Four names later, after a brief spell with the Gdynia America Line, she joined Osaka Shosen Kaisha's Pacific services as the *Fuso Maru*. She became a war casualty on 31 July 1944, when the American submarine USS *Steelhead* torpedoed and sank her off the north coast of Luzon, in the Philippine Islands, in the position 18°57′N–120°50′E. She was serving as a troop transport at the time.

YOSHINO (YOSINO) MARU ex-*KLEIST* (1906–1944)

Nippon Yusen Kaisha, Japan; F. Schichau, Danzig.
8,959 GRT, 463ft (141.1m) length, 57ft (17.4m) beam.
Quadruple expansion SR engines, twin screw, 14.5kts.
Date of disaster: 31 July 1944.

The Norddeutscher Lloyd steamship *Kleist*, which served in the Far East and Australian trades from Europe, passed into Nippon Yusen Kaisha ownership in 1919, as a Japanese war reparation, and continued working in the same service. On 31 July 1944, while serving as a Japanese naval transport, she was torpedoed and sunk off the west coast of Dalupiri, in the Philippines Islands, by the American submarines USS *Steelhead* and *Parche*. The position was 19°10′N–120°58′E.

BAUDOUINVILLE as *LINDAU* (1939–1944)

Cie. Maritime Belge, Belgium; John Cockerill, Hoboken.
13,761 GRT, 541ft (164.9m) LOA, 67ft (20.4m) beam.
395 passengers in two classes.
Diesel engines, twin screw, 16kts.
Date of disaster: 10 August 1944.

The Germans seized the almost new Belgian passenger ship *Baudouinville* at Bordeaux in June 1940, after she had eluded capture at Antwerp the previous month. She had completed only three commercial round voyages in the service from Antwerp to the Belgian Congo by the time war broke out. The German Navy took her over as the hospital ship *Lindau*, managed on their behalf by the Deutsche Ost-Afrika Line. These duties were terminated in January 1943 and she then became an accommodation ship at Nantes. During the retreat from Nantes, on 10 August 1944, the Germans deliberately set the vessel alight to scuttle her and she sank after an ammunition store ignited and exploded. She was refloated in 1946 and towed to Antwerp on 29 August for breaking up. Later, on 21 October 1947, the partly-demolished ship was moved to Boom for the completion of the scrapping work.

The Messageries Maritimes liner Aramis, *another example of the unusual square-funnelled ships which this company introduced in the late-1920s. She was lost while under the Japanese flag after she had been renamed* Teia Maru. (Author's collection)

ARAMIS as *TEIA MARU* (1932–1944)

Messageries Maritimes, France; Forges et Chantiers de la Mediterranée, La Seyne.
17,537 GRT, 566ft (172.5m) LOA, 69ft (21.0m) beam.
1,045 passengers in four classes.
Diesel engines, twin screw, 18kts.
Date of disaster: 18 August 1944.

The Messageries Maritimes liner *Aramis* was the last unit of the class of square-funnelled motor liners built for the premier service from Marseilles to the Far East. The other two ships were the *Felix Roussel* and the unlucky *Georges Philippar*. In September 1939, the *Aramis* was converted into an auxiliary cruiser at Saigon, only to be captured there by the Japanese in April 1942. Renamed *Teia Maru*, she was employed as a troop transport apart from a brief interlude in 1943 when, under the auspices of the International Red Cross, she made a number of so-called 'mercy voyages' in which prisoners-of-war were exchanged. The *Teia Maru* was finally sunk on 18 August 1944, the victim of torpedoes from the American submarine USS *Rasher*. She was attacked 150 miles west of Negra Point, Luzon, in the Philippines, and sank in the position 18°09'N–119°56'E.

KASUGA MARU as *TAIYO* (1941–1944)

Nippon Yusen Kaisha, Japan; Mitsubishi, Nagasaki.
17,127 GRT, 590ft (179.8m) LOA, 74ft (22.6m) beam.
285 passengers in three classes (designed).
Steam turbines, twin screw, 21kts.
Date of disaster: 18 August 1944.

The third ship of the trio of Nippon Yusen Kaisha liners ordered for the Yokohama to Hamburg trade in the late 1930s, the *Kasuga Maru* was still under construction when the Japanese Navy took her over for completion as an aircraft-carrier. Renamed *Taiyo* when delivered in September 1941, she was the first of the three ships to enter service in the carrier role and, unlike her sisters, she was never engaged in commercial work as originally conceived. She was torpedoed by the American submarine USS *Rasher* on 18 August 1944, about 22 miles south-west of Cape Bojeador, Luzon, Philippine Islands. She sank in the position 18°16'N–120°20'E.

CHENONCEAUX ex-*ARAMIS* (1922–1944)

Messageries Maritimes, France; Ateliers et Chantiers de la Gironde, Bordeaux.
14,825 GRT, 565ft (172.2m) LOA, 65ft (19.8m) beam.
317 passengers in three classes.
Triple expansion SR engines, twin screw, 15kts.
Date of disaster: 20–25 August 1944.

The *Chenonceaux* sailed on the Far East routes from Marseilles with her near-sister ships *Athos II* and *D'Artagnan*. She was renamed from *Aramis* in 1925, her original name going to a new ship that joined the company's fleet in 1931. The *Chenonceaux* was scuttled at Marseilles between 20 and 25 August 1944. Refloated in 1948, she was towed to Toulon on 17 June 1948 and broken up there.

Top *The* Chenonceaux *was scuttled by the Germans as they withdrew from Marseilles.* (World Ship Society)

Above *The* Jean Laborde, *another of Messageries Maritimes' distinctive square-funnelled motorships, was also scuttled at Marseilles by the Germans.* (World Ship Society)

JEAN LABORDE (1930–1944)

Messageries Maritimes, France; Soc. Provençale de Constructions Navales, La Ciotat.
11,591 GRT, 491ft (149.7m) LOA, 61ft (18.6m) beam.
900 passengers in four classes.
Diesel engines, twin screw, 19kts.
Date of disaster: 20–25 August 1944.

The *Jean Laborde* and her sister ship *Marechal Joffre* were motorships employed in the service from France to the Far East via the Suez Canal. The *Jean Laborde,* which had remained in the port of Marseilles throughout the war, was scuttled there by German forces at some time between 20 and 25 August 1944 as they withdrew from Southern France. Raised in early 1946, the wreck was towed to La Seyne in April the same year. It was finally sold for breaking up at Savona.

MASSILIA (1920–1944)

Cie. Sud-Atlantique, France; Forges et Chantiers de la Mediterranée, La Seyne.
15,363 GRT, 600ft (182.9m) LOA, 64ft (19.5m) beam.
1,041 passengers in four classes.
Triple expansion SR engines, quadruple screw, 20kts.
Date of disaster: 20–25 August 1944.

The *Massilia* was the last vessel of a three-ship class, including the *Gallia* which was torpedoed in the First World War, the third member of the trio being the *Lutetia*. They served on the route from Bordeaux to La Plata ports. After taking members of the French Government from Bordeaux to Casablanca in June 1940, the *Massilia* was laid up in the Basin Mirabeau for the next four years. German troops sank her there between 20 and 25 August 1944 in order to block the harbour. Refloated after the war's end, the wreck was broken up from 1948.

SINAIA (1924–1944)

Fabre Line, France; Barclay Curle, Glasgow.
8,567 GRT, 439ft (133.8m) length, 56ft (17.1m) beam.
Triple expansion SR engines, twin screw, 14kts.
Date of disaster: 20–25 August 1944.

The liner *Sinaia* was a sister ship to the French Line's *De la Salle*. She operated on the service from Marseilles to New York until the outbreak of the Second World War, when she was laid up in her home port. She was scuttled there between 20 and 25 August 1944 by retreating German army units. The *Sinaia* was refloated on 9 December 1946, her wreck being ultimately moved to the Leon Gourret quay in Marseilles in 1953, where she was broken up.

EXPLORATEUR GRANDIDIER (1924–1944)

Messageries Maritimes, France; Chantiers et Ateliers de L'Atlantique (Penhoët), St Nazaire.
10,267 GRT, 476ft (145.1m) LOA, 60ft (18.3m) beam.
299 passengers in three classes.
Triple expansion SR engines, twin screw, 15kts.
Date of disaster: 21 August 1944.

The *Explorateur Grandidier* and her sister ship *Bernardin de Saint Pierre* were employed in the service from Marseilles to Madagascar. Laid up in Marseilles from 1940, the *Explorateur Grandidier* was scuttled there on 21 August 1944. The wreck was cleared and broken up in 1948.

USARAMO (1920–1944)

Deutsche Ost-Afrika Line, Germany; Blohm & Voss, Hamburg.
7,775 GRT, 418ft (127.4m) length, 56ft (17.1m) beam.
250 passengers.
Steam turbine, single screw, 14kts.
Date of disaster: 25 August 1944.

The sister ships *Usaramo*, *Ussukuma*, and *Wangoni* were employed in the African services. The first two were

The Massilia *of Cie. Sud-Atlantique, one of a trio of stylish ships built for the South American run. Only the* Lutetia *escaped destruction in wartime.* (World Ship Society)

The Deutsche Ost-Afrika ship Usaramo *was scuttled at Bordeaux when the Germans evacuated the city.* (World Ship Society)

casualties of the Second World War, the *Usaramo* being deliberately sunk by the Germans in the River Gironde at Bordeaux on 25 August 1944. She was salvaged and sold for scrapping after the end of hostilities.

MEXICO MARU (1910–1944)

Osaka Shosen Kaisha, Japan; Mitsubishi, Nagasaki.
6,064 GRT, 407ft (124.1m) length, 49ft (14.9m) beam.
Triple expansion SR engines, twin screw, 13kts.
Date of disaster: 29 August 1944.

The transpacific steamship *Mexico Maru* maintained a passenger service to South American ports in conjunction with six sister ships, whose names mostly reflected the port or country the vessel served (the exception being the *Chicago Maru*). The *Mexico Maru* was sunk by the American submarine USS *Jack* on 29 August 1944, some 50 miles north of Buol in the Celebes, in the position 02°07'N–122°28'E.

ST LOUIS (1929–1944)

Hamburg Amerika Line, Germany; Bremer Vulkan, Vegesack.
16,732 GRT, 574ft (174.9m) LOA, 73ft (22.3m) beam.
973 passengers in three classes.
Diesel engines, twin screw, 16kts.
Date of disaster: 30 August 1944.

From March 1929 the German motorship *St Louis* sailed on the North Atlantic route and on cruises. She was in the headlines in the summer of 1939 when she was involved in a diplomatically sensitive mission taking 900 Jewish emigrants to Havana, Cuba. The full story has been chronicled in the book and film *Voyage of the Damned.* First the Cuban authorities, and later the Americans, refused to accept the desperate passengers. Subsequently, they were granted asylum in Great Britain, France, Belgium, and the Netherlands, but when the latter three countries were overrun by Germany, many of the former passengers fell prey to the Nazis.

In January 1940 the *St Louis* became a naval accommodation ship at Kiel. Three years later, on 30 August 1944, she was bombed and severely damaged. The partly burnt-out liner was beached, and was not refloated until 1946. She was then towed to Hamburg where, secured at the Altona landing stage, she was used to provide accommodation for the port's homeless. The *St Louis* departed Hamburg in tow for Bremerhaven for breaking up on 15 April 1950.

MARIETTE PACHA (1925–1944)

Messageries Maritimes, France; Soc. Provençale de Constructions Navales, La Ciotat.
12,239 GRT, 522ft (159.1m) LOA, 62ft (18.9m) beam.
949 passengers in four classes.
Triple expansion SR engines, twin screw, 15kts.
Date of disaster: ? August 1944.

With her sister ship *Champollion*, the *Mariette Pacha* operated on the service from Marseilles to Alexandria for 15 years prior to the Second World War. In 1940 she was laid up at Marseilles for the duration of the war, but when the

The Hamburg Amerika Line motorship St Louis *hit the headlines in mid-1939 when she was engaged to take Jewish refugees to Cuba.* (World Ship Society)

Germans withdrew from the port towards the end of August 1944 they scuttled her. Her wreck was demolished from 1948.

REX (1932–1944)

Italia Line, Italy; Ansaldo, Sestri Ponente, Genoa.
51,062 GRT, 880ft (268.2m) LOA, 97ft (29.6m) beam.

The Rex *was Italy's only Atlantic Blue Riband record-breaker.* (L.L. von Münching)

2,258 passengers in four classes.
Steam turbines, quadruple screw, 28kts.
Date of disaster: 8 September 1944.

The transatlantic express liner *Rex*, which was originally conceived by the Navigazione Generale Italiana Company prior to the reorganization of the Italian merchant marine, was the largest passenger liner to fly the Italian flag, and Italy's only holder of the Atlantic Blue Riband. She took the speed honours westbound in August 1933 with an average speed of 28.92kts. When war broke out between the Axis powers and Great Britain and France the *Rex* was laid up, first at Bari and, from August 1940, at Trieste although she must have been moved yet again, at a later, unknown date. Like her half-sister *Conte di Savoia*, the *Rex* was not involved in the war effort because her large size made her vulnerable to air attack. Even after she fell into German hands in September 1943, following Italy's capitulation, she remained idle until, a year later, she was spotted by Royal Air Force Beaufighter aircraft on 8 September 1944, proceeding close inshore along the coast south of Trieste, near Capo d'Istria. It was assumed that she was heading for Trieste, where she was to be scuttled to block the harbour entrance, so the Beaufighters attacked. The offensive continued into the next day and the *Rex* was hit by a total of 123 rockets. The first attack left her on fire from stem to stern and after the second she rolled over onto her port side, sinking in shallow water. The wreck was demolished on the spot by the Yugoslavs from 1947 to 1948.

Left *RAF Beaufighters attack the liner* Rex, *which is hugging Italy's Adriatic coastline.* (Imperial War Museum, Neg. C4622)

Right *After 123 rocket hits, the* Rex *lies on her beam ends in Capo d'Istria Bay, ablaze and billowing smoke. The position of the wreck, south of Trieste harbour and inside the Yugoslav border, frustrated Italian efforts to salvage the ship after the war.* (L.L. von Münching)

GIULIO CESARE (1920–1944)

Lloyd Triestino, Italy; Swan, Hunter & Wigham Richardson, Newcastle.
21,657 GRT, 634ft (193.2m) LOA, 76ft (23.2m) beam.
640 passengers in three classes.
Steam turbines, quadruple screw, 19.5kts.
Date of disaster: 11 September 1944.

After a mixed career for several owners, working with her

The Giulio Cesare, *painted in the colours of the International Red Cross for prisoner repatriation missions.* (Imperial War Museum, Neg. GM625)

The scene at Vallone di Zaule on 16 October 1947. The Giulio Cesare *is in the foreground and her near-sister* Duilio *is just beyond her bow. In the centre background lies the wreck of the* Sabaudia. (Maj Aldo Fraccaroli)

sister ship the *Duilio*, the passenger liner *Giulio Cesare* entered the Italy to Far East service for Lloyd Triestino in 1937. After the outbreak of war she was laid up. Like her sister, the *Giulio Cesare* undertook prisoner repatriation voyages for the International Red Cross in 1942, after which she was laid up again. Scuttled by her crew at the time of the Italian surrender, she was raised by the Germans only to be destroyed in bombing raids on Trieste in the late summer of 1944. In the first raid, on 25 August 1944, she received extensive damage but remained afloat. However, a further raid on 11 September sank her, leaving her lying on her side close to her sister *Duilio*. The wrecked remains of the *Giulio Cesare* were removed and demolished in 1949.

One of the worst Japanese shipping disasters of the Second World War involved the Rakuyo Maru. (Mitsubishi Heavy Industries)

PRESIDENT HARRISON ex-*WOLVERINE STATE* as *KACHIDOKI MARU* (1921–1944)

American President Line, USA; New York SB Corp, Camden, New Jersey.
10,509 GRT, 516ft (157.3m) LOA, 62ft (18.9m) beam.
78 passengers in single class.
Triple expansion SR engines, twin screw, 14kts.
Date of disaster: 12 September 1944.

From 1924 the American President Line's *President Harrison* operated on the round-the-world service from New York to New York, via the Far East and the Mediterranean. She was a United States Shipping Board standard design ship, her career having commenced under the management of the Pacific Mail SS Co. Dollar Line purchased her in 1923 and she passed to American President in 1938. On 8 December 1941 she was seized by the Japanese in the Strait of Pohai, bound for Chingwangtao from Shanghai. Her master, Capt Orel Pierson, had deliberately run her aground off Shaweishan Island in the hope that she would be beyond recovery. After 43 days the Japanese salvaged the ship and, following repairs, they placed her in service as the transport *Kachidoki Maru*. Capt Pierson and the other officers were taken to Japan as prisoners. The American submarine USS *Pampanito* sank the *Kachidoki Maru* on 12 September 1944, 50 miles east of the island of Hainan in the position 19°18′N–112°23′E.

RAKUYO MARU (1921–1944)

Nippon Yusen Kaisha, Japan; Mitsubishi, Nagasaki.
9,419 GRT, 460ft (140.2m) length, 60ft (18.3m) beam.
Steam turbines, twin screw, 12kts.
Date of disaster: 12 September 1944.

In consort with the *Anyo Maru*, *Bokuyo Maru*, and *Ginyo Maru*, the steamship *Rakuyo Maru* operated on the service from Japan to ports on the west coast of South America, via the United States. On 12 September 1944 she was torpedoed and sunk by the American submarine USS *Sealion II* about 100 miles north-east of the Paracel Islands, South China Sea, in the position 18°42′N–114°30′E. She had left Singapore eight days earlier, bound for Kobe with a mixed cargo of rubber, oil, and foodstuffs and 1,350 prisoners-of-war. How many of these survived the sinking is not known but it is suspected that the casualties were very heavy.

YAWATA MARU as *UNYO* (1940–1944)

Nippon Yusen Kaisha, Japan; Mitsubishi, Nagasaki.
17,128 GRT, 590ft (179.8m) LOA, 73ft (22.3m) beam.
285 passengers in three classes.
Steam turbines, twin screw, 22kts.
Date of disaster: 16 September 1944.

Built for the Yokohama to Hamburg service, the *Yawata Maru* instead entered the service to San Francisco because of the war in Europe. Like her sisters *Nitta Maru* and

Nippon Yusen Kaisha's Yawata Maru, *later rebuilt as the escort carrier* Unyo. (Nippon Yusen Kaisha)

Kasuga Maru, the *Yawata Maru* was taken over in January 1942 for conversion into an aircraft carrier and, only five months later, she re-emerged as the *Unyo*. On 16 September 1944 she was torpedoed and sunk in the South China Sea by the American submarine USS *Barb*, 220 miles south-east of Hong Kong in the position 19°18'N–116°26'E.

MIZUHO MARU ex-*INFANTA ISABEL* (1912–1944)

Osaka Shosen Kaisha, Japan; Russell & Co, Port Glasgow.
8,506 GRT, 460ft (140.2m) length, 58ft (17.7m) beam.
2,044 passengers in three classes (as a Spanish ship).
Quadruple expansion SR engines, twin screw, 15kts.
Date of disaster: 21 September 1944.

The cargo-passenger steamship *Mizuho Maru* was purchased from Cia Transoceanica of Spain in August 1926 to serve on the Pacific route from Japan to the United States of America. She was taken over as a troop transport following the outbreak of war in the Pacific in December 1941. In this role she was torpedoed and sunk by the submarine USS *Redfish* on 21 September 1944 off the north-west coast of Luzon in the Philippines, in the position 18°38'N–120°43'E. The former *Infanta Isabel* was sister ship to the *Principe de Asturias*, which was wrecked after running onto rocks off the Brazilian coast in March 1916.

ZUIDERDAM (1944)

Holland Amerika Line, Netherlands; Wilton Fijenoord, Schiedam.
12,150 GRT, 518ft (157.9m) LOA, 66ft (20.1m) beam.
134 passengers in single class (designed).
Diesel engines, twin screw, 16kts.
Date of disaster: 22 September 1944.

This sister ship to the *Westerdam* was less lucky than her consort, for she did not survive the Second World War. Still under construction when the Netherlands was overrun by the Germans in May 1940, the *Zuiderdam* immediately became the target of the Resistance and the Allied air forces to prevent the Germans from completing her for their own purposes. She was floated in her construction dock in the spring of 1941, but on 28 August of that year, while still incomplete, she was burnt out and capsized after a British air-raid on Schiedam. She was refloated on 25 July 1942 and laid up at Rotterdam. When, in 1944, the tide of war turned

The Japanese passenger ship Mizuho Maru, *depicted in her death throes in a painting by Ichiro Ohkubo.* (Mitsui-OSK Lines)

The incomplete Zuiderdam *was sunk as a blockship in the Nieuwe Waterweg, near Maassluis.* (L.L. von Münching)

against the Germans, compelling them to withdraw from the Netherlands, it was determined that the *Zuiderdam* and *Westerdam* should be scuttled in the Nieuwe Waterweg to block access to the port of Rotterdam. In the case of the *Westerdam* the Dutch Resistance was able to intervene, but not so with the *Zuiderdam*, which was towed to Maassluis and sunk there on 22 September 1944, though she failed to fulfil the German objective. She was raised on 13 November 1946 but it was not considered worthwhile repairing her, so she was sold for breaking up at Ghent in April 1948.

AUGUSTUS as *SPARVIERO* (1927–1944)

Italia Line, Italy; Ansaldo, Sestri Ponente.
30,418 GRT, 711ft (216.7m) LOA, 82ft (25.0m) beam.
2,034 passengers in four classes.
Diesel engines, quadruple screw, 19kts.
Date of disaster: 25 September 1944.

The Navigazione Generale Italiana motorship *Augustus*, sister ship to the turbine driven *Roma*, served on both the North and South Atlantic routes under the Italia Line

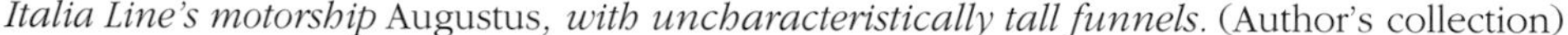

Italia Line's motorship Augustus, *with uncharacteristically tall funnels.* (Author's collection)

houseflag from January 1932. In 1939 the *Augustus* was laid up pending conversion to turbine propulsion in order to increase her speed. This was not undertaken, however, and the *Augustus* remained laid up until 1942, when the Italian Navy took her over for conversion into an aircraft-carrier. Renamed *Sparviero*, it was intended at first that her conversion should follow the lines of that of the *Aquila* ex-*Roma*, to a full fleet carrier. However, lack of finance, and bomb-damage suffered in November 1942, interfered with these plans, and a modified scheme was pursued instead, which would have resulted in the *Sparviero* becoming an escort carrier. At the time of the armistice with Italy in September 1943, work had progressed to the point where the ship's upperworks had been removed and she was flush-decked at hull level, but the conversion was then terminated. The Germans, who seized the *Sparviero*, sank her at Genoa on 25 September 1944 to block the entrance to the harbour. The wreck was refloated in 1946 to clear the channel and in April 1948 it was sold to be broken up.

ARABIA MARU (1936–1944)

Osaka Shosen Kaisha, Japan; Mitsubishi, Nagasaki.
9,480 GRT, 475ft (144.8m) length, 61ft (18.6m) beam.
Triple expansion SR engines, twin screw, 13kts.
Date of disaster: 18 October 1944.

The *Arabia Maru* was employed on various Pacific routes from the time of her completion, primarily the Hong Kong to Tacoma service. During the Second World War she was utilized as a naval transport, in which role she was torpedoed and sunk by the American submarine USS *Bluegill* on 18 October 1944, about 100 miles east of Manila, Philippine Islands. The position was 14°06'N–119°40'E.

ASAMA MARU (1929–1944)

Nippon Yusen Kaisha, Japan; Mitsubishi, Nagasaki.
16,975 GRT, 583ft (177.7m) LOA, 72ft (21.9m) beam.
822 passengers in three classes.
Diesel engines, quadruple screw, 20kts.
Date of disaster: 1 November 1944.

On 2 September 1937 the transpacific liner *Asama Maru* was caught up in a typhoon which struck Hong Kong, nearly ending her life prematurely. Left high and dry, two of her four main engines had to be removed before she could be refloated, an operation which lasted seven months. When war erupted in the Pacific in December 1941, the *Asama Maru* was requisitioned as a Japanese Navy transport. She was torpedoed and sunk on 1 November 1944 by the submarine USS *Atule*, the attack taking place approximately 100 miles south of Pratas Island in the South China Sea, in position 20°09'N–117°39'E.

GOKOKU MARU (1942–1944)

Osaka Shosen Kaisha, Japan; Tama SB Co., Tama.
10,438 GRT, 537ft (163.7m) LOA, 66ft (20.1m) beam.
400 passengers in three classes (designed).
Diesel engines, twin screw, 17kts.
Date of disaster: 10 November 1944.

The sister ships *Hokoku Maru*, *Aikoku Maru*, and *Gokoku Maru* were intended for the Japan to Europe service. However, the *Gokoku Maru* was never completed as a passenger ship, instead being completed as an auxiliary cruiser for the Japanese Navy in September 1942. In this capacity she was badly damaged by American aircraft on 18 December 1942 while at Madang. After repairs she resumed service as a troop transport, only to be severely damaged a second time on 27 December 1943 when she struck a mine

Nippon Yusen Kaisha's motorship Asama Maru. (Mitsubishi Heavy Industries)

A model showing the proposed appearance of the liner Gokoku Maru, *which was actually completed as an auxiliary cruiser.* (Mitsui-OSK Lines)

off Omae Zaki. Her luck finally ran out on 10 November 1944, when she was torpedoed and sunk by the American submarine USS *Barb* about 50 miles west of Sasebo, in the position 33°23′N–129°03′E.

SCHARNHORST as *SHINYO* (*JINYO*) (1935–1944)

Norddeutscher Lloyd, Germany; Deschimag AG Weser, Bremen.

18,184 GRT, 652ft (198.7m) LOA, 74ft (22.6m) beam.
293 passengers in two classes.
Turbo-electric propulsion, twin screw, 21kts.
Date of disaster: 17 November 1944.

Sister ship to the *Gneisenau* on Norddeutscher Lloyd's Far East service from Hamburg, the *Scharnhorst* was laid up in Japan in September 1939, following the outbreak of war in Europe. In February 1942 her owners sold her to the

The German liner Scharnhorst, *which was taken over by the Japanese after the outbreak of the Second World War.* (World Ship Society)

The aircraft-carrier Shinyo *ex*-Scharnhorst. (Author's collection)

Imperial Japanese Navy, which converted her into an aircraft-carrier at Kure. She entered service as the *Shinyo* in December 1943 and appears to have served primarily in the role of escort carrier or aircraft ferry. On 17 November 1944, the *Shinyo* was torpedoed 140 miles north-east of Shanghai by the American submarine USS *Spadefish*. She sank in the position 33°02′N–123°33′E.

MANILA MARU (1915–1944)

Osaka Shosen Kaisha, Japan; Mitsubishi, Nagasaki.
9,518 GRT, 475ft (144.8m) length, 61ft (18.6m) beam.
Triple expansion SR engines, twin screw, 13kts.
Date of disaster: 25 November 1944.

The transpacific liner *Manila Maru* was, like her four sister

The Manila Maru. (Mitsui-OSK Lines)

ships, a Second World War casualty, all but one of the class being the victims of torpedo attacks. The *Manila Maru* was sunk on 25 November 1944 by the American submarine USS *Mingo*. The attack took place about 120 miles west of Brunei, Borneo, in the position 05°30′N–113°21′E, while the *Manila Maru* was serving as a hospital ship.

SANTOS MARU (1925–1944)

Osaka Shosen Kaisha, Japan; Mitsubishi, Nagasaki.
7,267 GRT, 430ft (131.1m) length, 56ft (17.1m) beam.
Diesel engines, twin screw, 15kts.
Date of disaster: 25 November 1944.

The *Santos Maru* operated between Japan and the east coast of South America via South Africa and the Indian Ocean, until the outbreak of war in the Pacific. She was torpedoed and sunk by the United States submarine *Atule* on 25 November 1944, in the position 20°12′N–121°51′E, approximately 50 miles south-west of Basco on the island of Bataan.

HAWAII MARU (1915–1944)

Osaka Shosen Kaisha, Japan; Mitsubishi, Nagasaki.
9,482 GRT, 475ft (144.8m) length, 61ft (18.6m) beam.
Triple expansion SR engines, twin screw, 13kts.
Date of disaster: 2 December 1944.

The steamship *Hawaii Maru* carried passengers on various routes across the Pacific until the intervention of the Second World War, when she was requisitioned for war duties. The American submarine USS *Sea Devil*, under the command of Cdr R.E. Styles, torpedoed and sank the *Hawaii Maru* on 2 December 1944 when she was about 150 miles south-west of Kagoshima, Japan, in the position 30°51′N–128°45′E.

KASHIWARA MARU as *JUNYO* (1942–1944)

Nippon Yusen Kaisha, Japan; Mitsubishi, Nagasaki.
27,700 GRT, 722ft (220.1m) LOA, 88ft (26.8m) beam.
890 passengers in three classes (designed).
Steam turbines, twin screw, 24kts.
Date of disaster: 9 December 1944.

Originally conceived, with her sister ship *Izumo Maru*, as an express transpacific passenger liner for Nippon Yusen Kaisha, the *Kashiwara Maru* was converted, while still building, into the aircraft-carrier *Junyo* and commissioned into the Japanese Navy on 5 May 1942. After being involved in many of the naval actions in the Pacific, the *Junyo* was so severely damaged in a torpedo attack by the American submarines USS *Redfish* and *Sea Devil* on 9 December 1944 that she could take no further part in the war. The attack

Built in 1925 at Nagasaki, the motorship Santos Maru. (A. Duncan)

took place south of Nagasaki, off Cape Nomozaki, and, though the *Junyo* was able to reach Sasebo, it was impossible to repair her extensive damage with the limited facilities and materials available. She was further damaged during American air-raids in 1945. There was no contemplation of restoration or reconversion to a liner at the end of the war, and the *Junyo*'s wreck was instead broken up in 1947.

LEOPOLDVILLE (1929–1944)

Cie. Maritime Belge, Belgium; John Cockerill, Hoboken.
11,509 GRT, 517ft (157.6m) LOA, 62ft (18.9m) beam.
360 passengers in two classes.
Quadruple expansion SR engines, twin screw, 16.5kts.
Date of disaster: 24 December 1944.

The twin-funnelled sister ships *Albertville* and *Leopoldville* entered the Antwerp to Matadi, Belgian Congo (Zaire), service in 1928 and 1929. Both vessels were extensively reconstructed in 1936–1937, resulting in engine modifications, the lengthening of their hulls, and the replacement of their original funnels with a single squat one in each case. After the fall of Belgium in May 1940, the *Leopoldville* came under the control of the British Ministry of War Transport and was used as a troopship. On a voyage

Right *An artist's impression showing the intended appearance of the* Kashiwara Maru*, which was completed instead as the aircraft-carrier* Junyo. (Nippon Yusen Kaisha)

Below *The* Junyo*'s wreck seen disarmed and decommissioned at Sasebo, Japan, after the end of the Pacific war.* (United States National Archives)

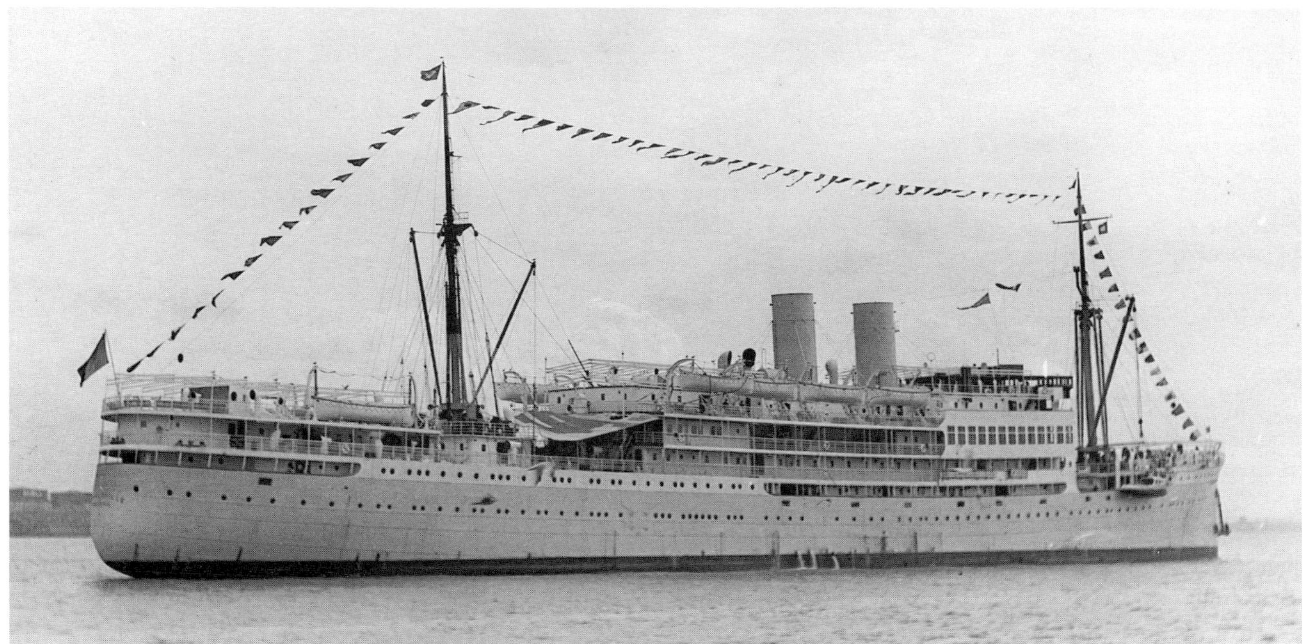

Photographed on 5 August 1924 as originally built, the Leopoldville *was fitted with a raked bow and a single modern funnel between 1936 and 1937.* (Tom Rayner)

from Southampton to Cherbourg with 2,235 American troops on 24 December 1944, the *Leopoldville* was torpedoed by the German submarine *U486* when only five miles from her destination. The torpedo exploded with an incredible force and the troopship's two after decks collapsed, trapping some of the men. In spite of this, the *Leopoldville* remained afloat and evacuation was begun with little sense of urgency. The destroyer HMS *Brilliant* came alongside and removed 1,500 people, troops and crew, who were taken to Cherbourg. The *Leopoldville* was left unattended as it was thought she was in no immediate danger, the intention being for the *Brilliant* to take off the remainder of those aboard on a second trip. However, only an hour after the destroyer had departed the bulkheads suddenly gave way and the *Leopoldville* foundered within 10 minutes. Unfortunately many of the crew abandoned ship through a misunderstanding over orders, leaving the inexperienced soldiers to lower the remaining lifeboats as best they could. Small craft sent out from the French coast arrived on the scene too late to save many of those in the water and 802 troops and six members of the 228-strong crew were drowned. The *Leopoldville*'s captain was among the dead. The wreck lay in the position 49°45′N–01°34′W. Lloyds' records state that the Admiralty at one point considered the loss of the *Leopoldville* to be attributable to a mine.

Chapter Twelve

1945

'HANNIBAL' AND THE ROAD TO JAPAN

The closing months of the Second World War were dominated by two principal campaigns which had a major influence on the continued losses to passenger ships: firstly, the desperate attempt to evacuate Germany's eastern territories in the face of the advancing Red Army; and secondly, the relentless onslaught in the Pacific as the Americans closed in on the Japanese homeland.

The Russians had entered East Prussia the previous October, pushing on towards Poland and the German capital. Recognizing the importance of consolidating all available forces for the final defence of the Fatherland, and that thousands of civilians vital to the regeneration of German post-war prosperity were cut-off in the East, a rescue operation was launched by Admiral Doenitz, code-named Operation Hannibal. This called for the services of all available shipping in the Baltic – some 494 merchant vessels of all sizes plus numerous naval craft. It was the greatest evacuation ever carried out, dwarfing Dunkerque, and rivalling the D-Day landings' 'Neptune' force in size as the largest armada of ships ever assembled for a naval operation.

From the time of its inception in late December 1944, it was beset with the most terrible dangers and difficulties – notably the icy cold of the Baltic winter and the ever-present Soviet submarines, now freed from their once besieged bases and able to attack at will. The worst passenger ship casualties ever occurred during this period, the losses of the *Wilhelm Gustloff, Goya,* and *Steuben,* as already stated in the Introduction, costing between 15,000 and 17,600 lives.

One of the most tragic losses in the closing days of the war in Europe, however, was the sinking by Allied aircraft of the *Cap Arcona* just five days before the cease-fire. Aboard her at the time were thousands of concentration camp inmates, making this terrible disaster the worst instance in history of casualties resulting from 'friendly fire' – although, of course, the flight-crews involved in the attack had no way of knowing the *Cap Arcona*'s cargo.

On the other side of the world the war in the Pacific was drawing to its inevitable conclusion, with losses to passenger ships mounting steadily as part of the overall destruction of Japanese shipping that formed part of this relentless drive to victory.

By comparison with the First World War, at the end of this second global conflict a total of 329 passenger ships had been destroyed, resulting in 50,329 known casualties. Of the total of ships sunk, 185 were owned or operated by Allied countries, the remaining 144 being vessels owned or in the possession of the Axis powers at the time that they were sunk.

Fortunately, since 1945 there have only been a few incidents of conflict which have necessitated the requisitioning of passenger ships for war duties, the principal occasions being the Suez Crisis and the Falklands War; and only one passenger ship has been sunk as a result of military action in the past 50 years, this being the *Raffaello*, destroyed by missiles fired from Iraqi warplanes during the Iran-Iraq War of 1980–1985.

ANYO MARU (1913–1945)

Nippon Yusen Kaisha, Japan; Mitsubishi, Nagasaki.
9,257 GRT, 460ft (140.2m) length, 58ft (17.7m) beam.
Steam turbines, twin screw, 13kts.
Date of disaster: 8 January 1945.

The Japanese company Toyo Kisen Kaisha introduced four new ships to the transpacific route to South America before and after the First World War. These were the *Anyo Maru, Ginyo Maru, Bokuyo Maru,* and *Rakuyo Maru.* All four were absorbed into the Nippon Yusen Kaisha when the two companies merged in 1926. The *Anyo Maru* was torpedoed by the American submarine USS *Barb* on 8 January 1945 and sank near to the Pescadores Islands, in the position 24°54′N–120°26′E.

DONAU (1929–1945)

Norddeutscher Lloyd, Germany; Deschimag AG Weser, Bremen.
9,035 GRT, 521ft (158.8m) length, 64ft (19.5m) beam.
Triple expansion SR engines with LP turbine, triple screw.
Date of disaster: 17 January 1945.

During the Second World War, the *Donau* was employed as an accommodation ship in Norwegian waters and later, as German units were evacuated back to the Fatherland in a bid to halt the Allied advance, as a troopship. On 17 January 1945 she was conveying 1,500 troops back to Germany

Norddeutscher Lloyd's Donau *in peacetime and wartime liveries. She was sunk in Oslofjord by an explosion of uncertain cause.* (Hapag-Lloyd *and* W.Z. Bilddienst)

along with a second ship, the *Rolandseck*. As the *Donau* was passing through Oslofjord, off Drobak, she was rocked by a huge explosion that was at first believed to have been an act of sabotage. Later reports stated that she had struck a mine, but it was ultimately revealed that it was either an internal explosion or the result of a limpet mine attached to her hull. The crippled vessel was beached but broke in two, the stern section sinking in deep water. Although there was loss of life in the incident, most of the troops aboard the *Donau* were rescued. The Germans sent the salvage vessel *Uraed* to assist, but she was captured by Norwegian patriots who escaped aboard her to Sweden. The *Donau*'s forward section was never recovered, but after the war was dismantled where it lay.

WILHELM GUSTLOFF (1938–1945)

Deutsche Arbeitsfront, Germany; Blohm & Voss, Hamburg.
25,484 GRT, 684ft (208.5m) LOA, 77ft (23.5m) beam.
1,465 passengers in single class.
Diesel engines, twin screw, 15.5kts.
Date of disaster: 30 January 1945.

The *Wilhelm Gustloff* was the first purpose-built cruise ship to be completed for the workers' cruises of the *Kraft durch Freude* (Strength Through Joy) association, one of the Nazi Government's more savoury propaganda diversions. She figures prominently in these pages, for to her belongs the dubious distinction of being the victim of the worst maritime disaster of all time. Managed by the Hamburg Sud-Amerika Line, her cruises were not so much for indoctrination purposes, as has been suggested, as for providing recreation for the Nazi party faithful. They were also used as a public relations exercise to the world at large, presenting a more acceptable image of the Third Reich. The outbreak of war brought an end to her short-lived pleasure-cruising era, and the *Wilhelm Gustloff* was commissioned as a hospital ship with the German Navy.

In November 1940 her role changed yet again when she was sent to Gotenhafen (Gdynia) for duties as a static accommodation ship for U-boat personnel. As Germany's fortunes declined, the *Wilhelm Gustloff* was reactivated in January 1945 in support of Operation Hannibal, the evacuation of East Prussia and Upper Silesia. On such a mercy voyage, on 30 January 1945, she was torpedoed and sunk by the Russian submarine *S13*, under the command of Capt Alexander Marinesko, when north of Stolpmünde in Danzig Bay. The ship was hit by a perfect spread of three torpedoes and sank inside 45 minutes. Numerous accompanying vessels came to her aid, including the heavy cruiser *Admiral Hipper*, the Norddeutscher Lloyd steamer *Gottingen*, and the naval escorts *Lowe*, *T36*, *TF19*, *TS2*, *M341*, and *V1703*. In spite of their considerable efforts, however, only 904 survivors, according to official records, were rescued from the icy Baltic waters.

The loss of life was staggering, far greater than on any other ship, but it is impossible to determine its precise extent. The circumstances under which the evacuation was conducted were extremely difficult, refugees clamouring to get aboard west-bound ships, in a state of near panic fed by the belief that the advancing Russians would exact a terrible retribution for German war atrocities. Those passenger manifests that were prepared were unreliable and most ships carried far in excess of their allocation. German records state that the *Wilhelm Gustloff* was carrying 6,100 people, mainly refugees and wounded. Lloyds' figures state that she had aboard some 5,000 refugees plus 3,700 U-boat personnel, besides her mixed naval/mercantile crew. It is clear, therefore, that at least 5,196 people lost their lives, but at worst the casualty figure could be in excess of 7,800. Over the years since the end of the war, Heinz Schoen, the

The Wilhelm Gustloff *in her role as a workers' cruise-ship. Though not a particularly distinguished vessel, her sinking by torpedo in January 1945, resulting in a record loss of life, has assured her a place in the annals of the sea.* (Author's collection)

ship's Purser and a survivor of the sinking, has amassed into a special archive a vast amount of information relating to the disaster. According to him, the *Wilhelm Gustloff* was carrying 6,600 people in total of whom 5,348 fell victim to the torpedo attack.

Contrary to popular belief the *Wilhelm Gustloff* was not raised and scrapped at Swinoujscie in September 1955, although Polish sources may be responsible for this false impression. In fact the wreck still lies on the sea bed, and the following verbatim quotation from a Polish diving team's report, dated 12 September 1979, describes the scene: 'The wreck is lying on flat and hard bottom in depth 44 metres. The top mast is [?] about 21 metres under water. The hull is broken in two places – ca. 50 metres from bow and ca. 40 metres from stern. All the wreck is lying on the port-side; however, every part of the ship has different angle of inclination – bow about 40°, waist (mid-section) about 60° and the stern about 30°. The waist (mid-section) is the most buried and this part of the wreck seems the most destroyed. Position of the wreck; 55°07′N–17°42′E.' The Bundesarchivs in Germany has the position of the *Wilhelm Gustloff* at the time of the disaster recorded as 55°28′N–17°31′E.

STEUBEN ex-*GENERAL VON STEUBEN* ex-*MUNCHEN* (1922–1945)

Norddeutscher Lloyd, Germany; Vulkan Werke, Stettin.
14,690 GRT, 551ft (167.9m) LOA, 65ft (19.8m) beam.
484 passengers in single class.
Triple expansion SR engines with LP turbine, twin screw, 17kts.

The Steuben *seen earlier in her career when she was the* Munchen, *berthed at New York in April 1930 after she had been refloated following a disastrous fire two months previously.* (Mariners Museum)

Date of disaster: 9 February 1945.

Following full restoration after a major fire aboard her in New York in February 1930, the *Munchen* spent much of the 1930s as the white-hulled cruise-liner *General Von Steuben*. In 1938 her new name was shortened to *Steuben*, and a year later she was taken over as a German Navy accommodation ship based at Kiel. The four years of idleness which ensued were ended when, in the summer of 1944, she put to sea in the role of a Baltic transport. She conveyed troops on her eastbound trips, and brought back wounded on the return voyages to Kiel. By early-1945 the situation in East Prussia had deteriorated to a point where the German Army was in full retreat on a broad front. Units of the German passenger fleet which had been dispersed to ports all along the Baltic were therefore mustered to evacuate civilians and military personnel alike from the war zone, and the *Steuben* found herself participating in this desperate operation. Her last voyage commenced on 9 February 1945 when she left Pillau (Baltiysk) bound for Kiel with 2,500 wounded and 2,000 refugees along with her crew of 450. Shortly before midnight the following day the Russian submarine *S13* attacked the heavily-laden ship off Stolpmünde (Ustka), sinking her with two torpedoes in the position 54°41′N–16°51′E. Despite the efforts of escorting naval vessels some 3,000 people were drowned. The *S13* had sunk the *Wilhelm Gustloff* in the same vicinity 11 days earlier with even greater loss of life.

HAKOZAKI MARU (1922–1945)

Nippon Yusen Kaisha, Japan; Mitsubishi, Nagasaki.
10,413 GRT, 520ft (158.5m) LOA, 62ft (18.9m) beam.
175 passengers in single class.
Steam turbines, twin screw, 16kts.
Date of disaster: 19 March 1945.

The *Hakozaki Maru* entered the Yokohama to Hamburg service in June 1922, maintaining the service with three sister ships. All four vessels were lost during the Second World War. The *Hakozaki Maru* became a naval troop transport in 1940 and was sunk in the East China Sea on 19 March 1945, in the position 33°09′N–122°08′E, the American submarine USS *Balao*, under Capt R.K.R. Worthington, being responsible.

USAMBARA (1922–1945)

Deutsche Ost-Afrika Line, Germany; Blohm & Voss, Hamburg.
8,690 GRT, 433ft (132.0m) length, 58ft (17.7m) beam.
250 passengers.
Steam turbine, single screw, 14kts.
Date of disaster: 20 March 1945.

The *Usambara* was employed in the round-Africa service from Germany with a sister ship, the *Njassa*. They could each accommodate 250 passengers. The *Usambara* was bombed and destroyed in an Allied air attack on Stettin (Szczecin) on 20 March 1945. At the time she was being

The General von Steuben *ex*-Munchen, *seen during a pre-war visit to Venice. Later renamed* Steuben, *she was a victim of the Russian submarine* S13 *during Germany's evacuation of her Eastern territories.* (Hapag-Lloyd)

used as a barracks ship, having been repaired sufficiently to serve this purpose following damage sustained in an earlier air-raid on 11 April 1944.

ROBERT LEY (1939–1945)

Deutsche Arbeitsfront, Germany; Howaldtswerke, Hamburg.
27,288 GRT, 669ft (203.9m) LOA, 79ft (24.1m) beam.
1,774 passengers in single class.
Diesel-electric propulsion, twin screw, 15kts.
Date of disaster: 24 March 1945.

Although some 20 purpose-built cruise-ships were planned for the *Kraft durch Freude* (Strength Through Joy) movement, in the event only two were constructed, the second of these commemorating the director of the Deutsche Arbeitsfront organization, Dr Robert Ley. The liner *Robert Ley* entered service in April 1939, managed by the Hamburg Amerika Line, but had completed only a few cruises when the outbreak of war diverted her to other activities. She then served as a hospital ship and, later, an accommodation ship in the Baltic, stationed at Gotenhafen (Gdynia) and Pillau (Baltiysk). During the evacuation of the eastern territories in early 1945, one of the *Robert Ley*'s westbound voyages took her as far as Hamburg, where she arrived on 24 March 1945. That night, prior to the disembarkation of the vessel, Hamburg was raided by Allied bombers, in the course of which the *Robert Ley* was hit and set on fire. She was completely burnt out and an

The Robert Ley *was employed as a hospital ship in the early part of the Second World War.* (W.Z. Bilddienst)

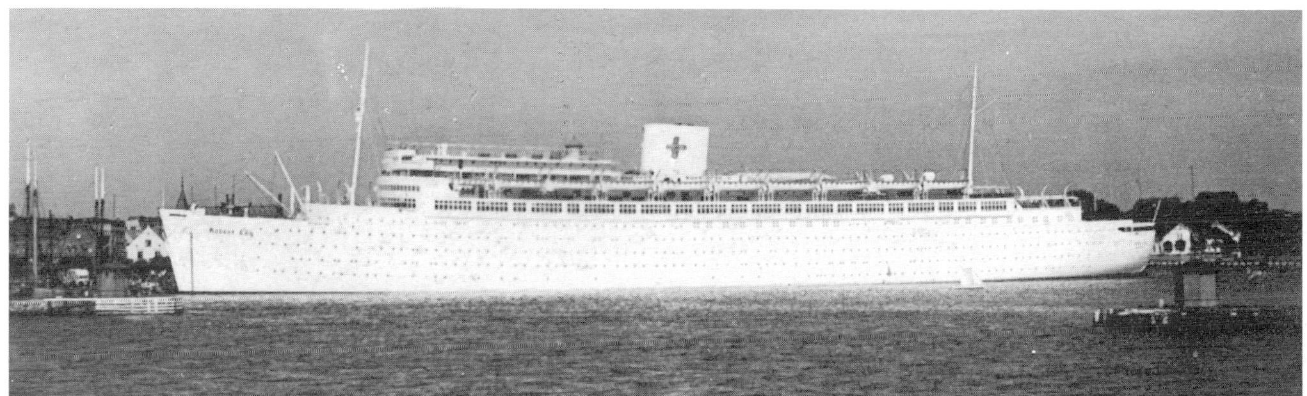

undisclosed, but large, number of refugees lost their lives. In 1947 the wrecked liner was towed to the United Kingdom for breaking up, arriving at the Thomas W. Ward yard at Inverkeithing on 6 June.

AWA MARU (1943–1945)

Nippon Yusen Kaisha, Japan; Mitsubishi, Nagasaki.
11,249 GRT, 535ft (163.1m) LOA, 66ft (20.1m) beam.
137 passengers in single class (designed).
Diesel engines, twin screw, 20kts.
Date of disaster: 1 April 1945.

The *Awa Maru* was intended for Nippon Yusen Kaisha's Japan to Australia service but, due to the outbreak of war in the Pacific, she was completed as a transport instead. In February 1945 Japan sought and obtained diplomatic status for the *Awa Maru* and she was subsequently disarmed and accordingly repainted with a green hull and white crosses. In this guise, she commenced a long voyage from Moji to Kaohsiung, Hong Kong, Saigon, Singapore, and Djakarta with the return to Tsuruga. Outward bound, she transported a vast quantity of Red Cross parcels for prisoners-of-war but it was intended that on the return leg she would use her safe flag of immunity to provide protection for her to convey valuable cargoes back to the Japanese homeland.

ABOVE LEFT *The* Robert Ley *after she had been raised, lying alongside a quay at Hamburg in July 1945.* (Imperial War Museum, Neg. A29692)

LEFT *The scene at the Thomas W. Ward breaker's yard at Inverkeithing on 26 March 1948. All that remains of the* Robert Ley, *right, is her lower hull and double bottom. Alongside her in the outer mooring is the battleship HMS* Rodney, *also in the process of demolition.* (Thomas W. Ward)

BELOW *The loss of the* Awa Maru *ranks as Japan's worst passenger shipping disaster of the Second World War, the more so because her passengers were mainly civilians.* (Nippon Yusen Kaisha)

While engaged in Operation Hannibal, the Monte Olivia *was bombed and sunk at Kiel.* (Hamburg Sud-Amerika Line)

She also attracted over 2,000 passengers, Japanese nationals eager to get home who felt more secure aboard a ship flying the flag of the International Red Cross. However, when she was sighted in overcast weather on 1 April 1945 by the United States submarine *Queenfish*, she was mistaken for a warship. The *Queenfish* attacked, firing four torpedoes, all of which struck. Only a few minutes later the *Awa Maru* was gone, just one survivor being rescued, making her sinking the worst Japanese maritime disaster ever. Among those killed was a new-born baby that had been delivered while the ship was at sea. The tragic sinking occurred in the position 25°26′N–120°08′E, as the *Awa Maru* was passing through the Straits of Formosa. Various attempts to locate the wrecked ship have been made, all unsuccessful, and the Japanese Government has exclusively reserved ownership of it for themselves. It has been claimed that this is an indication of the extreme value or embarrassing nature of the cargo in her holds. Earlier, on 19 August 1944, the *Awa Maru* had survived a torpedo attack off the Philippine Islands by the American submarine USS *Rasher*.

MONTE OLIVIA (1925–1945)

Hamburg Sud-Amerika Line, Germany; Blohm & Voss, Hamburg.
13,750 GRT, 524ft (159.7m) LOA, 65ft (19.8m) beam.
2,528 passengers in two classes.
Diesel engines, twin screw, 14.5kts.
Date of disaster: 3 April 1945.

The five-ship *Monte* class of the Hamburg Sud-Amerika Line, introduced to the River Plate service between 1924 and 1931, experienced varying fortunes. One was wrecked in 1930, three were bombed and sunk during the Second World War, and the last was seized by the British as a war prize only to fall victim to fire in 1954. The *Monte Olivia* was one of those lost in aerial attacks, being destroyed by bombing at Kiel on 3 April 1945. Prior to this she had served as an accommodation ship and a hospital ship. It was her involvement in the transportation of evacuees and wounded from Prussia in early 1945 that had brought her to Kiel. The scrapping of the *Monte Olivia*'s wreck commenced in June 1946.

NEW YORK (1927–1945)

Hamburg Amerika Line, Germany; Blohm & Voss, Hamburg.
23,337 GRT, 677ft (206.3m) LOA, 72ft (21.9m) beam.
960 passengers in three classes.
Steam turbines, twin screw, 16kts.
Date of disaster: 3 April 1945.

After returning from New York to Hamburg via Murmansk in late-1939, the liner *New York* became an accommodation ship at Kiel. She remained laid up there, employed in this capacity, for virtually the duration of the war. Reactivation came in January 1945 when the *New York* joined Operation Hannibal to evacuate refugees and military personnel from Germany's eastern territories. While involved in this work she was hit by bombs during an air-raid on Kiel on 3 April 1945, and she capsized onto her port side on fire. The wreck was refloated on 21 March 1949 and towed to Dalmuir on the Clyde, where it arrived on 2 August 1949 for breaking up.

Hamburg Amerika Line's New York *was also destroyed at Kiel by Allied warplanes.* (Blohm & Voss AG)

CUBA (1923–1945)

French Line (CGT), France; Swan, Hunter & Wigham Richardson, Newcastle.
11,420 GRT, 495ft (150.9m) LOA, 62ft (18.9m) beam.
1,086 passengers in four classes.
Steam turbines, twin screw, 16kts.
Date of disaster: 6 April 1945.

For many years the *Cuba* operated on the French Line service from St Nazaire to the West Indies and Vera Cruz, Mexico, in consort with the *Mexique*. The *Cuba* was another passenger ship that remained with the Vichy authorities from June 1940, but only until 31 October of that year. She was then arrested and seized by a British warship while on a voyage from Martinique to Casablanca. The Ministry of War Transport placed the *Cuba* under Cunard Line management as a troopship. On a crossing from Le Havre to Southampton on 6 April 1945, she was torpedoed and sunk by the *U1195*. The attack took place about 50 miles south of St Catherine's Point, in the position 50°36′N–00°57′W. Of the *Cuba*'s complement of 252 crewmen and 13 military passengers, one individual was killed. The *U1195* was herself sunk by the destroyer HMS *Watchman*. The wreck of the *Cuba* was later dispersed to a depth of 48ft.

GENERAL OSORIO (1929–1945)

Hamburg Sud-Amerika Line, Germany; Bremer Vulkan, Vegesack.
11,590 GRT, 528ft (160.9m) LOA, 65ft (19.8m) beam.
980 passengers in two classes.
Diesel engines, twin screw, 15kts.
Date of disaster: 9 April 1945.

The French turbine steamship Cuba *was one of the last Allied passenger ship losses of the Second World War.* (World Ship Society)

Formerly a Hamburg Amerika ship, the Hamburg Sud-Amerika Line continued to use the General Osorio *on the La Plata service after they acquired her in 1936.* (World Ship Society)

The twin-funnelled motorship *General Osorio* was built for Hamburg Amerika Line's service to South America. Five years after entering service she was chartered to Hamburg Sud-Amerika Line, to whom she was later sold outright. In common with most other German passenger vessels, the *General Osorio* became a naval accommodation ship in April 1940. She was stationed at Kiel, where bomb hits she received during two air-raids on the port left her fit only for scrap. The first occurred on 24 July 1944, when a bomb-strike set her on fire and partially gutted her. She was beached with her aft end high and dry. Raised that October and given temporary repairs, the *General Osorio* received more extensive damage in a British air-raid on 9 April 1945, resulting in her being completely burnt out and sunk. The wreck was refloated in 1947 and in August of the same year it was towed to Great Britain for demolition.

NIKKO MARU (1903–1945)

Nippon Yusen Kaisha, Japan; Mitsubishi, Nagasaki.
5,559 GRT, 428ft (130.5m) length, 49ft (14.9m) beam.
219 passengers in three classes.
Triple expansion SR engine, single screw, 16kts.
Date of disaster: 9 April 1945.

The Japanese liner *Nikko Maru*, which spent almost 40 years in the Japan to Australia trade, was sunk on 9 April 1945 by the American submarine USS *Tirante* while she was serving as a troop transport. The attack took place in the Yellow Sea, in the position 36°50′N–123°55′E.

GOYA (1942–1945)

J. Ludwig Mowinckels Rederei, Norway; Akers Mekanika Verksted.
5,230 GRT, 430ft (131.1m) length, 57ft (17.4m) beam.
Diesel engines.
Date of disaster: 16 April 1945.

Strictly speaking, as a cargo-carrying shelter-decker the motorship *Goya* falls outside the limits imposed on the contents of this book, but she is included because of the exceptional loss of life suffered when she was sunk. Indeed, the *Goya*'s loss ranks only second to the *Wilhelm Gustloff* as the worst maritime tragedy of all time.

The sister ships *Goya* and *Molda* were ordered by a Norwegian company, A/S J. Ludwig Mowinckels Rederei, from the A/S Akers Mekanika Verksted shipyard. The *Goya* was launched in 1940, but after the conquest of Norway she passed into German ownership and on completion was taken over by the German Navy, managed on their behalf by the Hamburg Amerika Line as a troop transport. Like all other available ships in the area she was drafted into Operation Hannibal to evacuate German nationals from East Prussia and occupied Poland near the end of the Second World War. She joined a convoy bound for Copenhagen from Hela, in the Gulf of Danzig (Gdansk), on 16 April 1945, under the command of Capt Plunneke. Just before midnight, only a few hours after sailing, the *Goya* was torpedoed when she was about 50 miles north of Rixhoft (Rozewie) on the Stolpe Bank. Her attacker was the Russian submarine *L3*, whose commander, Capt Vladimir Konovalov, was later promoted to Rear Admiral. The two torpedoes struck the *Goya* amidships and astern on her starboard side, with such devastation that the ship broke in half and sank within four minutes. Typical of the hurried and ill-organized manner in which these mercy voyages were arranged, there had been no opportunity to prepare a proper manifest of the vast human complement the *Goya* was carrying – at the time, getting people aboard and away took a much higher priority. Survivors have estimated, however, that the *Goya*

The startlingly camouflaged Goya. *She gained the dubious distinction of being lost in the second worst maritime disaster of all time.* (A. Kludas)

had at least 7,000 people on her. Of these, a mere 183 were rescued.

ROMA as *AQUILA* (1926–1945)

Italia Line, Italy; Ansaldo, Sestri Ponente.
32,583 GRT, 759ft (231.3m) LOA, 82ft (25.0m) beam.
1,675 passengers in three classes.
Steam turbines, quadruple screw, 21kts.
Date of disaster: 19 April 1945.

Prior to 1939 the passenger liner *Roma* served on the Genoa to New York run with her near-sister *Augustus*, first for Navigazione Generale Italiana and then, from 1932, for Italia Line. In October 1940 she was taken over by the Italian Navy for conversion into an aircraft-carrier. The conversion was of the fullest order, involving the replacement of her original turbines with a set first intended for a cruiser, the fitting of a new bow and anti-torpedo bulges, and the construction of an off-set island superstructure. On completion as the *Aquila*, she did not bear the slightest resemblance to the liner from which she had originated. In that respect the *Aquila* makes an interesting comparison to the Japanese carriers *Hiyo* and *Junyo*, the former *Izumo Maru* and *Kashiwara Maru* respectively. Due to the extent of the reconstruction, progress on the *Aquila* was slow so that by the time Italy capitulated on 8 September 1943 she was only just nearing completion. She was then seized by the Germans but no further work was carried out on her: although virtually ready for sea trials, the *Aquila* was of no practical value for her crew had methodically sabotaged vital on-board installations, besides which she had not received her complement of aircraft. She was bombed and damaged during air-raids on Genoa on 20 June 1944 and 6 January 1945. On 19 April 1945 she was attacked by Italian one-man torpedoes and sunk at her moorings, thus preventing the Germans from using her to block the harbour entrance at Genoa. The wreck was refloated in 1946 and towed to La Spezia in 1949 when consideration was given to completing her as a carrier or converting her to some other role. When both options were abandoned she was broken up in 1951.

The Italia Line passenger ship Roma *seen prior to the drastic reconstruction which transformed her into the aircraft-carrier* Aquila. (Author's collection)

The Aquila, *seen at Genoa following salvage but before the decision had been made that she should be demolished.* (Ufficio Storico)

NEURALIA (1912–1945)

British India Line, Great Britain; Barclay Curle, Glasgow.
9,082 GRT, 480ft (146.3m) length, 58ft (17.7m) beam.
Quadruple expansion SR engines, twin screw, 14.5kts.
Date of disaster: 2 May 1945.

The *Neuralia* was employed with her sister ship *Nevasa* on the India and East Africa services, in addition to which she was also engaged as a Ministry of Transport peacetime troopship. On the outbreak of the Second World War, the *Neuralia* was taken over for full-time trooping. On 2 May 1945 she struck a mine off the coast of Southern Italy, in the position 40°11'N–17°44'E, while bound from Split, Yugoslavia, to Taranto. Out of her complement of 265 crew and 12 passengers, four people lost their lives.

CAP ARCONA (1927–1945)

Hamburg Sud-Amerika Line, Germany; Blohm & Voss, Hamburg.
27,561 GRT, 675ft (205.7m) LOA, 84ft (25.6m) beam.
1,315 passengers in three classes.
Steam turbines, twin screw, 20kts.
Date of disaster: 3 May 1945.

The *Cap Arcona* was the biggest German liner ever to be placed on the run to ports on the River Plate, South

View of the Uberseebrucke, Hamburg Harbour, in 1938, showing in the foreground the Cap Arcona, *with in the middle the* Monte Rosa, *and far left the* Monte Olivia. (Hamburg Sud-Amerika Line)

America, at a time when there was considerable competition on the route and other companies were introducing increasingly larger vessels. The same period witnessed the emergence of the *Augustus* and *L'Atlantique*. From November 1940 the *Cap Arcona* was employed as a German Navy accommodation ship stationed at Gotenhafen (Gdynia). As with so many other German liners locked in the Baltic for the duration of the war, the *Cap Arcona* was reactivated in early 1945 to assist in the evacuation of the eastern territories, and in three voyages she transported 26,000 people. A less auspicious task in April 1945 was to provide accommodation for the concentration camp internees from Neuengamme. About 5,000 prisoners were embarked including the majority of the inhabitants of the Dutch village of Putten, who had been incarcerated in the Autumn of 1944 as a reprisal for the murder of some high-ranking German officers. The *Cap Arcona* remained anchored off Neustadt, in the Bay of Lübeck, crowded with in excess of 6,000 prisoners, guards, and crewmen. On 3 May 1945 she became the target of RAF fighters, which hit her repeatedly with rockets and machine-guns, setting her on fire. All means of escape were destroyed and panic broke out among those trapped inside. Shortly afterwards she capsized, claiming the lives of 5,000 people. It is bitterly ironical that these wretched souls who had suffered so much at the hands of their captors should have met their end at the hands of those who would have liberated them just five days later. The *Cap Arcona* drifted ashore in the position 54°04′N–10°50′E, where she became a total wreck. She was broken up from 1949.

DEUTSCHLAND (1923–1945)

Hamburg Amerika Line, Germany; Blohm & Voss, Hamburg.
21,046 GRT, 677ft (206.3m) LOA, 72ft (21.9m) beam.
1,515 passengers in three classes.
Steam turbines, twin screw, 16kts.
Date of disaster: 3 May 1945.

The four liners of the *Albert Ballin* class, introduced to the transatlantic service from 1923, fared badly during the Second World War. The *Hamburg* and *Hansa* ex-*Albert Ballin* struck mines, although they were salvaged and rebuilt after the war, while the *New York* and *Deutschland* were sunk in aerial attacks. The *Deutschland* had completed five years as a naval accommodation ship at Gotenhafen (Gdynia), followed by seven voyages ferrying 70,000 refugees from the German eastern territories, when she was bombed by British aircraft at Neustadt on 3 May 1945. Like the nearby *Cap Arcona*, the *Deutschland* had a large number of concentration camp inmates and political

The Deutschland *was sunk off Neustadt while being used as a floating prison for political internees.* (Hapag-Lloyd)

prisoners aboard. She caught fire and capsized, sinking in a munitions dumping area in the position 54°03′N–10°48′E. The extent of any casualties is not known. The wreck was raised and scrapped in 1948.

CAP VARELLA ex-*KERSAINT* as *TEIKA MARU* (1921–1945)

Chargéurs Reunis, France; Ateliers et Chantiers de la Loire, Nantes.
8,169 GRT, 417ft (127.1m) length, 55ft (16.8m) beam.
850 passengers.
Steam turbine, single screw, 12kts.
Date of disaster: 7 May 1945.

The Chargéurs Reunis passenger liner *Cap Varella* was one of a class of five ships engaged in the Far East trade from France on the route via the Suez Canal. She was captured by the Japanese at Yokohama on 10 April 1942 and returned to service on their behalf under the name *Teika Maru*. On 7 May 1945 she sank at Genkai Nada, between Karatsu and Shimonoseki, off north western Kyushu, after striking a mine laid by the American submarine USS *Finback*.

CONTE VERDE as *KOTOBUKI MARU* (1923–1945)

Lloyd Triestino, Italy; William Beardmore, Glasgow.
18,765 GRT, 593ft (180.7m) LOA, 74ft (22.6m) beam.
640 passengers in three classes.
Steam turbines, twin screw, 18.5kts.
Date of disaster: 8 May 1945.

After being refloated and repaired following a stranding incident in Hong Kong in September 1937, the *Conte Verde* resumed her Trieste to Shanghai passenger service until 1940, when she was laid up in the Chinese port. In 1942, under charter to the Japanese Government, she made a number of voyages conveying exchanged prisoners-of-war between China and Japan, but after these she was again laid up. On 11 September 1943, following the Italian armistice, the *Conte Verde* was scuttled by her crew at Whangpoo to deny the Japanese possession of her. The ship was salvaged, however, and following temporary repairs at Shanghai she was taken to Maizuru, Japan, for rebuilding as the troop transport *Kotobuki Maru*. While she was being rebuilt at Maizuru in 1944 she was damaged during an American air-raid. The following year, on 8 May 1945, she was sunk in the position 34°30′N–126°30′E, in Nakata Bay, following

The Conte Verde, *seen in Lloyd Sabaudo colours between the wars. Like the* Asama Maru, *she was severely damaged in 1937 by a typhoon which struck Hong Kong.* (Author's collection)

The hulk of the Kotobuki Maru *lies in Japanese waters in 1949 awaiting a decision on her future. Although not distinct in this picture, her original name,* Conte Verde, *can still be seen on her hull.* (World Ship Society)

another raid. The cause of her loss on this occasion was not definitely established and there was suspicion that the true cause may have been an aircraft-laid mine. Lloyds had her reported as an oil-tanker. She was refloated in 1949 and taken to the Maizuru shipyard. In 1950 she was formally returned to the Italian Government, but she remained laid up as she was considered to be beyond economic reconstruction. She was finally sold to Mitsui in 1951 and breaking up commenced that August.

TRANSBALT ex-*RIGA* ex-*BELGRAVIA* (1899–1945)

Sovtorgflot, USSR; Blohm & Voss, Hamburg.
11,439 GRT, 516ft (157.3m) LOA, 62ft (18.9m) beam.
2,700 passengers in two classes (as a German ship).
Quadruple expansion SR engines, twin screw, 13kts.
Date of disaster: 13 June 1945.

The *Belgravia* was one of the five vessels of Hamburg Amerika Line's 'B' class of steamers. In May 1905 she was sold to the Russian Navy and renamed *Riga*, only to return to commercial passenger-carrying duties the following year. After the First World War she spent three years as a hospital ship before resuming passenger and cargo sailings for the state-owned Sovtorgflot shipping line. Her name was changed to *Transbalt* in 1919. She was the victim of mistaken identity when, on 13 June 1945, the American submarine USS *Spadefish* torpedoed her, believing her to be a Japanese ship. The *Transbalt* was returning to Vladivostok from Port Townsend and Seattle when the attack occurred at the western end of the La Perouse Channel. She sank in the position 45°42′N–140°41′E, but all 99 members of her crew were picked up by Japanese ships.

TALTHYBIUS as *TARUYASU MARU* (1912–1945)

Blue Funnel Line, Great Britain; Scott's, Greenock.
10,224 GRT, 518ft (157.9m) LOA, 60ft (18.3m) beam.
600 passengers in single class.
Triple expansion SR engines, twin screw, 13.5kts.
Date of disaster: 30 June 1945.

The Blue Funnel liner *Talthybius*, built for the Far East run from Liverpool, was captured by the Japanese at Singapore in February 1942, in a damaged and waterlogged condition. Raised and repaired, she was placed in service as the *Taruyasu Maru*. She struck a mine off Toyama on 30 June 1945 and sank in the position 37°07′N–137°04′E. After the war, the British salvaged her and sent her to Hong Kong for repairs, where she arrived on 23 November 1948. Patched up and renamed *Empire Evenlode* for the voyage home, she was sent to the scrapyard at Briton Ferry, Glamorgan, on her arrival in September 1949. Although she made this final voyage in a seaworthy condition of sorts, the former *Talthybius* has been included here because, for all practical purposes, her commercial career had been ended by the war and on arrival in the United Kingdom she was fit only for scrapping.

ARGENTINA MARU as *KAIYO* (1939–1945)

Osaka Shosen Kaisha, Japan; Mitsubishi, Nagasaki.
12,755 GRT, 544ft (165.8m) LOA, 68ft (20.7m) beam.
901 passengers in three classes.
Diesel engines, twin screw, 21.5kts.
Date of disaster: 24 July 1945.

The Japanese aircraft-carrier *Kaiyo* was formerly the

The Soviet passenger ship Transbalt *in wartime livery. In the closing days of the war she was sunk by an American submarine, which had reportedly mistaken her for a Japanese vessel.* (World Ship Society)

The Osaka Shosen Kaisha passenger liner Argentina Maru. (A. Duncan)

Osaka Shosen Kaisha diesel passenger ship *Argentina Maru.* Prior to the Second World War she spent three years in the Japan to South America service. After this, she spent a year as a troop transport before she was converted into a carrier, commissioning on 23 November 1943. The *Kaiyo* was sunk by United States naval aircraft on 24 July 1945 in Beppu Bay, 10 miles north-west of Oita, Kyushu. The wreck, lying in the position 33°21′N–131°32′E, was broken up on the spot after the war.

CHRISTIAAN HUYGENS (1928–1945)

Nederland Line, Netherlands; Nederlandsche Dok en Scheepsbouw, Amsterdam.
16,287 GRT, 570ft (173.7m) LOA, 68ft (20.7m) beam.
572 passengers in three classes.
Diesel engines, twin screw, 18kts.
Date of disaster: 26 August 1945.

The *Christiaan Huygens*, which was constructed for the Amsterdam to Batavia (Djakarta) service, survived the

The small Japanese aircraft-carrier Kaiyo *ex*-Argentina Maru. (Imperial War Museum, Neg. MH 5932)

Above *The* Christiaan Huygens *was actually sunk after hostilities had ended, but, being the victim of a mine, is still categorized as a war loss. Hers was, therefore, the very last wartime disaster at sea.* (World Ship Society)

Left *The wreck of the* Christiaan Huygens *on the Zuid Steenbank.* (L.L. von Münching)

Second World War, in which she served as a troopship under Orient Line management, only to become a mine casualty shortly after the cessation of hostilities. She is officially recorded by Lloyds as a war loss and for this reason has been included here. In effect she was the very last passenger ship to be sunk in consequence of military action until the former Italia Line ship *Raffaello*, whose loss in November 1982, unlike that of the *Christiaan Huygens*, had no connection with either of the World Wars.

The *Christiaan Huygens* was heading from Antwerp to Rotterdam on 26 August 1945 when she struck an uncleared mine near Westkapelle in the estuary of the River Scheldt, the explosion killing one crewman. The badly-damaged ship was beached on the Zuid Steenbank, in the position 51°37′N–03°16′E. On 5 September 1945 she broke in two and became a total loss.

Appendix 1

SUMMARY OF WARTIME DISASTERS

Cause of Loss	**1914**	**1915**	**1916**	**1917**	**1918**	**WW1 Total**	**1939**	**1949**	**1941**	**1942**	**1943**	**1944**	**1945**	**WW2 Total**	**TOTAL**
Submarine	–	14	21	56	44	135	5	22	22	44–45	32	31	9	165–166	300–301
Mine	–	1	5	12	–	18	4	8	–	2–3	3	1	4	22–23	40–41
Raider	4	3	3	1	–	11	2	5	1	6	–	–	–	14	25
Aircraft	–	–	–	–	–	0	–	15	12	16	22	14	9	88	88
Scuttling/ sabotage	–	–	–	–	–	0	3	7	4	1	1	12	–	28	28
Collision	–	–	–	1	1	2	–	–	–	–	–	–	–	0	2
Fire	–	–	–	–		0	–	–	1	1	–	–	–	2	2
Stranding	2	–	–	1	–	3	–	–	–	2	–	1	–	3	6
Foundering	–	1	–	–		1	–	–	–	–		–	–	0	1
Other	–	–	–	–	–	0	–	–	–	2	2	–	2	6	6
TOTAL	6	19	29	71	45	170	14	57	40	75	60	59	24	329	499

Appendix 2A

WORST 25 DISASTERS BY CASUALTIES

	Name	Nationality	Date	Casualties
1.	*Wilhelm Gustloff*	German	30 January 1945	*c.*7,800
2.	*Goya*	German	16 April 1945	*c.*6,800
3.	*Cap Arcona*	German	3 May 1945	*c.*5,000
4.	*Lancastria*	British	17 June 1940	*c.*3,050
5.	*Steuben*	German	9 February 1945	*c.*3,000
6.	*Laconia*	British	12 September 1942	2,279
7.	*Awa Maru*	Japanese	1 April 1945	*c.*2,000
8.	*Bahia Laura/Donau*	German	30 August 1941	*c.*1,700
9.	*Gallia*	French	4 October 1916	1,350
10.	*Rakuyo Maru*	Japanese	12 September 1944	*c.*1,350
11.	*Lusitania*	British	7 May 1915	1,198
12.	*Rohna*	British	26 November 1943	1,149
13.	*Royal Edward*	British	13 August 1915	935
14.	*La Provence* (as *Provence II*)	French	26 February 1916	930
15.	*Amiral Magon*	French	25 January 1917	*c.*900
16.	*Nova Scotia*	British	28 November 1942	863
17.	*Slamat*	Dutch	27 April 1941	843
18.	*Leopoldville*	Belgian	24 December 1944	808
19.	*Arandora Star*	British	2 July 1940	805
20.	*Conte Rosso*	Italian	24 May 1941	*c.*800
21.	*Francesco Crispi*	Italian	19 April 1943	*c.*800
22.	*Taiyo Maru*	Japanese	8 May 1942	780
23.	*Ceramic*	British	6 December 1942	655
24.	*Mendi*	British	21 February 1917	636
25.	*Aragon*	British	30 December 1917	610

Appendix 2B

WORST 25 DISASTERS BY SIZE OF VESSEL

	Name	Nationality	Date	Size (GRT)
1.	*Normandie* (as *Lafayette*)	French	9 February 1942	83,423
2.	*Bremen*	German	16 March 1941	51,656
3.	*Rex*	Italian	8 September 1944	51,062
4.	*Conte di Savoia*	Italian	11 September 1943	48,502
5.	*Britannic*	British	21 November 1916	48,158
6.	*Empress of Britain*	British	26 October 1940	42,348
7.	*Vaterland*	German	25 July 1943	41,000
8.	*Augustus* (as *Sparviero*)	Italian	25 September 1944	32,650
9.	*Roma* (as *Aquila*)	Italian	19 April 1945	32,583
10.	*Columbus*	German	19 December 1939	32,354
11.	*Statendam*	Dutch	20 July 1918	32,234
12.	*Lusitania*	British	7 May 1915	31,550
13.	*Statendam*	Dutch	11 May 1940	29,511
14.	*Stockholm* (as *Sabaudia*)	Swedish	6 July 1944	29,307
15.	*Champlain*	French	17 June 1940	28,124
16.	*Kashiwara Maru* (as *Junyo*)	Japanese	9 December 1944	27,700
17.	*Cap Arcona*	German	3 May 1945	27,561
18.	*Izumo Maru* (as *Hiyo*)	Japanese	20 June 1944	27,500
19.	*Robert Ley*	German	24 March 1945	27,288
20.	*Wilhelm Gustloff*	German	30 January 1945	25,484
21.	*Duilio*	Italian	10 July 1944	24,281
22.	*Strathallan*	British	21 December 1942	23,722
23.	*Orcades*	British	10 October 1942	23,456
24.	*New York*	German	3 April 1945	22,337
25.	*President Coolidge*	American	26 October 1942	21,936

Appendix 3

COMPARISON OF TOTAL LOSSES

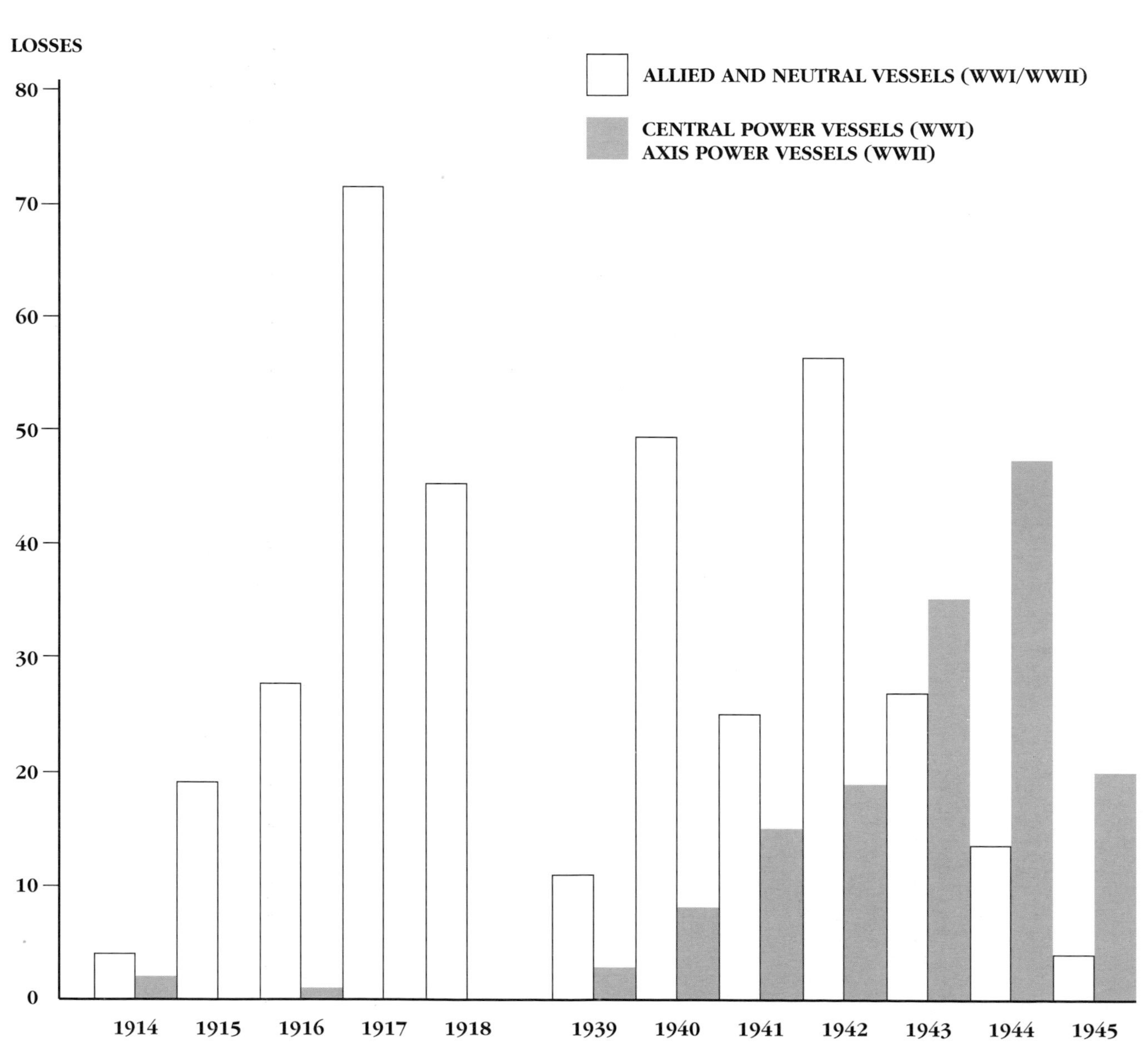

BIBLIOGRAPHY

Braynard, Frank O. *Lives of the Liners* (Cornell Maritime Press, 1947).

Hocking, Charles. *Dictionary of Disasters at Sea During the Age of Steam* (Lloyds Register of Shipping, 1969).

Kludas, Arnold. *Great Passenger Ships of the World* volumes 1–4 (Patrick Stephens, 1975–1977).

Lloyds War Losses, The First World War (Lloyds of London Press, 1990).

Lloyds War Losses, The Second World War (Lloyds of London Press, 1989).

Seabrook, William C. *In the War at Sea* (1946).

Smith, Eugene W. *Passenger Ships of the World, Past and Present* (George H. Dean, 1963).

Williams, David L., and de Kerbrech, Richard P. *Damned by Destiny* (Teredo Books, 1982).

Williams, David L. *Liners in Battle Dress* (Conway Maritime Press, 1987).

Wilson, Richard M. *The Big Ships* (Cassell, 1956).

Also:

'Steamers of the Past' articles by John H. Isherwood, which were featured in *Sea Breezes* magazine from September 1949 to December 1987.

Features in *Steamboat Bill*, the journal of the Steamship Historical Society of America; in *Sea Lines*, the journal of the Ocean Passenger Ship Society; and in *Marine News*, the journal of the World Ship Society.

ACKNOWLEDGEMENTS

I would like to express my appreciation to the following persons and organizations for the help they have given to me in the preparation of this book:

Mr Frank Braynard; Major Aldo Fraccaroli; Captain Otto Giese; Mr Arnold Kludas; Mr Bjorn Pederson; Mr Heinz Schoen; and Mr Edward Wilson.

American President Lines; Blohm & Voss AG; Blue Star Line; Chantiers de L'Atlantique; East Asiatic Company; Ellerman Lines; Furness Withy Group; Hamburg Sud Shipping Group; Hapag-Lloyd AG; Harland & Wolff; Italcantieri SpA; Kawasaki Heavy Industries; Mitsubishi Heavy Industries; Mitsui-OSK Lines; Nippon Yusen Kaisha; P&O Group; Royal Schelde Group and Vickers Limited.

Particular thanks go to Mr Cliff Parsons of the World Ship Society and to Mr L.L. von Münching in the Netherlands, the well-known authority on Dutch merchant shipping, for their magnificent efforts helping me with photographs.

My warm thanks, too, to my good friend Richard de Kerbrech, for his customary support and encouragement, and to my wife Jane, for her assistance with what turned out to be marathon word-processing and text editing tasks.

Finally, I have reserved a very special thank you to Mrs Izabel Rayner, on behalf of her husband Tom, a valued colleague on many previous projects, who sadly passed away during the course of my writing this book and was therefore denied the opportunity of seeing the finished result, in which many of his pictures feature. I trust, nevertheless, that Tom would have approved of this volume, which has been dedicated to him in recognition of his personal contribution to the history of passenger shipping.

INDEX OF SHIPS' NAMES

Note: Page numbers in parentheses refer to photographs

Abosso, (built 1922) 50
Abosso, (built 1935) 159, (159)
Accra 108, 116
Achates, HMS, destroyer 114
Adda 134
Admiral Hipper, cruiser 101, 227
Admiral Scheer, pocket battleship 115–16
Aeneas 107, 124, 146
Afric 43, (44)
Africa Maru 157
Aikoku Maru 165, 199, (199), 219
Aki Maru 208–9
Alaskan 170
Alaunia 34–5, 68
Albertville 101
Alcantara, (built 1913) 31, (31)
Alcantara, (built 1927) 126
Alesia 61
Algerie 39
Almeda Star 122–3, (123), 155
Alnwick Castle 46–7
Amasis 95, (95)
Amazon 65,70, (71)
America Maru 201
Amerika 132, 179–80, (180)
Amiral de Kersaint 42
Amiral Ganteaume 42
Amiral Magon 18, 42, (42), 78, 242
Amiral Olry 42
Amiral Zede 42
Anchises 124
Ancona 26–7, (26), 73
Andalucia Star 155, (155)
Andania, (built 1913) 68
Andania, (built 1922) 103
Anselm 135, (135)
Antares, torpedo boat 121
Antony 46, (47)
Anyo Maru 216, 225
Aotearoa, as HMS Avenger 55, (55)
Apapa, (built 1914) 64, (65)
Apapa, (built 1927) 108, 116, (117)
Aquila, see Roma
Aquileja 196
Arabia 22, 28, 36
Arabia Maru 219
Arabic 24–5, (24), 38
Aragon 65–6, (65–6), 242
Aramis, as Teia Maru 210, (210)
Arandora Star 106–7, (106), 155, 242
Araquara 153
Arcadian 49, (49)
Archimede, submarine 155
Argentina Maru, as Kaiyo 152, 238–9, (239)
Arizona Maru 168, (168)
Arno 154
Asama Maru 175, 219, (219), 237
Asie, as Rossano 202
Aska 110
Athenia, (built 1905) 60, (60)
Athenia, (built 1923) 86–7, (86)
Athos 43–4, 162
Atlantis, commerce raider 107–8, 111
Atsuta (Atuta) Maru 148
Atule, USS, submarine 219
Augustus, as Sparviero 218–9, (218), 234, 236, 243
Aurania 68, (69)
Ausonia 74
Australien 79–81, (79)
Avenger, HMS, see Aotearoa
Avila Star 149–50, (150), 155
Awa Maru 230–1, (230), 242
Awatea 162–3, (163)

Baden 121
Baependy 153–4, (153)
Bage 187, (187)
Bahia Laura 136, (136), 242
Balao, USS, submarine 228
Ballarat 51, (51)
Baloeran, as Strassburg 187–8, (188), 201
Barb, USS, submarine 220, 225
Baudouinville, as Lindau 209
Bayano 19–20, (19)
Bellau Wood, USS, aircraft carrier 205
Belle Isle 193
Bengal, minesweeper 165, 199
Berakit, see Vogtland
Bernardin de Saint Pierre, as Teibi Maru 190–1, 212
Birkenhead, HMS, cruiser 25
Bluegill, USS, submarine 219
Boadicea, HMS, destroyer 166
Bonefish, USS, submarine 190–1
Brazil Maru 152–3, (153)
Brazza 99
Bremen 92, 124–5, (125), 243
Bretagne 87
Brilliant, HMS, destroyer 224
Britannia 125, (126)
Britannic 36–7, (36–7), 243
Brooke, HMS, destroyer 127–8
Buenos Aires Maru 194, (195), 199
Burdigala 36
Burza, destroyer 113

C. de Eizaguirre 54
Cairo, see Royal Edward 23, (24)
Calabria 119
Caledonia, (built 1905) 39–40, (39), 43
Caledonia, (built 1925) as HMS Scotstoun 102–3, (102)
Caledonien 57, (57)
Calgarian 70, (70)
California, (Anchor Line, built 1907) 43
California, (Anchor Line, built 1923) 184, (185)
California, (Lloyd Triestino, built 1920) 136
California, (Pacific SN CO, built 1902) 62
Californian 27
Camelon, destroyer 53
Cameronia 43, 49, (49)
Canada 88, (88), 132
Cap Arcona 225, 235–6, (235), 242–3
Cap Padaran 196
Cap Trafalgar 13, 15–16, (15)
Cap Varella, as Teika Maru 237
Capellini, submarine 154
Carare 99
Caribbean 25
Carinthia 99–100
Carmania 15–16, (16)
Carnarvon Castle 126
Carolina 74
Carpathia 79, (79)
Carthaginian 56
Cathay 127, 163–4, (163–4)
Centaur 181–2, (181)
Ceramic 172–3, (173), 242
Challenger, HMS 32
Champagne, see Oropesa
Champlain 103–4, (103), 243
Chantala 33
Chateaurenault, cruiser 34
Chenonceaux 210, (211)
Chicago Maru 191, 198, 208, 213
Chihaya Maru, see Tjisaroea
Christiaan Huygens 239–40, (240)
Chrobry 99
Chuyo, see Nitta Maru
Cincinnati, as Covington 77, (77)
City of Athens 59
City of Baroda 178
City of Benares 110–111, (111)
City of Birmingham 37–8, (37)
City of Cairo 161, (161)
City of Los Angeles, as George F. Elliot 153
City of Nagpur 130–1, (131)
City of New York 145–6, (145)
City of Paris 47, (48)
City of Simla 112, (112)
City of Venice 182–3, (182)
Coamo 171–2, (172)
Colombia 176
Colombo 128, (128)
Columbus 86, 92–3, (93), 243
Commissaire Ramel 111–12, (112)
Comorin 127–8, (127), 163
Conegliano, see Min
Conte di Savoia 188, (188–9), 214, 243
Conte Rosso 134, (134), 139, 242
Conte Verde, as Kotobuki Maru 237, (237)
Conynham, USS, destroyer 63
Cornwall, HMS, cruiser 13, 16, 45
Costa Rica 130
Covington, see Cincinnati
Crevalle, USS, submarine 209
Crijnssen 98, 149
Cuba 232, (232)
Cymric 33–4, (33)

D'Artagnan, as Teiko Maru 201, 210
D'Estrees, cruiser 64
Darro 45
De La Salle 183, (183)
Dempo 187, 201
Deutschland 236–7, (236)
Devonian 60–1
Devonshire, HMS, cruiser 108
Diamond, HMS, destroyer 130
Djemnah 77, (78)
Dnyepr (138), 139
Domala, as Empire Attendant 151–2, (151)
Donau, (Flensburger Dampfer Co) 136, 242
Donau, (Norddeutscher LLoyd) 225–7, (226)
Dorsey, USS, destroyer 84
Douglas, destroyer 184
Dover Castle 53–4, (53)
Drina 45–6, (46)
Drum, USS, submarine 193
Duca di Genova 69
Duchess of Atholl 156–7, (156)
Duchess of York 184, (184)
Duilio 207–8, (208), 216, (216), 243
Dumana 151, 196
Dunbar Castle 94, (94)
Dunvegan Castle 109–10, (109)
Dwinsk 74–5, (75)

Edward Rutledge, see Exeter
Egypt 22, 28, 36
Elizabethville 62
Elysia 148–9

Empire Attendant, see Domala
Empire Citizen, see Wahehe
Empire Evenlode, see Talthybius
Empire Trader, see Tainui
Empress of Asia 142, (142)
Empress of Britain 113–14, (113), 243
Empress of Canada 176, (176)
Esperia 136
Ettrick 169–70, (170)
Europa 132, (133)
Excalibur, as Joseph Hewes 164, (164), 167, 190
Excambion, as John Penn 190
Exeter, as Edward Rutledge 166–7, 190
Explorateur Grandidier 212

Falaba 20, (20)
Finback, USS, submarine 157, 178, 237
Flandre 110, (110)
Flier, USS, submarine 203
Floride 19
Flying Fish, USS, submarine 196
Forfar, HMS, see Montrose
Foucauld 106, 165
France 27
Francesco Crispi 179, (179), 242
Franconia 34, (35), 45
Fuji (Huzi) Maru 191–2, (191)
Fushimi (Husimi) Maru 175
Fuso (Huso) Maru 209

Galeka 35–6
Galicia 52
Gallia 18, 30, 34, (35), 78, 242
Galway Castle 83, (83)
Gandia 140–1
Gange 48–9
Garoet 203–4, (204)
General Artigas 185
General Metzinger 101
General Osorio 232–3, (233)
George F. Elliot, see City of Los Angeles
Ginyo Maru 196, 216, 225
Giulio Cesare 207–8, 215–16, (215–16)
Glenart Castle 70
Gloucester Castle 152, (152)
Gneisenau 180–1, (181), 220
Gneisenau, battlecruiser 90–1, 101
Gokoku Maru 219–20, (220)
Golconda 34
Goya 225, 233–4, (234), 242
Grayback, USS, submarine 192
Greenling, USS, submarine 153
Grenadier, USS, submarine 148
Grief, commerce raider 31
Griffin, HMS, destroyer 130
Guadeloupe 19
Gudgeon, USS, submarine 180

Hake, USS, submarine 198
Hakone Maru 151, 194, (195)
Hakozaki Maru 151, 203, 228
Hakusan Maru 151, 203
Haruna Maru 151, (151)
Hawaii Maru 222
Hector 114, 146
Heian Maru 199, (200)
Heiyo Maru 174
Hesperian 25
Highflyer, HMS, cruiser 13
Highland Brae 18–19, (18)
Highland Brigade 70–1, (71)
Highland Corrie 52, (53)
Highland Hope 16
Highland Patriot 113
Hilary 46, 53
Himalaya 56

Hirano Maru 83–4, (84)
Hitachi Maru 63–4, (63), (64)
Hiye (Hie) Maru 193
Hiyo, see Izumo Maru
Hokoku Maru 165, (165), 199, 219
Horai Maru 145
Hugh L. Scott, see President Pierce
Hurricane, HMS, destroyer 111
Hyacinth, HMS 32–3
Hyperion, HMS, destroyer 92–3

I29, submarine 170
India 22–3, (23), 28, 36
Ioannina 65
Iroquois, destroyer 184
Italia 206
Ivernia 41–2, (41)
Ixion 132–3
Izumo Maru, as Hiyo 204–5, (204–5), 222, 234, 243

Jack, USS, submarine 213
Jagersfontein 149, (150)
Jan Pieterzoon Coen 98, (98)
Jean Laborde 211, (211)
Jervis Bay 114–16, (115–16)
John Penn, see Excambion
Joseph Hewes, see Excalibur
Junyo, see Kashiwara Maru
Justicia, see Statendam

Kaiser Wilhelm der Grosse 13–14, (14), 36, 70
Kaiyo, see Argentina Maru
Kamakura Maru 180
Kamo Maru 206
Karanja 167, (167)
Karlsruhe, commerce raider 16–17
Karnak 38
Kashima (Kasima) Maru 190
Kashiwara Maru, as Junyo 204–5, 222–3, (222–3), 234, 243
Kashmir 84–5
Kasuga Maru, as Taiyo 194, 210, 217
Katori Maru 87, 139, (139)
Kemmendine 107–8, (107), 146, 182
Kingfish, USS, submarine 177
Kitano Maru 146
Komet, commerce raider 118
Koningin Emma 25, (25)
Kormoran, commerce raider 142
Kotobuki Maru, see Conte Verde
Kronprinz Wilhelm, commerce raider 18–19
Kulmerland, commerce raider 118
Kusonoki, destroyer 59

L3, submarine 233
La Coruna 96, 201
La Plata 178–9
La Provence, as Provence II 18, 30, (30), 78, 242
Laburnam, HMS, destroyer 43
Laconia, (built 1911) 45, (45)
Laconia, (built 1922) 100, 154–5, (154), 194, 242
Lady Drake 135, 148
Lady Hawkins 135, 141, (141)
Lady Somers 135–6
Lafayette, see Normandie
Lake Michigan 72
Lancastria 94, 104–5, (104), 155, 194, 242
Lanfranc 46, 50, (50), 53
Laurentic, (built 1909) 42 (43)
Laurentic, (built 1927) 114, (114)
Leasowe Castle, see Vasilissa Sophia

Leedstown, see Santa Lucia
Leonardo da Vinci, submarine 176
Leopoldville 101, 223–4, (224), 242
Letitia 59, (59)
Leuthen, see Nankin
Liguria 123, 187
Lima, destroyer 150
Lincoln, HMS, destroyer 127
Lindau, see Baudouinville
Lipari 165
Llandaff Castle 171
Llandovery Castle 76–7, (76)
Lombardia 179
Lusitania 18, 20–2, (21), 34, 80, 242–3

Maasdam 91, 135, (135)
Madrid 139
Magellan, (Messageries Maritimes) 40, (40)
Magellan, (Pacific SN Co) 81
Malda, (built 1913) 43, 61, (62)
Malda, (built 1922) 146, (147)
Maloja, (built 1911) 30–1, (30), 81
Maloja, (built 1923) 96
Manila Maru 221–2, (221)
Mantola 43
Marco Polo 202, (203)
Mariette Pacha 213–4
Marmora 81
Marne, HMS, destroyer 81
Marnix Van Sint Aldegonde 192–3, (192–3)
Marquette 26, (26)
Mashobra, (built 1914) 49–50
Mashobra, (built 1920) 99
Massilia 212, (212)
Matsu, destroyer 52
Mauretania 20
Medina 51–2, (51)
Meknes 108, (108)
Mendi 44–5, (44), 242
Mendoza 160
Merion 22, (22), (23)
Mesaba 82
Mexico Maru 213
Mexique 105, (105), 232
Michel, commerce raider 152
Miike Maru 201–2
Millbrook, HMS, destroyer 81
Min, as Conegliano 182
Mingo, USS, submarine 222
Minneapolis 32, 38
Minnehaha 62
Minnetonka 68, (68)
Minnewaska 32, 38, (38)
Missanabie 82–3, (83)
Miyazaki Maru 54, (54)
Mizuho Maru 217, (217)
Moldavia 56, 73
Mongara 57
Mongolia 56, (56), 58, 73
Mongolian 81
Monte Cervantes 144
Monte Olivia 231, (231), (235)
Monte Pascoal 198–9, (198)
Monte Sarmiento 144–5, (144)
Montfort 83
Montreal 47
Montrose, as HMS Forfar 119, (119)
Mooltan 58–9, (58)
Mounsey, HMS, destroyer 85
Mount Temple 40
Mowe, commerce raider 39–40, 81, 126
Munchen 190, 228, (228)
Munster, HMS, destroyer 31

Namur 63

Nankin, as Leuthen 171, (172)
Narkunda 168–9, (168)
Narvik, commerce raider 118
Nautilus, USS, submarine 201
Nazario Sauro 128
Nellore 205, (205)
Nemesis, destroyer 53
Neptunia 134, 136–9, (137)
Nerissa 132, (132)
Neuralia 235
New York 231, (232), 236, 243
Newfoundland 170, 188–9, (189)
Niagara 105–6, (106)
Nieuw Zeeland 165, (166)
Nikko Maru 233
Nitta Maru, as Chuyo 194–5, (195), 216
Normandie, as Lafayette 142–4, (143), 243
Norseman 29–30, (29)
Northern Prince 126
Nova Scotia 170–1, (171), 188, 242

Oceania 134, 137–9, (137)
Oceanic 14–15, (14)
Olympic 37
Omrah 73, (73)
Orama, (built 1911) 58, 62–3, (63)
Orama, (built 1924) 99–100, (100–101)
Orcades 157, (157), 243
Orford 99, (100)
Orion, commerce raider 105, 118
Orissa 75, (76)
Oronsa 72
Oronsay 99, 155, (156)
Oropesa, (built 1895) as Champagne 62, 75
Oropesa, (built 1920) 122, (122)
Oslofjord 118, (119)
Otranto 67, 84–5, (84–5)
Otway 58, (58)

Palermo 38–9
Pampa 81–2
Pampanito, USS, submarine 216
Panama Maru 198
Parana 61
Parche, USS, submarine 209
Patia 74, (75)
Patria 116–18, (117)
Patroclus 114, (115)
Pegu 57
Pennland 130, (130)
Persia 22, 28, (28), 36
Perugia 39
Petunia, HMS, corvette 155
Piemonte 123, 187
Pigeon, HMS, destroyer 81
Pilsudski 91, (91)
Piranha, USS, submarine 208
Piriapolis 101
Platino, submarine 169
Pluton, cruiser 26
Po 124, (125)
Polynesien 80–1, (82)
Pomeranian 71–2, (72)
Pompano, USS, submarine 148
Porthos 43, 161–2, (162)
President Cleveland, as Tasker H. Bliss 167
President Coolidge 157–8, (158), 243
President Doumer 159–60, (159)
President Grant 201
President Harrison, as Kachidoki Maru 216
President Lincoln 76, (76)
President Pierce, as Hugh L. Scott 167

President Taylor 144, (144)
President Van Buren, as Thomas R. Stone 161
Principe Umberto 34
Prinz Eitel Friedrich, commerce raider 19
Proteus, submarine 121
Provence II, see La Provence

Quebec 42
Queenfish, USS, submarine 231

Rajputana 89, 129, (129)
Rakuyo Maru 216, (216), 225, 242
Rangitane 118, (118)
Rasher, USS, submarine 210, 231
Ravenna 47
Rawalpindi 89–91, (90), 129
Redfish, USS, submarine 217, 222
Regina Elena 67
Remuera 47, 108–9
Rewa 67–8, (67)
Rex 188, 214, (214–15), 243
Rhein 120
Rio de Janeiro 95, (95)
Rio de Janeiro Maru 199–201, (200)
Robert Ley 229–30, (229–30), 243
Rohilla 17, (17), 67
Rohna 193–4, (194), 242
Roma, as Aquila 218–19, 234, (234–5), 243
Romolo 116
Rossano, see Asie
Rotorua, (built 1910) 47
Rotorua, (built 1911) 120, (120)
Royal Edward 23–4, 242
Ruth Alexander 139

S13, submarine 227–8
Sabaudia, see Stockholm
Sado Maru 169
Sagaing 146, 152
Sagamore 46
Sailfish, USS, submarine 195
Sakaki, destroyer 52
Salopian, HMS, see Shropshire
Salsette 57–8, (58)
Salta 48, (48)
San Jacinto 147–8, (148)
Sannio 128
Sant'Anna 72
Santa Clara, as Susan B. Anthony 203, (203)
Santa Cruz, commerce raider 127
Santa Elena 192, 193
Santa Lucia, as Leedstown 162, 193
Santos Maru 222, (222)
Sardegna 121, (121)
Savoie 162
Scharnhorst, as Shinyo 180, 220–1, (220–1)
Scharnhorst, battlecruiser 90–1, 101
Scotstoun, HMS, see Caledonia
Sea Devil, USS, submarine 222
Seadragon, USS, submarine 178
Seahorse, USS, submarine 192
Sealion II, USS, submarine 216
Seattle Maru 191, 198, 208
Shad, USS, submarine 192
Shinyo, see Scharnhorst
Shirala 77, (78)
Shropshire, as HMS Salopian 133–4
Sicilia 180
Simla 32–3
Simon Bolivar 88, (89)
Sinaia 212
Sirdhana 88
Slamat 130, (131), 242
Snook, USS, submarine 189
Sontay 50
Southland 54–5
Spaarndam 91, (91), 135
Spadefish, USS, submarine 221, 238
Sparviero, see Augustus
Sperrbrecher 10, see Vigo
Sphinx, as Subiaco 43, 197–8, (197)
Spreewald 141–2, (141)
St. Laurent, destroyer 107
St. Louis 213, (214)
Stampalia 34
Statendam, (built 1917) as Justicia 80–1, (80), 243
Statendam, (built 1929) 96–7, (96–7), 243
Steelhead, USS, submarine 209
Steuben 7, 190, 225, 228, (228–9), 242
Stockholm, as Sabaudia 206–7, (206–7), (216), 243
Strassburg, see Baloeran
Strathallan 173, (173), 243
Stuttgart 190, (190–1)
Subiaco, see Sphinx
Sunfish, HMS, submarine 95
Surada 67, 85
Susan B. Anthony, see Santa Clara
Suwa Maru 178, (178)

Tabora 13, 32, (33)
Tacoma Maru 191, 198, 208
Tainui, as Empire Trader 176
Tairea 92, (92), 183
Taiyo, see Kasuga Maru
Taiyo Maru 148, (149), 242
Takachiho (Takatiho) Maru 176–7
Talamba 183–4, (183)
Talthybius, as Taruyasu Maru 238
Tanda 208, (209)
Tanganjika 192
Tango Maru 193
Tarpon, USS, submarine 175–6
Taruyasu Maru, see Talthybius
Tasker H. Bliss, see President Cleveland
Tatsuta (Tatuta) Maru 175–6, (175)
Teia Maru, see Aramis
Teibi Maru, see Bernardin de Saint Pierre
Teika Maru, see Cap Varella
Teiko Maru, see D'Artagnan
Teison Maru, see Ville de Verdun
Teiyo Maru 176
Terukuni Maru 86, 88–9, (89), 198
Tevere 174, (175)
Thames, HMS, destroyer 119
Theophile Gautier (138), 139
Thomas R. Stone, see President Van Buren
Thor, commerce raider 126–7, 171
Tilawa 170, (170)
Tinosa, USS, submarine 206
Tirante, USS, submarine 233
Titanic 7, 20, 27, 37, 79
Tjikarang 145, (145)
Tjinegara 152, 192
Tjisaroea, as Chihaya Maru 192
Toscana 47
Transbalt 238, (238)
Transylvania, (built 1914) 52, (52), 68
Transylvania, (built 1925) 108, (109)
Trigger, USS, submarine 198, 201, 205
Tsushima, cruiser 64
Tubantia 31–2, (32)
Tullibee, USS, submarine 191
Tunny, USS, submarine 178
Turakina 59–60, (60)
Tuscaloosa, USS, cruiser 92–3
Tuscania 68, (69)

U19 70
U20 22, 25, 34
U24 24–5, 42
U25 103
U27 19–20
U28 20
U30 87
U32, (WWI) 38
U32, (WWII) 114
U33 49
U34 27
U35 26, 30, 32, 34
U37 87, 99
U38, (WWI) 26–8
U38, (WWII) 113
U39 30
U45 87
U46, (WWI) 68
U46, (WWII) 100, 109
U47 107
U48, (WWI) 62
U48, (WWII) 111
U50 45
U52 47, 70
U53 56, 61
U55 79
U56 108
U60 42
U62 63
U63 52
U64 68
U65 40, 44
U69 55
U70 55
U73 36–7
U75 131
U82 83
U86 77
U90 74
U94 133
U96 120, 122–3
U99 114, 119
U107 149, 155
U108 129
U130 167
U155 170
U156 154
U160 146
U172 157
U173 164
U174 161
U177 171
U178 157
U181 204
U201 149
U306 179
U371 201
U407 165–6
U413 169
U486 224
U506 154
U507 154
U515 173
U516 176
U562 173
U575 159
U582 152
U604 160
U1195 232
UA70 103
UB8 22
UB13 32
UB14 24
UB47 34, 42
UB64 81
UB67 68
UB77 68
UB87 83
UB124 81
UC7 25
UC17 47
UC49 58
UC56 70
UC66 43
Ultonia 56
Ulysses 146, (147)
Umbria 101
Ume, destroyer 59
Umtata 151
Unique, HMS, submarine 136
Unyo, see Yawata Maru
Upholder, HMS, submarine 134, 137–9
Usambara 192, 228–9
Usaramo 212–13, (213)
Ussukuma 92, 212

Valparaiso 62
Van Kinsbergen, cruiser 120
Van Rensselaer 98, 149
Vandyck, (built 1911) 16–17, (16)
Vandyck, (built 1921) 101, (102)
Vasilissa Sophia, as Leasowe Castle 73
Vaterland 185–7, (185–6), 243
Vengeance, HMS, cruiser 32
Verdi 61, (61)
Verona 72–3
Viceroy of India 166, (166), 169
Victoria 141
Vigilancia 46
Vigo, as Sperrbrecher 10 96, 201, (202)
Vigrid 135
Ville de Bruges 98–9
Ville de la Ciotat 28, 80–1
Ville de Verdun, as Teison Maru 157
Viminale 174–5
Virgilio 205–6
Vogtland, as Berakit 181
Voltaire, (built 1907) 39, 126
Voltaire, (built 1923) 101, 126–7, (127)

Wahehe, as Empire Citizen 123–4, (124)
Warilda 81, (82)
Waroonga 179
Warwick Castle 169, (169)
Watchman, HMS, destroyer 232
Watussi 91
Western Prince 120–1
Wilhelm Gustloff 7, 225, 227–8, (227), 233, 242–3
Windsor Castle 177–8, (177)
Wolf, commerce raider 45, 54, 56, 59, 63
Worcestershire 44
Wryneck, HMS, destroyer 130

Yamato Maru 189
Yarra 54
Yasaka Maru 27, (27)
Yasukuni Maru 198
Yawata Maru, as Unyo 194, 216–17, (217)
Yokohama Maru 146
Yoma 182, (182)
Yorkshire 87, (87)
Yoshino (Yosino) Maru 209

Zaandam 135, 160–1, (160)
Zam Zam 129–30
Zennia, HMS, destroyer 74
Zieten 64
Zuiderdam 217–18, (218)